Handbook of Faith

Contributors

Monika K. Hellwig

John Carmody

Louis Dupré

Jacqueline Mariña

H. Newton Malony

Carroll Stuhlmueller

James L. Price Jr.

Avery Dulles

Alexander J. McKelway

Louis Weil

Randolph A. Nelson

Melvin Blanchette

James Michael Lee

Handbook of Faith

edited by

James Michael Lee

Religious Education Press
Birmingham, Alabama

Library of Congress Cataloging-in-Publication Data
Handbook of faith / edited by James Michael Lee.
  Includes bibliographical references.
  ISBN 0-89135-075-6
  1. Faith. 2. Faith—Comparative studies. I. Lee, James Michael.
BT771.2.H34   1990   90-31685
234'.2—dc20   CIP

Religious Education Press, Inc.
5316 Meadow Brook Road
Birmingham, Alabama 35242
10 9 8 7 6 5 4 3 2

Religious Education Press publishes books exclusively in religious education and in areas closely related to religious education. It is committed to enhancing and professionalizing religious education through the
publication of serious, significant, and scholarly works.

PUBLISHER TO THE PROFESSION

Contents

Introduction   vii
James Michael Lee

PART I—FOUNDATIONS OF FAITH

1. A History of the Concept of Faith   3
   Monika K. Hellwig

2. The Concept of Faith in Comparative Religions   24
   John Carmody

3. The Concept of Faith in Philosophy   47
   Louis Dupré and Jacqueline Mariña

4. The Concept of Faith in Psychology   71
   H. Newton Malony

PART II—FAITH IN THEOLOGY

5. The Biblical View of Faith: A Catholic Perspective   99
   Carroll Stuhlmueller

6. The Biblical View of Faith: A Protestant Perspective   123
   James L. Price Jr.

7. The Systematic Theology of Faith:
   A Catholic Perspective   142
   Avery Dulles

8. The Systematic Theology of Faith:
   A Protestant Perspective   164
   Alexander J. McKelway

PART III—FACILITATING GROWTH IN FAITH

9. Facilitating Growth in Faith through
   Liturgical Worship   203
   Louis Weil

10. Facilitating Growth in Faith through Social Ministry   221
    Randolph A. Nelson

11. Facilitating Growth in Faith through
    Pastoral Counseling and Spiritual Direction   242
    Melvin Blanchette

12. Facilitating Growth in Faith through
    Religious Instruction   264
    James Michael Lee

   Profile of Contributors   303

   Index of Names   309

   Index of Subjects   317

Introduction

Whether one regards faith as the central category of human existence as many religionists like James Fowler does, or whether one views love as the central category as other religionists like myself do, the fact remains that faith is an extraordinarily important construct in religion. Because of its pivotal role, faith surely deserves that kind of attention which is at once inclusive, profound, and unremitting.

The purpose of this book is twofold. The first of these purposes is to provide in one convenient location a somewhat comprehensive overview of faith from a wide variety of contrasting but complementary perspectives. Unless one looks at faith from many basically different perspectives, one is in grave danger of falling prey to a narrow and probably a warped concept of faith. The second of the two purposes of this volume is to explicitly consider some major forms of pastoral ministry solely from the perspective of faith so that this book will be eminently useful not only for scholars, students, and interested laypersons who wish to enlarge their knowledge about the construct of faith but also for those persons in pastoral ministry who wish to facilitate growth in faith through the exercise of their own special apostolates.

Handbook of Faith is divided into three major parts, each part consisting of four chapters.

Part I deals with the foundations of faith and provides a broad horizon on faith from the vantage points of the history of this concept in Christianity from the ancient church until today, the way in which major world religions have conceptualized faith within their own traditions, philosophical faith as understood by philosophers from pre-Socratic times until the present, and various psychological outlooks on religious faith.

Whereas Part I considers faith from a wide variety of complementary religious and scientific standpoints, Part II sharpens the book's focus to consider how faith is conceptualized by biblical theology and by systematic theology. In order to ensure that this focus is expansive as well as intense, one of the chapters on the concept of faith as presented in the Bible is written by a Catholic biblicist and the other by a Protestant. The same pluralistic mix obtains in the two chapters on the systematic theology of faith.

Part III deals with the actual facilitation of growth in faith, a task which has always been central to the mission of the church. One chapter apiece is devoted to enhancing faith in four major areas of church life, namely, liturgical worship, social ministry, pastoral counseling, and religious instruction.

There is a sense in which the first two parts of this book (Chapters 1-8) stand alone, since by themselves these two parts form a complete book. Chapters 1-8 do not need the remaining four chapters to finish their unified task. But a fuller understanding of Part III requires the existence of Parts I and Parts II as the necessary contextual embedment for that kind of pastoral activity which is productively admixed with the best thinking from a wide variety of complementary scientific perspectives.

There is a distinct difference between Parts I and II and Part III. The first two parts are descriptive whereas Part III is primarily prescriptive (as befits pastoral activity). Parts I and II, then, are geared to a deeper and more meaningful understanding, while Part III is oriented to wiser and more competent action.

Each of the chapters in Parts I and II gives a meaty overview of the topic it covers, while each of the chapters in Part III, though providing somewhat of an overview, nonetheless tends to concentrate on a cluster of related but less-than-the-whole focal points and zones of activity. Such concentration is probably inevitable in a short treatment of various forms of pastoral activity because these types of action cannot be as neatly circumscribed, as is the case with a delimited area of scientific endeavor such as the psychology of religion or biblical theology.

In Chapter 1, Monika Hellwig provides a panoramic but concise history of faith as it has been conceptualized in Christianity from New Testament times down to the present day. Hellwig's chapter was placed first in this book because an understanding of the history of the construct of faith is contextually essential to a proper understanding of its nature, structure, contours, and development. This chapter traces the growth as well as the shifts in understanding of the notion of faith in the

Patristic era, the Middle Ages, the Reformation, and in modern times.

In Chapter 2, John Carmody situates the construct of faith in an even wider perspective, namely, the way faith has been conceptualized in the major religions of the world. This chapter is very helpful because it enables us to place the Christian concept of faith within a broader matrix, namely, the way in which faith is viewed in other world religions. This broader context is important if faith is to be truly appreciated as a general category of existence permeating all religions rather than solely a Christian gift flowing exclusively from Christian revelation. This chapter shows the way faith is conceptualized in nonliterate religions such as shamanism and in world religions like Hinduism, Buddhism, Chinese religion, Islam, and of course Judaism.

Chapter 3 is different from the other chapters in that it devotes its attention exclusively to philosophical faith rather than dealing with religious faith as such. Yet this chapter is very germane to this volume, not only because theological thinking has classically depended almost exclusively on philosophy for its fundamental categories and investigative methodology, but also because there is a large sense in which philosophy presents a legitimate ultimate explanation for faith independent of religion or theology. In this chapter Louis Dupré, assisted by Jacqueline Mariña, provides a short yet insightful history of philosophical faith from the pre-Socratics right down to contemporary philosophers.

Chapter 4 on the psychology of faith rounds out the first major part of this volume. An understanding of the psychology of faith is as necessary as it is foundational because faith is a humanly devised construct summarizing a set a interrelated human behaviors. Consequently faith is inextricably linked with psychology in a pervasive and highly influential way. In this chapter, H. Newton Malony presents a wide range of varying psychological views in the nature, source, structure, uniqueness, and operations of faith. These psychological theories and data have to be taken seriously into account in all realistic explanations of faith and in all pastoral ministries which hope to be effective.

In Chapter 5, Carroll Stuhlmueller examines the biblical view of faith from the Catholic perspective. He unfolds the various but complementary biblical conceptualizations of faith including confidence, trust, knowledge, and waiting—conceptualizations which, when taken together, underscore faith as a personal relationship. Stuhlmueller links the word *'āman* in the Old Testament with the word *pistis* in the New Testament in a way which sheds important light on the biblical concept of faith. He highlights another pervasive motif in the New Testament, namely, the linkage between adherence to doctrine and adherence to Jesus as these two are juxtaposed with faith and works. In the final section of this chapter, Stuhlmueller contrasts scholarly methods of un-covering the biblical concept of faith with existential methods such as liturgical practice.

Chapter 6 is the Protestant counterpart to Chapter 5. Because there is a great deal of common agreement between Protestant and Catholic biblicists at the highest level of scholarship, this chapter and the one before it are complementary rather than opposed. Nonetheless, in this chapter James Ligon Price provides a distinctly Protestant accentuation and flavor to the biblical notion of faith. Thus he highlights the persis-tent biblical intertwining of faith and righteousness. Other major themes in this chapter are human faith as a divine gift reflecting the faithfulness of God, the Pauline emphasis on the obedience of faith, and the Old Testament concept of covenantial faith contrasted with the New Testament emphasis on personal faith in him who fulfilled the cove-nant.

Chapter 7 offers an extensive treatment of the Catholic concept of faith as held by the official church as well as by Catholic theologians who might or might not be in agreement with officially held views. Avery Dulles deals with Catholic views on the nature of faith, including the definition of faith, intellectualism and faith, and the virtue/act of faith. He details Catholic views on the contents of faith. He also treats major issues such as the necessity of faith, the ecclesial dimension of faith, grace, and credibility, together with the major properties of faith such as freedom, certitude, and obscurity. As would be expected, there is a recurrent consideration, sometimes salient, sometimes less notice-able, of the relationship between ecclesiastical authority and the concept of faith.

Chapter 8 is the Protestant counterpart to the previous chapter. As is natural for any truly Protestant overview of the concept of faith, Alex-ander McKelway places faith and justification in existential and func-tional apposition. Thus he appropriately begins his chapter with the leitmotiv of the whole essay, namely, the Protestant principle of justifica-tion by faith alone. He gives the background of the Reformation con-cept of faith and then flavorfully summarizes the views of faith held by Luther, Calvin, and the Protestant Confessions. McKelway goes on to highlight the dissolution of the classic Protestant doctrine of faith as exemplified by the post-Reformation movements of orthodoxy, pietism, rationalism, and later, nineteenth-century liberalism. He winds up the chapter with a treatment of contemporary Protestant conceptualizations of faith and contrasts these views both with the Reformers and with the possibility of an "end-of-the-road."

In Chapter 9, Louis Weil deals with facilitating growth in faith through liturgical activity. The main theme of this chapter is the inter-

dependency of liturgy and faith, regardless of whether faith is conceptualized as intellectual adherence to doctrine or as trusting acceptance.
Weil shows that though the church's concept of faith shapes its worship,
worship also shapes the church's concept of faith. *Lex orandi, lex credendi.* Implicit throughout this chapter, though not necessarily stated
directly, is that religious faith would not be true or even possible without
the liturgy. Interlacing his chapter with numerous practical examples,
Weil discusses how the liturgy is a potent source and framework for
faith, how both the act and the content of faith are conditioned by
liturgy, and how the liturgy is a specially privileged enactment of faith.
This chapter also shows how liturgy fosters faith effectively through
living, holistic worship rather than through heavy didacticism.

Chapter 10 explores the intimate connection between faith and social
ministry and how social ministry can lead to growth in faith. As is the
case with most sophisticated treatments of social ministry, Randolph
Nelson's chapter takes as its major axis the theme that faith is not apart
from social ministry but is simultaneously a product of social ministry
and forms/directs social ministry. Permeating this chapter is the view
that faith is not only personal faith; it is also, necessarily, social faith.
Nelson delineates the various dimensions of social ministry and devotes
a section to showing how the church has persistently neglected social
ministry because it wrongly identifies social ministry with social welfare
such as almsgiving. This chapter also shows how faith is made whole, is
made concrete, and is made proactive through social ministry.

Chapter 11 deals with enhancing faith through pastoral counseling
and spiritual direction. As would be expected, this chapter is very per-
sonalistically oriented. Melvin Blanchette shows how pastoral counseling is a key avenue for producing a faith which can become whole, and a
faith which frees the personality to become fully itself. An important
theme of this chapter is that pastoral counseling is intimately linked
with faith because both have freedom and self-clarification as essential
characteristics. Blanchette provides two illustrative case histories of persons in suffering and pain and goes on to reveal how pastoral counseling
helped these individuals to work out their faith in conjunction with the
structure and limitations of their respective personalities.

In Chapter 12, James Michael Lee examines why and how religious
instruction can facilitate faith. This chapter starts off by examining the
question of whether faith can be taught and reviews the various positions taken on this question by prominent Catholic and Protestant
religious educationists. Lee also treats the thorny issue of whether religion teaching can lead to faith or can only enhance existing faith. A
large section of this chapter is devoted to faith as a construct and how a
major task of religious instruction is to go from construct to learning

outcome by moving from the notional to the operational. The last part of this chapter uncovers the four major components in every religious instruction act and indicates what religious educators can do to select appropriate pedagogical procedures to teach faith effectively.

In preparing this book, I tried to assemble the best persons I could find to write chapters. I also endeavored to assemble a group of contributors that would represent a diversified mix of older and younger scholars as well as individuals from various faith traditions and from different orientations from within the same faith tradition. Deep is my gratitude to all my collaborators for their fine contributions to what we all hope will be an important volume in the field of religion.

If, as a result of this book, persons of all religious persuasions will better understand the concept of faith, the purpose of this volume will have been accomplished. And if, as a result of this book, persons of all religious persuasions will not only better understand the concept of faith but also deepen their own personal faith, then the purpose of this volume will have been doubly accomplished. And if, as a result of this book, persons of all religious persuasions will not only better understand the concept of faith and deepen their own personal faith but additionally help facilitate faith in others, then the purpose of this volume will have been triply accomplished.

JAMES MICHAEL LEE
Birmingham, Alabama

PART I

FOUNDATIONS OF FAITH

CHAPTER 1

A History of the Concept of Faith

Monika K. Hellwig

INTRODUCTION

The term "faith" ranges in meaning from a general religious attitude on the one hand to personal acceptance of a specific set of beliefs on the other hand. There are many shades and nuances of meaning on the continuum between these two poles. Taken out of context, therefore, statements about faith may be ambiguous or even misleading. Furthermore, because context is constitutive of meaning, the history of both the word faith and the idea of faith is also important. For most Christians, this history is typically known sketchily from a denominational perspective. However, for constructive dialogue and collaboration it is necessary to round out the picture. This entire volume is devoted to that task, and this introductory chapter will simply outline the historical background to the contemporary effort at a broader and more ecumenical understanding.

The ancient world of Greek and Roman culture does not seem to have had the concept of faith within the range of meaning indicated above. Indeed, the concept of faith has its direct and single origin in the Hebrew scriptures. In the Hebrew scriptures the vocabulary of faith is built up from a root that has to do with firmness, reliability, trustworthiness—the same root from which we take the affirmation, "Amen." The stories of faith, focusing most sharply on the figure of Abraham, are stories of human responses to God's promises, and therefore of acceptance of God's self-revelation as powerful and loving. The history of faith as understood in the biblical texts is the history of God's covenant

3

gradually revealed to and accepted by human beings. The faith that is presented by the sacred texts as characteristic of Abraham is a very active, creative force that constantly moves him to bold and radical measures involving great risk. We are given to understand that Abraham took these risks out of an unshakable conviction that God is utterly faithful.

What is written about Abraham is reinforced throughout the history of Moses and the people of ancient Israel with their judges, kings, and prophets. In the story of Moses at the Burning Bush the exchange about the name of God suggests the insight that it is in one's own response of faith that one comes to know the divine attributes of covenant fidelity and truth. In the story of the Sinai covenant and the giving of the law there is the suggestion that the people's "Amen" or response of faith welcomes the covenant love and power of God into the world of human history in a way that offers a channel to the fidelity of God's purpose. Although Israel was always more inclined to speak of its relationship with God in story and image than in abstract conceptual definitions. Yet it might be said that the Hebrew concept of faith was such that the wholehearted openness to receive the self-revelation of God could only exist as a commitment to live according to the covenant under all circumstances because God is faithful and will fulfill all the great promises.

THE NEW TESTAMENT

The New Testament takes up the theme of faith with reference to Jesus as the Word of God which is the pledge and expression of the divine fidelity. The gospels present Jesus as calling forth faith in himself. In the many stories of healing and exorcism, and in those other stories of calls to discipleship, faith is again presented as a move forward that involves risk taken because the other is trustworthy and faithful. The trustworthy one is God and Jesus mediates the presence of the transcendent God in the lives of those with whom he comes in contact. The reciprocity involved in the concept of faith and of God's fidelity appears both in the sayings of Jesus and in the evangelists' sayings about him. But Paul (2 Cor 1:19-21) captures the sense that this reciprocity is contained within Jesus himself. Thus Paul writes of Jesus both as the "Amen" of God to us, but also as our way of saying "Amen" to God. The same idea appears in the Johannine literature in Revelation 3:14. Summing up the notion of faith implied in the stories, sayings, and images of the New Testament, one might say that faith is a response to Jesus that will risk a whole new way of life on the conviction that Jesus is the all-powerful, redeeming word of God spoken into the midst of creation and history and as such is utterly trustworthy, faithful, and powerful to fulfill his promises and restore God's presence and rule among the peoples of the earth.

However, the development of the idea of faith in the scriptures would not be complete without reference to the Letter to the Hebrews. This extended homily contains an elaborate Christology and soteriology and concludes in chapters 11 through 13 with an exhortation to faith that begins with a definition and continues by fleshing out the definition with a plethora of examples from the history of Israel. Faith is defined as that which "gives substance to our hope and makes us certain of realities we do not see" (Heb 11:1).[1] This definition, of course, is an English translation from the ancient Greek text. The Greek term which is translated as "substance" can just as well be translated as "assurance." If "substance" is taken as the meaning, then the concept of faith as set forth in this passage from Hebrews might well accentuate faith as the belief in that Christology and soteriology which the inspired writer had expounded earlier in his letter. In this case, the second half of the definition of faith given in Hebrews might properly be understood as relating faith to realities which we do not see. If on the other hand the meaning of the sacred text is closer to "assurance," then the emphasis would be on faith in the trustworthiness of God. From such a perspective, the second half of the definition of faith given in Hebrews would be interpreted in a manner which would place emphasis on faith as confidence rather than on belief.

The legitimate variations in the interpretation of the definition of faith given in Hebrews 11:1 are perhaps even more interesting than the definition itself. By faith, the text continues, "We perceive that the universe was fashioned by the word of God" (11:1); Abel and Enoch were pleasing to God, for "anyone who comes to God must believe that he exists and that he rewards those who search for him" (11:6). By faith, Noah, Abraham, Sarah, Isaac, Jacob, and Joseph believed the promises of God about a future that was not only unseen but humanly speaking unlikely, and they acted, staking everything on those promises. By faith the parents of Moses, and Moses himself, chose loyalty to the God and traditions of their ancestors over obedience to the Pharaoh with all his power. Judges, kings, and prophets, and even Jesus himself, are added to the list of examples of faith. In all of these examples the emphasis is that those mentioned staked everything on the reliability of God's promises

---

1. The translation of scripture quotations used in this chapter is taken from *The New English Bible* (New York: Oxford University Press, 1976).

concerning the future, but that seems to rest on the aforementioned presupposition: It is necessary to believe that God exists and rewards those who search for God.

THE PATRISTIC ERA

Given the range of meanings that already exists in the scriptures, it is not surprising that the Church Fathers of the second century give us some evidence that the Christian community of those times tended to an interpretation of faith based on Greek expectations. Justin the Martyr, for instance, presents Christianity as a philosophy, though he reinterprets philosophy when he maintains that God spoke to the Hebrews through the prophets and to the Greeks through the philosophers.[2] In general, we can find a good deal written at this time about the content of faith but little about the act or virtue of faith. The expression "the rule of faith" which emerges in this era clearly means the content of what is to be believed. Yet while the emphasis appears to be on believing certain propositions about what has happened, what God has done, and what exists beyond our present scrutiny, all this cannot be separated in practical living from the determination of where one places one's trust, what one depends on, what one's expectations are.

There is no doubt that two factors exerted a strong influence on the writings of the earlier Church Fathers when they wrote about faith. One was the prevailing metaphysical dualism of the world in which they lived. This dualism affirmed a radical and clear-cut separation between the world of mind and spirit and the world of body and matter. In such a context the biblical expression of faith as the evidence of things not seen may well shift its meaning from the temporal sense of something not yet realized but promised to something that is in another realm not subject to ordinary observation. The other factor that influenced patristic thought about faith is Gnosticism, which took the metaphysical dualism to the extreme by advocating a doctrine of salvation that required withdrawal in all possible ways from involvement with the material and historical. But this doctrine raised the problem, particularly acute for the Alexandrians, Clement and Origen, early in the third century, of the relationship between faith and knowledge. As they saw it, this relationship was not simple, because there were two quite different kinds of knowledge. There was ordinary knowledge, based on observation of the world about us. Faith for Clement and Origen meant believing something on the word of others. Both in ordinary usage and in a religious context, faith could reach further toward the truth than ordinary knowl-

---

2. *The First Apology* of Justin the Martyr, ch. 46.

edge. For these Church Fathers there is also a *gnosis* (knowledge) that is beyond faith, to which God called at least some Christians. Such knowledge was the mature outcome of a life dedicated to the pursuit of Christian wisdom. Thus Clement writes:

> Knowledge is a state of mind resulting from demonstration, but faith is a grace which begins with what is undemonstrable and rises to what is both universal and simple—to something which is not matter, is not with matter and is not under matter.[3]

While this statement appears as dry and abstruse, there is quite a different trend discernible in the catechetical sermons of Cyril of Jerusalem (c. 315-c. 386) to those about to be received into full membership in the church in the fourth century. Cyril devotes an entire lecture to faith and begins by pointing out analogies between faith and the secular life in society.[4] Marriage contracts are based on faith. So are farming and seafaring. Cyril offers these comparisons between faith and secular life as a help in understanding the faith which is required of, and given to, Christians.[5] But he points out that faith has two meanings:

> There is one kind of faith that has to do with doctrines, and involves the assent of the mind to such and such a doctrine. . . . For if you believe that Jesus Christ is Lord and that God raised him from the dead, you shall be saved and translated to paradise by him who led the robber into paradise.[6]

And he continues, more subtly,

> But the second kind of faith is that given by Christ by a particular grace. . . . This faith that is given by the Spirit as a grace is not only doctrinal faith, but one that empowers activities surpassing human nature. . . . For such a one places the thought of God before his mind . . . and with the end of this age not yet come, beholds the judgment already and the bestowal of the promised rewards.[7]

Cyril's analogies and his second definition of faith restore the sense of trust in the promises and in the coming future which seems to have

---

3. *Miscellanies*. Book 2, Ch 4, trans. Allan Douglas Galloway, *Basic Readings in Theology* (New York: Meridian, 1968), p. 39.
4. Cyril of Jerusalem, *The Catechetical Lectures*. Lecture 6. trans. William Telfer (Philadelphia: Westminster, 1955).
5. Ibid. p. 121.
6. Ibid. p. 123.
7. Ibid.

been the dominant element in the New Testament texts and in the utterances of the martyrs of the early centuries. Moreover, Cyril concludes his lecture by exhorting the newcomers to hold fast to the "articles of faith." He is referring to the Nicene Creed, which suggests both an interpretation of what has happened and is happening in history and also a confident expectation concerning the outcomes in the future. There again Cyril implies an understanding of faith in which belief in the truth of certain claims is inextricably interwoven with trust in the divine promises as mediated by Jesus Christ and by the Holy Spirit in the church of believers.

In the Western, Latin-speaking church of the patristic era the most penetrating and consequential reflections on faith were certainly those of Augustine of Hippo in the early fifth century. Augustine's reflections on this topic were strongly autobiographical. He was constantly amazed that out of the welter of the confused Roman world of the Mediterranean basin in his time he should have been converted to faith in God through Christ and the church. He was keenly aware that he had not in any way earned or deserved this grace and that many of his friends who were certainly no worse than he in their behavior and attitudes had not been brought to such faith. Thus, when Augustine is writing about faith, he seems to mean conversion to Christ, a conversion involving the whole person. But Augustine also speaks of the eyes of faith, that is, of faith as a special kind of seeing. In so doing he draws on existing liturgical practice and instruction in his own time, which refers to the Spirit (or to Christ) opening the eyes of the mind in faith and enlightening the baptizands with the radiance of faith.[8] It has been suggested, therefore, that Augustine thought of faith as a kind of affective knowledge. It is in this vein that he writes:

Faith is the virtue by which we believe things not seen.[9]

To profess one's faith is to put into words what one's heart holds. . . . He who believes in Christ believes with his heart; and no one does that against his will. . . . We are drawn not only willingly but with delight. . . . And so the man who can see, who can taste and savor

---

8. This imagery is pervasive in both Ambrose (who instructed Augustine in the Christian faith) and Augustine himself, suggesting that this imagery may have been in wider usage. Multiple references are given and explained in John Coventry, *The Theology of Faith* (Notre Dame, Ind.: Fides, 1952), Ch. 3.

9. Augustine of Hippo, *Treatise 79 on St. John*. This brief quotation gained in importance because Thomas Aquinas quoted it in the *Summa Theologiae* IIa IIae, q. 4, a. 1.

with his faith, that he in whom he puts his faith is equal to God, that is he whom the Father draws to his son.[10]

From passages such as this, in which Augustine seems to have stayed very close to liturgical texts that were common to the church, the emphasis is on faith as a gift of God that is at the same time a response from the human person. In the longer quotation above we do not have a clear definition because Augustine was writing in a pastoral and not in a scholarly context. He is inviting others to appreciate, and to be open to, something that he himself knows from experience and which he assumes he shares with his readers or listeners. His words, therefore, are suggestive and evocative rather than strictly definitive. Consequently, Augustine's words on faith can be read in two rather different ways. Some readers may either emphasize a psychological state of receptivity combined with the acceptance of certain specific revealed truths. Others might with equal justice to the texts regard Augustine's notion of faith as self-surrender to God through Christ. This ambiguity was to reappear later in the Reformation arguments over justification by faith.[11]

As the patristic era was coming to an end some residual anxiety over the Pelagian controversy (which emphasized human freedom and responsibility for a godly life) prompted the church in the Second Council of Orange in 529 to take up one aspect of the definition of faith in a particularly emphatic way in a solemn statement:

> Even after the coming of Our Lord, the grace of faith is not just a matter of man's free choice, but is also conferred by the generosity of Christ on all who wish to be baptized.[12]

THE MIDDLE AGES

With the transition to the medieval period, the aspect of grace as gift of God given without prior claim of any merit was emphasized even

---

10. Augustine of Hippo, *Treatise 26 on St. John*, commentary on John 6:43-44.

11. For a detailed discussion of the interpretation of Augustine in the light of his Neo-Platonist background, see Stewart Means, *Faith: a Historical Study* (New York: Macmillan, 1933), Ch. 5.

12. The Second Council of Orange, *The Canons on Grace*. The text is preserved in Henricus Denzinger and Adolfus Schönmetzer, eds., *Enchiridion Symbolorum* (Freiburg: Herder, 1967), no. 396. Translation available in Josef Neuner and H. Roos, *The Teaching of the Catholic Church* (New York: Alba House, 1967), p. 380.

more in the process of explaining faith in relation to the baptism of infants. But the mind of the Scholastics could scarcely rest without analyzing also what kind of modification of human beings and action was involved in faith. Although the medieval attention was more on the content of faith (that which is believed) than on faith as virtue, act or, gift, the whole era was permeated with the struggle to understand the relationship between faith and reason. This is evident already in the writings of Anselm of Canterbury, who died in 1109. Though not directly concerned with defining faith, he is preoccupied with the question whether it is possible reasonably to deny that there is a God, and he responds to that question with a rational demonstration that the denial of God is not a reasonable stance.[13] This seems to initiate a period of "scholastic theology" for it seems that the question is not of immediate pastoral concern in the place and time in which Anselm lived, but is of speculative interest as foundational to other discussions. What Anselm really thought faith was may be inferred from his approach to theology which he saw as faith in quest of understanding. Indeed he carried this so far that he attempted to demonstrate the rational necessity of the major Christian doctrines—a stance in which he was not followed by later scholastic theologians but which shows that he took very seriously the notion that faith opens the eyes of the mind to the truth, and that he must have had a strong conviction of the necessary unity of the truth.

The medieval reflection on faith as gift, act, and virtue reached its greatest elaboration in the thirteenth century, and the formulations which have subsequently been most influential are, of course, those of Thomas Aquinas (1225-1274). By this time there was general agreement that with the grace conferred at baptism the baptized Christians received as a gift three theological virtues, so called because they relate that person directly to God—faith, hope, and charity. That listing, of course, is as old as the letters of Paul in the New Testament. Of interest to the schools of medieval theology was the question concerning the specific characters of these three virtues and the distinction between them. Thomas is very clear and succinct in setting up these specifications:

> They are the virtues which make us well-adjusted to our last end, which is God himself: hence they are called theological, for they not only go out to God but also reach him. To be well-adjusted to an end we must know and desire it; the desire demands that we are in love with this end and are confident we can attain it. The theological virtues are therefore three—faith, which makes us know God; hope,

---

13. This argument appears in the *Proslogion* of Anselm.

which makes us look forward to joining him; charity, which makes us his friends.[14]

More at length Thomas defines faith like this:

> The virtue of faith causes the mind to assent to a truth which, transcending human understanding, is held in divine knowledge. . . . Men accept God's knowledge by faith and are joined thereby to him. Faith's principal object is God himself; other things are subsidiary and dependent.[15]

In these quotations, however, it is clear that when Thomas writes that the principal object of faith is God he is not referring to the belief that there is a God, but rather to an attitude of the mind inclining it to welcome the self-communication of God as ultimate or first truth.

Thomas has something more to say about the believing subject, and this also pertains to his definition of faith:

> To believe is an act of the mind assenting to divine truth because it is commanded by the will which is moved by God through grace; thus the act is under the control of the free will and is directed toward God.[16]

This formulation is intended to safeguard both the gratuity of God's gift and the authentic freedom of the person who gives the assent of faith. While the will is involved, however, there is absolutely no doubt that in the thinking of St. Thomas faith is essentially a "habit" or quality of the mind, and the act of faith is an act of the mind. Aquinas gives this point a great deal of attention precisely because he is aware that Augustine, for whom he has the greatest respect and whom he quotes frequently, leaves the matter somewhat ambiguous. Moreover, Thomas is sympathetic with the ambiguity when, in commenting on the Apostles' Creed, he writes, "By faith the Christian soul enters as it were into marriage with God." But the reason for which he allows a certain breadth in the definition in some contexts is that he acknowledges two kinds of faith: a first kind of faith that is informed by charity, which is the fullness of faith and leads to salvation, and a second kind of faith not so informed, which therefore cannot avail for salvation. That distinction is only possible because Aquinas' basic definition focuses on the mind as the human faculty in which the virtue of faith resides.

---

14. *De Virtutibus in communi*, 12, trans. and ed. Thomas Gilby, *St. Thomas Aquinas. Theological Texts* (Durham, N.C.: Labyrinth Press, 1982), p. 182.
15. *de Veritate*, XIV, 8, trans. Gilby, *Theological Texts*, p. 186.
16. *Summa Theologiae*, Ia IIae, q. 2, a. 9.

Because he takes this basic position, Thomas like other Scholastics must determine the relation between faith and reason. He writes:

> Between knowledge through science and knowledge through faith there is this difference: science shines only on the mind, showing that God is the cause of everything, that he is one and wise, and so forth. Faith enlightens the mind and also warms the affections.[17]

and again:

> Faith presupposes reason as grace presupposes nature, or as any perfection supposes a subject capable of betterment. Nevertheless nothing bars a truth which is demonstrable in itself and open to scientific knowledge from being accepted as a matter of belief before its proof has been grasped.[18]

A particularly interesting parallel is drawn as follows:

> The infused light of the habit of faith discovers the meaning of the articles of the Creed just as the mind's natural power of abstraction discovers the first evidences of reason.[19]

Moreover, Thomas is convinced that faith involves assent to particular propositions:

> Some urge: Cannot we believe different dogmas and yet hold the same underlying reality? Faith, they say, assents to a thing, not to a proposition about it. . . .
> Yet they are in error, for the assent of faith operates only through a judgment of reason. . . . When I profess, I believe in the Resurrection, you rightly take me to be committed to an assertion about a past historical event.[20]

In the last analysis, Thomas claims that he accepts as definitive the definition of faith offered in Hebrews 11:1 (which he attributes to Paul), but he knows himself that he has given far more philosophical precision to it:

> "Faith is the substance of things hoped for, the evidence of things not seen." Some writers are of the opinion that St. Paul was not

---

17. *Commentary, II Corinthians.*, 2, Lecture 3, trans. Gilby, p. 184.
18. *Summa Theologiae*, Ia, q. 2, a. 2, ad 1.
19. *III Sentences*, XXIII, q. 2, a. 1, ad 1, trans. Gilby, p. 190.
20. *de Veritate*, XIV, 12, trans. Gilby, p. 192.

proposing to describe what faith is but what faith does. But may he not provide what amounts in effect to a final definition? True, proper scholastic form is lacking, but all the essential requisites are touched on.[21]

Thomas Aquinas was not, of course, the only theologian of his time writing on the topic of faith, but in the course of time his writings stood out among those of his age for their clarity and coherence, so that he became by far the most influential thinker of his age for subsequent centuries. The trend of thought that was poised against his in his own time, the Augustinian school which wanted to maintain the Neo-Platonic base and thought-structure for theological discussion, produced some very important thinkers in the fourteenth and fifteenth centuries. These writers tended to emphasize the will and the activity of loving very strongly over the intellect and the activity of knowing and believing truth. This was built into a magnificent synthesis by John Duns Scotus (1265-1308) about the turn of the century and developed further by William of Occam (c. 1300-1349) and others in the fourteenth century. Their way of thinking presented God as determining the actual dispositions of creation and redemption rather arbitrarily so that there was less room for a theology that tried to understand the divine wisdom and more reason to focus on the absolute lordship of God.

This did not immediately or directly affect the definition of faith, but indirectly and in the course of the fourteenth and fifteenth centuries it did have a pervasive effect on the implicit definition. It rendered superfluous the rather elaborate discussions which had been conducted on the subject of the *praeambula* or preconditions of faith. In thirteenth-century theology these preconditions were understood to be: a judgment of the intellect that revelation as such is credible and that there is a duty to believe; a free act of the will commanding the intellect to assent; and finally the intellect's act of assenting, establishing it, so to speak, in the state or condition of faith. A voluntaristic way of thinking about God's action in history and about the human response is bound to find this too rationalistic a concept of faith. Moreover, the earlier concept of faith had been linked in the Thomistic synthesis with the final happiness of the blessed in heaven which was described as beatific vision—a seeing face to face with the eyes of the mind—and therefore the final fruition of the seeing dimly with the eyes of faith. As the predominantly Franciscan view gained momentum—the view that final blessedness was in love and the will rather than in knowing and in the mind—there was a subtle transformation in the implicit sense of the content of justification

---

21. *Ibid.*, 2, trans. Gilby, p. 195.

(the coming into the state of grace) and of the role faith played in Christian life and relationship with God.

Meanwhile in the popular piety of the time there was a definite, though scarcely self-conscious, inclination toward the voluntaristic sense of God's action. Faith in the omnipotence of God was rather dissipated by the preoccupation with miracles, a trivial sense of sacramental grace, a multiplicity of beliefs many of which were quite peripheral to faith in Jesus Christ, and a credulous but uninformed pursuit of indulgences. Implicitly, the popular definition of faith was belief in the extraordinary whenever the truth of the claims seemed to be endorsed by church authority. Implicitly, therefore, the object of faith was the inscrutable arbitrariness of God who was nevertheless savior. Explicitly, the concrete and immediate objects of faith could be the most horrendous and ludicrous frauds and deceptions, because the only grounds of credibility sought were the appearance of some sort of endorsement by church officials at any level.

THE REFORMATION

Under those circumstances it is scarcely surprising that mass movements such as those of John Wykliff (c. 1328-1384) and John Hus (c. 1369-1415) should arise in which the ground for credibility was established as the word of scripture. Such responses had arisen from the laity even earlier, as in the movements initiated by Peter Waldo and by Francis of Assisi (c. 1182-1226), but with Wykliff and Hus the understanding and reinterpretation came from significant scholars with strong university connections and direct influence on the theology of the schools. In their thought, faith was still in quest of understanding, but the relationship was modified by the experiences of their time. They no longer sought grounding for faith in a kind of natural theology in which reason supplied the grounds of credibility on which the move (the leap as it was later named) of faith might be made. The ground of credibility was simply the word of God in scripture. However, the role of reason was in the applying of the word of God in the New Testament in particular to the life of the believers and the activity of the institutional church of the time.

The primary effect of this, as is well known, was the dawning of a horrified awareness of how far the church of that time had distanced itself institutionally from the gospel of Jesus Christ. An indirect effect was a growing tendency to define terms, whether implicitly or explicitly, from the biblical contexts in which devout readers and listeners to sermons were now hearing these terms much more frequently. The concept of faith therefore widened once again to the range of meaning and to the benign ambiguity belonging to it in scripture. And this certainly set the stage for what was to come in the Reformation of the sixteenth century.

It is well known that Martin Luther (1483-1546), a devout and anxious Augustinian friar, was an avid biblical scholar whose special preoccupation was with the Pauline epistles. It is not strange that he should have seized upon the broader biblical sense of faith, noting the many passages in scripture in which faith is intimately linked to salvation. His main theological contention, however, was not about the definition of the concept but about the adequacy of faith (as defined contextually in scripture) for justification, that is, the entrance into the grace of God. The times were bristling with misunderstandings and mutual accusations, and it is surely at least in part due to the failure to reexamine the definition of faith early, irenically, and thoroughly that the problems and differences were never resolved. In any case, it is clear that Luther and his accusers were constructing their positions on the basis of two quite different definitions of faith.

Luther's concept of faith is aptly summarized by Bernhard Lohse as follows:

Man has nothing to do but gratefully to receive God's gift. Precisely this is faith. To have faith means not to trust in our own works, but humbly and gratefully to take the hand of God which reaches out to us. It means to trust and love God as a child its father.[22]

Melanchthon, in the Augsburg Confession, wrote:

Faith is not merely a knowledge of historical events but is a confidence in God and in the fulfillment of his promises. . . . We should understand the word faith in the scriptures to mean confidence in God, assurance that God is gracious to us, and not merely such a knowledge of historical events as the devil also possesses.[23]

In spite of this insistence on faith as being first and foremost confidence in God, Luther and the other Reformers clearly included some intellectual content to be believed. In the *Schmalkald Articles* of 1537, for instance, Luther wrote:

Jesus Christ, our God and Lord, "was put to death for our trespasses and raised again for our justification" (Rom 4:25). . . . Inasmuch as

---

22. Bernhard Lohse, *A Short History of Christian Doctrine* (Philadelphia: Fortress, 1966), pp. 161-162.
23. See John H. Leith, ed., *Creeds of the Christian Churches* (Atlanta: Knox, 1973), *The Augsburg Confession*, XX. "Faith and Good Works," p. 77.

this must be believed and cannot be obtained or apprehended by any work, law, or merit, it is clear and certain that such faith alone justifies us. . . . On this article rests all that we teach and practice. . . . Therefore, we must be quite certain and have no doubts about it. Otherwise all is lost.[24]

Moreover, the care which Luther took in preparing the *Small Catechism* and in expounding articles of the Creed elsewhere makes it abundantly clear that he is also concerned with the orthodoxy of the content of faith, more particularly in the doctrines of Christology and soteriology and in the way these doctrines are linked to the understanding of the sacraments.

This concern with the orthodoxy of the content of faith (the content of an intellectual grasp) is even more pronounced in the writing of John Calvin on behalf of the Swiss Reform. Thus in the *Institutes of the Christian Religion* he writes:

> The true knowledge of Christ consists in receiving him as he is offered by the Father—namely as invested with his gospel, For, as he is appointed as the end of our faith, so we cannot directly tend toward him except under the guidance of the gospel. . . . There is an inseparable relation between faith and the word. . . . For faith includes, not merely the knowledge that God is, but also, nay chiefly, a perception of his will toward us. . . . Faith is the knowledge of the divine will in regard to us, as ascertained from his word. . . .
> We shall now have a full definition of faith if we say that it is a firm and sure knowledge of the divine favor toward us, founded on the truth of a free promise in Christ, and revealed to our minds and sealed on our hearts by the Holy Spirit.[25]

In response to these voices of the Protestant Reformers, the Council of Trent (1545-1563), in its efforts to maintain the fullness of the Catholic tradition, turned largely to the synthesis made by Thomas Aquinas. In the *Decree on Justification* the Council insisted on an understanding of faith that involved intellectual assent to revealed truth, and therefore of course it also insisted that justification was not by faith alone but also by hope and charity:

---

24. *The Schmalkald Articles*, II, 1. See Theodore Tappart, ed., *The Book of Concord* (Philadelphia: Fortress, 1959), p. 292.

25. John Calvin, *The Institutes of the Christian Religion*. Book III, ch. 2. Translation taken from John T. Hunt, ed., *Library of Christian Classics*, Vol. XX (London: SCM, 1961).

Faith, unless hope and charity be added to it, neither unites man perfectly with Christ, nor makes him a living member of his body. For which reason it is most truly said that faith without works is dead and of no profit.[26]

The concern lying behind this Tridentine statement becomes clearer later in the text, in the canons concerning justification:

If anyone says that man is absolved from his sins and justified because he firmly believes that he is absolved and justified, or that no one is truly justified except him who believes himself justified, and that by this faith alone absolution and justification are effected, let him be anathema.[27]

But a slightly different concern also emerges which has to do with the definition of faith:

If anyone says that justifying faith is nothing else than confidence in divine mercy, which remits sins for Christ's sake, or that it is this confidence alone that justifies us, let him be anathema.[28]

There is no doubt that one of the primary concerns of the Council Fathers was to preserve normative intellectual content as a constitutive element of the theological virtue of faith. This emphasis on faith as intellectual assent to a set of dogmas has been held in the Roman Catholic Church down to the present time—at least as far as the official teaching of the institutional church is concerned.

The teaching of Trent on faith might be summed up as follows: Faith is not only confidence but assent of the mind to whatever God has revealed and promised; faith is a gift of God which is the beginning of salvation but must be combined with hope and charity if it is not to be a dead thing. This position was reaffirmed at the First Vatican Council (1869-1870). But by the time the First Vatican Council was convened, the most pressing issues with regard to faith came not so much from the theological discussions of the sixteenth century Protestant Reformation and the Catholic Counterreformation as from the cultural and intellectual movement known as the Enlightenment. From the early seventeenth century until the end of the eighteenth, there was a groundswell

---

26. The Council of Trent, 6th Session, 1547. *Decree Concerning Justification*, Ch. VII, See Leith, *Creeds of the Christian Church*, p. 412.
27. Ibid., Canon 14. (Leith, p. 422)
28. Ibid., Canon 12. (Leith, p. 421)

in European culture and thought which placed its confidence in human reason and rejected any authority other than human reason. The foundations of modern science and the philosophical trends initiated by René Descartes (1596-1650) set great store by philosophical skepticism. Along with the newfound confidence in reason, the culture with its many aspects—political, economic, social, etc.—was rapidly emancipating itself from theological control or direct influence. The autonomy of human reason spread through all aspects of life and gave rise to attempts to build a religion of reason out of the Christian tradition.

THE MODERN ERA

The new attempts at a religion of reason came upon the scene when seventeenth-century Protestantism as well as the contemporary Catholicism had again developed a scholastic type of theology that was itself rather rationalistic in its mode of argument by logical deduction from first principles that seemed little connected with religious experience of any kind. But the theology of the various denominational traditions was still a divisive force, and people seemed to have wearied of the endless persecution and strife. In England a number of writers and preachers began the quest for a common faith based on "innate principles" of a very general nature, such as that there is a God who ought to be worshiped mainly by virtuous behavior, that it is necessary to repent of sins, and that there are rewards and penalties after death as sanction for the need to behave virtuously and repent for one's sins.[29] Building upon such very general innate principles, a group of thinkers generally known as Deists came to the logical conclusion that there was no need of divine revelation because unaided human reason is a sufficient basis for religion. These people were evidently not tortured by Luther's anxiety and self-condemnation. In any case, faith is nothing but the human side of revelation, and this holds true whether the definition of faith stresses a movement of the intellect to accept the self-revelation of God as truth, or whether the definition stresses a movement of trust in response to a self-revelation of God as merciful. If there is no revelation, or if revelation is simply identical with the whole of creation and of human experience in the world, then there is no call for faith, but only for a reasonable response to reality.

---

29. This particular list of basic truths was proposed by Lord Herbert of Cherbury in *De Veritate*, published in 1624. Text quoted at greater length in James C. Livingston, *Modern Christian Thought* (New York: Macmillan, 1971), p. 14.

Those Christian thinkers, however, who wanted to preserve the authority of the Christian scriptures and some traditional doctrines, tried to establish ways of combining the scrutiny of reason with some possible role for faith.[30] John Locke (1632-1704) for instance, a devout believer as well as an eminent philosopher, wrote at the end of the seventeenth century that there are propositions that are according to reason, others that are above reason, and yet others that are against reason. When faith assents to truths of revelation it is the assent of the mind to propositions that are above reason. He wrote:

> Faith is the assent to any proposition, not . . . made out by deductions of reason, but upon the credit of the proposer, as coming from God in some extraordinary way of communication. This way of discovering truths to men we call revelation.[31]

This definition, though made in an entirely different intellectual context, is not very different from Thomas Aquinas' definitions. Moreover, it places heavy emphasis on faith as an intellectual response, making no mention of the element of confidence or trust.

The continuing movement, however, to a religion based on reason alone continued in England, France, and Germany until it finally began to collapse on the one side because it drifted into atheism, on the other side because it did not take into account the affective side of religious experience. Adding to the collapse of a religion based solely on reason was the fact that the various institutional Christian churches clung resolutely to their respective traditional orthodoxies and successfully urged many Christians to follow the official teachings of these churches.

Two nineteenth-century authors who strove to redress the balance lost by excessive intellectualism in matters of religion were Friedrich Schleiermacher (1768-1834) and John Henry Newman (1801-1890). Schleiermacher defined the essence of religion in a way not very different from Luther's definition of faith:

> The common element in all diverse expressions of piety, by which these are conjointly distinguished from all other feelings, or in other words the self-identical essence of piety is this: the consciousness of

---

30. For extensive development see Livingston, *Modern Christian Thought*, ch. 2.

31. *An Essay Concerning Human Understanding* (New York: Oxford University Press, 1956), p. 355. (Extensive excerpt given in Livingston, *Modern Christian Thought*.)

absolute dependence, or, which is the same thing, of being in relation with God.[32]

It is true that this particular definition does not relate piety to redemption in Christ—a link that Schleiermacher makes elsewhere when addressing Christianity more specifically. But what is important in the impact which Schleiermacher has had on the understanding of the concept of faith is that he has reintroduced affectivity into the one-sidedly intellectual interpretation of faith which had been brought to the fore by the constant concern over the relationship between faith and reason in an atmosphere in which it was faith which had to justify itself.

Newman, writing as a member of the Tractarian Movement in the Anglican Church (though he later became reconciled with Rome) discussed the nature of faith in various writings in the context of his own time. This context was still one in which rationalism made constant inroads on people's perceptions of the very possibility of faith and of the intelligibility of the concept. He and the other Tractarians saw faith as grounded in moral obedience and in a quest for righteousness. Newman wrote:

> Faith is created in the mind, not so much by facts, as by probabilities; and since probabilities have no definite ascertained value, and are reducible to no scientific standard, what are such to each individual, depends on his moral temperament.[33]

Elsewhere, Newman draws the important distinction between notional assent and real assent. Notional assent follows upon acts of inference and other logical processes. Newman points out, however, that notional assent falls far short of the kind of assent that is evidently intended by a truly Christian view of faith. That kind of assent that is authentically named faith is what Newman tries to describe when he speaks of real assent. Real assent is founded upon the experience of conscience which leads to the apprehension of a Divine Judge and to the perception of divine goodness and trustworthiness, out of which is born a personal relationship—a commitment very different from the purely intellectual character of notional assent.[34]

---

32. Friedrich Schleiermacher, *The Christian Faith* (Edinburgh: T & T Clark, 1948), p. 12. An excerpt in which this and other relevant passages occur is reprinted in the anthology by Bernard M. G. Reardon, *Religious Thought in the Nineteenth Century* (Cambridge: University Press, 1966).

33. *University Sermons. Sermon X* (1839). Here quoted from Reardon, *Religious Thought in the Nineteenth Century*, p. 272.

34. John Henry Newman, *An Essay in Aid of a Grammar of Assent* (1870). Available in many editions.

Though they had characteristic contributions, Schleiermacher and Newman were certainly not the only nineteenth-century authors to concern themselves with the concept of faith and to defend it against the inroads of an all-consuming rationalism. Almost every theological writer of that period wrestled with this particular problem in one form or another. Many of them, like Newman and Schleiermacher, did not write or think with the methodical precision and style of the Scholastics, but rather in a personal, meditative style that keeps insisting on what is known from experience, in a way that anticipates the twentieth-century existentialist writers in some aspects. What is common to most of these writers is their focus upon the act of faith and its very possibility.

Meanwhile, however, official pronouncements and confessions of the institutional churches regularly focused on the content to be believed rather than on the act of faith or the meaning of the concept of faith. However, the *Constitution on the Catholic Faith* of the First Vatican Council did contain three chapters on faith and reason. The text includes what may be considered to be a definition of faith and reads as follows:

> Since man is wholly dependent on God, his Creator and Lord, and created reason is entirely subject to uncreated truth, we are obliged to render God revealing the perfect obedience of our intellect and will in faith. This faith, which is "the beginning of human salvation," the Catholic Church acknowledges to be a supernatural virtue whereby, impelled and sustained by grace, we believe those things to be true which God has revealed, not because we have perceived the intrinsic truth of these things by the light of our natural reason, but on the authority of God himself who reveals them, who can neither deceive nor be deceived.[35]

The strengths of this definition are obvious, inasmuch as it takes into account and incorporates much of the discussion of previous centuries. The weakness was soon to be apparent again in the misadventures of the so-called Modernist crisis at the turn of the century: namely, it is very problematic to isolate "those things which God has revealed" to which "we are obliged to render God revealing the perfect obedience of our intellect and will in faith" from the human and culture-bound, histori-

---

35. Denzinger-Schönmetzer, *Enchiridion Symbolorum*, no. 1789. An excellent summary of official Catholic teaching on faith is available in English in Karl Rahner and Herbert Vorgrimler, *A Concise Theological Dictionary* (New York: Herder, 1965). For a fuller explanation of the concept of faith in Vatican I, see John O'Donnell, "Faith," in *The New Dictionary of Theology*, ed. Joseph A. Komonchak, Mary Collins, and Dermot A. Lane (Wilmington, Del.: Glazier, 1987).

cally conditioned ways in which that revelation has been understood and formulated in times past. The question of our continuing experience, our growing historical and scientific consciousness, our changing philosophy and language, and so forth, is not addressed by the definition of faith given by the First Vatican Council.

The teaching of the Second Vatican Council in the Constitution *Dei Verbum*, concerning revelation, goes a long way toward meeting this deficiency. While reaffirming Vatican I's definition of faith, the Second Vatican Council nonetheless recasts this definition into a dynamic and existential mode showing faith as a continuing personal relationship:

> The obedience of faith must be given to God who reveals, an obedience by which man entrusts his whole self freely to God, offering "the full submission of intellect and will to God who reveals," and freely assenting to the truth revealed by him. . . .
> There is a growth in the understanding of the realities and of the words that have been handed down. This happens through the contemplation and study made by believers, who treasure these things in their hearts . . . through the intimate understanding of spiritual things they experience, and through the preaching of those who have received through episcopal succession the sure gift of truth.[36]

Meanwhile, more recent Protestant confessional statements, such as those of the World Council of Churches, tend to reaffirm faith in Jesus Christ as the hope of the world (emphasizing the element of confidence and trust) while also setting forth specific content of belief. This much is traditional, but what is noteworthy is that the context in these more recent statements is often a concern with major social problems in the world, so that the reaffirmation of Christ as hope of the world relates the act and disposition of faith rather directly to redemptive transformation of wordly realities. Moreover, these statements are made within an intense sensitivity to ecumenical questions, and even to the claims of other religious traditions to divine revelation through channels other than Jesus Christ. Though not addressing the definition of faith explicitly, therefore, these new confessions and official statements have broadened the implicit definition of faith considerably.[37]

CONCLUSION

This chapter has provided the historical background (in outline sketch) to the present Protestant and Catholic understanding of the

---

36. *Dei Verbum*, 5, 8. Translation taken from Walter Abbott, ed., *The Documents of Vatican II* (New York: America Press, 1966), pp. 113, 116.
37. See Leith, *Creeds of the Christian Church*, pp. 566-597.

concept of faith in the churches of the West—an understanding that is explored in depth in the essays in Part II of this volume. This summary presentation has not considered the development of the concept of faith in the Eastern churches, nor has any consideration of the churches of the Radical Reform been attemped. Each of these is a worthwhile study, the more so as each tradition has its own way of tracing and evaluating the historical developments. Nor, yet again, has any attempt been made here to deal with new developments in the understanding of the concepts of faith which have resulted from contemporary Jewish-Christian dialogue, though these are immensely important.[38]

In the contemporary theological exchange there is a new approach to the shaping of a foundational theology in which the notions of revelation and of faith are pivotal.[39] Today the concern is not so much with faith and reason as it is with faith and history and with faith and worldly experience in the socio-economic and political dimensions.[40] In order to begin to understand this contemporary exchange and effort, it is rather important to consider the history of the concept of faith in the Christian community and to avoid repeating the misunderstandings of the past, based as they were on ignorance of one another's positions. The ecumenical possibilities of the present offer a veritable window of opportunity to all who are engaged in both theological reflection and church ministries.

---

38. The richness of this exchange and its fruit for Christian reflection is well explored and explained in John C. Merkle, *The Genesis of Faith* (New York: Macmillan, 1985). A study of the depth theology of Abraham J. Heschel, this volume highlights in very readable fashion many of the issues concerning faith which have preoccupied Christians through the ages and shows how Jewish tradition offers many new insights.

39. Contemporary theological reflection on this topic is summarized and explained (in a rather technical fashion) in Francis Schüssler-Fiorenza, *Foundational Theology* (New York: Crossroad, 1984).

40. This link is pervasive in the work of Jürgen Moltmann, Johann-Baptist Metz, and of the large cluster of Third World theologians grouped under the designation "liberation theologians."

CHAPTER 2

The Concept of Faith in Comparative Religions

John Carmody

This chapter deals with the concept of faith held in various non-Christian religious traditions. In this vein, the chapter will concentrate on nonliterate religious traditions, Hinduism, Buddhism, Chinese traditions, Judaism, and Islam. Let it be said, only once but seriously, that each of these traditional religious blocs is at once immense and diverse, and so it is very difficult adequately to provide a highly accurate overview in just a few pages. It should also be noted that this chapter deals only with those non-Christian religious traditions which are alive in the present age. A fully comprehensive treatment of the concept of faith in comparative religion would also include the religions of such perished cultures as the ancient Egyptian, Persian, Greek, and Roman.[1]

---

1. The best general reference work on world religions now is the 16 volume *The Encyclopedia of Religion*, ed. Mircea Eliade (New York: Macmillian, 1987). A still serviceable older handbook, especially good on the perished civilizational religions, is the 2 volume *Historia Religionum*, ed. C. Jouco Bleeker and Geo Widengren (Leiden: E. J. Brill, 1969, 1971). Other useful reference works include *Historical Atlas of the Religions of the World*, ed. I. al Faruqi and D. Sopher (New York: Macmillan, 1974); *World Christian Encyclopedia*, ed. David B. Barrett (New York: Oxford University Press, 1982); *The Times Atlas of World History*, ed. Geoffrey Barraclough (Maplewood, N.J.: Hammond, 1979); *The Concise Encyclopedia of Living Faiths*, ed. R. C. Zaehner (Boston: Beacon Press, 1967); *Abingdon Dictionary of Living Religions*, ed. Keith Crim (Nashville: Abingdon, 1981); and *A Dictionary of Non-Christian Religions*, by Geoffrey Parrinder (Philadelphia: Westminster, 1971). On recent views of method-

24

NONLITERATE RELIGIOUS TRADITIONS

A typical comparative religion survey of nonliterate religious traditions embraces American Indians, Africans, Australians, and Eskimos. Some surveys also deal with prehistoric peoples and the peasant substratum (the "little tradition") that has lived on in "higher traditions" such as those treated in the other sections of this chapter.

One of the realities common to nonliterate traditions is shamanism. Roughly speaking, the shaman is the predominant religious figure throughout the nonliterate world. Working with a Siberian prototype, Mircea Eliade defined the shaman as a specialist in archaic techniques of ecstasy.[2] Much nonliterate religious faith boiled down to trust that the shaman could contact spirits who would help the tribe survive. Survival primarily meant gaining food, through hunting and gathering, and producing offspring through female fertility. Secondarily, survival meant assuring the dead of a peaceful afterlife, purging the tribe of guilt (incurred through breaches of taboos), tamping down strife, curing sickness, and providing a coherent worldview that made human existence seem meaningful, bearable, even beautiful. The concept of faith in nonliterate religious traditions, then, stressed trust in the shaman and in the efficacy of his activity.

The Eskimo shaman, who is close to the Siberian prototype, would go into ecstasy through such techniques as beating a drum and dancing,

---

ology, see *The World's Religious Traditions*, ed. Frank Whaling (New York: Crossroad, 1986), and Jonathan Z. Smith, *Imagining Religion* (Chicago: University of Chicago Press, 1982). The most ambitious historical interpretation is Mircea's Eliade's multivolumed *A History of Religious Ideas* (Chicago: University of Chicago Press, 1978 ff). The most useful American journal is *History of Religions*, published by the University of Chicago Press.

2. See Mircea Eliade, *Shamanism* (Princeton, N.J.: Princeton University Press, 1964). Other works relevant to this section include two collections of myths, Eliade's *From Primitives to Zen* (New York: Harper & Row, 1967), and Barbara Sproul's *Primal Myths* (San Francisco: Harper & Row, 1979). On Eskimo culture, see Barry Lopez, *Arctic Dreams* (New York: Scribner's, 1986), which not only is fine reading in itself but also has a good bibliography. On American Indian religion, see Ake Hultkrantz, *The Religions of the American Indians* (Berkeley: University of California Press, 1979). A primer on African religions is Noel Q. King's *African Cosmos* (Belmont, Calif.: Wadsworth, 1986). On the intellectualist side, see John Mbiti, *African Religions and Philosophy* (Garden City, N.Y.: Doubleday, 1969). For Australian religions, see Mircea Eliade, *Australian Religions* (Ithaca, N.Y.: Cornell University Press, 1973). Eliade's *A History of Religious Ideas, Vol. 1: From the Stone Age to the Eleusinian Mysteries*, deals with prehistoric themes, while the other volumes of this work regularly attend to the little tradition. Other good sources on the little tradition are works by anthropologists such as Clifford Geertz and Victor Turner and by folklorists.

fasting, plunging into icy water, meditating on a skull, or ingesting tobacco. The Eskimo sense of reality, like that of most nonliterate peoples, was tripartite. The heavens contained many of the spiritual forces thought responsible for creation and fate: the sun, the wind, the snow. Some Eskimo tribes thought the spirits of the dead went to the heavens, while other tribes placed them under the earth. For coastal Eskimo peoples, whose livelihood depended on fishing and hunting sea animals, the under-earth tended to house the mistress of the sea creatures, who could withhold or release them. On earth, between heaven and the under-world, human beings moved through a realm of numerous souls. Plants, animals, and even rocks had souls, sometimes several different ones for each individual. It was important not to offend these souls, especially the ones animating important animals like the seals or the deer. Thus when one killed a seal, one apologized and gave back to the sea a part of the seal in which the soul was thought to lodge.

The shaman had the power to go into trance and move to the heavens or the under-earth. This power made it possible to learn what was bothering a sick person, to learn where the game had gone, or to guide the dead to their resting place. Shamanistic faith virtually always assumed that sickness, or a dearth of game, was a matter of imbalance in the system of dynamic ongoing interactions among the spirits, the tribe, and nature. The sick person had been hexed by an enemy, or the tribe had offended the mistress of the sea animals. In trance, the shaman would travel to the spirit in charge and try to set things right. Often the practical response would be to dance the sick person's spirit back to health, or to get the tribal members who had broken a taboo (for example, by eating meat out of season or aborting a fetus) to repent.

American Indian variations on this pattern, in both the North and the South, included the practice in many tribes of encouraging all members, not just the predominant shamanic healers (medicine-men), to gain a directive vision and recruit spirits who would be familiars and helpers. Indian males regularly sought the warrior's power to kill. They were engaged in a battle of survival with the animals they hunted and the enemies they fought. Indian females carried within them a complementary power, namely the power to bring forth new life. It was important to keep these two powers from clashing. Hence warriors returned from battle would be segregated, as would menstruating women. The concept of faith held by the American Indians centered around the following: By keeping the rules and petitioning the spiritual powers, human beings could maintain harmony with the cosmic whole in which they were immersed. Peace and prosperity came from such harmony. Disharmony would bring disaster.

African variations on this shamanic pattern included a more optimistic view of the natural world than tended to obtain among Eskimos and American Indians, less stress on ecstatic journeying to the gods, and more stress on mediums who could represent the dead and divine the cause of illness or bad luck. As with American Indians, the concept of faith held by traditional nonliterate Africans included a fear of witches, who served powers of evil. Nonliterate Africans also shared with Native Americans a great reverence for dreams, which they considered prime sources of revelation. The sacrificing of animals also held an important place indeed. These people probably sacrificed animals to the gods or spiritual forces more than Eskimos or American Indians, but the occasions and sorts of sacrifices varied from African tribe to tribe. By sacrificing something of worth, animal or vegetable, it was thought in faith that one could appease angry spirits and express one's gratitude for life's blessings. Some tribes had high gods, who created the world and then left daily business to lesser spirits. Most tribes venerated the ancestors, thinking that the departed continued to be available to their descendants. Fertility—in crops, animals, and children—was the theme of many prayers and rituals. Warding off sickness and death was a second major concern.

The aboriginal Australian's faith in the powers of shaman-like functionaries to gain the help of favoring spirits and so protect the tribe from infertility, sickness, death, and ill-fortune had a distinctive focus on a return to the "dream time" of creation. Throughout the life cycle, ceremonies of one kind or another initiated Australians deeper and deeper into the mysteries of this dream time. The concept of faith held by nonliterate Australians was deeply enmeshed with myths and rituals. These myths and rituals told how humanity originally had been a cluster of souls, how the divine spirits had formed the landscape, and how the spirit of a deceased person entered into the body of a newborn child. In ceremonies that involved blood-letting, men tried to preserve the fertility cycles of nature and imitate the spontaneous fertility that women achieved through blood. Women's ceremonies made puberty, childbirth, and menopause thresholds to new levels of immersion in the dream time.

Paleontologists conjecture that prehistoric hunters and gatherers lived by shamanic patterns similar to those sketched thus far. Paintings on the walls of European caves 20,000 years ago may represent the typically shamanic concern for fertility in women and animals as well as those religious ceremonies designed to increase this fertility or to secure a successful hunt. Arrangements at grave sites suggest that tribal members were buried with hope of an afterlife, and figurines found across paleolithic Eurasia suggest a widespread cult of a mother goddess, who most likely was revered as the source of all life and fertility. Thus the concept of faith among prehistoric peoples usually included an emphasis on fertility and a belief in a mother goddess.

In Europe, India, Asia, and the Americas, many of these shamanic motifs—contests with spiritual forces, concern for fertility, need to placate the dead—continued after a canonical Christianity, Judaism, Islam, Hinduism, Confucianism, or Buddhism had arisen. Peasants and illiterate people continued to believe that one had to protect children from the evil eye, or that stone, because of its permanency (thought of as a solid form of life), could help women conceive. Farmers prayed to spirits of the field, fishermen prayed to spirits of the waters, and midwives prayed to spirits or saints who cared for childbirth.

The concept of faith among nonliterate peoples therefore has stressed the actions of spiritual forces, good and bad, and the need to stay on the side of the good spiritual forces. If one could keep harmony with the positive balance in nature, one could hope to survive and prosper. On the whole, nonliterate people have believed that nature, the main face of divinity, gave them good grounds for such hope.

HINDUISM

Hinduism is a term of convenience rather than an exact description of a single religious tradition. More than Judaism or Christianity, Hinduism has been an umbrella under which numerous native traditions have sheltered. The main criterion for admission to the Hindu family has been accepting the Vedic scriptures as the prime religious authority, but Hindus often have interpreted such acceptance quite loosely. Thus only those such as the Buddhists who directly challenged the Vedic authority have been judged unacceptable by Hindu orthodoxy (and some lists of *avatars* [embodiments of Hindu divinity] even include the Buddha).

Perhaps the notion most important to the Hindu concept of faith has been *dharma*. This term has two related meanings. More generally, it denotes Truth, Instruction, Revealed Teaching. In this denotation, dharma is typically placed by scholars in comparative religion alongside Jewish Torah, Christian Revelation, and Islamic *Sharia*. The Vedas are the font of such dharma, but the later law codes, philosophies, religious epics, and other Hindu teachings all expressed and amplified it.

More specifically, dharma has meant the responsibilities of one's caste, one's inherited place in the complicated structure of Indian social life. The main castes traditionally have been four: priests, warriors, producers (farmers and merchants), and workers. A fifth group fell outside the caste structure and as such were outcastes (out-of-caste) and so were untouchable to those persons in a caste. In reality, however,

Indian society has been much more complicated than this simple five-fold division suggests, because one's occupation also tended to become a niche that restricted or expanded one's dealings with people in other social sectors. Thus rice farmers were different from wheat farmers, with implications for marriage, worship, and other interactions the two groups might contemplate.

The main responsibilities of Hindu priests have been to perform religious ceremonies and offer religious instruction. The main responsibilities of the warriors have been to protect the realm against criminals and enemies and to provide civil order. The main responsibilities of the producers have been to furnish food, goods, and economic prosperity. The main responsibility of the workers has been to serve the three higher castes. To outcastes fell the worst jobs—collecting garbage, sweeping sewers, burying the dead—and the fate of representing uncleanness, pollution. (This concept of pollution cuts across many religious traditions. In general, pollution means a state of being, not necessarily culpable, that renders one unfit for most dealings with divinity or holy things.)

Central to the Hindu concept of faith is the belief and trust that by fulfilling the responsibilities of their caste they could improve their karma and advance toward *moksha*. Moksha is a state of freedom from all of the constraints—physical, moral, intellectual, ontological—that earthly creatures suffer. Moksha therefore is the Hindu equivalent of the salvation sought by Western religions. Until one has gained moksha, karma—the influence of one's prior deeds, including those performed in previous existences—keeps one in *samsara*: the realm of birth and death. Since birth and death are painful, the release brought by moksha is very attractive. The Hindu faith holds that the chains binding people to samsara boil down to personal desire. Because human beings want various things, they become attached to samsaric existence. If human beings can stop desire, they can gain detachment, improve their karmic condition and step closer to moksha. Another Hindu way of putting the problem is to say that people are ignorant of their situation and so seek the wrong things. Progress toward moksha therefore is a process of enlightenment.

Perhaps the prototypical Hindu religious figure has been the yogin. As the shaman stands to nonliterate traditions, so does the yogin stand to Hindu traditions. By withdrawing from most activities, by engaging in the practice of meditation, and by trying to quench desire, the yogin pursues moksha full-time. In contrast to the shaman, however, the yogin believes in faith that the way to salvation leads inside. Shamans are ecstatic, going out of themselves, traveling to the gods or masters of the animals to gain help. Yogins are, in Mircea Eliade's term, "enstatic."

They go within, trying to gain control of their bodily movements, to quiet their senses, to still their imaginations, to pass below the level of rational thought, and finally to rest at the bottom of pure consciousness (the awareness that is awareness of nothing in particular). This last state is called *samadhi*. In it the yogin can experience the truth taught by many of the Upanishads: the ground of reality and the ground of the self are one and the same.

For priests and yogins, the Hindu dharma implies considerable study and meditation. For warriors, merchants, and workers, meditation has been commendable; however, a discipline of action has seemed more pertinent for members of these castes. The ideal life cycle for the warriors and merchants, who along with the priests were eligible for initiation as twice-born people who realistically could hope to gain enlightenment and moksha, began with apprenticeship to a guru, from whom one learned the Vedic traditions. After studying and meditating under a guru's direction, one returned to secular life, married, raised a family, took part in business and civil affairs, cared for one's parents, and generally kept Indian society going. The third phase of the ideal life cycle was retirement to meditate on the meaning of life, as experience had shown the Vedic tradition to illumine one's experiences. In the final stage in a successful life cycle, the person gained enlightenment and wandered as a free beggar instructing others in the primacy of moksha. The Hindu concept of faith, then, focuses on the life cycle and its ultimate fulfillment in moksha.

The disciplines for work obviously applied most directly to the second stage in the life cycle, that of the householder. Essentially these disciplines boiled down to learning to work or to act with detachment, neither greatly desiring success nor greatly fearing failure. (Mohandas Gandhi, the Mahatma, adapted this tradition, which went by the name *karma-yoga*, to his campaign for India's political liberation from British rule, teaching his followers that if they boycotted British goods, marched in protest against British policies, and suffered British retaliation with detachment their fight for freedom would advance them toward salvation.)

In addition to meditation and purifying one's action or work, a third way that Hindus have expressed their faith in the dharma and have sought moksha has been through devotional love (*bhakti*). This has been popular with women, the lower classes, and the outcastes. The object of bhakti typically has been a god or goddess who promises protection to the devotee, help in practical matters, and assistance toward moksha. The most popular gods have been Krishna, Shiva, and the many local versions of an Indian Great Goddess. Often the devotees became impassioned adherents of the deity in question, singing its traditional songs, attending its annual cycle of festivals, and performing its household rites (*puja*) much as Christians have honored Jesus, Mary, or the saints: as sharers of their hopes, fears, sorrows, and joys.

The most popular Hindu writing, the Bhagavad Gita, probably owes its influence to its catholic blend of these three different paths to moksha. The Gita is part of the Mahabharata, a great Indian epic about a prehistoric war. Its literary form is a dialogue in which Krishna instructs Arjuna, a warrior who is repulsed at the prospect of killing, in both his caste responsibilities and the paths to salvation. Krishna describes yogic meditation, freeing oneself from desire, how to handle different humors, karma yoga, the true nature of the inmost spirit (*Atman*), and bhakti. The two high points of the Gita are the god's revelation of his splendid presence throughout all of creation and his revelation of his love for those who love him.

The core of the Hindu concept of faith, therefore, has been the tenet that by following the rich dharma handed down by the sages (both those sages whose visions are enshrined in the Vedas and those sages who commented on the Vedas) one could gain moksha: release from both a painful present life and condemnation to more painful lives in the future. Believing that karma framed the problem of human existence, Hindus have found various ways of trying to free themselves from karma. For the majority, however, the way has been focusing their faith, their religious ardor and need, on a deity such as Krisha. They have believed they could escape bondage and gain all happiness by loving nothing worldly, only the god.[3]

BUDDHISM

Gautama, the Buddha (536-476 B.C.E.), studied with various Hindu meditation masters but found neither their teachings nor the ritualistic religion of the Vedic priests effective. His difficulty flowed from the typical Hindu problem: how to overcome samsaric suffering. The solu-

---

3. The following general works offer a good introduction to Hinduism: A. L. Basham, *The Wonder That Was India* (New York: Grove Press, 1959); Thomas J. Hopkins, *The Hindu Religious Tradition* (Encino, Calif.: Dickenson, 1971); David R. Kinsley, *Hinduism* (Englewood Cliffs, N.J.: Prentice-Hall, 1982); Troy Wilson Organ, *Hinduism* (Woodbury, N.Y.: Barron's, 1974); Edward C. Dimock et al., *The Literature of India: An Introduction* (Chicago: University of Chicago Press, 1978); S. N. Dasgupta, *Hindu Mysticism* (New York: Frederick Ungar, 1959); Heinrich Zimmer, *Philosophies of India* (Princeton, N. J.: Princeton University Press, 1969); S. Radhakrishnan and C. Moore, eds., *A Sourcebook in Indian Philosophy* (Princeton, N.J.: Princeton University Press, 1957); and Mircea Eliade, *Yoga* (Princeton, N.Y.: Princeton University Press, 1970).

tion that he found, through a regime of moderate asceticism and determined meditation (yoga), was expressed in his Four Noble Truths: 1) all life is suffering, 2) the cause of suffering is desire, 3) stopping desire will stop suffering, and 4) one can stop desire by following the noble eightfold path of right views, right intention, right speech, right action, right livelihood, right effort, right mindfulness, and right concentration. These Four Noble Truths are central to the concept of faith in classical Buddhism.

When Buddhists formally embrace their religion, in a ceremony equivalent to Christian baptism and confirmation, they "take refuge" in the Buddha, the dharma, and the sangha. These three "jewels" are extremely important in the mainstream Buddhist concept of faith, forming as they do the object of faith. The Buddha is Gautama, the historical figure who lived in the sixth and fifth centuries B.C.E. But the Buddha is also the ontological principle of enlightenment that gives all of reality its meaning. The dharma is the truth taught by the Buddha but also the ontological Truth by which the universe stands. The sangha is the Buddhist community—in the first instance, the community of monks and nuns who have been the mainstay of Buddhist life; in the second instance all Buddhists, laypeople as well as monks and nuns.

The concept of faith taught in classic Buddhism is enmeshed with faith in the Buddha. For its part, faith means trusting that the Buddha's analysis of the human condition is accurate and that his prescription for solving its problems is effective. Just as Buddhists share with Hindus an analysis that stresses the enslaving results of desire, so they share the millennial Hindu convictions about karma and samsara. The Buddhist equivalent of Hindu moksha is *nirvana*: an ineffable state of unconditionedness and freedom. Buddhists also have explained the religious problematic in terms of ignorance and so have conceived of their pathway as an enlightenment.

Three of the most significant ways in which the Buddhist concept of faith differs from the Hindu concept of faith are the Buddhist repudiation of Vedic religion as authoritative, the Buddhist dismissal of the Hindu gods, and the Buddhist denial that the human personality is a substantial self. In place of the Vedas, Buddhists have relied on the teachings of Gautama. The followers of Gautama eventually expanded these original teachings into a vast corpus of Buddhist scriptural texts (the *Tripitaka*). In place of the Hindu gods they relied on either personal effort or the merits of both the Buddha and the *bodhisattvas* (Buddhas-to-be, saints). In place of a substantial self they have found only a temporary collection of elements that are always changing, are never permanent. Mahayana Buddhism, the branch that developed a fuller speculative philosophy and more devotions for the laity, stresses that all beings are fleeting, painful, and selfless—empty of substance and ultimate significance. Removing desire therefore is removing the ignorant assumption that anything one experiences is fully real, good, or reliable.

The three pillars on which Buddhist practice has rested are meditation, wisdom, and morality. They have been mutually reenforcing. Meditation enables the person to experience the cogency of the Buddha's analysis of the human problematic and realize one's true nature as a being made for freedom and enlightenment. Wisdom has expressed the fruits of meditation in conceptual form, mapping the contours of reality and giving Buddhist disciples their metaphysical texts. Morality has spelled out the practical implications of the dharma, imposing on all Buddhists the fivefold obligation of *sila*: 1) not to kill, 2) not to lie, 3) not to steal, 4) not to be unchaste, 5) not to take intoxicants. Monks and nuns have had further obligations, but all Buddhists have been bound to this ethical core.

When Buddhism traveled from India to the East, it adapted to new cultural perspectives. Thus in China the Buddhist concept of faith (as well as its practice) accommodated to Confucian ethics, to the traditional clan-structure of society, and to a preference for concrete terms and symbols rather than abstractions. In Japan it blended with Shinto aesthetics, which expressed a great love of natural beauty and a conviction that *kami* (divine forces) permeated the landscape. Schools such as Ch'an/Zen epitomized the dharma in a single practice. In the case of Zen this practice has been meditation. In the case of devotional schools such as Nichiren Buddhism, the principal practice has been veneration of a single scripture (the Lotus Sutra). But through all of these developments the concept and the practice of faith have continued to rivet upon the Buddha, the dharma, and the sangha. Even when Zen masters told students to slay the Buddha (cut undue attachments and assume responsibility for their own enlightenment), Gautama has been present in the halls of the monastery, his statues assuring students that enlightenment is possible. Even when the metaphysical and ethical pillars of the tradition have not been the central focus, doctrines about emptiness and the fundamental demands of sila have structured devotional life.

In the devotional schools, the compassion of the Buddha and the bodhisattvas has been the main force specifying adherents' faith. Thus Buddhists who have worshiped Amida, the Buddha of light, and begged for admission to his Pure Land (the Western Paradise) have believed that divine mercy would count their reliance on Amida as sufficient for salvation. Indeed, Shinran (1173-1263), the Japanese priest who most eloquently expressed trust in Amida, sounds quite like a Protestant

Reformer plumping for justification by faith alone.

The concept of faith held by Tibetan Buddhists has been shaped by Indian *tantra*. In both Hinduism and Indian Buddhism, tantric schools have drawn upon the imagination and libidinal powers to propel disciples toward enlightenment. Thus Tibetan Buddhist meditations have used mantras and mandalas to help disciples imagine themselves as deities, vessels of enlightenment. Tibetan masters occasionally have urged disciples to forsake social conventions, depart to the solitude of the snowy mountains, and break taboos concerning meat, alcohol, and sex as a way of overcoming dualistic thinking and experiencing emptiness or the identity of nirvana and samsara (two themes of Mahayana philosophy). Other Tibetan Buddhists have worshiped the goddess Tara, bringing to her their troubles and hopes much as East Asians have petitioned the goddess/bodhisattva Kuan-yin, their paramount symbol of the divine mercy.

The variations of the Buddhist concept of faith, as well as the ways and means by which devotees live their faith, are therefore legion. Constantly, however, the sangha has repeated the mainstream traditions about the four noble truths, the three jewels in which Buddhists take refuge, and the three pillars of Buddhist practice, trying to bring them up to date for both monks and laity. The monastic life itself has symbolized the primacy of meditation, detachment, and study. Monks and nuns have lived in vowed celibacy, ideally begging their food from supportive laity, living simply, and offering the laity religious service. The monastic sangha therefore has greatly bolstered lay Buddhist faith, giving good example and wise counsel.

In East Asian cultures, Buddhist priests have cornered the market on funeral services, in part because the Buddhist concept of faith has dealt more profoundly with death than native traditions had, in part because Buddhist burial rites have seemed more impressive and consoling. Buddhist faith in the efficacy of meditation stimulated Confucians and Taoists to ponder the place of retreat and interiority in their own worldviews, while the common people frequently combined reverence for Confucian mores with Buddhist convictions about karma, transmigration, nirvana, and merit. Indeed, the anthropologist Melford Spiro has stressed the great significance of merit in a Buddhist land like Burma, where most of the laity are not expecting nirvana but only hoping to improve their karma and gain a favorable rebirth. In their case one might say that the Buddhist concept of faith suggests confidence, based on the traditional dharma, that good deeds—prayers, devotions, acts of kindness—can shape one's fortunes for the better. If so, the suffering that afflicts all the life they can see need not be terrifying. Through the eyes of faith, these persons can believe, and perhaps experience, that the

Buddha really has taught people how to make suffering—pain, despair—lessen, and so perhaps one day cease.[4]

CHINESE TRADITIONS

Buddhism had established itself in China by the middle of the second century C.E. Because the native tradition to which it showed greatest affinity was Taoism, Chinese translations of Buddhist scriptures often assimilated Buddhist notions to Taoist. On its own terms, Taoism competed with Confucianism for the allegiance of both the rulers and the educated classes in China. Throughout Chinese history the peasantry lived by an amalgamation of shamanistic, Confucian, Taoist, and Buddhist views. Perhaps the best way to generalize about what the concept of faith meant in Chinese religious history is first to sketch how Confucianism evolved from the earliest Chinese models and then to synthesize its view of the Tao with the view of classical Taoists such as Lao Tzu and Chuang Tzu.

Confucianism

In the *Analects*, which come closest to presenting his own voice, Confucius (551-479 B.C.E.) takes the position that he is not an innovator but a traditionalist. He is handing on, and explicating for his own time, the traditions of the legendary rulers who presided over the golden age of the earliest Chinese dynasties. These rulers held sway by the nearly magical potency of their virtue. They were so fully in tune with the Tao, the Way that the universe ran, that their subjects well-nigh inevitably acceded with their wishes. No doubt Confucius greatly romanticized these early rulers, but he passionately believed that by doing what was right, by being swayed by no unseemly motive, by acting for the common good, by avoiding destructive violence, and by gracefully performing the religious and social rites, rulers and gentlemen could keep the commonwealth peaceful and prosperous. Relatedly, he inter-

---

4. On Buddhism I recommend: Richard H. Robinson and Willard L. Johnson, *The Buddhist Religion* (Encino, Calif.: Dickenson, 1977); Trevor Ling, *The Buddha* (London: Temple Smith, 1973); Edward Conze, *Buddhist Scriptures* (Baltimore: Penguin, 1959); Edward J. Thomas, *The History of Buddhist Thought* (New York: Barnes & Noble, 1951); Henry Clarke Warren, *Buddhism in Translations* (New York: Atheneum, 1973); Charles S. Prebish, ed., *Buddhism: A Modern Perspective* (University Park, Pa.: Pennsylvania State University Press, 1975); Edward Conze, *Buddhism: Its Essence and Development* (New York: Harper Torchbooks, 1959); Heinrich Dumoulin, ed., *Buddhism in the Modern World* (New York: Macmillan, 1976); Heinrich Dumoulin, *A History of Zen Buddhism* (Boston: Beacon Press, 1969); and Melford Spiro, *Buddhism and Society* (New York: Harper & Row, 1970).

preted the strife of the times in which he lived as an object lesson in how not to run a state or build up a people. Confucius believed there had to be a better way, and he found it in the virtuous example of the statesmanly sages of yore.

Commentators frequently make the point that Confucius was a humanist, not a theologian. The point has merit, but one should not infer from it that Confucianism has not been a religion. The Master was a humanist in the sense that his great interest was human affairs: how to bring about order and harmony in the lives of individuals and groups. Confucius accepted the shamanism and ritualism of his era only to the extent to which these influential religious forces were geared to promoting order and harmony in the lives of individuals and groups. In those cases in which shamanism and ritualism were directed toward this goal, Confucius clearly stressed that only a proper respect for "Heaven" (the ultimate sanctioner of the patterns of nature and the wisdom of the ancient statesmen) could bring about justice in social relations.

In the wake of their Master, Confucians have believed that there is a way to peace and prosperity—the path that Confucius himself marked out. Thus Mencius, the great disciple who advanced Confucian thought a century after the Master, continued to preach to rulers and gentlemen the wisdom of leading the people by virtuous example. As well, he continued to stress *jen* and *li*, humaneness and etiquette, the leading Confucian virtues. If people fostered benevolence toward other human beings and observed the customs that civilized social life, things could go well. In the middle centuries of the Common Era, neo-Confucians amplified the small canon of the Confucian scriptures with treatises on the philosophy of nature, metaphysics, politics, and meditation. So doing, they broadened the significance of Confucian humanism. Yet they retained the Master's own basic concept of faith which placed great confidence in reason and virtue—his faith that one could discover the Way Heaven intended human beings to walk and that following this way would result in a social existence justifying human time.

Taoism

The Taoists did not disagree with the Confucian convictions about the Way, but they did dispute the somewhat formalized ethics that Confucianism had developed within a few centuries following the Master's death. Both Lao Tzu, the legendary author of the *Tao Te Ching*, and Chuang Tzu, the author of a collection of stories bearing his name, thought that in ancient times life had been simpler and more vigorous. The Taoist understanding of the Way, in fact, reflects greater interest in how Heaven moves nature. For these philosophical Taoists (later we shall speak of religious Taoists), the Way moving through nature was patient, unobtrusive, and much more effective than the ways human beings tended to move. The central attribute of the Tao, in fact, was *wu-wei*: active inaction, controlled not-doing. Symbols were water wearing away rock, an infant dominating a household, the emptiness contained by the walls of a house being more important than the walls themselves. Lao Tzu likened the Tao to womanly wisdom: subtle, indirect, apparently powerless but often predominant. Chuang Tzu noted that the gnarled, ugly tree survived while the tall, straight tree was chopped by builders. He saw that people in important positions at court lost many more limbs (in punishment for falling out of favor) than nobodies living in the provinces.

These philosophical Taoists believed that if one cast aside the prevailing (Confucian) wisdom and went back to the basics of simple living in harmony with the Tao, vitality would return with renewed vigor. They scoffed at the pretensions of scholars and courtiers, because they experienced the vastness and grandeur of a nature that dwarfed all human enterprises. Human beings came from the earth and went back to the earth. Only if they lived close to the earth, attuned to the inner music of the Tao that moved the 10,000 things of creation, could human beings hope to mature to the measure of nature's promise.

The religious Taoists took literally the symbolic, poetic writings of foundational thinkers such as Lao Tzu and Chuang Tzu, seeing in them a license to pursue immortality. Their belief was that if one could store up the germ of life (which some located in the breath and others located in the semen), one could maintain one's bodily integrity endlessly. Other religious Taoists dabbled in alchemy, seeking the elixir of immortality, or prayed to a bureaucracy of gods presiding over various bodily organs. The result was a hodge-podge of rites, researches, philosophical and political movements which, under the impact of Buddhist competition, resulted in a Taoist priesthood and "church."

When one tries to generalize about the concept of faith held in the Chinese religious tradition, the notion of harmony with nature bulks large. It is no accident that both Confucians and Taoists spoke of the Way. However differently the word resonated in the two traditions, they shared a more than empirical conviction that reality comprised a living whole which invited human beings to live in order with it. Unlike animals and plants, human beings had to choose such order. They had to learn in what it consisted and to freely join themselves with it. Confucians stressed the social benefits of such learning and free choice, while Taoists emphasized the naturalistic and meditational aspects. But both native Chinese traditions intuited that disharmony with the living cosmic whole was the root of social and personal disorders.

To understand this cardinal tenet of traditional Chinese faith, we must not only recall its kinship with the shamanic and prehistoric traditions but also appreciate the numinous, theological overtones that "cosmic whole" carried. When traditional Chinese spoke of the Tao they did not mean the sort of constant which the individual might catch in today's relativity theory or quantum mechanics. They meant the patterns, the music, the grain, the heartbeat of Reality itself—the composite of cosmos and divinity that is the sacred whole in cultures that have not differentiated a deity transcending the natural world. Tao therefore carries overtones of the Christian Logos and the Buddhist *Dharmakaya* (the Truth-Body of the Buddha that regulates all of reality). To search for the Tao, believe in the Tao, and entrust oneself to the Tao or its foremost expositors was to say, however implicitly, that neither political life nor private life had to be chaotic. Both could be peaceful, harmonious, beautiful, if human beings would discern the Way and follow it.

The last thing to be said about the traditional Chinese concept of faith vis-à-vis the Tao is that it undergirded the various hierarchies through which Confucianism structured Chinese society. Bred in the bone of Chinese people for centuries, and exported to the rest of East Asia (Japan, Korea, Vietnam), Confucian mores decreed that children should honor their parents, no matter how aged. Women were to submit to men, younger siblings were to submit to older, subjects were to revere rulers, and lower social classes were to submit to upper social classes. Between each of these groups an etiquette ideally prevailed, such that a Chinese person almost always would know what was expected. To be sure, there were informal safety valves and counterbalances. For example, a woman who normally had to obey her husband in all things could on occasion scream her head off. Or she could muster support for her causes by gossiping with other women, who would then tell their husbands her grievances and so bring pressure to bear on her husband to stop abusing her, lest he lose face among his male peers. But on the whole, faith in the Tao meant accepting the traditional social hierarchies, coupled with the right to indulge in private a debunking of social pretensions like that practiced by the classical Taoists.[5]

5. For Chinese religion see: Laurence G. Thompson, *The Chinese Religion: An Introduction* (Belmont, Calif.: Wadsworth, 1979); Laurence G. Thompson, *The Chinese Way in Religion* (Encino, Calif.: Dickenson, 1973); Wing-Tsit Chan, *A Sourcebook in Chinese Philosophy* (Princeton, N. J.: Princeton University Press, 1963); Sebastian de Grazia, ed., *Masters of Chinese Political Thought* (New York: Viking, 1973); Arthur Waley, *Three Ways of Thought in Ancient China* (Garden City, N.Y.: Doubleday, 1956); Marcel Granet, *The Religion of the Chinese People* (New York: Harper Torchbooks, 1975); C. K. Yang, *Religion in Chinese Society* (Berkeley: University of California Press, 1970); H. G. Creel, *What Is Taoism?* (Chicago: University of Chicago Press, 1970); Arthur Waley,

JUDAISM

By Judaism I shall mean the entire swath of Jewish religious history, from Abraham and the biblical period through rabbinic Judaism and modern times. So taken, Judaism clearly has focused its faith on the Torah, the Law or Instruction, of God. Like the Christian gospel or creed, the Torah cannot be separated from God. By accepting the Torah as the form of their lives, traditional Jews did the most they could to please God.

In the narrowest interpretation of its scope, the Torah consisted in the five books often attributed to Moses. In its widest interpretation, the Torah included all of the Hebrew Bible, plus the major rabbinic collections (the Mishnah and the Talmud), plus the major philosophical, theological, ethical, legal, and devotional writings that developed through the centuries.[6] Within the Hebrew Bible, one can usefully dis-

---

The Nine Songs: A Study of Shamanism in Ancient China (London: Allen & Unwin, 1955); Arthur F. Wright, *Buddhism in Chinese History* (Stanford, Calif.: Stanford University Press, 1959); and Donald J. Munro, *The Concept of Man in Early China* (Stanford, Calif.: Stanford University Press, 1969).

6. See Jonathan Rosenbaum, "Judaism: Torah and Tradition," in *The Holy Book in Comparative Perspective*, ed. Frederick M. Denny and Rodney L. Taylor (Columbia, S.C.: University of South Carolina Press, 1975), pp. 10-35. Other books on Judaism helpful for the theme of this chapter include *The Encyclopedia Judaica*; Barry W. Holtz, ed., *Back to the Sources* (New York: Summit Books, 1984); Paul J. Achtemeier, ed., *Harper's Bible Dictionary* (San Francisco: Harper & Row, 1985); Norman K. Gottwald, *The Hebrew Bible: A Socio-literary Introduction* (Philadelphia: Fortress, 1985); Douglas A. Knight and Gene M. Tucker, eds., *The Hebrew Bible and its Modern Interpreters* (Philadelphia: Fortress, 1985); W. Gunter Plaut, ed., *The Torah: A Modern Commentary* (New York: Union of American Hebrew Congregations, 1981); Brevard S. Childs, *Introduction to the Old Testament as Scripture* (Philadelphia: Fortress, 1979); Jacob Neusner, ed., *Take Judaism, for Example* (Chicago: University of Chicago Press, 1983); A. Cohen, *Everyman's Talmud* (New York: Schocken, 1975); Jacob Neusner, *The Life of Torah* (Encino, Calif.: Dickenson, 1974); Jacob Neusner, *The Way of Torah* (Encino, Calif.: Dickenson, 1974); Cecil Roth, *A History of the Jews* (New York: Schocken, 1961); Mark Zborowski and Elizabeth Herzog, *Life Is with People* (New York: Schocken, 1962); Isadore Epstein, *Judaism* (London: Penguin, 1959); Victor Tcherikover, *Hellenistic Civilization and the Jews* (New York: Atheneum, 1974); William Scott Green, ed., *Approaches to Ancient Judaism* (Missoula, Mont.: Scholars Press, 1978); Nahum N. Glatzer, *Essays in Jewish Thought* (University, Ala.: University of Alabama Press, 1978); Jacob B. Argus, *The Meaning of Jewish History* (New York: Abelard-Schulman, 1963); Gershon G. Scholem, *Major Trends in Jewish Mysticism* (New York: Schocken, 1961); Louis Finkelstein, ed., *The Jews: Their History* (New York: Schocken, 1970); and Salo Wittmayer Baron, *A Social and Religious History of the Jews* (New York: Columbia University Press, 1952 ff).

tinguish prophetic, priestly, and sapiential emphases. Prophetic faith depended on the initiative of God, who called the prophet to be a spokesman for the divine Word. In the briefest of summaries, the oracles of the biblical prophets were a summons to pure cult and social justice, although of course Isaiah, Jeremiah, Ezekiel, and the twelve dealt with many other matters. Throughout, however, the major and the minor prophets all believed that God had chosen Israel for a special convenantal relationship. The great paradigm justifying this faith was the exodus from Egypt and entry upon the promised land. The Law given to Moses on Mount Sinai was the charter of faith which the chosen people had to obey if they were to prove worthy of their signal election.

For the Deuteronomistic theology that dominates the block of the Bible running from Deuteronomy to Second Kings, covenantal faith involved a certain *quid pro quo*. If Israel was faithful to the Torah of Moses, it could expect to prosper. If it was unfaithful to the Torah, it could expect to suffer. The Davidic covenant was less conditional, securing the monarchy and the people in God's free love. On the whole, though, when the prophets castigated Israel for its sins, they worked within the Deuteronomistic vision of the covenant of faith.

Priestly faith also accepted such a vision, although its principal interest consisted in laws for cleanliness, sacrifice, and cult. The priestly account of creation is quite tidy, parceling God's works through six days and establishing a cosmogonic foundation for the Sabbath. In the Holiness Code (Lv 17-26), the priestly authors gave Jews the foundations of their understanding that faith was a call to be holy like the God to whom they were covenanted. Consistently, the concept of faith in Judaism has been inextricably tied up with a resolute pursuit of such fitting holiness, usually by trying to keep exactly and generously the injunctions of the Torah (later enumerated as 613 prescriptions).

Sapiential faith added cosmological overtones and some winning skepticism. In the Book of Job we find Judaism wrestling with the problem of evil and questioning the pertinence of the stock reply that since God is the architect of the cosmos whatever befalls human beings must be fitting. Qoheleth proffers some of the cynicism of old age, which has heard a lot of talk about virtue being rewarded and vice being punished but has seen no excess of examples. Proverbs proposes a modest, commonsensical faith: Do not stick your neck out, find the virtue that is a golden mean. The sapiential psalms turn on the lovely notion that the delight of the wise person is meditating on the Torah day and night.

Biblical Jewish faith therefore was quite various and nuanced, as one would expect from more that a thousand years of traditions. The core, though, was trying to live by God's Word, trying to do God's expressed will, and so be holy like the One Lord of hosts.

The demise of prophecy in later biblical history went hand in hand with the rise of rabbinic emphases. Some scholars find precedents for rabbinic theology in priestly and sapiential themes, while others note that the interruption of the official cult at the Temple in Jerusalem at the time of the exile of many Jewish leaders to Babylon paved the way for the synagogue. Postexilic Judaism was largely a story of trying to survive under foreign rule, while after the destruction of the Second Temple by the Romans in 70 C.E., Jewish faith always was a thing of the diaspora (until the establishment of the modern state of Israel).

From the earliest collected rabbinic writings, such as the *Pirke Aboth*, one finds a concern for keeping to the traditions of the prior teachers about both the letter and the spirit of the Torah. The sayings of the most revered ancients, like the sayings of eminent rabbis in later eras, confound any charge that the Jewish concept of faith was simply a bundle of laws. In both the Mishnah and the Talmud, the rabbis show themselves well aware that genuine religion has love as its soul and justice as its body. However, the rabbis do think that persons who are truly motivated by love and seeking justice will keep the letter of the law. They do take seriously the traditional precepts about how to hallow the Sabbath, to eat as befits a holy people, to maintain the purity of marriage and family life. The pressures of living in the diaspora made keeping such distinctively Jewish ideals as kosher food, Talmudic learning, and separation from Gentile profanities a means of survival. Nothing testifies to the strength of rabbinic faith more clearly than the fact that Jews survived centuries of foreign rule and repeated bursts of persecution all over the globe.

The concept and indeed the act of devotional and mystical Jewish faith more embellished the rabbinic interpretation of Torah then supplanted it. The Hasidim, for example, accepted the main features of the Talmudic concept of faith, even as they developed for their teaching stories and venerated such incarnations of holiness as the Baal Shem Tov. The Kabbalists speculated rather broadly on the presence of divinity throughout creation, and their exegeses of scripture verged on the esoteric. Still, a leading Kabbalistic text such as the Zohar makes it plain that biblical theology is only being expanded into raw material for imaginative meditation, not at all being replaced.

From Enlightenment times, Jews have struggled to accommodate their faith to modernity. The main result of this move toward accommodation has often been some withdrawal from the ideal of strict fidelity to traditional interpretations of the prescriptions of Torah and a tendency, most pronounced among Reformed Jews (in contrast to Conservative and Orthodox), to reinterpret Torah as a rational morality. Where Orthodox Judaism has seen the Bible as directly dictated by God, Reformed Judaism has accepted historical criticism and tried to translate Jewish practice for pluralistic modern cultures. Nonetheless, virtually all religious Jews continue to revere Torah as the revelation and ethical commands of God, the content of faith. What God gave Israel as the charter of the covenant continues to be the pearl of great price, the word of life that the people are to pass on to their children and their children's children.

The doctrinal content of Jewish faith has never been so important as the behavioral prescriptions. Certainly Jewish teachers have thought it crucial to think correctly about God and human nature, but Judaism has granted more leeway in intellectual interpretation than in matters of religious practice. If people came to synagogue and kept the traditional rules for the Sabbath, diet, marriage, and other influential matters, they were Jews in good standing. Their theology and legal interpretation were more private matters.

One famous summary of the content of Jewish faith, representing the entire Jewish tradition at a pre–modern point of maturity, is the thirteen articles elaborated by the twelfth-century Jewish philosopher Moses Maimonides. Even today these are listed in the standard Jewish prayer book. For Maimonides, it is incumbent on all Jews to believe in 1) the existence of God, 2) the unity of God, 3) the incorporeality of God, 4) the eternity of God, 5) the obligation to worship God alone, 6) prophecy, 7) the superiority of the prophecy of Moses, 8) the Torah as God's revelation to Moses, 9) the immutability of the Torah, 10) the omniscience of God, 11) reward and punishment, 12) the coming of the Messiah, and 13) the resurrection of the dead. The predominance of articles dealing directly with God shows that the Torah was taken as blessed truth about the maker of the universe, while the relative silence about specific matters of daily practice suggests that these could be taken for granted.

ISLAM

Most commentators on Islam find its concept of faith succinctly summarized in the so-called "Five Pillars." The first pillar, which goes directly to the heart of the Muslim concept of faith, is a profession of faith: "There is no God but Allah, and Muhammad is his prophet." The other pillars are the obligation to pray five times a day, the obligation to fast during the daylight hours of the month of Ramadan, the obligation to give alms, and the obligation to make the pilgrimage to Mecca at least once in one's lifetime, if at all possible.

Like Judaism, Isalm is a strict monotheism. The revelations that Muhammad (570-632) received from God through the mediation of the Angel Gabriel sharpened a strong repugnance for the polytheism of traditional Arabia. These revelations, collected as the Qur'an, insist that God can have no rival, no fellow-partaker in divinity. This is the principal reason the Qur'an rejects the Christian doctrine about Christ's divine sonship. Although Islam reveres Jesus as a great prophet, its concept of faith rejects any notion that he was divine. There is only one God, only one sovereign Lord of the Worlds. Allah is the maker of all that exists. The will of Allah is the blueprint for nature and society alike. Any concept of faith that contests the sovereignty of Allah is heretical and has few rights. Because Jews and Christians share many convictions with Muslims, they are called "people of the book" and have more rights than adherents of other faiths when they are under Muslim rule. But the crux of Islamic religion is the absolute dominion of Allah, so much so that Muslim theology sometimes has seemed to forfeit human freedom.

The prophecy of Muhammad is the seal of a process that began with Abraham, if not indeed with Adam. The Qur'an has its own slant on many stories of the Hebrew Bible, but it accepts Abraham and Moses as true spokesmen for the divine Word. On the other hand, such prophecy, like that of Jesus, was not fully efficacious. With the revelations to Muhammad, however, God has brought the prophetic process to completion. Muhammad therefore is the *rasul*, the prophet *par excellence*. The Qur'an that God gave through Muhammad is the direct expression of the divine mind and will—so much so that later Muslim theologians gave the Qur'an an eternal existence alongside Allah. Nothing in it can be altered, and strictly speaking it cannot be translated: The Arabic in which Muhammad expressed it is an intrinsic part of the revelation.

To know the will of God, and so avoid the coming Judgment that will cast idolaters into the Fire, one has to accept Qur'anic revelation. Still, this necessity to follow Muhammad's preaching did not lead to the divinization of the Prophet. The Qur'an makes it clear that Muhammad was not the son of God, in the sense of a divine offspring. He was, however, the exemplary Muslim, so frequently Muslims have venerated him with something close to worship. (The Muslim practice in this matter parallels the practice of Roman Catholic and Eastern Orthodox Christians regarding the Virgin Mary.) The little tradition among Muslims has venerated many locals saints, again sometimes verging upon what many comparative religion scholars would call worship. Angels and troublesome spirits called *jinn* have also populated the Muslim landscape, forcing one to place some nuance upon Islamic monotheism. While there is no question that officially only God is divine, the Muslim religious reality is considerably richer than a Deistic understanding of such a statement would imply. Not only is God fully active in the world, the angels of God, Muhammad, and the Qur'an constantly mediate his will. In the Islamic concept of faith, God is a very active force.

There is a certain geographic dimension in the Islamic concept of faith. Thus the prayer that Muslims ought to make five times a day is sent toward Mecca, the psychological center of the Muslim world. By such prayer one practices the foundational virtue of remembrance (*dhikr*). Above all, one ought to remember that Allah is nearer to human beings than the pulse at their throats. To be sure, the entire creation does not contain Allah. He completely transcends all that he has made. But by bowing low five times each day and "submitting" (the etymological meaning of both "Islam" and "Muslim") to Allah, one offers him the praise he deserves and remembers the true proportions of reality.

The fasting incumbent on Muslims during the lunar month of Ramadan is meant to help them discipline their bodies and fight the good fight of faith. It is a joyous fasting, as the partying that goes on after dark witnesses. Yet it reminds Muslims that their faith, however distinctively this-worldly and unwilling to make the distinctions between sacredness and profaneness that many other faiths make, calls them to subordinate things of the flesh to things of the religious spirit. The Sufis, who are the Islamic group that came closest to establishing a monastic life (they formed communities, but they did not insist on celibacy, which is considered un-Qur'anic), nurtured and indeed produced many ascetics and mystics who took this teaching most to heart. These persons are the ones who came closest to sacrificing this-worldly prospects for the love of Allah. Most other Muslims approached Allah less in love than in profound obedience. The archetypal Muslim psychology centers in the awed obeisance of the servant overwhelmed by the splendor of the Lord. Submissive obedience is part-and-parcel of the Islamic concept of faith.

The alms that Muslim faith has required have varied in amount, perhaps 2 to 3 percent of one's income being the norm. The alms have concretized the Muslim conviction that all members of the House of Islam are brothers and sisters. Social solidarity and social responsibility therefore lie at the foundations of the Qur'anic concept of faith. Muhammad himself proposed many social reforms, trying to shift the Arab culture of his time from the clan-structure that had long prevailed to a broader community based on sharing the same faith.

The pilgrimage to Mecca is another way that Islam has unified its adherents. On pilgrimage all Muslims wear the same simple dress and ordinary social distinctions melt away. Women, who usually are quite subordinate to men (although Muhammad improved their status considerably, compared to what it had been in pre-Qur'anic times), more nearly approach equality. On the whole Muslim women have had spiritual equality with men; however, some traditions about what the Prophet said and did (*Hadith*) justified the second-class social standing women usually have experienced in Muslim countries, while other traditions pictured more men in the Garden and more women in the Fire. The main reason why such women did not pass the Judgment was disobedience toward their husbands.

The God whom Muslims consider the sole divinity in the universe therefore is a stern judge, as well as a compassionate and merciful guide to "the path that is straight." Muhammad assured his audiences that God would soon smite the idolater, as well as other lesser sinners. The concept of faith in Islam does not expressly consider human nature as sinful, nor has it developed a doctrine of original sin. But it does regard human nature as weak and forgetful. Unless Muslims keep the five pillars and constantly remember both Allah and the injunctions of his Qur'an, they are liable to wander away from true faith and end up in the fire. (However, the Muslim hell is not eternal, at least for believers. Those who have sinned through weakness one day will get out.)

The simplicity of the Muslim program of the five pillars undoubtedly has greatly contributed to Islam's great success. With a concept of faith which is predominantly fundamentalist, if not strictly literal, believers have taken the sole divinity of Allah to mean that all created things have limited significance. This has helped them to create a community in principle quite democratic (no sacrificial ceremonies required a priestly elite), although in practice mullahs and sheiks took spiritual precedence, while caliphs, sultans, and ayatollahs exercised a theocratic rule.

To complement the relativizing of all created affairs introduced by its strict monotheism, Islam has focused all religious truth in the prophecy of Muhammad, as represented in the Qur'an. The other sources of religious authority, such as the Hadith, the consensus of the community down the ages (codified in the *Sharia*, the Law), and analogical reasoning, all derived their legitimacy from their consonance with the Qur'an. Muslim faith therefore has had a remarkably concise and cogent content. Certainly Islamic theology, law, philosophy, religious practice, and other cultural expressions through the ages became as rich and diversified as those of its Hindu, Buddhist, Jewish, Christian, or Chinese equivalents. But the bare pith of Muslim faith, as classically expressed in both the first pillar and the first surah of the Qur'an, is uniquely simple: Allah/Muhammad.[7]

---

7. On Islam see: Cyril Glasse, *Concise Encyclopedia of Islam* (Atlantic Highlands, N. J.: Humanities Press International, 1986); Isma'il R. al Faruqi and Lois Lamya' al Faruqi, *The Cultural Atlas of Islam* (New York: Macmillan,

1986); Ali A. Mazrui, *The Africans* (Boston: Little Brown, 1986); W. Montgomery Watt, *Muhammad: Prophet and Statesman* (New York: Oxford University Press, 1974); Ignaz Goldziher, *Muslim Studies* (Chicago: Aldine, 1967); Marshall G. S. Hodgson, *The Venture of Islam* (Chicago: University of Chicago Press, 1974); Kenneth Cragg, *The House of Islam* (Encino, Calif.: Dickenson, 1975); Arthur Jeffrey, ed., *Islam: Muhammad and His Religion* (New York: Bobbs-Merrill, 1975); Geoffrey Parrinder, *Jesus in the Qur'an* (New York: Oxford University Press, 1975); Bernard Lewis, *The Arabs in History* (New York: Harper Torchbooks, 1966); Bernard Lewis, ed., *Islam and the Arab World* (New York: Knopf, 1976); P. M. Holt et al., eds., *The Cambridge History of Islam* (Cambridge: University Press, 1970); Joseph Schacht and C. E. Bosworth, eds., *The Legacy of Islam* (New York: Oxford University Press, 1979); Fazlur Rahman, *Islam* (Garden City, N.Y.: Doubleday, 1968); Martin Lings, *What is Sufism?* (Berkeley: University of California Press, 1977); John J. Donohue and John L. Esposito, eds., *Islam in Transition* (New York: Oxford University Press, 1982); Annemarie Schimmel, *Mystical Dimensions of Islam* (Chapel Hill: University of North Carolina Press, 1975); Clifford Geertz, *Islam Observed* (Chicago: University of Chicago Press, 1971); Elizabeth Warnock Fernea and Basima Qattan Bezirgan, *Middle Eastern Muslim Women Speak* (Austin: University of Texas Press, 1977); Kenneth Cragg and Marston Speight, *Islam from Within* (Belmont, Calif.: Wadsworth, 1980); Merlin L. Swartz, *Studies on Islam* (New York: Oxford University Press, 1981); Frederick Mathewson Denny, *An Introduction to Islam* (New York: Macmillan, 1985); Jane I. Smith, ed., *Women in Contemporary Muslim Societies* (Lewisburgh, Pa.: Bucknell University Press, 1980); and V. S. Naipaul, *Among the Believers* (New York: Vintage, 1982).

CHAPTER 3

The Concept of Faith
in Philosophy

Louis Dupré and Jacqueline Mariña

INTRODUCTION

In this chapter we shall consider the meaning and history of what
Karl Jaspers has coined "philosophical faith." The term "philosophical
faith" is conditioned by the adjective "philosophical"; as such, our
exploration does not consider the positive content of revealed religion
but rather the universal wisdom accessible to all peoples at all times.
This is not to say that philosophical faith has nothing to do with the
content of revealed religions; often throughout the history of Western
thought theologians have claimed that human reason, primarily as it
manifests itself as love of wisdom and as striving for truth, can sometimes serve as the preparation for the reception of the positive content
of revealed religion. This understanding of human reason finds strong
articulation in the theology of the Ante Nicene Fathers (pre 325 C.E.).
In their theology, the doctrine of creation through the second person of
the Trinity plays a large role. All of creation is thought to participate in
the divine Logos. Consequently any search for wisdom departing from
creation can in principle find the traces of God's truth, for the world
was created in wisdom, and the God of revelation had from the very
beginning left his indelible mark upon it.

Our investigation of philosophical faith is, however, not concerned
with the positive content of revealed religion, but rather with the universal quest for religious truth. As such, philosophical faith may or may

not lead to an acceptance of the positive contents of revelation. It does, however, have this much in common with revelation, that like the positive contents of revealed faith it concerns the human being's ultimate search for meaning. Much of philosophy, particularly early Greek philosophy, is a thinking about the divine, about that which is most really real and which offers a firm foundation and a guide for practical action in the world and theoretical attitude toward existence. As love of wisdom it is a search for truth, and this search for truth is always a movement beyond oneself and what is readily accessible as vulgar or common knowledge.

GREEK PHILOSOPHY

Early Greek philosophy evolved as a rational critique of Homer and Hesiod, but a critique faithful to the fundamental theological and existential thrust of the Greek mythical worldview. This was not only because the philosophy of the early Greek philosophers was conditioned by an attempt to arrive at a unified and intelligible understanding of a cosmos which was itself divine but also because the Greek myths themselves contained the beginnings of a rationality that would burgeon into a philosophical theology critical of the mythic, particular, and a moral character of the gods of the Homeric pantheon.

For the Greeks, the drive to understand, as expressed in the myth and later in philosophical thought, was always conditioned by religious concerns. The Homeric epics, for instance, are not simple storytelling, but rather concern themselves with the deeds of human beings and how these deeds are related to powers which move the human soul. In the *Iliad*, for example, Agamemnon explains himself in the following way:

> Often the Achaeans made this proposal to me and reproached me; but I am not at fault, but Zeus and Fate and the Fury that walks in darkness, who inspired a savage, fatal folly in my heart in the assembly on that day when I took away Achilles' prize myself. A goddess brings all things to pass, the revered daughter of Zeus, blind Folly, who misleads all, the baneful one.[1]

Moreover in Book XVI of the *Iliad* Homer portrays Zeus as bound to his own deeper will, namely, Fate and Destiny. Even Zeus' personal preferences cannot displace such depths from within himself. When it is fated that Zeus' beloved son Sarpedon must die, Zeus cannot intervene

---

1. Homer, *The Iliad*, trans. Alston Hurd Chase and William G. Perry Jr. (New York: Bantam, 1950), Book XIX, pp. 302-303.

but must allow Destiny to run its course. It is then in relation to an ultimate principle, *Moira* or Fate, that all deeds, those of gods and men, are understood.

In Hesiod's *Theogony*, a thoroughly mythical work, coherence in the universe is found through the principle of generation. This understanding of the cosmos is more rational than that of Homer. Whereas Homer attempts to interpret the cosmos in relation to human action, Hesiod transcends this view by attempting to understand everything that has come to be in relation to itself, although it goes without saying that Hesiod's cosmos includes both gods and men. His method of linking the individuals of the divine world by means of successive generations prepares the way for the less mythic attempt to come to terms with the φύσις of the Milesian philosophers, for Hesiod's poem reveals a "type of causal thinking unmistakably rational in the consistency with which it is carried out, even though it takes the form of myth."[2] It is important to note that Hesiod conceives of his gods as part of nature; they are subject to the same kind of natural law as are all visible objects. Eros, as old a divinity as Heaven and Earth, binds all things and is the guiding principle of all generation.

Pre-Socratic philosophy, particularly Milesian monism, being itself a thinking about the divine was very much concerned with the same kind of problems that the myth addressed. The Milesian philosophers not only strove to find some principle of intelligibility but they linked that intelligibility to one all encompassing principle, the very being of all that is. To know something as it really *is* is also to know its ontological foundation; it is thus to apprehend the foundation unifying all of reality. The divine is not conceived of as that which stands beside nature: nature herself is divine. How much the vitality and flux of the world which captures their attention and evokes their religious wonder is reflected in the saying attributed to Thales: "Everything is full of gods."[3] Their understanding of reality as it appears is not scientific in the modern sense of the word. Whereas modern science concerns itself with empirical reality as it is given, the Greek philosophers questioned the very givenness of reality itself. By the word physis the Milesian monists meant not merely what is but also the process of how it came to be, thereby extending their inquiry to the question of the ultimate source of things.[4]

---

2. Werner Jaeger, *The Theology of the Early Greek Philosophers* (London: Oxford University Press, 1947), p. 12.

3. *The Basic Works of Aristotle*, ed. Richard McKeon; *De Anima*, trans. J. A. Smith, 411a 7 (New York: Random House, 1941).

4. Jaeger, *Early Greek Philosophers*, p. 20.

The movement from myth to rational discourse is therefore not one from which religious considerations are altogether removed. Behind the thinking of the pre-Socratics lies the intuition that the "things that are" are not self-explanatory, that indeed that which allows them to emerge can be characterized as "immeasurable, undivided, inexhaustible; it encompasses everything, and is immortal and not ageing, it is divine."[5] Continuities with Greek myth are evident; the divine attributes of the Homeric gods are simply transferred to a singular and most high meta-physical principle, *theion*, that from which all things arise. In this trans-ference of divine qualities to a singular principle, eternal, and omnipres-ent, the divine achieves a much nobler grandeur than the anthropomorphic gods ever could attain. In assuming an ultimate ratio-nality even in the destruction of passing things a movement of transcen-dence which seeks rest in some surpassing power is set in motion. Anaximander (ca. 600 B.C.E.), for instance, connects the principle of original oneness which unites all things with a concept of harmony. None of the four elements could be primary, for if one were it would eliminate the others and the original "justice" would be broken. The indefinite both gives birth to and dissolves all oppositions. All definite elements must eventually be destroyed and return to their origin, the indefinite, according to necessity, "for they must pay the penalty and make atonement to one another for their injustice according to time's decree."[6] Every coming to be is viewed as an encroachment upon that which existed prior to its emergence, but this coming to be must also pass away. Thus there is an inherent rationality even in the destruction and dissipation of that which is, and beyond this dissipation there is the divine, aloof and superior, but whose simple eternity abides forever, transcending the changeable and promising a secure foundation from which ultimately nothing can slip away.

Heraclitus (ca. 500 B.C.E.), who according to legend deposited his writings in Artemis' temple, also established as an ultimate principle a primeval, self-sufficient oneness. Moreover, he equated it with *Logos* itself, the self-contained principle of both law and explanation. "This world that is the same for all, neither any god nor man has shaped it, but it ever was and is and shall be everliving fire that kindles by mea-sures and goes out by measures."[7] As in Anaximander the One develops

5. Walter Burkert, *Greek Religion, Archaic and Classical* (London: Blackwell, 1985), p. 307.

6. Fragment taken from Simplicius, *Physics*, 6r, 24, 19. We follow mainly John Burnet, *Early Greek Philosophy* (New York: Meridian, 1958), p. 54.

7. Hermann Diels, *Fragmente der Vorsokratiker*, 7th ed. (Berlin, 1954), Frag-ment 30., trans. Richmond Lattimore in Matthew Thomson McClure, *The Early Philosophers of Greece* (New York: D. Appleton-Century, 1935), p. 120.

through a harmony of opposites. However, Heraclitus gives more weight to the continuous changes in nature and postulates a constant movement and countermovement to maintain an original balance. This balance is achieved by "thought by which all things are steered through all."[8] It is thus through this divine thought, symbolized by fire, that the world achieves its unity, and moreover, "all human laws are nourished by one, the divine; for it rules as far as it will and is sufficient for all and remains superior."[9] The divine Logos fulfills the function of a law of nature which moves all things while preserving the initial energy. Implicit in it appears to be an idea of divine justice which rules over the changing phenomena and holds them in balance. In it all oppositions are reconciled and cease to exist.

Even for the most rational minds of early Greek culture philosophy was a religious as well as an intellectual pursuit. Parmenides (fifth century B.C.E.), the first authentic metaphysician, has often been considered an ontologist devoid of religious interest. Certainly Parmenides' gigantic metaphysical achievement has overshadowed his religious significance. However, Parmenides himself considered his truth divine and attributed it to a revelation. He describes the absolute—Being (το ὄν)—almost exclusively in religious terms. Being is one, transcendent, perfect, eternal, and identical.

Whereas the pre-Socratics strove to ascertain the nature of *what appears*, and through this knowledge to come to an acceptance of its terms, Plato (427?-347? B.C.E.) introduces a new element into Greek religion and thought. Being itself is divided into two realms: what appears and what truly is. The former is mutable and destructible, the latter characterized by changelessness and eternity. The properties of the divine are beyond the changeable and perishable world; the divine is associated with the realm of forms from which all material existences derive their intelligibility. Beyond these forms lies the form of the good, which is beyond even being. The form of the good is introduced in Plato's *Republic* in a passage worth quoting at length:

> This reality, then, that gives their truth to the objects of knowledge and the power of knowing to the knower, you must say is the idea of good, and you must conceive it as being the cause of knowledge, and of truth insofar as it is known. . . . But as for knowledge and truth, even as in our illustration it is right to deem light and vision sunlike but never to think that they are the sun, so here it is right to consider these two their counterparts, as being like the good or boniform, but

8. We follow mainly Burkert, *Greek Religion*, p. 309; B41 = 85M.
9. Ibid., p. 309; B114 = 23M.

to think that either of them is the good is not right. Still higher honor belongs to the possession and habit of the good[10]

All objects of knowledge are known through the presence of the good, and their very existence and essence is derived from it. The good itself, however, is not being but still transcends being "in dignity and surpassing power."[11] That the idea of the good displays some affinities with the Judeo-Christian God is largely due to the fact that Platonism itself had an impact on the developing self-reflection of the faith of both Jews and Christians. Moreover, the form of the good should not be conflated with the creator god of the *Timaeus*, for this eternal mind depends upon the ideas existing outside of himself in order to stamp the refractory necessity of matter with intelligibility. On the other hand, the good is beyond all essences, while all essences depend upon it for their very being. Yet even if the form of the good cannot simply be equated with God, it transcends all beings and is imbued with a divine aura. All goodness depends upon it. Moreover, it is especially important to note the name that Plato gives the highest of all forms, "the Good." In calling it "the Good" Plato emphasizes the transcendent religious nature of a principle that, in order to be known, must involve the whole person; it evokes an attitude of desire or *eros* and it is only through this desire that it can be known. As such, the good is imbued with value from the outset. Through its inherent value the good is related to the soul; *that* the soul can desire it and thereby know it demonstrates the possibility of relationship between the two. As recent scholarship has claimed, for Plato reason and desire are not two distinct principles, but reason is itself a particular form of desire.[12] The satisfaction of the desire to know the good leads to *eudaimonia*, the highest and most sublime kind of happiness a human being can achieve. The driving force of Plato's philosophy can thus fundamentally be understood as a doctrine of salvation, for it is only in knowing the good that the person can arrive at true happiness.

Important also is the fact that Plato uses mythical language to describe the upward journey of the soul. The term *eros*, which we used to characterize his philosophy, is mythical and so are the descriptions of its ultimate goal in the *Republic*, the *Symposium*, the *Phaedrus*, and the *Phaedo*. These myths are no mere allegorical devices elucidating a

---

10. *Plato: The Collected Dialogues*, eds. Edith Hamilton and Huntington Cairns, *Republic*, trans. Paul Shorey, 508e-509a, (Princeton, N.J.: Princeton University Press, 1961), p. 744.

11. Ibid., 509b, p. 744.

12. Charles H. Kahn, "Plato's Theory of Desire," *Review of Metaphysics* 41 (1987), pp. 77-103.

logical system. The myth is central to Plato's philosophy because it reveals the existential import of the mystery of life while at the same time protecting and veiling it. Existence is too deep, and the questions of life too profound, for them to be simply captured and defined in a precise logical system. Yet Plato was himself aware of the limitations of the myth. After the mythical description of the kingdom of the dead at the end of the *Phaedo* he cautions the reader: "Of course, no reasonable man ought to insist that the facts are exactly as I have described them. But that either this or something very like it is a true account of our souls and their future habitations . . . is both a reasonable contention and a belief worth risking."[13] Plato was aware of the relative nature of the myth as a form of knowledge. He knew that the myth, although irreplaceable, is uncritical. Yet in using the myth as a form of expression which is at once indispensable and insufficient, he used it in exactly the same way that religious persons use it.

Aristotle (384-322 B.C.E.) has often been considered the least religious of all Greek philosophers. Although his thinking hardly employs the categories of myth, it would be unfair to characterize his philosophy as devoid of religious concerns. A former student of Plato, Aristotle offered a reformulation, along with certain correctives, to Platonism. Unlike for Plato, for Aristotle the principles of intelligibility (the forms) are immanent in the world and do not transcend it. They are imbedded in particulars, and it would be as absurd to think of forms existing independently of matter as it would be to attempt to think of a color without shape. For Aristotle, therefore, an investigation of the good cannot begin through the positing of some transcendent principle. The good must be the good *for* the person, and in order to discover it one must begin to do so through an empirical investigation of the human being.

According to Aristotle, "The soul must be a substance in the sense of a form of a natural body having life potentiality within it."[14] In order to discover what the good *for* a person is, one must begin by investigating the nature of the soul as the substantial form of the body. Now according to Aristotle's theory of forms, the form contains in an incipient or potential way its proper end. Moreover, happiness is defined as the actualization of the proper end of the form of a being. The proper end of a human being is a life lived in accordance to reason. "And we state the function of a man to be a certain kind of life, and this to be an activity

---

13. *Plato: The Collected Dialogues*; *Phaedo*, trans. Hugh Tredennick, 114d., p. 94.
14. *The Basic Works of Aristotle, De Anima*, 412a 20ff; p. 555.

or action of the soul implying a rational principle, and the function of the good man to be the good and noble performance of these."[15] For Aristotle, moreover, the most perfect happiness is found in contemplation, for it is this activity that most fully realizes the nature of the human being as a rational creature. To be most fully oneself, therefore, is to contemplate the highest truths about the universe. Moreover, this very contemplation involves what is highest and most divine in man:

> Whether it be reason or something else that is this element which is thought to be our natural ruler and guide and to take thought of things noble and divine, whether it be itself also divine or only the most divine element in us, the activity of this in accordance with its proper virtue will be perfect happiness. That this activity is contemplative we have already said.[16]

It is, however, in relation to Aristotle's unmoved mover that the religious thrust of his philosophy can best be appreciated. For Aristotle philosophy is theology when it inquires into the highest cause of being. The idea of the unmoved mover is thus fundamentally religious, for this thought thinking its self-sameness (*noesis noeseos*) moves all other things as the supreme object of desire and love. Thus, in contemplation, *eros*, a movement of the soul beyond itself through love and longing, is involved. For Aristotle, however, this eros is transplanted onto a cosmic scale; the whole universe is itself moved through its desire to emulate the beauty and perfection of the unmoved mover. The human being, however, fulfills its desire for the unmoved mover in a peculiar way. Whereas the heavens revolve in a circular motion as a result of their desire to imitate the perfection of the unmoved mover, the human being emulates the unmoved mover in a much more direct way, namely, through contemplation. The unmoved mover is perfect insofar as it is thought thinking its self-sameness; its activity is, therefore, a contemplation of itself, and its perfect blessedness results from this contemplation. "Therefore the activity of God, which surpasses all others in blessedness, must be contemplative; and of human activities, therefore, that which is most akin to this must be most of the nature of happiness."[17] According to Aristotle, then, the human being achieves happiness, that is, realizes its form, insofar as it participates in the contemplation of the unmoved mover.

It is, however, Plotinus (205?-270 C.E.) who brought out the full

---

15. Ibid., *Nichomachean Ethics*, trans. W. D. Ross, 1098a 13ff.
16. Ibid., 1177a 14ff.
17. Ibid., 1178b 22ff.

religious implications of Plato's philosophical vision. In Plotinus the upward flight of the Platonic eros receives its ultimate justification from a downward process of emanation. The soul longs for the divine because it is itself of divine origin. Not only does Plotinus complete a line of thinking initiated by the Pythagoreans and culminating in Plato, he also brings out the full religious implications of this tradition. In emphasizing this aspect he may have modified the overall perspective but not so as to inaugurate an entirely new tradition. In particular, Plotinus did not discard reason for ecstasy. On the contrary, he showed how the process of reason attained its summit in mystical contemplation. In accordance with the entire Greek tradition reason remains the primary power of the mind and Plotinus offers no substitute for it. He only adds to its impact by presenting the last step in the reasoning process as a higher stage of consciousness in which the opposition inherent to the reflective attitude ceases to exist. Nor is this final stage unrelated to the reasoning which precedes it. Once the ultimate object of the mind is defined as transcendent, the upward movement *must* eventually leave the intellectual order.

As the above outline of some of the major figures in Greek philosophy suggests, the drive for wisdom was thoroughly permeated by religious concerns. Even for Aristotle, *boulesis*, the rational form of desire, finds its proper end in the contemplation of truth. This truth is linked with the contemplation of the ultimate source of all movement and, since it is the final object of desire and love, of all meaning. Generally speaking, for the Greeks epistemological concerns play only a secondary role, and the ontological and moral qualities of truth are given preeminence over the purely cognitive ones. For the Greeks, truth refers to *being*. But an inquiry into the truth of being, if faithfully carried through, is always religious. For in the attempt to understand in terms of global and comprehensive unities, the human being transcends the limits of experience and questions that which ultimately founds all that is. Since the quest for meaning is itself existential in scope, such a drive to understand cannot but include in its considerations elements of value; the human being *finds* that it is a meaning-seeking animal; this is a *fact* given to its existence, and any analysis of the nature of reality must take account of this fact. Being a part of this reality which it strives to understand, with an understanding at once unitary and all-comprehensive, the human being concludes that the ultimate reality which it seeks to comprehend must have some value *for it* and that, moreover, the ultimate principle of reality is in itself value-laden. To consider the ultimate source of all things as void of value would be to introduce a diastasis in the order of things which, in the final analysis, human reason cannot tolerate. Ultimately the very possibility of reason rests on the implicit assumption that everything known is unitary in nature. The ultimate source of all things, therefore, must have value, because the human being finds itself longing *for* it. When considered in this way, the drive for truth is religious. As Mohandas Gandhi once wrote, "It is more correct to say that 'Truth is God' than to say that 'God is Truth.' "[18] This is why the early Christians, in attempting to recommend themselves to the Hellenistic culture of the Roman world, found in Greek philosophy a tool so amenable to their apologetic concerns. Certainly the ensuing tensions between reason and revelation throughout the centuries should not be ignored. An equation between God and truth cannot fail to entail major philosophical and theological antinomies. Nevertheless, precisely such an equation lies at the root of much of Western theology's willingness to link itself with philosophy.

THE CHRISTIAN PHILOSOPHY OF THE MIDDLE AGES

Augustine (354-430 C.E.), the greatest of the Latin Fathers, began his search for truth through a philosophical exploration, yet wound up asserting the priority of faith over reason. Still that priority does not abrogate reason; rather is it the requisite condition for the exercise of a reason faithful to the truth. This is the meaning of Augustine's famous formula: "Understanding is the reward of faith. Therefore seek not to understand that thou mayest believe, but believe that thou mayest understand."[19] This priority of faith over reason, is however, not as divergent from the Platonic philosophy that nurtured Augustine's thinking as might first appear. Plato, too, speaks of "beliefs worth risking," in the passage quoted above. The passage continues, "We should use such accounts to inspire ourselves with confidence."[20] For Plato, however, this confidence is not merely one which allows one to get along duly in life but rather enables one to find the truth. The desire for, and the belief *that* the truth can be found, and that all existence is ultimately ordered toward beauty, truth, and goodness is a fundamental prerequisite to one's ability to know the truth. On this score Augustine follows Plato closely, although of course the 'beliefs worth risking' which Augustine adopts are different from those of Plato. The issues here are closely related to the unity of desire and reason mentioned above in our section on Plato. Augustine explores the question at length in Books 8 and 9 of

---

18. Mohandas K. Gandhi: *Yeravda Mandir* in *Gandhi: Selected Writings*, (New York: Harper & Row, 1972), p. 41.

19. Saint Augustine, *On the Gospel of Saint John*, XXIX, 6; in *Homilies on the Gospel of St. John*, trans. H. Brown, J. H. Parker (Oxford: A Library of the Fathers, 1848), vol. 1, p. 440.

20. *Plato: The Collected Dialogues*; *Phaedo* 114d., pp. 94-95.

the *De Trinitate.* Augustine first assumes that in order to love God there must be some innate principle through which we can know him, for one cannot love what one does not know. Yet his argument assumes a peculiar twist, for he then equates this form of knowledge with love. The inner truth present to the mind which enables us to love God is the image of God, but this image is love itself; it is, in fact, the love of God and neighbor. Augustine thereby tends to identify love and knowledge. Moreover, in Chapter 12 of Book 9 he argues that love must precede knowledge; knowledge is attained in the quest for wisdom, but this presupposes a love for knowledge, for if knowledge was not loved, one would not search for it. In order to know something, then, it must first be loved.

The love that is a prerequisite to knowledge has close affinities with faith. Love is a movement toward that which is as yet not possessed, even as faith "is the assurance of things *hoped* for, the conviction of things unseen."[21] Augustine's injunction "to believe that thou mayest understand" can only be fully appreciated in the light of his discussion of knowledge and love in the *De Trinitate.* For belief, or more precisely, faith, is nothing other than a species of love, just as truth cannot begin to be grasped unless it is first loved. Moreover, it is the *love* of truth itself which discloses its object, and only in and through this love can it be known.

Another element in Augustine's thinking that merits consideration is his attitude toward the world and the immanent character of truth and beauty found therein. For Augustine, although truth and beauty are in some sense immanent in the world (since the world was created through the *Logos*), the truth and beauty of the world cannot be self-contained. In the *Confessions* Augustine rejects his own earlier work, *On the Beautiful and the Fitting.* In this work Augustine had imagined that things are beautiful in and of themselves, without thereby referring them to the source that transcends them.[22] Yet when things are loved for themselves, even if they are beautiful, if they are not referred to their source, the truth is not known and the heart knows no rest; it is riveted in sorrows, for it is held back from its origin. Moreover, it is the very image of God in the soul, the love or desire for God, which insures that the heart will not rest until it rests in that which transcends all creaturely beings. The heart's longing is never quelled by the things *in* the world. All created things derive their being from God, and to love the changeable creature without loving it in and through him who made all things is to deceive

---

21. Hebrews 11:1
22. *The Confessions of St. Augustine,* trans. Hal M. Helms (Orleans, Mass.: Paraclete, 1986), p. 67; Book IV; chapter 13.

oneself and to throw the heart into torment, for it is to checkmate its most sacred desire, its innermost longings for him who is unchangeable above all changeable things.[23] The beautiful things of this earth can shine with beauty and truth, and yet if it is their own brightness which one turns to, the heart of the seeker shall not be illumined. Augustine explains this most clearly when he writes: "For I had my back to the light and my face toward the things enlightened, so even when I discerned things enlightened, my face itself was not enlightened."[24] The light and truth of the things of the earth are not their own; rather are they illumined from above, so that their beauty depends on God for their very sustenance. Such beauty being merely imparted, it is not the source or wellspring of truth, and as such, the created things of this world, although participating in the truth, cannot impart truth; they cannot cause "one's face to shine," for their shining is merely derivative. All things by virtue of their existence in some sense participate in the truth of the Logos. However, if their truth and beauty are not referred to the Logos, but are looked upon as if they had an existence in their own right, then truth is not known.

With the immanence of divine truth comes the mandate to explore it interiorly but also the risk of reducing a transcendent message to an acquisition of reason. Augustine always remained aware of both the need and the limits of rational exploration. With him the emphasis remains on the "intellectus quaerens fidem" and faith never ceases to be the ultimately decisive argument. Thus his daring speculations about the Trinity are always accompanied by a spirit of healthy skepticism about their final success and a cavalier lack of concern concerning their ultimate compatibility. With Anselm (1033-1109) the quest for truth takes a new turn. His "faith seeking understanding," despite its Augustinian tone, moves in a different direction. There is no reason to question the loyalty to St. Augustine which he explicitly professes in the *Monologion*. There Anselm echoes Augustine: "Right order requires that we should believe the deep things of the Christian faith before we undertake to discuss them by reason."[25] Yet the very revelation in which we believe urges us to reflect on its implication and to draw its conclusions.

One such reflection is Anselm's attempt to prove the necessity of the incarnation and atonement. This mode of posing the problem will, by

23. Ibid., p. 66; Book IV; chapter 12.
24. Ibid., pp. 72-73; Book IV; chapter 16.
25. Eugene R. Fairweather, ed., *A Scholastic Miscellany: Anselm to Ockham.* (Philadelphia: Westminster, 1956), p. 102; *Why God Became Man*; Book I, Chapter 1.

its very nature, impress its stamp on the solution. The fact that Anselm deals in such terms as "necessity" and "possibility" witnesses to the effect the categories of Aristotelian logic had upon theology; but this impression, which is disclosed by the very nature of the problem posed, also directs its solution. Almost every page of Anselm is brimming with arguments informed by the Aristotelian logic, and the very fact that Anselm engages in this mode of doing theology reveals a certain confidence on his part, a confidence concerning the rational order, not only of the cosmos, but of the divine life itself. Anselm's universe and his God seem to exist within the sphere of the perfect symmetry of logic, or rather, for Anselm to speak of God and the universe logically is possible because they *are* so. Yet to speak of the relationship between God and the world as merely "logical" would be misleading, for it would reduce the unity and harmony of the divine life and its created order to the human categories of logic. In fact, logical arguments are a mere shadow of the grandeur and symmetry of this divine life but a shadow which nevertheless apprehends, in a groping and tentative manner, the harmony existing within the divine life and its relations to the created order. That this is the case can be witnessed by Anselm's repeated deference to higher authorities and to revelation but, more importantly, by his insistence on the feeble powers of human reason. "Indeed, we must recognize that, whatever a man can say on this subject, the deeper reasons for so great a thing remain hidden."[26]

On the basis of this procedure Anselm develops a logic of immanence and transcendence complete with the historical event of Christ's incarnation. Since God is necessary in his very being, his redemptive activity must also result from an inner necessity in his relation with creation. In addition, creation itself must follow a pattern of conduct that does not destroy the divine plan and thereby jeopardize God's honor. Yet in deducing the inner necessity of God's dealings with the historical contingencies resulting from human decisions Anselm goes in fact well beyond the limits of what a consistent explication of the data of revelation allows. Thus he reduces God's choice after the fall to the following: "And since to deal rightly with sin without satisfaction is the same thing as to punish it, if it is not punished it is remitted irregularly."[27] Here as in other instances, Anselm, on the basis of a particular conception of justice, makes fundamental assumptions concerning divine freedom that are neither stated nor implied in the revealed text. These assumptions contain the seeds of all future religious rationalism. Anselm thereby surpasses what revelation assisted by reason enables one to say about

---

26. Ibid., p. 103; Book I, Chapter 2.
27. Ibid., p. 120; Book I, Chapter 2.

God's disposition to the world. An Aristotelian logic of propositions has manifestly impelled Anselm to give an *exhaustive* account of the relations between God and creation. Thus a project proclaimed to be based on the *data revelationis* in an unambiguous profession of faith changed its nature in the course of its execution.

Still, Anselm's rationality remains throughout a *devout* rationality illumined by a monastic vision and never consciously deviates from the principle stated in the *Proslogion: Quaero credere ut intelligam, non autem intelligere ut credam.* Faith remains the basic presupposition of all genuine understanding. Yet a trend was set and the rationalism that emerged with Abelard was far less pious. No theological knowledge of scripture was needed, he thought, to investigate the truth of religious mysteries. Logic alone sufficed to understand even such recondite dogmas as the eucharist or the Trinity. The reception of Aristotle's systematic works made the study of theology itself something it had never been before, namely, a science in the Aristotelian sense. With it came the ontological distinction between two orders of Being, one of which, being supernatural, would of necessity have to be "accidentally" related to the natural in an Aristotelian scheme of thought.

St. Thomas (1225-1274) confronted the problem head-on. In the very beginning of the *Summa Theologiae* (Question 1, article 2) he raises the question whether sacred doctrine is a science. Of particular interest is the purely Aristotelian definition by which he supports his affirmative answer, namely, science progresses from self-evident principles. Aquinas places the principles "known by the natural light of reason" on an even footing with the principles "established by the light of higher science, namely, the science of God and the blessed." To us such an equation may appear surprising, since it proves by means of what has to be proven. Need the so-called "science of God and the blessed" not itself first be established? But Aquinas takes the epistemic solidity of the manner in which we gather the "first principles" of sacred doctrine for granted. A little later he fully admits that they are *articuli fidei* (articles of faith), hence direct objects of revelation. "As other sciences do not argue to prove their premises, but work from them to bring out other things in their field of inquiry, so this teaching does not argue to establish its premises, which are the articles of faith, but advances from them to make something known."[28] The higher "science," then, turns out to be revelation—an interpretation of his text which Aristotle would have found surprising. Since Thomas is concerned only about the formal procedure from principles (however certified) to conclusions, he unhesi-

---

28. Thomas Aquinas, *Summa Theologiae: Part One, Questions 1-13* ed. Thomas Gilby (New York: Doubleday, 1969), p. 54; I, Question i, a. 8.

tatingly transplants the method from one to the other.

Such a scientific definition of religious truth differed too obviously from the one advocated by Augustine and the entire Greek Christian tradition that preceded him to remain unchallenged. The Paris condemnation of 1277 as well as the nominalist development in theology profoundly shook it. Still in the end Aquinas's "scientific" presentation of religious truth may not be as far removed from the Augustinian tradition as it seems. In themselves the articles of faith are only "external" principles; to be convincing at all they must be accompanied by an "interior light that induces the mind to assent." The principles themselves function as sense data which do not become intelligible until the mind illumines them. The light of faith provides the formal element that converts the objective data of faith into religious truth.[29] For Aquinas as for Augustine what ultimately determines the act of faith is God's own internal witness. The truth about God can only come from God, and in faith man responds to God's witness about himself. Aquinas moves within a well-established tradition initiated by the Fourth Gospel: Religious truth derives its constitutive evidence from a divine illumination. The external object of belief (the "principles") reveals itself as *true* only within the act of faith.

The synthesis between faith and reason achieved by Aquinas dissolved toward the end of the Middle Ages. Thomism had postulated that the world was created according to eternal exemplars. John Duns Scotus (1266?-1308), a Franciscan born almost a decade before the death of St. Thomas, pointed out that such a view compromised the freedom and omnipotence of God, since God's creative act would then be bound by these exemplars. This voluntarist view was taken to its radical conclusion by another Franciscan who had studied Scotus's views, William of Ockham (1290?-1349?). If God is to create from nothing, (*ex nihilo*) then even the reality of universal, preexisting forms must be denied. Each new entity which comes into existence is a totally new creation and not a conjunction of an identical form with a differing element of matter. Such a doctrine concerning the nonreality of universals leaves thought in a singularly embarrassing position. In the absence of universals which really reflect the nature of reality, the mind is forced to posit its own categories of order, an order that may not necessarily agree with the reality of nature as it is in itself or as it relates to God's creative act.

---

29. Hans Urs von Balthasar, *The Glory of the Lord*, volume I, trans. Erasmo Leiva-Merikakis (San Francisco: Ignatius Press, 1982), p. 162. As Von Balthasar notes, "For Thomas, neither Christian doctrine nor the miracles that attest to it would say anything to man without the *interior instinctus et attractus doctrinae.* (In John C. 6, 1. 4, n. 7; C. 15, i. 5, n. 5; In Rom. C. 8, i. 6), which he also calls *inspiratio interna* and *experimentum.*"

The nominalist development is important in that it sets the trend for all future philosophical thought. From now on human reason becomes more certain of itself, at least concerning what is required of it in order to get along in the world and to make natural judgments. As opposed to Augustine's unitary theory of knowledge, where even knowledge of things *in* the world depends upon divine illumination, nominalism separated what could be known through faith from what could be known by human reason alone; thus, according to nominalism, natural judgments about things in the world are possible without illumination. What is of particular import here, however, is the subtle change that the nature of truth undergoes under nominalism. Judgments made by human reason are no longer thought of in relation to an ontological order that is disclosed to it. Rather, since the employment of universals is merely a logical device enabling the human being to make judgments about reality, the truth arrived at by human reason alone comes more and more to be viewed in functional terms. Unaided by divine illumination, human reason is thought to have fulfilled its function if it allows a person to make the judgments necessary to get along in the world. On the other hand, in this scheme faith is conceived of primarily as a movement of the will to assent to mysteries which human reason cannot comprehend. After nominalism, then, reason and faith are concerned with two distinct objects, the respective nature of which determine the methods of procedure through which they can be known.

MODERN PHILOSOPHY

Modern philosophy is often claimed to begin with René Descartes (1596-1650). But his thought still owes much to the scholastic philosophy which he so firmly rejects. Descartes' insistence on cognitive certainty through clear and distinct ideas arising from the powers of human understanding *alone* had been prepared by nominalism's justification of a domain of knowledge free from the intrusions of revelation or theology. Yet Descartes went further in deriving a purely philosophical and natural concept of God from human reason unassisted by revelation. It is in Descartes' philosophy that "the God of the philosophers" is born. With Descartes, the basics of certainty is no longer found in God, but man. In other words, the medieval way of reasoning from certainty of God to certainty of the self is replaced by the modern approach: from certainty of the self to certainty of God."[30] Increasingly in the modern epoch, truth, if still granted to religious affirmations, no

---

30. Hans Küng, *Does God Exist? An Answer for Today*, trans. Edward Quinn (New York: Doubleday, 1980), p. 15.

longer springs from within faith but is extrinsically conveyed to faith by pure reason. Faith, on the other hand, is not the result of thought, but rather of the will's obedient assent to what the mind is unable to grasp. Even though for Descartes the domains of reason and faith remained separate, he assumed an ultimate harmony between the two.

Of primary significance is the function of the philosophical idea of God in Descartes' system. Descartes' radical doubt led him to question everything that could possibly be doubted. That included the reality of the world itself. To safeguard the epistemic reliability of knowledge of the world, Descartes first had to prove philosophically the existence of a good God who insured that the created reason, if used properly, sufficed to provide *certain* knowledge of the material world. The idea of God is taken out of its religious context in order to guarantee the veracity of the human knowledge of the world. It has ceased to be an inherently religious idea and instead is put in the service of purely cognitive interests.

Descartes' "clear and distinct ideas" set the stage for what has been called a "rationalist" philosophy. In the philosophy of Baruch Spinoza (1632-1677), for instance, the human understanding attains the fullness of truth only when it understands all that exists through the rational implications of some very simple ideas. According to Spinoza, the real is fully rational; indeed it is rational in the same way that mathematics or geometry are rational. In order to arrive at this conclusion Spinoza postulated a substantial unity between mind and reality. Moreover, Spinoza's philosophy included an exhaustive knowledge of God. Since God is eminently real, his existence is the primary object of reason. Indeed, he is the only one, for all other reality necessarily follows from this one and must be understood through it. Yet if that ultimate principle of rationality is a *substance*, that is, a reality existing in and through itself, then no other reality can be more than a mode of this one substance. Spinoza appropriately equates his God with nature. "God" thereby becomes, in effect, the beginning and end of a deductive system of propositions. Despite Spinoza's personal piety, his understanding of God and the world is so thoroughly rational that reason leaves no room for faith. Nor can we speak of any genuine transcendence in the idea of a God of whom we are all parts: God is both the initial idea and the necessary conclusion of consistent thought. It goes without saying that this "God" is hardly convertible with the God of religious faith.

Within the same rationalist tradition stands Gottfried Wilhelm von Leibniz (1646-1716) although, contrary to Spinoza, Leibniz attempts to safeguard a divine transcendence. Yet just as in the philosophies of Descartes and Spinoza, God fulfills a purely rational function. For Leibniz, God is the principle securing cosmic harmony in a universe consisting of independent substances. It is, in fact, through the miraculous attunement of these substances or "monads," as Leibniz calls them, with one another that we may infer the existence of God. Leibniz's concern with teleology and the internal coherence of the world brought him to attempt to answer questions arising from the existence of evil and imperfection in the world. Leibniz first establishes the existence of God through a purely rational deduction. Since nothing outside of God can impede the possibility of God's existence, God is necessarily possible, and this necessary possibility implies his actuality as the most perfect Being. Since God is wise, good, and omnipotent, he could not have but created the best of all possible worlds. Whatever evil exists *in* the world must therefore contribute to the greater perfection of the world as a whole. Again, the function of God in Leibniz's system is to guarantee the coherence of the world.

Descartes, Spinoza, and Leibniz, each in his own way, contributed to the idea of a purely natural religion, that is, of an idea of God which could be arrived at by human reason unaided by revelation. This way of posing the religious problem led to innumerable conflicts, not only with faith itself, but with the facts of experience, which, according to rationalist arguments, implied the existence of an all-powerful and good Creator. David Hume (1711-1776), both in the *Enquiry Concerning Human Understanding* and in the *Dialogues Concerning Natural Religion* showed that from the experience of the world alone it was impossible to derive an adequate concept of an omnipotent and good God. The *facts* of our experience of the world could only evoke a neutral attitude toward the world, not only because our experience of the cosmos is itself limited, but also because the world as we know it contains some good, but also much that is bad. The experience of evil in the world is a major stumbling block to a purely rational acceptance of the existence of God. In the *Dialogues* Hume writes, "But inspect a little more narrowly these living existences. . . . How contemptible or odious to the spectator! The whole presents nothing but the idea of blind nature, impregnated by a great vivifying principle, and pouring forth from her lap, without discernment or parental care, her maimed and abortive children."[31]

Gotthold Ephraim Lessing (1729-1781), influenced by the rationalism of Spinoza and Leibniz but as skeptical as Hume, maintained that a revealed religion based on historical contingency could not justify its claims before the tribunal of reason. Reason admits of only necessary logical truths and "the accidental truths of history can never become the

---

31. David Hume, *Dialogues Concerning Natural Religion*, ed. Henry D. Aiken (New York: Hafner, 1948), pp. 78-79, Part XI.

proof of the necessary truths of reason."[32] Lessing thereby brings to its logical conclusion a development of thought that separated reason from faith. Once the two were torn asunder, there was no way that the twain could be but back together again.

Lessing and Hume exemplify the skeptical attitudes resulting from a purely rational approach to religion. As Hume pointed out, reflection on our experience of the world does not enable us to ascertain the nature of that which transcends the world. On the other hand, Lessing's dilemma showed that the idea of God as a "necessary truth of reason" could relate only tangentially, if at all, to our contingent, historical experiences. Thus the divorce of reason from faith also resulted in the divorce of a "reasonable" religion from experience.

The philosophy of Immanuel Kant (1724-1804) marks the end of rational deductions of the existence of God. In the Preface to the second edition of the *Critique of Pure Reason* appear the famous words:

> From what has already been said, it is evident that even the assumption—as made on behalf of the necessary practical employment of my reason—of God, freedom, and immortality is not permissible unless at the same time speculative reason be deprived of its pretensions to transcendent insight. For in order to arrive at such insight it must make use of principles which, in fact, extend only to objects of possible experience, and which, if also applied to what cannot be an object of experience, always really changes this into an appearance, thus rendering all practical extensions of pure reason impossible. I have therefore found it necessary to deny *knowledge* in order to make room for faith.[33]

In the second half of the *Critique* Kant shows the inadequacy of the three kinds of proofs for God's existence, the ontological, the cosmological, and the teleological. According to Kant, the ontological proof remains a mere analysis of *a priori* concepts and God's existence cannot be proved by an analysis of the concept God. Likewise, the cosmological proof fails in its effort to deduce the existence of some necessary cause from the contingency of the world. The principle of causality applies only to appearances *in the world* and loses its meaning when it purports to define what lies beyond the world. Moreover, even if we allowed that from the contingency of the world we could arrive at a concept such as

---

32. *Lessing's Theological Writings*, trans. Henry Chadwick (Stanford: Stanford University Press, 1956), p. 53.

33. Immanuel Kant, *The Critique of Pure Reason*, trans. Norman Kemp Smith (New York: St. Martin's Press, 1929), p. 29.

that of a "necessary being," the empirical premises tell us nothing about the properties that such a necessary being might possess. As against the teleological argument, Kant argues that order in the world does not imply a single intelligent principle at its origin; there may in fact be many such principles. Kant's critique of knowledge discredited the traditional "proofs" for the existence of God and gave a whole new direction to the understanding of faith. In the practical order, Kant saw an opportunity to extend the realm of certainty beyond the rigorous limits which he had set to the domain of objective knowledge. Although no theoretical knowledge of God's existence is possible, God's existence can be shown to be a necessary condition of the practical realization of the highest good for man. God's existence must be postulated in order to insure that a person can achieve the final happiness that his moral worthiness requires. This postulate is particularly necessary since morality, being purely internal, guarantees no worldly success. Thus religion's exclusion from scientific knowledge was no ground, as Hume thought, for dismissing it as unworthy of the mature mind. Kant's decision to reintroduce God as a postulate of the moral imperative, and religion as a complement to ethics, may strike us as an unusually narrowing one. It was in fact, a daring attempt to extend the realm of consciousness so as to include legitimately the entire area of religion. Meanwhile, it created some problems of its own.

The concept of moral autonomy, on which Kant's ethical system was based, tolerated no transcendent foundation. So when Kant later defined religion as the recognition of all duties as divine commands, either this recognition introduces a new element into morality whereby the moral law becomes God's law, thus destroying the human being's autonomy, or the recognition remains extrinsic to the moral law, whereby religion loses its moral impact. Kant's solution of this dilemma satisfied no one, not even himself if we may believe his posthumous papers. But at least he had clearly stated a problem which proved to be of vital importance to the philosophy of religion. Kant's pioneering work resulted in three conclusions which have affected all subsequent philosophy of religion.

1. Since reliable theoretical knowledge is restricted to the objective, phenomenal sphere, the religious consciousness can expect no direct support of its beliefs from theoretical reason.

2. Since the transcendent does not belong to the objective, phenomenal sphere, it must be approached through the subject's awareness of itself rather than through that of its world.

3. Since the subject must be conceived as essentially autonomous, no transcendent reality can ever interfere with the exercise of human freedom.

Kant's critique of the limits of reason did not, however, discourage Georg Wilhelm Friedrich Hegel (1770-1831) from constructing a metaphysics based on the representational content of revealed religion. The question of the relationship between revealed religion and speculative thought erupts once more with the appearance of Hegel's philosophy. Hegel accepts the unique authority of the Christian revelation. Yet he also argues that faith does not fully come into its own until it has philosophically *thought* the representational content of this revelation. Such a view may appear similar to that proposed by Augustine: Faith must seek understanding. However, for Hegel philosophy is not merely a reflection upon faith; it is faith reaching its own truth. This does not mean, as has been argued in the past, that philosophy is a substitute for religion; philosophy cannot substitute that which it presupposes. However, it does mean that religion cannot be fully true *in its own right* until it has become philosophy. To many such a conclusion seems objectionable since it places an exclusive emphasis on the cognitive, that is, the gnostic element of the religious act. Certainly, a desire for clarification is essential to the act of faith, but it is not the whole act, nor can it ever change the act into a different one, an act of knowledge. Religious faith spontaneously tends toward philosophical reflection, but it never gives up its own identity in order to become philosophical reflection. To identify the two is to change the nature of the act of faith. It then becomes primarily an intellectual insight—which it was not before—claiming to understand its object exhaustively—which faith never does. To remain religious the gnostic drive of faith must be kept within the boundaries of faith. A religious act can never be transformed into one of reflection and still preserve its original identity. Hegel seems to set no limits to the gnostic drive. This appears even in the order of development of the *Philosophy of Religion*, based on their philosophical significance, that is, their role in bringing the idea to manifestation, rather than on their intrinsically spiritual significance. Thus the Greek and Roman religions marked a higher stage of development than the Hebrew or the Buddhist.[34]

The exhaustive character of the philosophical-religious insight is the other trait which makes Hegel's position suspect to the believer. The God of faith remains hidden, at the end of the clarification process as much as in the beginning. It is essential to faith *not* fully to understand. Hegel's philosophical religion has no such restrictions. The cognitive dynamism toward the absolute is pursued in the religious act until there remains nothing of the original darkness of faith. But is this still true

34. G. W. F. Hegel, *Lectures on the Philosophy of Religion*, ed. Peter Hodgson (Berkeley: University of California Press, 1987), vol II.

religious insight? Hegel's case shows how difficult it is to keep the relations between philosophy and religion such that both preserve their full integrity.

The Twentieth Century

Two important philosophers of the twentieth century to shed light on the meaning of religious faith are Martin Heidegger (1889-1976) and Karl Jaspers (1883-1969).

For Heidegger the God of metaphysics is the result of a misunderstanding and must be discarded with the misunderstanding itself. To answer the question *Why is there something rather than nothing?* by referring to a First Cause is to reveal the basic flaw of metaphysics: its inability to go beyond beings to Being itself. For by regarding the *ground* of all beings as their cause, I simply add another being to the series. Even less appropriate is it to call God his own cause. Philosophy, Heidegger writes in the *Letter on Humanism*, is incompetent to deal with God. Its task is to define the essence of man in relation to the truth of Being. On the relation to God it can make neither positive nor negative assertions, although it is highly interested in it. However, philosophy does deal with the divine realm of Being. This realm directly concerns the religious mind, for man cannot relate to God at all unless he stands in a correct relation to the truth of Being.

Theologians and philosophers alike have puzzled over the place of God in Heidegger's philosophy. Is God Being, or a being? The question is too complex to attempt an answer here, and moreover, the question of God is not central to Heidegger's philosophy. More pertinent to the question of philosophical faith is Heidegger's description of the religious attitude required by an authentic being-in-the-world.

Being, in order to be disclosed, must first and foremost confront the individual as that which cannot be *grasped* by the understanding. Such a conception of the nature and scope of philosophical activity substantially differs from the rationalist one, wherein it was thought that truth could be comprehended by moving from one inference to the next. Rather is Being precisely that which hides and recedes in the very apprehension of finite objects. As the horizon of thinking Being cannot be comprehended by the human mind, but all thinking presupposes it. And yet *that* there should be something rather than nothing is not only the most mysterious aspect of our finding ourselves in the world, but it is also the most essential. This is the meaning of Heidegger's urging us to wonder at Being.

The philosophy of Karl Jaspers, like Heidegger's, is existential in tone. At the very beginning of his *Philosophical Faith and Revelation*, Jaspers makes a distinction between two kinds of being-in-the-world, existence and Existenz. To these two subjective modes of being correspond respectively the world and Transcendence. Thus existence is mainly preoccupied with closed and immanent structures of everyday concerns. Moreover, the world of existence is clear and perspicuous; it is objectively graspable precisely because it remains at the level of that which has a definite shape, a knowable definition. The individual who remains at the level of existence moves from one finite thing to the next, and it is the world of finite things in its totality that fills his or her life. At the level of existence the person merely reacts, remains within the structures of cause and effect, and communicates by means of modes of thinking and speaking which he or she already finds present in the public domain of consciousness at large.

To the subjective mode of Existenz belongs freedom. Jaspers describes Existenz in the following way:

> Whatever has been said, done, unfolded in regard to Existenz stays indirect. . . . At bottom, knowing that it is a gift—Existenz remains hidden. Why do I love? Why do I believe? Why am I determined?
>
> These questions are unanswerable, no matter how many premises, conditions, motivations may be set forth for what appears in the world. Each answer makes us realize the radical unanswerability.
>
> There is no reason why we should not ask; but experience shows that for our cognition the reality of Existenz is bottomless.
>
> To us, anything so unfathomable is an origin rather than a visible, determinable object.[35]

Existenz is not determined by the realm of objects inside our world. Its object, or rather, that toward which the subject is directed, is Transcendence. The nature of Transcendence is, however, such that it defies all categorical objectifications. To objectify it is to make it finite and to thereby make it a part of the world that *appears* to human consciousness; but then it is no longer that which grounds all appearances yet merely a part of the world.

The philosophies of both Heidegger and Jaspers attempt to overcome the modern turn to the subject by showing that authentic participation in existence must always involve a realm of openness to that which transcends and founds the given. For Heidegger transcendence occurs through an openness to Being, that is, through an openness to that which recedes in the very apprehension of finite objects, but which is nevertheless the ground that must be presupposed for their very appear-

---

35. Karl Jaspers, *Philosophical Faith and Revelation*, trans. E. B. Ashton, (New York: Harper & Row, 1967), p. 68.

ance. For Jaspers too, both Existenz and Transcendence remain hidden. The realm of Transcendence can never be objectified without doing it violence, and this is why Jaspers is so opposed to the absolute claims made by historical revelation, even though he is deeply interested in the believer's faith in revelation. Nevertheless, Jaspers admits that a philosophical faith, that is, a faith which remains open to Transcendence and thereby does not seek to fix its object in the realm of what appears, may still be operative in the believer's faith in revelation. As such, Jaspers' "philosophical faith" is the faith that recognizes the radical contingency permeating all our existence, indeed, the radical contingency and particularity of all that we even can know. Yet in the very recognition of this contingency, philosophical faith makes it possible for the human being not to fall prey to either nihilism or despair. This faith in and openness to Transcendence ultimately sustains us in doubt and despair.

CHAPTER 4

The Concept of Faith in Psychology

H. Newton Malony

Since psychology is commonly understood to be that discipline which attempts to understand, predict, and control behavior, the "psychology of faith" can be defined as the study of faith as human behavior. As such, psychology intentionally exempts itself from any investigation of the object of faith. It makes no attempt to answer the "validity question," i.e., whether there is a God or not. It confines itself to a study of the act of faith.

IS FAITH NECESSARY?

While psychology cannot determine the truth or falseness of faith's object, it can reflect on the question of whether faith is a necessary human act since mystics suggest that religious truth is immediately apprehended and since some theologians have asserted that God makes himself known quite apart from human intent or belief.

If God, or spiritual reality, were instantaneously experienceable, then faith would be no more than an instinct at worst or a reaction at best. Instincts are those behaviors which occur in all members of a species quite apart from intention or awareness. Reactions are those behaviors which, like the sensations of sight, touch, and sound occur without thought. Sensations, unlike responses, do not involve mid- or fore-brain interactions. To conceive of faith as an instinct or as a reaction would be tantamount almost to abolishing its traditional meaning.

71

James Leuba, an early twentieth-century psychologist of religion, clearly perceived this possibility when he wrote: "If the fundamental truths of religion are either immediately given in inner experiences or induced from them, one does not see why something additional called "faith" should be a necessary condition of religious belief. . . . If God manifests himself immediately and clearly in consciousness . . . why should a conscious process additional to those in which the truths of religion are revealed intervene, and what may be the function of this process?"[1]

Is Faith a Discovery? a Perception? or Neither?

Athough he did not acknowledge it, Leuba was bringing to the fore the realist/idealist controversy which had been addressed often in intellectual history. A brief discussion of this controversy leading up to Immanuel Kant's propositions about the nature of faith have import for psychology's understanding of whether faith is more instinctual or more responsive.

Such seventeenth-century skeptics as Locke, Berkeley, and Hume, for example, challenged the Newtonian scientists who confidently assumed that they were apprehending the absolute laws of God through their experiments.[2] According to these skeptics, the Newtonians failed to see that human reason functioned as something more than as an empty receptacle of truth. Reason molded truth, according to the skeptics. In fact, the skeptics insisted that the object could only be known in the form which reason gave it. The object of truth was never known in any pure form. In regard to faith, the skeptics would probably have agreed with Carl Jung that people not only have their gods, they make them.

Although the skeptics were primarily concerned with the truths of scientific discovery, the issues they noted are extremely pertinent to the psychology of faith, as Jung's assertion and Leuba's question note. In fact, Kant's answer to the doubts of the skeptics addressed this issue by distinguishing between "theoretical" and "practical" reasoning.[3] His dis-

---

1. James H. Leuba, *The Psychological Study of Religion* (New York: Macmillan, 1912), pp. 261-262.
2. See John Herman Randall Jr., *The Making of the Modern Mind: A Survey of the Intellectual Background of the Present Age*, rev. ed. (Cambridge, Mass.: Houghton Mifflin, 1940), especially the chapter on "The Newtonian World-Machine," pp. 253 ff.
3. Immanuel Kant, *Critique of Pure Reason*, trans. Norman Kemp-Smith (London, 1929). See also Newton P. Stallknecht, "Kant's Critical Philosophy," in *A History of Philosophical Systems*, ed. Vergilius Ferm (New York: Philosophical Library, 1950), pp. 280-290 and Randall, *Making of the Modern Mind*, pp. 304ff.

tinction is a model which continues to influence the psychology of faith as well the philosophy of science.

Faith as Practical Reasoning

According to Kant, the human mental activity termed "theoretical reasoning" referred to the truths gleaned from the scientific study of nature, exemplified by the conclusions of the Newtonians. Kant agreed with the skeptics that these truths were shaped by an active, not a passive, mental process. Nature, the type of reality studied by theoretical reason, was grasped, or apprehended, through the categories of the mind: time, space, causality, and substance. These categories were the innate ways that the mind organized the world. He agreed with the skeptics that humans created, rather than discovered, the laws of nature. Nature was never known in its pure form but was known only through the ways in which theoretical reason shaped it.

Kant agreed with the skeptics in a second assertion they had made. He agreed that because these scientific laws were only human descriptions of causality, there was no way one could be certain these assumptions were in fact the ways God acted. Thus, contrary to Newtonian assertions, scientific laws could not be used as a basis for reasoning back to any first cause and, therefore to claim proof for God. These cause-effect laws were nothing more than descriptions which emerged from the ways in which reason organized the world. They were not immediate apprehensions of the way things really were before humans attempted to study them.

In sharp contrast, Kant contended that humans DID have direct access to God through "practical" reason. His famous dictum that he "believed in the starry heavens above and the moral law within" refers to this type of reasoning which he felt led to an immediate apprehension of God not filtered through the imposition of mental categories; i.e., time, space, causality, or substance.

Known as the moral proof for God, this form of reasoning Kant understood to be "practical" rather than "theoretical." Practical reason provided humans guidance for the way life should be lived rather than an understanding of the natural world. The truth that God existed was, therefore, thought by Kant to be immediately and directly given through the voice of the human conscience.

In terms of traditional philosophical categories, Kant could be called an "idealist" with regard to scientific or theoretical reasoning and a "realist" with regard to religious or practical reasoning. He would basically agree with Leuba that faith, as a human act, was not necessary.

Yet, Kant's understanding included a subtle distinction which has import for contemporary psychological understanding of faith. On the one hand, faith for Kant was the immediate awareness that God was speaking through one's conscience. On the other hand, faith was what one did in response to this awareness that God was calling one to the moral life. In a sense, faith was, to Kant, more a matter of volition than of perception. Faith was something one did in response to God.

Kant would not agree with Jung's statement that people make their gods. According to Kant, people experience God directly. However, people also respond to God. Faith was not simply a way of thinking "about" God, but an intention to act based upon a previous awareness.

In terms of the question of whether faith was necessary, Kant would seem to answer both yes and no. He combines instinct and response. People's experience of God is universal and not determined by human intention or thought. Thus, faith is instinctual. However, people's response to this experience varies. Faith requires thought. Thus, faith is responsive.[4]

Faith as Mystical Awareness

Kant provided the basis for most subsequent psychological thinking as can be seen in the early twentieth-century theorizing of the celebrated psychologist of religion William James. James answered the question regarding faith's necessity in a manner that was heavily dependent on Kant for its rationale. Reasoning from a mystical, rather than a moral, point of view, James regarded faith as a response to the human awareness of a higher, spiritual universe.[5] Although he did not so note it, it is commonly assumed that James was describing his own mystical experience when he gave a vivid description of the "consciousness of a presence" over several nights and in a variety of locations.[6]

James felt that a universe wider than that available to humans through the five senses was as universal and innate as Kant's moral sense. Hence faith, understood as mystical awareness, was instinctual.

James also felt that the awareness of this wider universe was something humans recognized and acknowledged rather than constructed,

---

4. Kant's distinction between the ways God and the natural world are known still influences contemporary discussions about the differences between scientific and religious language; knowledge and faith. Certainly, the moral proof for God and the responsibility of human action in response to conscience has been the foundation for the social gospel movement as well as psychology's study of the relationships between beliefs, attitudes, and behavior. See Richard L. Gorsuch, "Religion as a Significant Predictor of Important Human Behavior," in *Research in Mental Health and Religious Behavior*, ed. W. J. Donaldson Jr. (Atlanta, Ga.: Psychological Studies Institute, 1976), pp. 206-221.

5. William James, *The Varieties of Religious Experience* (New York: Mentor, 1902, 1958), especially p. 367 and chapter 3 "The Reality of the Unseen."

6. Ibid., pp. 62-63.

even in part, by their mental processes. Faith did not make this awareness possible. Faith accepted it and was sensitive to it. Faith was like "extrasensory perception." However, faith was more an awareness of a wider universe than it was an experience of the call to the moral life, as it was with Kant.

Faith had a consequential dimension for James, as it did for Kant. Understood as a response, faith for James was the intention to become more responsive to this extrasensory, spiritual environment. Once again, this was different from Kant's understanding of faith as the intent to be moral. James felt that the reponse of faith had a broader outcome, namely, personality integration. In fact, James is best known for his emphasis on the "fruits" of faith defined less in moral than in psychological adjustment terms.[7] This idea has had much influence on psychology's understanding of the relation of religion to mental health.[8]

Is Faith a Gift?

Yet another variation on this question of the necessity of faith is the statement in Ephesians 2:8 where the writer states that faith is a necessary component of the Christian religion yet quickly corrects any impression that faith is something persons do through their own efforts. This scripture states, "For it is by grace that you are saved, THROUGH faith and this not from yourselves, it is the gift of God—not by WORKS so that no one can boast." (emphasis mine)

For the psychologist, crucial questions arise from this biblical verse. Is faith a "faculty" separate from the mind as can be seen, for example, in Kant's conscience? Is faith a "sixth sense" as can be seen, for example, in James' spiritual awareness? Or is faith an imparted capacity given by God at a certain time to individuals when they are in crisis? If this last option is the case, is faith thereby a capacity that is qualitatively different from and independent of any innate or acquired physical or mental capacity? This would make faith something different from instincts, reactions, or responses.

Faith as the Answer to Problems

Another option might be that the "faith" about which the biblical verse speaks is a normal human response capacity whose object or focus in this situation is God as contrasted with the answers to life's problems provided by medicine, society, or philosophy. The "gift" in this case

---

7. Ibid., p. 191, p. 257.
8. See C. Daniel Batson and W. Larry Ventis, *The Religious Experience: A Social-Pychological Perspective* (New York: Oxford University Press, 1982), particularly chapter 11, "Mental Health or Sickness," pp. 211 ff.

would not be the capacity to have faith, but the love or "grace" of God. The unanswered issue from this point of view would be the nature of "grace." Since Ephesians is part of the Christian scriptures, grace refers to the assertion that the God who is experienced through faith is one who "saves" humans through his mighty act in Christ Jesus.

As contrasted with both the moral and mystical foci of Kant and James, this biblical passage introduces a conflict theme into psychological theorizing about faith. Hereby, faith is not something one discovers, as with theoretical reasoning, or something one becomes aware of and responds to, as with moral or mystical experience. Faith, in the Ephesians' sense, is something that one *believes* or *affirms* in the midst of great personal need. Faith saves. It provides answers to questions; it solves conflicts.

From this viewpoint, faith is neither instinct nor reaction. It is response. It involves thought. But the thought of faith is not, as with Jung, the "making" of the gods. The thought of faith, herein conceived, is believing or accepting the nature of the divine as given through the gift of grace; i.e., the Christian revelation. In theological phraseology, faith has dogmatic cognitive content. This is a type of faith response which perceives and accepts *a certain type* of God as an answer to life problems.

Although, as we noted earlier, the Bible does not clarify the nature of faith, at the very least it could be said that the writer of Ephesians agrees with modern psychology in saying that grace must be received or perceived. He states that persons are saved "by grace *through* faith." Both modern psychology and the writer of Ephesians would agree that faith is a response, not a reaction or an instinct. Faith is indeed necessary from this point of view. It is a thoughtful act involving the mind of the person.

Faith: A Reaction to an Occasional or Constant Stimulus?

Whether "grace," as used in the Ephesians passage, implies that sometimes God, like an advertiser in a newspaper, chooses to reveal himself to humans on one occasion while at other times he does not, is left unanswered. The answer to this dilemma has much import for the larger issue of whether faith is necessary or not. Arminian and Calvinist theologians have long debated these issues.[9]

However, psychologists of sensation, while not dealing directly with the response of faith, assert that if God were present in persons' environment at a level above the subliminal there would be neural transmissions to the brain resulting from stimulation of one or more of the five

---

9. See William R. Cannon, *The Theology of John Wesley* (New York: Abingdon, 1946), pp. 31-33.

senses.[10] The "sensation of God" would be received by the human brain. This cranial reception would be automatic, certain, and involuntary unless persons were asleep or drugged. Distraction would not prevent the brain from receiving the stimulation although the brain might not recognize or label it.

The organizing of these sensations into perceptions and the reconstruing of these perceptions into concepts would be a different matter. The Ephesians' understanding of faith refers to this final conceptualizing process. In contrast to Kant's understanding that faith is an ethical response to God who speaks through the voice of conscience and in contrast to James' understanding that faith is the recognition of a spiritual universe above physical reality, the faith referred to in Ephesians has dogmatic cognitive content. It refers to the belief that Jesus is the Son of God, the long hoped for Messiah, the Savior of the world, one's personal Redeemer.

In characterizing faith as "grace" and "gift," the writer of Ephesians is perhaps asserting that the threefold process of sensation-perception-conceptualization, resulting in the affirmation that "Jesus is Lord," is entirely guided by the power of God and is not dependent on any logical reasoning by humans.

To accept that this is the way the grace of God works would require a giant leap of logic for psychologists of learning. The difficulty would not arise because the stimulus object which prompted the sensation-perception-conception process could not be consciously identified. Psychologists of learning readily accept concepts that can be based on stimulus-reponse pairings which have been forgotten, become sub-conscious— even unconscious, and which have become gestalt-like conglomerates resulting from tendencies of the mind to simplify reality.[11]

What would be difficult for these psychologists to accept is that the stimulus was extrasensory or metaphysical.[12] Since the time of Locke the mind has been assumed to be a blank tablet on which experience with the physical, not the metaphysical, world was based. Extrasensory perception, much less metaphysical perception replete with dogmatic content, is still not widely accepted by most psychologists, William

---

10. See Roger Brown and Richard J. Herrnstein, *Psychology* (Boston: Little, Brown, 1975), pp. 410ff., for a review of this issue.

11. See Philip G. Zimbardo, *Psychology and Life*, 11th ed. (Glenview, Ill.: Scott, Foresman, 1985), pp. 108-149, for a presentation of the physical basis of all sensation/perception.

12. Ibid. In spite of the long-term interest in extrasensory perception (ESP) at Duke University and in the popular press, there is no mention of this phenomenon in this widely respected general psychology text. This omission is typical of the attitude in mainline psychology toward ESP.

James and modern transpersonal psychology notwithstanding.

The great contribution of Sigmund Freud was to bring even higher mental processes, e.g., those thoughts which have complex conceptual content, under the umbrella of stimulus-response learning theory grounded in physical sensation.[13]

Jean Piaget gave a convincing analysis of the development of morality which concluded that even the voice of conscience is a learned, rather than an innate phenomenon—as Kant had suggested.[14]

Whether the tendencies of the mind to organize sensations and perceptions into concepts are limited to Kant's categories of time, space, causality, and substance is still being debated. What is not being debated in contemporary psychology is that the mind is active. The mind neither passively receives stimulation nor is it filled with innate ideas. The mind does something to the stimulations it receives and the stimulations it receives are limited to those it receives via the five senses which, in turn, are attuned to the physical, not the metaphysical world. To think of faith as somehow bypassing this process through some kind of response to a nonphysical stimulus or some kind of immediate prehension would be difficult for cognitive psychologists to affirm.

In the Ephesians passage, persons are cautioned against boasting that they have reached these conclusions on their own effort, i.e., by "works." If we assume that works refers to some kind of mental process, the writer of Ephesians seems to be disapproving of the Newtonians' reasoning about God as first cause seventeen hundred years before the fact! It is also clear that this kind of Ephesian faith which includes dogmatic cognitive content may be different not only from the moral determination of Kant's faith and the extrasensory spiritual awareness of James but also from the tenets of modern learning theory.

Faith as Revealed or Grasped?

Nevertheless, the Ephesian kind of thinking that pictures dogma-full faith as bypassing all human effort can be seen in the theologian Karl Barth's reaction to the existentialist psychology inherent in the thinking of his contemporary Emil Brunner. In their well-known dialogue entitled *Nature and Grace*,[15] Brunner and Barth argued over the question with which the Ephesians' quotation deals, namely: Is faith something

---

13. See Ruth Monroe, *Schools of Psychoanalytic Thought: An Exploration, Critique and Attempt at Integration* (New York: Dryden, 1955).

14. Jean Piaget, *The Moral Judgment of the Child*, trans. Marjorie Gabian (Glencoe, Ill.: Free Press, 1960).

15. Karl Barth and Emil Brunner, *Nature and Grace* (Zurich: Zwingli, 1935).

humans grasp by mental effort or by immediate awareness, i.e., a "gift" from a metaphysical source?

Arguing on the basis of the human need to find a resolution to the anxiety of finitude and death, Brunner suggested that the God-stimulus must speak of these needs, or else humans will pay no attention to it. Barth, affirming the Ephesians position, answered "Nein!" to Brunner's point of view. He contended that if God revealed himself only in answer to human anxiety, then God would have to wait for humans to experience this anxiety before he could make himself known. And Barth said that this was unthinkable from a theological point of view. Barth reasoned: If God is all-powerful then he is not dependent on the awakening of human need to awaken faith in people. Human anxiety would not lead people to God. Human anxiety would lead to idolatry at worst or a misuse of God for human ends at best. Barth contended that God continued to make himself known to humans on his own initiative, not in response to peoples' recognition of their need for him.

For Barth, this did not mean that the life, death, and resurrection of Jesus was not an answer to the human problem. It simply meant that, from Barth's point of view, human sin, resulting from the fall, was so pervasive that humans could not even ask the proper questions much less know when they had received the gospel answer through their own mental processes. Barth did not believe that faith was instinct, reaction, or response. Faith, understood in these three latter ways, was neither possible nor necessary.

The question might be asked, "Then how is faith possible from Barth's point of view?" The answer is: "It is God who gives faith; it is God who enables faith." From time to time God comes to the hearts of believers and awakens faith in them. Barth seems to adopt the Ephesian position that the sensation-perception-conception process was entirely under divine control.

Faith as Selective Perception

It can be seen that Brunner took a different tack from the Newtonians, Kant, or James. He was not arguing that human reason construed God, as did the Newtonians. Nor did he contend that persons had a moral sense, as did Kant, or a spiritual sense, as did James. Brunner's is explicitly a conflict, need-based, motivation-driven model in which persons must have God to survive.

Contemporary psychology supports Brunner's point of view. Brunner's contention that human beings seek answers to their questions makes sense out of the obvious facts that perception is selective. Although sensations may be indiscriminately registered on the brain, only those which have met the needs of individuals are acknowledged and utilized in the perception-conceptualizing process, according to contemporary psychology.[16]

Unless physical stimuli are so loud, so light, so pungent, so painful, or so distasteful that they overwhelm whatever else is on the mind, they will be ignored unless they meet human need. Of course, Barth might contend that this is just the character of the God-stimulus, i.e., overwhelming. However, when he contends that persons must be where the gospel is read and preached, we are left with the unexplainable facts that 1) people must be at church, and 2) the whole event starts with their hearing the good news about God. The faith event, for Barth, seems inextricably related to human mental processes, try though he did to divorce the two.

Brunner's point of view seems much more compatible with contemporary cognitive psychology. His model firmly sees faith as a necessary process in religion. Furthermore, faith, for Brunner, is clearly a response—not an instinct or a simple reaction. Faith is a thoughtful, problem-solving process. Moreover, Brunner's model clarifies why persons are selectively attentive to the God-stimulus. They are conscious of their anxiety over death, guilt, and meaninglessness at some times more than others.

Thus, while the God-stimulus may be always available, people become aware of it and put themselves in places where it is more obvious *when* they are anxious. Brunner's model helps us avoid the metaphysical dilemma of questioning God's character if he made himself available at some times but not at others and if he chose to awaken faith in some people but not in others.

Summary

In this section we have considered the question of whether faith is essential or not. Several alternatives were proposed. Although Brunner and contemporary psychologists all contend that faith follows an inevitable and necessary mental process, Kant, James, and Barth maintain that faith is a process independent of and qualitatively different from normal thinking mechanisms.

Despite the fact that the issues are more complex than this, it could be said that we have considered whether faith should be looked upon as instinctive, reactive, or responsive behavior. In general, it could be concluded that faith is a "response," one more thoughtful than spontaneous, more planned than automatic. In an earlier publication, I pro-

---

16. Floyd Allport, *Theories of Perception and the Concept of Structure* (New York: Wiley, 1955).

posed a Stimulus-Organism-Response model for religious experience which I feel sums up this position. This model is as follows:[17]

Table 1: Perspectives on the three events in religious experience			
	EVENT 1	EVENT 2	EVENT 3
THEOLOGICAL PERSPECTIVE	Revelation →	Faith	→ Work
BEHAVIORIST PERSPECTIVE	Stimulus →	Organism	→ Response
PHENOMENOLOGICAL PERSPECTIVE	Need →	Perception/conception	→ Action

Some of the terms and issues in this model will be considered later. However, to return to Leuba, he asked the question for all psychologists of faith, "What does faith mean?" Just what kind of behavior is "faith"?

In an effort to answer these concerns, a second question must be posed, "Is faith a behavior that can be qualitatively distinguished from other human acts?" The following discussion will be based on the presumption that regardless of how faith occurs, it is basically a human act that can be described.

Is Faith Unique?

Although he felt "religious experience" itself is based on a unique awareness of the unseen world, William James understood "religion" in a less idiosyncratic manner. It is clear that James did not consider religion to be human behavior that was qualitatively different from other human experiences. His definition of religion was "the feelings, acts, and experiences of individuals [persons] in their solitude, so far as they apprehend themselves to stand in relation to whatever they may consider the divine."[18]

James felt that religious feelings, acts, and experiences differ from other feelings, acts, and experiences only in terms of their object, i.e., the divine. They do not differ in terms of the mental processes involved.

---

17. H. Newton Malony, "An S-O-R Model of Religious Experience," in *Advances in the Psychology of Religion*, ed. L. B. Brown (New York: Pergamon, 1985), pp. 113-126.

18. James, *The Varieties of Religious Experience*, p. 42.

Athletic, literary, religious, or musical emotions are the feelings and thoughts persons have in relation to these interests. The underlying emotional process is the same from one to the other. Only the object of interest differs. Perception is perception for James, regardless of whether perception was of a sunset or a spiritual presence. Many, if not most, contemporary psychologists of religion would agree with this point of view[19] although not all of them would reduce faith to the human search for cognitive meaning, as James Fowler seems to do.[20]

However, even if one adopts Fowler's[21] position that faith is essentially the search for cognitive meaning and coherence in life, it is obvious that there are other answers to this quest which humans can believe and accept. This act of believing and affirming is a higher mental process which can be applied to a number of options other than God. The objects of belief differ but the act of believing is the same.

Whether beliefs about and attitudes toward these other interests could be termed "faith" is a debatable question. Many would do so. Others would limit "faith" to those beliefs and attitudes focused on transempirical realities such as God. The distinctions are not easy to make as the statement that "some live for God, some for country, and some for Yale" poignantly illustrates. Where everyday belief ends and faith begins is unclear.

It is interesting to note, however, that James moderated his opinion significantly when he discussed the import of the "faith-state" for human life. What James still insisted was merely a difference in degree or intensity, appeared to be a difference in kind when one considers the transforming, life-changing power of the religious experiences which he described.[22]

James' position that faith is unique becomes clearer when we consider his distinction between faith-states and beliefs.

Basing his theorizing on Leuba's designation of intense religious experience as a "faith-state" replete with biological as well as emotional components, James concluded that such a state had little or no intellectual content.[23] He recounted experiences of persons who had a sudden awareness of the divine presence and who had a vague excitement that wondrous things were about to happen. These experiences, however, routinely became "stamped" with intellectual content, namely beliefs.

---

19. Batson and Ventis, *Religious Experience.*
20. See Bernard Spilka, Ralph W. Hood Jr., and Richard L. Gorsuch, *The Psychology of Religion* (Englewood Cliffs, N.J.: Prentice-Hall, 1985), ch. 7, "Religious Experience," for a discussion of this issue.
21. James W. Fowler, *Stages of Faith: The Psychology of Human Development and the Quest for Meaning* (San Francisco: Harper & Row, 1981), p. 33.
22. James, *Varieties of Religious Experience,* pp. 381-382.
23. Ibid., pp. 157-206.

These beliefs became creeds. According to James, faith-states coupled with creeds equaled religions. But the two involved different mental processes, in his opinion.

However, belief is that behavior most typically associated with faith. The two terms have often been used interchangeably. The ways in which faith and belief are related have been considered by a number of psychologists of religion in addition to James.

For example, Gordon Allport noted that although we tend to use the word faith to refer to things about which we are less than sure, nonetheless when we say that we believe in God we are implying something more perfunctory and less serious than when we say we have faith in God. Allport probably understated the issue when he wrote that "faith is more complex psychologically than is simple belief."[24]

Later contemporary psychologists of religion, Daniel Batson and Larry Ventis,[25] extended this comparison of faith and belief in a discussion of true versus false religion. They identified false religion with just believing or being religious in traditional, customary ways. They noted that Jesus, as well as Old Testament prophets such as Amos, discounted the hypocrisy of traditionally religious people. With Batson and Ventis, as with Allport, true religion or faith seemed to imply something more than belief.

The implication of the above comments is that faith involves something in addition to or different from intellectual assent to certain creeds or the performance of certain rituals. It involves an enthusiastic and/or emotional commitment to a way of life. It refers to a person's identity. Faith is not so much something one believes as it is something one is and does. Faith is an active verb rather than a sterile noun. Interestingly enough, however, James Fowler in his volume *Stages of Faith*[26] pointed out that the original meanings of belief and faith were not all that different. Both implied commitment and passion—not just tacit cognitive assent.

Psychotheologist Don Browning proposed a distinction between faith and lower-order beliefs that is helpful for this discussion. He suggested that faith is more inclusive, primarily applies to the self, and affords a degree of certainty that transcends the "deferential, calculative, and probabilistic character of hypotheses and beliefs guiding more immediate adaptation."[27]

---

24. Gordon Allport, *The Individual and His Religion* (New York: Macmillan, 1950), p. 123.
25. Batson and Bentis, *Religious Experience*, p. 138.
26. Fowler, *Stages of Faith*, p. 12.
27. Don Browning, "Faith and the Dynamics of Knowing," in *The Dialogue between Theology and Psychology*, ed. Peter Homans (Chicago: University of Chicago Press, 1968), p. 126.

84 H. NEWTON MALONY

Browning's three distinctives of faith provide a model for asserting that faith is, indeed, a unique human act. Faith differs qualitatively from other behaviors and, although it contains elements of belief, it goes beyond beliefs in that, as Browning suggests, 1) faith combines a number of beliefs into a whole worldview, i.e., it is inclusive; 2) faith is that act which provides one's basic identity, i.e., it is focused on the self; and 3) the certainty of conviction that emerges from faith differs radically from the cause-effect assumptions that are used in daily problem-solving, i.e., faith is not dependent on repeated empirical verification of the five senses.

In this regard, the European psychologist of religion, André Godin, proposes a distinction that is very informative for an understanding of the unique meaning of CHRISTIAN faith.[28] Although faith in general results in all three of the outcomes mentioned by Browning, Godin insists that Christian faith accomplishes these goals in a distinctive manner.

Godin differentiates "functional religion" from "Christian faith." According to Godin, functional religion is wish-based. Functional religion is synonymous with the conflict model discussed earlier when Brunner was considered. It is based on a natural human wish to experience comfort and security in the face of existence. It is grounded in the desire for experience of a reality that both transcends earthly limits and gives guidance in the face of problems.

Functional religion is the type of religious faith that Freud concluded was based on the illusion that certainty and security are obtainable.[29] This is the type of religion that contemporary psychologist Albert Ellis critiques in his "Case Against Religion."[30]

Although his assessment is more benign, Godin would agree that functional religion has as its aim adjustment through wish fulfillment. Functional religion is faith based on the desires of "irreligious man," according to Godin. Although it meets all of Browning's criteria, its underlying motive is the desire to find reassurance and safety.

Although Godin recognizes that many who call themselves Christian are actually functionally religious, he feels that true Christian faith is of a different order of reality. As contrasted with functional religion which is based on the desires of humans, Christian faith is based on the desires of God as seen in Jesus Christ. He terms this "conforming one's life to the wish of the Other," i.e., to Christ.[31]

---

28. André Godin, *The Psychological Dynamics of Religious Experience* (Birmingham, Ala.: Religious Education Press, 1985), pp. 194 ff.

29. Sigmund Freud, *The Future of an Illusion* (New York: Doubleday, 1964).

30. Albert Ellis, *The Case Against Religion* (New York: Center for Rational Emotive Therapy, 1975).

31. Godin, *Psychological Dynamics of Religious Experience*, pp. 196-197.

Godin used the experience of Saul of Tarsus as his paradigm. He notes that Saul's experience with God did not "come out of nothing." It was not contentless mysticism, as was William James' experience. It occurred as a counter to Saul's firm desire to protect the Jewish faith from the Christian revelation.

By this observation, Godin identifies himself with mainline psychology in suggesting that the stimuli to which Saul was responding was communicated to him through his five senses. Saul's own cultural experience prepared him for his bias. Moreover, his sense of threat to what he held dear, his religion, focused his perception on the sensations which were coming into his brain.

His conversion, was less a fulfillment of his natural desires, i.e., functional religion, and was more a transformation of his own desires by the desires of God—not simply to oppose those whom he had been serving, the Jews, but to seek their salvation. His ego-ideal was changed from his own need to be the defender of his cultural faith to that of servant of the God of love revealed in Jesus Christ.

Godin suggests that the psychological process involved in Paul's (and all Christian) faith is an "active synthesis of presence and interpretation."[32] In the first place, this active synthesis involves the linking together of the natural wishes of humans for security with the wishes of God which reach persons through the life and teachings of Jesus. Godin recognizes that the motivation for seeking God in the first place is the natural wish of irreligious humans for safety and security. This motive propels humans toward God and makes them attend to God. But in Christian faith this motive is transformed by the presence of Jesus Christ. Persons meet God in Christ just as Saul did on the Damascus road. This is the active synthesis of "presence." The human desire for assurance is met in God's steadfast love rather than in some human effort.

In the second place, this active synthesis involves an identification of persons with Jesus' love for and commitment to the persecuted and poor. The purpose of life becomes less one of achievement and more one of faithful service to the less fortunate. More importantly, Christians see *themselves* as the poor. In giving themselves to others they are doing what was done for them. They identify with Christ and the meaning of their lives becomes refocused in a radically different manner. Godin calls this the synthesis of interpretation. It might better be called REinterpretation.

These psychological processes involved in Christian faith make it a qualitatively unique experience, according to Godin. Godin's argu-

---

32. Ibid., pp. 202 ff.

ments have merit. His model has some affinity with Barth's views. Whether Godin would see functional religion as also unique is debatable. He would perhaps agree with James in saying that functional religion is simply common human emotion and thought focused on a religious object.

Having asserted that faith is an act that can be thought to differ in kind, not just in degree, from other human behavior, let us consider more fully the nature of the faith act.

THE "ACT" OF FAITH

Since not everyone is religious in a traditional sense, it has been questioned whether the act of faith is universal. Paul Tillich, the theologian, thought it was. Everyone has an "ultimate concern," according to him.[33] This is somewhat different from James Fowler's statement that people are born with a nascent capacity for faith.

However, both Fowler and Tillich would seem to be referring to what Godin calls "functional religion" rather than Christian faith. The basic motivational force in both Tillich and Fowler is a sense of need and of incompleteness. Nevertheless, as the late Harvard psychologist, Gordon Allport concluded, behaviors which have their genesis in human need can become "functionally autonomous" in their later expressions.[34]

This concept of functional autonomy has much import for understanding how the act of faith can be initiated by a human desire for safety and security yet also be transformed into behavior grounded in unselfish ideals such as Godin conjectures are integral to Christian faith. Allport realized that human action is goal-directed at both the perceptual and the behavioral levels. He agreed that the directing of attention to stimuli in the environment was initially provoked by a sense of need, or as Godin would state about functional religion, "a human wish." However, Allport contended that mature adult behavior could not be simply reduced to a satisfying of these early needs. Allport contended that those psychologists and psychotherapists such as Freud, who reduce religion to meeting childish needs for security, distorted the motivations which maintain mature adult religion.

In Allport's view, mature religion, like much of adult behavior, is cut off and free from its tie to earlier self-centered motives. Although its

33. Paul Tillich, *Systematic Theology*, three volumes in one (Chicago: University of Chicago Press, 1967), pp. 12-14.
34. Allport, *The Individual and his Religion*, p. 64. For a fuller discussion of the construct of "functional autonomy" see Gordon Allport, *Becoming: Basic Considerations for a Psychology of Personality* (New Haven, Conn.: Yale University Press, 1955).

roots lie in these early motivations, mature religion is "functionally autonomous" or basically free from this earlier connection. Mature religion may be started by one motivation but be sustained and maintained by another. Allport concluded that this is the distinction between behavior that is pushed from the past and behavior that is pulled by the future. He suggested that mature religion is pulled toward the future, a future of the realization of ideals such as the kingdom of God and of the realization of unselfish human potential.

Such a model as Allport's would explain Godin's contention that Christian faith begins with human desire but is later transformed by an encounter with God's desires seen in Christ. This would also explain Kant's proposal that God was primarily experienced as moral obligation.

Faith: Decisive or Emergent?

Returning to the question of how faith arises, Tillich seemed to imply that faith, or having an ultimate concern, is a life necessity. Everyone has a faith, in his opinion.

While Fowler might agree that there is a faith "urge" in everyone, he would not say that faith is the same from person to person except for the underlying motivation to order life or to find meaning. Faith is more a capacity or ability than a reality, in Fowler's opinion.

The difference between Tillich and Fowler lies in their definition of the faith *act*. Faith for Tillich, as seen in his books *The Courage to Be*[35] and *Dynamics of Faith*[36] should be understood in Kierkegaardian terms. Faith is that risky leap into the possible but not proven, a leap which one takes when one is sick unto death with the anxieties of finiteness. Tillich's faith would appear to be an experience reserved almost entirely for late adolescence and adulthood, those times in life when the disillusionment is most apparent.

David Elkind summarized the contention of developmental psychologists that only in adolescence are persons able cognitively to introspect on their own histories and construct ideals by which to live. Utilizing the cognitive-developmental model of Jean Piaget, he suggested that in infancy persons search for conservation or object permanency which is met religiously in the belief in the Holy Spirit which is religion's answer to this quest for certainty. In early childhood the search is for a language to represent reality which is met by religion with concepts of God as well as symbols of the transcendent. In later childhood, the search is for

---

35. Paul Tillich, *The Courage to Be* (New Haven, Conn.: Yale University Press, 1948).
36. Paul Tillich, *The Dynamics of Faith* (New York: Harper, 1957).

relationships with both the physical and interpersonal worlds. This need is met through worship and community. In adolescence, the search is for comprehension or meaning. Religion meets this need by providing a view of the world and the meaning of human life which goes beyond daily problem solving and mundane existence.[37]

For Tillich, faith does not exist much earlier than adolescence. Those experiences Elkind suggests occur in childhood would not be faith in Tillich's eyes. Fowler would disagree.

Fowler sees faith as a lifelong venture beginning in early childhood. Basing his thinking on Jean Piaget's theory of cognitive development, Lawrence Kohlberg's cognitive theory of moral development, and Erik Erikson's psychoanalytic theory of identity formation, Fowler concludes that faith is an innate urge of persons to relate themselves to the transcendent.

Although Fowler, like Tillich, sees faith as a dynamic function which gives meaning and courage to life, he has a more benign view of the impulse which provokes it. For Fowler, faith is less conflict-laden and more an outgrowth of natural developmental needs.

Faith: Essential to Ego Identity

These differences between Tillich and Fowler may be more apparent than real, however. Both authors see faith as integrally related to ego-identity. Whether faith is seen as rooted in the basic trust of infancy or in the disillusionment of adulthood, at all times both Fowler and Tillich suggest that faith functions to provide an inner sense of selfhood and a pervasive framework of meaning to human existence. As Gordon Allport stated, such a faith-act becomes the "mainspring of the individual's life from which radiate all manner of intentions whose purpose is to fulfill the values compromising the sentiment."[38]

It is intriguing to reflect on how the understanding of faith as related to ego identity resembles Freud's view that religious faith is an "illusion."[39] It is important to note that Freud did not use the word "delusion" in referring to religion. Illusions were those yet-to-be-proven understandings of what should be the goals and purposes of life. Some have termed these understandings "worldviews" or "ideologies." In his treatise *The Future of an Illusion* Freud's contention was that religion is a poorer illusion than science.

---

37. David Elkind, "The Origins of Religion in the Child," in *Current Perspectives in the Psychology of Religion*, ed. H. Newton Malony (Grand Rapids, Mich.: Eerdmans, 1978), pp. 269-278.
38. Allport, *The Individual and his Religion*, p. 126.
39. See H. Newton Malony, *Understanding your Faith: A Christian Psychologist Helps You Look at Your Religious Experience* (Nashville: Abingdon, 1978), pp. 111-113.

Freud was not unaware that persons live for and must have illusions. He simply felt they should identify with superior, rather than inferior, illusions. The thirty-year correspondence between Freud and the Swiss pastor, Oskar Pfister, reveals that Freud's deliberations over whether science or religion held more promise for humankind was more an ongoing dialogue rather than a cut-and-dried judgment on his part.[40]

Implicitly, Freud was agreeing with Fowler and Tillich in affirming the importance of faith for selfhood. He would probably agree that faith, or illusion, functioned to give identity and meaning to life. It should also be said that Freud's negative judgments about religion were focused primarily on what Godin would call "functional religion" which was uninformed by higher motives. As noted earlier in this essay, his judgments would probably be shared by a number of writers, not-the-least of whom was William James who suggested religion should be judged by its results, or "fruits," rather than its "roots," or basic motivations.[41]

On the basis of the above discussion, it can be assumed that faith is the act whereby persons go beyond daily problem solving and establish their selfhood by affirming their identity within a context of ultimate meaning.

Faith Development

Turning from a discussion of how the act of faith arises to changes in its content, James Fowler has provided psychology with the most comprehensive model available for understanding the development of faith. It is helpful to have in mind the exact definition of faith proposed by Fowler. For him faith is:

"The process of constitutive-knowing;
underlying a person's composition and maintenance of comprehensive frame (or frames) of meaning;
generated from the person's attachments or commitments to centers

---

40. It is interesting to note that Oskar Pfister, the Swiss pastor who embraced psychoanalysis and who was Sigmund Freud's partner in dialogue for the first three decades of this century, reviewed *The Future of an Illusion* in *Imago*, the first journal of the movement, under the title "The Illusion of the Future." In this essay, he contended that religion was the only illusion that had a future. In disagreement with Freud, Pfister felt that faith in science was ill-advised and self-defeating. See H. Newton Malony and Gerald North, "The Future of an Illusion: The Illusion of the Future: A Historic Dialogue on the Value of Religion between Oskar Pfister and Sigmund Freud," *Journal for the History of the Behavioral Sciences* 15 (1979), pp. 179-186, for a discussion of this correspondence between Freud and Pfister.

41. James, *The Varieties of Religious Experience*. See Lecture VIII "The Divided Self, and the Process of its Unification," pp. 140ff.

of supraordinate value which have power to unify his or her experience of the world;

thereby endowing the relationships, contexts, and patterns of every life, past and future, with significance."[42]

This definition clearly meets the criteria proposed by Don Browning. Faith, as so construed, is at the core of ego development. Some critics have concluded that faith, for Fowler, cannot be distinguished from the search for meaning.[43] There is some warrant for this interpretation. In fact, the subtitle to Fowler's best known book entitled *Stages of Faith* is "The Psychology of Human Development and the Quest for Meaning." This subtitle could imply that faith is no more than the search of all persons for order, structure, and coherence in their experience. This proclivity was identified by Kant as simply the tendency of the mind to order the world. In the 1950s the psychologist George Kelly called this the universal inclination of persons to be "scientists," i.e., to seek predictability and order in their experience.[44]

Notwithstanding, Fowler protests that faith is different in degree, if not in kind, from problem solving. Fowler suggests that faith is "an apparently genetic consequence of the universal burden of finding or making meaning."[45] He insists that while the *impulse* toward faith is grounded in the process of human meaning-making, faith goes beyond this in that it is invested in powerful, supraempirical images which provide core values and which unify all experience.[46] These qualifications would seem to imply a difference in degree, if not in kind, between faith and the making of meaning. It is helpful to note, in this regard, that the quote with which this paragraph began has Fowler stating that faith is the CONSEQUENCE of finding meaning, not its equivalence.

Stages of Faith Development

This conclusion that, for Fowler, faith begins with the human impulse to order life but goes beyond it leads naturally into the major concern with which Fowler has dealt, namely, the development of faith. Like

---

42. James W. Fowler, "Faith and the Structuring of Meaning," in *Faith Development and Fowler*, ed. Craig Dykstra and Sharon Parks (Birmingham, Ala.: Religious Education Press, 1986), pp. 25-26.

43. J. Harry Fernhout, "Where is Faith: Searching for the Cube," ibid., p. 67.

44. George A. Kelly, *The Psychology of Personal Constructs* (New York: Norton, 1955).

45. Fowler, *Stages of Faith*, p. 33.

46. James W. Fowler, "Moral Stages and the Development of Faith," in *Moral Development, Moral Education, and Kohlberg*, ed. Brenda Munsey (Birmingham, Ala.: Religious Education Press, 1980), p. 135. See the whole article for a summary of Fowler's ideas.

Elkind, noted earlier, Fowler sees faith as beginning in infancy with ego development. Changes in the character of faith are determined by the person's relationship with significant others as well as contact with supraordinate value systems, such as are mediated to persons through culture and traditional religions. Further, these changes are shaped by emerging cognitive capacities such as those described by Jean Piaget.[47] Faith development continues through six stages defined as follows:[48]

Infancy and Undifferentiated Faith: This is a pre-stage in which the infant learns the basic capacity to trust the world through interdependent relationships with those providing care and love.

Intuitive-Projective Faith (Stage 1): This is the time during which early powerful images implant themselves within the child's psyche. They give a permanent shape to the emotional and imaginative dimensions of faith. The child imitates the faith expressions of others.

Mythic-Literal Faith (Stage 2): Faith at this stage is replete with the child's growing ability to make logical cause-effect relations. Distinctions between good and bad are based on external structures of good and bad. The child experiences a sense of belonging to a community.

Synthetic-Conventional Faith (Stage 3): The important aspect of faith at this stage is the initial formation of a personal "myth." Persons adopt for themselves ideologies that relate them to wider communities and to history. Persons situate their identity within these structures.

Individuative-Reflective Faith (Stage 4): Faith at this stage involves critically examining the group identities that characterized the previous stage. Faith roles become chosen rather than compulsory. Ideologies are demythologized and become personal affirmations more than concrete descriptions of reality.

Conjunctive Faith (Stage 5): Appreciation for paradox becomes the dominant facet of faith at this stage. Incorporation of assertion and waiting, of logic and mystery, also characterize this stage. A new type of inculcation of symbols with meaning results.

Universalizing Faith (Stage 6): This stage is the culmination of the development of faith. The dialectical nature of partial truths in all positions and in all religions is affirmed. The norm becomes a commitment to living with paradox in which both passion and openness are affirmed.

Fowler and his colleagues in the Center for Faith Development at Candler School of Theology contend that this pattern of development has been confirmed by hundreds of structured interviews with a wide

---

47. See Jean Piaget, *The Child and Reality* (New York: Penguin, 1976), for example.
48. For a fuller discussion of these stages see Fowler, *Stages of Faith*, pp. 119ff.

variety of individuals. Ongoing research is attempting to extend these investigations to non-Western populations. Although it is unclear to what extent faith development, as conceptualized here, is dependent on the resolution of ego crises such as described by Erik Erikson,[49] Fowler and his associates are convinced that most people do not progress beyond stages three or four. These are the stages of conventional or individual faith.

In addition to the question of whether and how Fowler confuses faith with the search for meaning, a variety of other concerns have been expressed about Fowler's model.[50] Foremost among these expressed concerns have been such questions as: "Is the shape of faith as dependent on the emergence of cognitive structures as Fowler implies?" "Is faith primarily an emergent or a decisive act?" "Does Fowler's research have adequate reliability and validity from a measurement point of view?" and "Can maturity be equated with a preference for relativism and universalizing?"

Is the shape of faith as dependent on the emergence of cognitive structures as Fowler implies? Fowler grounds his model on the theorizing of Jean Piaget.[51] Piaget's theory is concerned with the intellectual structures which individuals impose on their experience of reality. It is a model for how persons know the world.

As contrasted with the nativism of Kant which assumed that the categories of the mind are innate, Piaget contended that these structures emerge over time through maturational process. Although experience defines the content, the biological maturation of mental structures determines the shape of knowledge. The claim made by many persons that Piaget completely countered Kant's implicit nativism is only partially true. Piaget substituted a maturational model which was still dependent more on biology than experience.

Fowler does, indeed, subordinate the development of faith to these maturational processes. His descriptions of faith stages are replete with descriptions which are limited by the individual's capacity for making

---

49. Erik H. Erikson, *Childhood and Society* (New York: Norton, 1958).

50. See Dykstra and Parks, eds., *Faith Development and Fowler* for a compilation of these critiques. Several of these essays express doubt that Fowler appreciates his implicit affirmation of contemporary Western individualism or the lack of precision in his measurement of faith stages. Other essays are basically affirming of his approach and are appreciative of his sensitivity to the relationships among identity formation, cognitive development, and faith.

51. See Jean Piaget and Barbel Inhelder, *The Psychology of the Child* (New York: Basic Books, 1969) and Herbert Ginsbuerg and Sylvia Opper, *Piaget's Theology of Intellectual Development* (Englewood Cliffs, N.J.: Prentice-Hall, 1969) for a more complete discussion of this model of cognitive development.

certain inferences and reaching certain conclusions. These are clearly identified with Piaget's theories of the development of mental operations. Cognitive change can only occur when biological development makes it possible.[52]

However, this limiting of the character of faith to the cognitive capacities of a given age is not new as can be seen in traditional Christian religious confirmation and Jewish bar mitzvah practices. Nor is such a limitation foreign to contemporary neuropsychological thinking, as exemplified in the writings of Donald McKay.[53] McKay suggested that though the brain always imposes boundary limits on the mind, nonetheless the "I story" is always qualitatively different from the "O story." By this he meant that the limits of the organism, seen in the brain events of the "O story," provided the parameters within which persons experience life and think about it, their "I story." But the "I story" continues to have an existence that could not simply be reduced to the "O story." Fowler, and perhaps Piaget, would possibly agree.

Turning to the second question of whether faith is an emergent or a decisive act, it would seem that here Fowler is most vulnerable. He seems to imply that faith emerges in a somewhat unidirectional manner alongside biological maturation. His inclination to partially identify faith development with the urge toward ordering reality lends further support to this vulnerability. In his defense, however, it should be noted that the last two stages do not, by any means, emerge automatically with increasing age. Here, Fowler implies that intention and life experience overwhelm the importance of neurological structures.

I, among others, am convinced that the decisive character of faith is present in faith development at a much earlier stage than Fowler implies. In an essay entitled "Dogma(tic) Pastoral Counseling"[54] I noted that, contrary to Fowler's contention that everyone has a faith, many persons' accounts of their lives are mere "chronologies" rather than "stories." Chronologies are mere reports of consecutive experiences while stories have plots and themes. Only life stories could be said to include "faith."

Further, Fowler's theorizing seems to not take fully into account the conflict implications of ego development which are explicit in the theorizing of Erik Erikson, on whom he reportedly depends heavily.[55] While Fowler might deny this evaluation, it does seem as if the type of inter-

---

52. See Fowler's descriptions of Stages 2, 3, and 4 in *Stages of Faith*, pp. 135ff.

53. Donald M. McKay, *Freedom of Action in a Mechanistic Universe* (London: Cambridge University Press, 1967).

54. H. Newton Malony, "Dogmatic Pastoral Care," *Journal of Pastoral Counseling* 22:2 (1987), pp. 89-97.

55. See Erikson, *Childhood and Society*, for a discussion of this approach.

views that he conducts as well as the examples he gives in his writings fall prey to the judgment that he tends to see faith as emergent rather than decisive. This tendency makes his understanding of faith easily confused with other mental processes as has been noted earlier.

Fowler's interview approach by which he gathers his data leads to the question of how reliable and valid is his method of research. Ellis Nelson and Daniel Aleshire wrote a sympathetic, yet objective, evaluation of Fowler's methodology in the Dykstra and Parks volume.[56] Although they noted the difficulties involved in rating free response, anecdotal material such as that given in open, semistructured interviews, Nelson and Aleshire affirmed this research approach over more objective methods such as questionnaires. However, they questioned the standardization of the administrations, the selectivity of the subjects, the unexamined reliability of the ratings, the lack of uniformity of the test situations, and the overgeneralization of the theory on the basis of limited data. In fact, Carl Schneider, in another essay in the Dykstra-Parks volume, reported significant differences in the scoring of the interview of one of the cases to which Fowler gave much weight in his writings.[57]

An interview assessing level of religious maturity which exemplifies greater attention to these important measurement issues is the "Religious Status Interview" which has been subjected to a number of studies of reliability and validity.[58] Fowler could well appropriate some of these methodological strategies into his own research procedures.

Finally, there is the question of whether religious maturity can be equated with that openness, uncertainty, and tolerance for lack of final answers which is implied in Fowler's Stage 6. Although Fowler contends that Stage 6 includes commitment, one gets the distinct impression that "Universalizing Faith" implies a judgment that all faiths are implicitly equal and are to be judged pragmatically in terms of whether they are beneficial for a given individual or not.

The last-mentioned viewpoint enjoys a long-standing history in the treatment of religion by the social/behavioral sciences. Such a cultural relativism intermixed with a bias toward equating maturity with lack of closure has influenced many researchers. James Dittes and Daniel Batson are but two examples.

Dittes reported research in which students made sense out of nonsense material more quickly if they were led to believe that they were

---

56. C. Ellis Nelson and Danile Aleshire, "Research in Faith Development," in *Fowler and Faith Development*, ed. Dykstra and Parks, pp. 180-201.

57. Carl D. Schneider, "Faith Development and Pastoral Diagnosis," in ibid., pp. 231ff.

58. See H. Newton Malony, "The Clinical Measurement of Optimal Religious Functioning," *Review of Religious Research* 30:1 (1988), pp. 3-17.

judged less positively by their peers or were assessed to be less intelligent than they thought they were.[59] In discussing these results, Dittes implicitly suggested that those persons with lower self-esteem are more likely to seek closure on the important issues of life and, thus, to affirm the dogmatic answers of traditional faith. The corollary of this is that more mature persons remain uncertain and open. They could tolerate ambiguity and did not feel a need to have final answers to the enigmas of life.

A similar conclusion has been reached by Daniel Batson in his adaptation of Gordon Allport's extrinsic-intrinsic orientation model into a threefold approach: means, ends, quest.[60] On the basis of a number of psychological investigations, Batson concluded that those whose approach to religion was characterized by "questing" were more religiously mature. Questing was typified by a lack of certainity and an openness to others' points of view.

Fowler would seem to have adopted a similar point of view to that of Dittes and Batson. The approach has been heavily criticized by Hood and Morris[61] and others as one which is empirically unproven and biased. There is little evidence to suggest that those who are less certain in their faiths are inclined to be more moral in their behavior or to exhibit more mature behaviors. Fowler may need to examine this assumption and make more room in his theory for maturity WITHIN religious traditions as opposed to ABOVE them. Our efforts to measure optimal religious functioning have been based on a clear presumption that maturity exists alongside passion and certainty.[62] This does not preclude tolerance. It simply incorporates it.

CONCLUSION

This has been a chapter on the psychology of faith. Although at points some metaphysical assertions were included, the intent of the chapter has been to abide by psychology's self-imposed limits to confine itself to the understanding, prediction, and control of that human behavior called "faith." A number of epistemological questions concerning the necessity and the process of faith were considered. The nature of the faith response was also discussed. The chapter ended with a discussion of current theorizing about faith development.

---

59. James E. Dittes, "Justification by Faith and the Experimental Psychologist," *Religion in Life* 28 (1960), pp. 567-576.

60. Batson and Ventis, *The Religious Experience*, pp. 149-161.

61. Ralph W. Hood and Ronald J. Morris, "Conceptualization of Quest: A Critical Rejoinder to Batson," *Review of Religious Research* 26:4 (1985), pp. 391-397.

62. Malony, "The Clinical Measurement of Optimal Religious Functioning," *Review of Religious Research* 30:4 (1988), pp. 3-17.

PART II
FAITH IN THEOLOGY

The Biblical View of Faith: A Catholic Perspective

Carroll Stuhlmueller

INTRODUCTION

Because Protestants and Catholics share the same Bible, their differing perspectives on the biblical view of faith will turn mostly around emphases, priority of details, and postbiblical tradition. These variations become significant over centuries of devotion and worship, church government, and theology. Catholic tradition, as we will indicate in the second part of this chapter, highlights: 1) the liturgical or sacramental setting for celebrating and understanding one's faith; 2) the primary role of the church in celebrating the liturgy and interpreting the scriptures; and 3) the authorization for those who preach the word of faith in the liturgical assembly. In order to manifest the biblical roots of these specifically Catholic emphases, the first part of this chapter investigates the two, most important words for faith: *'āman* in the Hebrew Bible,[1] and *pisteuō* in the Greek New Testament.[2]

---

1. Major references include: Johannes Alfaro, "Fides in terminologia biblica," *Gregorianum* 42 (1961), pp. 463-505; P. Antoine, "Foi," *Dictionnaire de la Bible Supplément* 3 (1938), pp. 276-310; Jean Duplacy, "Faith," *Dictionary of Biblical Theology*, ed. Xavier Léon-Dufour, 2nd ed. (New York: Seabury, 1973), pp. 158-163; Albert Gelin, "La foi dans l'Ancien Testament," *Lumière et Vie* 22 (1955), pp. 431-442; Alfred Jepsen, *"'aman,"* *Theological Dictionary of the Old Testament* 1, ed. G. Johannes Botterweck and Helmer Ringgren (Grand Rapids, Mich.: Eerdmans, 1977), pp. 297-323; Artur Weiser, *"pisteuō*: B. The Old Testa-

In studying each of these verbs and their derivatives we will be impressed at once that faith includes but reaches beyond the intellectual acceptance of divinely revealed truth. We read in the Epistle to the Hebrews: "Faith is the assurance of things *hoped for,* the conviction of things *not seen*" (Heb 11:1); "hope that is seen," we are told in the Epistle to the Romans, "is not hope. For who hopes for what they see?" (Rom 8:24). Faith is not determined by reasons, as helpful as these may be, but reaches beyond visible evidence to what is unseen, or as the Bible stresses, to the person of God, strongly present yet unseen either to the naked eye or to the probing intellect.

Faith then requires more than an act of the intellect. This double approach, the underscoring of the intellect but the activation of other human responses, shows up in all major Catholic presentations. Thomas Aquinas defined faith as "an act of the *intellect,* assenting to divine truth, impelled by the *will* which God moves through grace" (*Summa Theologica* II-II, Q. 2, a. 9). We read in the documentation of Vatican II: " 'The obedience of faith' (Rom 16:26; cf. 1:5; 2 Cor 10:5-6) must be given to *God* who reveals, an obedience by which a person entrusts *their whole self freely* to God, offering 'the full submission of intellect and will to God who reveals,' and freely assents to the truth revealed by Him."[3] In one of his weekly audiences during the Year of Faith (begun June 29, 1967) Paul VI stated: "Faith . . . makes us welcome the truths . . . which the Word of God has revealed to us. . . . It is at once an act of conviction and truth, which pervades *all the personality* of the believer and by now engages one's *entire manner of living.*"[4] Finally, Karol Wojtyla (later to become John Paul II) wrote in his doctoral dissertation, "Faith is a supernatural virtue that operates in the intellect and has the power of uniting this faculty with God. . . . To be perfect, faith must be a living faith, vivified by charity and the gifts of the Holy Spirit. [It] must be open to the *other virtues and powers* that can offer the plenitude and perfection of union" with God.[5]

In these references, typical of Catholic tradition, the intellect acts in

ment Concept," *Theological Dictionary of the Old Testament* 6, ed. Gerhard Friedrich and Geoffrey W. Bromiley (Grand Rapids, Mich.: Eerdmans, 1968) pp. 183-196.

2. Major references include: Johannes Alfaro, "Fides in terminologia biblica"; "Foi"; Rudolf Bultmann, "*pisteuō*: D. The *pistis* Group in the New Testament," *Theological Dictionary of the New Testament* 6, ed. Friedrich and Bromiley, pp. 203-228; Jean Duplacy, "Faith."

3. "Dogmatic Constitution on Divine Revelation, n. 5," *Bible Interpretation,* ed. James J. McGivern (Wilmington, N.C.: Concortium Books, 1978), p. 405.

4. *Faith—Response to the Dialogue of God* (Boston: Daughters of St. Paul, 1967), p. 82.

5. *Faith According to Saint John of the Cross* (San Francisco; Ignatius Press, 1981), pp. 265, 267.

consort with other human faculties, especially the will which is moved by God's grace; the object of faith reaches beyond dogma to the person of God who is revealing a mysterious way of life.

THE BIBLICAL BASIS OF FAITH

The Hebrew Text

In the Hebrew text we find a whole series of words related to faith, all indicating some form of trust or confidence. Faith, therefore, rests more in a personal attitude of hope and fidelity toward God than in a body of doctrine: i.e., *bāṭaḥ*, to be confident (Dt 28:52; Is 31:1); *qāwāh*, to look or even to call out hopefully (Gen 49:18; Is 40:31; 49:23); *yāḥal*, to wait (Pss 31:25; 33:22); *ḥāsah*, to trust or confide (Dt 32:37; Judg 9:15); *ḥākāh*, to wait (Is 8:17; 30:18). Personal relationship is evident in all these texts.[6]

These words originated in a nonreligious setting of everyday life[7] and were gradually transferred into expressions for Israel's stance before God. Typical of biblical religion, cognitive doctrine originates in the arena of human life. It is in everyday life that Israel through divine guidance seeks to love the Lord, her God, and to engrave the name of God upon the heart, in the minds of the children, and across the doorposts of the home (Dt 6:4-9; Jer 31:31-34), thereby centering their entire existence in God. Through it all God is leading the chosen people to the fulfillment of mysterious plans, far beyond human expectation (Ps 139). For the sake of communication and encouragement, laws and ritual were devised, prophetic exhortations and threats were preached, and important sections of the Hebrew Bible began to emerge. Faith involved doctrine but mostly attitude and practice.

The Hebrew word for faith which began to dominate especially the religious scene was *'āman* and its derivatives. This important word was translated into the Greek Old Testament, the Septuagint, exclusively as *pisteuō* or *pistis* and as such became the major Old Testament word behind the New Testament theology of faith.[8]

'āman, so far as our documentation from ancient Semitic languages

---

6. Cf. C. H. Pickar, "Faith," *New Catholic Encyclopedia* 5 (New York: McGraw-Hill, 1967), pp. 792-796.

7. Antoine, "Foi," p. 276.

8. Martin Buber, *Two Types of Faith* (New York: Macmillan, 1951; Harper Torchbook, 1961) tends to separate Judaism and Christianity too radically, excessively differentiating between: a) the Hebrew background of *'aman* in which Israel's faith was born from the stirrings of a nation to be an elect people and to persevere in this calling; and b) the Greek meaning of *pisteuō* or *pistis* in the New Testament which he understood to be a faith independent of historical experience, residing more in the soul of individuals.

permits us to state, originated with the Israelite people[9] and therefore offers a clue to what is innately Israelite. In its early, nonreligious use *'āman* referred to a man or a woman who nurtures and cares for children: Isaiah 49:23, "Kings *shall look after* your children"; Ruth 4:16, "Naomi . . . became the infant's *foster mother.*" The word exuded a warm, strong relationship in which the child developed according to what it was receiving from its parents and guardians. *'āman* reached into the mysterious origins of life and life's true direction.[10]

Used more frequently in the passive (or *niphal*) form, *'āman* disclosed a condition continuously and firmly in place, like sickness (Dt 28:59), water (Is 33:16), a tent peg (Is 22:23, 25). Religiously it confessed God's long-term faithfulness or the people's fidelity toward God (Is 49:7; Neh 9:8). When associated with words or statements, *'āman* declared them to be true and reliable: Joseph's testing of his brothers' promise (Gen 42:20); God's pledge to David (1 Kgs 8:26; cf. 2 Sm 7:16; Ps 89:37). In studying these latter texts we notice that there is something special about God's promise, undeserved and obviously unexpected.[11] The constancy and stability of the promise then derives from the person who speaks, in this case God. The examples speak to individuals only in their relation to a community of God's elect people and therefore to God's plans for bonding and for authority within the community.

By far the most important use of the verb *'āman* is grammatically the *hiph'il* form, introducing a strong nuance of causality and effectiveness into the practice of faith. It occurs twenty-four times in the narrative sections, seven times in prophecy, and eleven times in wisdom literature. In the Wisdom books the situation is usually nonreligious (Prov 14:15; 26:25; Job 15:22). In the narrative sections the negative generally occurs, as though something were impossible to believe, yet is actually happening and its effects live on. In Exodus, for instance, Moses is arguing with God that the people "*will not believe me* when I say that the LORD appeared to me and ordered me to lead you out of Egypt." There is even doubt if they will believe the signs and wonders which God will work through Moses (Ex 4:5, 8-9, 30-31). The verb, "to believe," also occurs in the positive form, though less frequently. After Moses led the people out of Egypt, "Israel saw the great work which the LORD did . . . and the people *feared* the LORD; and *they believed* in the LORD and in his servant Moses" (Ex 14:31). This act included the

---

9. Jepsen, "*'aman,*" p. 292.
10. This notion that not only life but its important direction are mysteriously planned by God before conception and certainly during the time of pregnancy is evinced in many biblical passages: Gen 25:19-34; Judg 13; Ps 139:13-18; Is 7:14; Jer 1:5; Is 49:1.
11. Jepsen, "*'aman,*" p. 298.

exodus as an object of faith, yet much more than that; fear and other human responses are associated with such a wonder. Most of all, the exodus becomes a remembrance to be celebrated liturgically, as we see immediately in Moses' and Miriam's hymns of praise to God, recorded in the next chapter of Exodus.[12] Positive statements about faith occur again in Psalm 119:66; Jonah 3:5; Genesis 15:6.[13]

Another somewhat enigmatic verse moves our discussion of 'āman into prophecy.[14] It comes from Isaiah 7:9, "If you are not firm [by relying totally upon the Lord, despite all odds], you will never be confirmed." This line is expanded in 2 Chronicles 20:20, "Rely firmly upon the LORD your God and you will be confirmed; rely firmly upon his prophets and you will be made secure" (CS).[15] Especially in Isaiah, Israel is being corrected against over-reliance upon promises and upon the grandeur of dynasty and temple.[16] Faith, in other words, must be part of everyday life, especially in areas of justice and compassion (cf. Mi 6:1-8).

When God begins to punish the people and to sweep away their human bastions of power, the prophet Habakkuk argues with God for chastising the unjust Israelites by foreign hordes still more unjust and cruel. Again the answer is faith: "The righteous shall live by their faith" (Heb 2:4).[17] Even though Israel's confessions of faith embraced the remembrance of God's great deeds within the liturgy, faith required

---

12. The movement from an initial act of salvation into a liturgical celebration of it so that it can be repeated in the lives of future generations is discussed by: Ingo Hermann, *The Experience of Faith* (New York: Kenedy, 1966), pp. 7-21, for the New Testament; and by Donald Senior and Carroll Stuhlmeuller, *Biblical Foundations for Mission* (Maryknoll, N.Y.: Orbis Books, 1983), pp. 11-15, for the Old Testament.

13. Gen 15:6 will be discussed later in this chapter; it became fundamental to St. Paul's thinking about faith: Abraham "believed the LORD; and he reckoned it to him as righteousness," as in Rom 4:3.

14. Weiser, *"pisteuō,"* pp. 182-183, too quickly moves from the narrative and formative sections of Old Testament religion, particularly as found in the Books of Moses, to highlight the individual believer and the role of prophecy, as when he writes: "Thus a wealth of usage begins to appear only when the individual breaks free from the collective bond and on the basis of his own experience devotes special attention to the attitude of man to God. The prophets, by a deepening of content, gave a new creative impulse to the vocabulary and imagery of faith."

15. Translations which are marked "CS" are adapted from the RSV by the author.

16. Cf. S. Virgulin, "Isaian and Postisaian Faith," *Euntes Docete* 16 (1963), pp. 522-535; 17 (1964), pp. 109-122.

17. Another Old Testament statement (see note 13), pivotal to St. Paul's theology of faith (Rom 1:17; Gal 2:11), to be discussed later in this chapter.

more than remembrance and liturgy. Israel must live honorably and compassionately within the bonds of family and community. Prophecy stressed personal responsibility against superstition and false confidence.

A derivative from *'āman* is the liturgical refrain, transliterated and used repeatedly in our prayers: "Amen!" It occurs twelve times in the cultic setting of cursing wicked deeds against the integrity of family and community (Dt 27:14-26),[18] in bestowing blessings (Neh 8:6; 1 Chr 16:36), and as a conclusion to the first four books of psalms (Pss 41:13; 72:19; 89:52; 106:48). All of these settings are liturgical. Still another derivative of *'āman* is the word *'emeth*, which occurs 126 times, very frequently with *ḥesed*,[19] a word signifying the Lord's bonded, warm love for Israel. *'emeth* declares how reliable and constant is that love. The phrase, *ḥesed we'emeth,* is met very often in the psalms, again in a liturgical setting (Pss 25:10; 40:11, 12; 57:4; 61:8).

From this word study of faith in the Hebrew scriptures, we recognize first an insight from everyday life of warm and loving care, as strong as that of parents for their children. This meaning is transferred to the religious domain of God's affectionate and constant love for Israel, the chosen people. This love induces God to make promises which seem impossible to Israel and to accomplish them marvelously. The remembrance of these wondrous deeds, like the exodus out of Egypt or the promises to the Davidic dynasty, created the basic creeds of Israel (Ex 15; Dt 26:5-10). As the narratives and songs were repeated in the sanctuaries, not only did a body of sacred traditions gradually take shape as the object of faith, but a group of dedicated priests, prophets, and singers emerged as religious leaders. Without sanctuary and its personnel much of our Hebrew Bible would have been lost. Faith, moreover, involved Israel in a complete dedication to the Lord and to one another, so that if this loyalty was compromised, then prophets like Isaiah and Jeremiah lashed out against the infidelity (cf. Is 7; Jer 2:21). Israel's faith, therefore, certainly included an intellectual element in these promises. But these promises elicited much more than an intellectual response; indeed, they elicited a consecration of the entire person to Yahweh's hopes for the community of Israel.

---

18. Here the Torah of Moses anticipates what will be a pronounced development within prophecy; cf. note 14. It shows one of many points of contact between Deuteronomy and prophecy.

19. For the force of *ḥesed* see Katherine Doob Sakenfeld, *The Meaning of ḥesed in the Hebrew Bible* (Missoula: Scholars Press, 1978); Francis I. Andersen and David Noel Freedman, *Hosea* (Garden City, N.Y.: Doubleday, 1980), p. 336; Hans Walter Wolff, *Hosea* (Philadelphia: Fortress, 1974), p. 52.

The Greek Scriptures of the New Testament

In the Greek scriptures of the New Testament the impact of the Hebrew Bible, especially of the basic word, *'āman*, is evident.[20] The multifaceted meaning of faith shows up at once. While it included a creed or body of doctrine, nonetheless central to the meaning of faith was confidence in God, compassionate and faithful, saving a chosen people in marvelous, unexpected ways. A tradition emerged in the fourth gospel of liturgically celebrating this marvelous assistance in each new generation.

Other contacts of the New Testament with the Hebrew scriptures appear in the way that the prophetic mantle fell upon the rabbis who functioned as miracle workers, or in the way Judaism interpreted the scriptures as being fulfilled in their contemporary moment;[21] this reinterpretation was especially evident at Qumran in the Dead Sea Scrolls.[22] Apocalyptic literature with its extravagant imagery of God's awesome activity, already present within the later Hebrew scriptures like Daniel 7-12, flourished in the last century before Jesus. In other words faith was alive in God's marvelous intervention among the chosen people and in the celebration of it in communal worship. Jesus was born and reared in this tradition of faith within Judaism.[23]

As mentioned already, the Septuagint or ancient Greek translation of the Old Testament always used the Greek verb *pisteuō* (to believe) and its derivative *pistis* (faith) in translating the principal Hebrew word for belief, *'āman*. This Greek word was already current within classical and Hellenistic Greek.[24] Classical authors from Homer to Plato to Xenophon employed it to express the trustworthiness of a treaty, as well as a person's firm conviction or confidence. When later writers of the Hellenistic period like Plutarch (c. 46-120 C.E.) and Plotinus (c. 205-270 C.E.) began to argue against the existence of the ancient gods, they spoke negatively about faith. Those pagan religions which engaged in

---

20. Cf. note 8 and the accompanying text of this chapter.

21. Cf. Rudolf Bultmann, *"pisteuō*: C. Faith in Judaism," *Theological Dictionary of the New Testament* 6, ed. Friedrich and Bromiley, pp. 197-202.

22. Cf. Joseph A. Fitzmyer, "The Use of Explicit Old Testament Quotations in Qumran Literature and in the New Testament," *Essays on the Semitic Background of the New Testament* (Missoula; Scholars Press, 1974) pp. 3-58. For a handy translation, Theodor Herzl Gaster, *The Dead Sea Scriptures,* 3rd. ed. (Garden City, N.J.: Doubleday Anchor Books, 1976).

23. Harvey Falk, *Jesus the Pharisee. A New Look at the Jewishness of Jesus* (New York: Paulist, 1985); David Edward Aune, *The New Testament in its Literary Environment* (Philadelphia: Westminster, 1987).

24. Cf. Rudolf Bultmann, *"pisteuō*: A. The Greek Usage," *Theological Dictionary of the New Testament* 6, ed. Friedrich and Bromiley, pp. 175-182.

propaganda evoked the need of faith. A passage from Celsus mocks such efforts, as different groups proclaimed their savior and declared that one must believe without evidence in order to be saved. Christianity was not the only new religion coming out of the East. In their style of proselytizing and specifically in making use of *pisteuō,* Christian preachers showed themselves part and parcel of their Greek culture. Yet as the various New Testament writers began to explain the meaning of Jesus as Lord and Savior, drawing upon themes and attitudes of Judaism and its Sacred Scriptures as well as upon the impact of Jesus' teaching and his death-resurrection, Christian faith became dramatically different from other Eastern religions. Greek philosophical influence, however, enabled Christianity to develop its Christology and faith in Jesus in ways different from Judaism.[25]

In the synoptic gospels (Matthew, Mark, and Luke) *pisteuō* and *pistis* occur nineteen or twenty times each.[26] The word is frequently linked with the amazement of the people at the wonders performed by Jesus, with a deepening faith in Jesus' compassionate determination to act, and with a stylized way of expressing this faith. Amazement relates to the Hebrew use of the negative with *'āman* (one could hardly believe that . . .). Compassion links up with Israel's faith in a merciful God. Stylization occurs with the development of liturgical formulas as happened in the emergence of the Old Testament.[27]

Mark's account of Jesus' ministry begins with the announcement: "The time is fulfilled, and the kingdom of God is at hand; repent, and *believe* in the gospel" (1:15). This gospel includes the healing of the sick which is associated with the conquest of demons.[28] Jesus is continuing the eschatological tradition of Judaism, a point made several paragraphs previously. Jesus' first miracle in Mark consists of an exorcism. After Jesus drove out the unclean spirit, the people "were all amazed, so that they questioned among themselves, saying, 'What is this? A new teaching! With authority he commands even the unclean spirits' " (Mk 1:27).

25. For the centering of New Testament faith upon Jesus, see John O'Donnell, "Faith," in *The New Dictionary of Theology,* ed. Joseph A. Komonochak, Mary Collins, and Dermot A. Lane (Wilmington, Del.: Glazier, 1987), pp. 376-378.

26. Cf. Alfaro, "Fides in terminologia biblica," p. 475.

27. Cf. Bruce Vawter, "The Development of the Expression of Faith in the Worshiping Community: (a) in the New Testament," *Liturgical Experience of Faith,* ed. Herman Schmidt and David Power, (New York: Herder and Herder, 1973), pp. 22-29.

28. For the role of exorcisms in the ministry of Jesus and in the gospels, cf. Senior and Stuhlmueller, *Biblical Foundations for Missions,* pp. 149-150, 155-156, 213, and accompanying references.

In verse 34 after casting out "many demons . . . he would not permit the demons to speak because they knew him." Again before healing a paralytic man we are told that "Jesus saw their faith," and afterwards that "they were all amazed and glorified God, saying, 'We never saw anything like this!' " (Mk 2:5, 12). Faith thus included knowledge and an object of belief but most of all fear and wonder.

The gospel of Mark intensifies the faith in the person of Jesus, as someone strong and compassionate in reaching out to the unfortunate. In 1:40-41, "a leper came to him beseeching him, and kneeling, said to him, 'If you will, you can make me clean.' Moved with pity, he stretched out his hand and touched him, and said to him, 'I will; be clean.' " A still more striking episode occurs in 9:14-29, where Jesus addresses a "faithless generation." The father of a demented boy begs of Jesus, "If you can do anything, have pity on us and help us," to which Jesus replied: "If you can! All things are possible to the one who believes." The father exclaimed: "I believe; help my unbelief!" When the disciples inquired why they could not have cured the boy, Jesus' answer was: "This kind cannot be driven out by anything but prayer and fasting." Faith involves not only total confidence in Jesus' compassion but also identification through prayer and fasting with the God of suffering people.

In the synoptic gospels faith reached beyond attitudes and practice, to the details of a creed. Jesus is to be confessed as the promised Messiah (Mk 15:32; Mt 16:16) whose sufferings and resurrection (Mk 16:11-14) were announced by the Sacred Scriptures of Judaism (Lk 24:25). It is necessary to receive and ponder the preaching of Jesus (Lk 8:12-13). Depending whether one believes like Mary or doubts like Zachary, the promises of God will or will not be fulfilled (Lk 1:12-20, 26-38, 45).

The Acts of the Apostles insist even more upon faith, introducing the word twenty-one times absolutely without any object, simply the need to believe. The first group of disciples are described as those "who believed . . . and had all things in common." Such a generic use of belief without any qualifications makes the word all-embracing. Faith also reached into areas of worship. Not only did these followers daily attend temple services, but they also gathered in their homes for the breaking of bread (Acts 2:43-47). Through their presence in the temple they showed themselves in direct continuity with the Jewish setting of Jesus' life and ministry, with his Sacred Scriptures. They also began the evolution of a specific form of worship, the eucharist, and their own forms of leadership (Acts 6:1-6; 7; 8:5-8).

Faith was included in the preaching of the apostles and, as the concluding chapters of the synpotic gospels show, Jesus' resurrection from the dead (Acts 2:44; 4:1-4) became the centerpiece of apostolic teaching. Every other instruction was seen in a new light because of Jesus' resurrection from the dead.

The apostles continued the healing ministry of Jesus, as we read in this early prayer: "Lord . . . grant to thy servants to speak thy word with all boldness, whilst thou stretchest out thy hand to heal, and signs and wonders are performed through the name of thy holy servant Jesus" (Acts 4:29-30). This faith required obedience (Acts 6:7). According to Acts, faith must reach the farthest corners of the earth. More so than in the synoptic gospels, the mission of spreading the faith becomes central in Acts.[29] The doctrinal elements are simple enough: Jesus is Lord and Messiah whose death and resurrection have fulfilled the scriptures and have become a redemptive power in people's lives (Acts 2:14-41; 13:16-41). Acts also insists upon the commissioning of witnesses and church leaders (3:15; 6:1-7; 10:41-42; 13:1-3).

The epistles of Paul[30] show a continuity but equally a distinctive development. Continuity is professed by Paul: "Now I remind you, brethren, in what terms I preached to you the gospel . . . by which you are saved, if you hold it fast—unless you believed in vain. For I delivered to you as of first importance what I also received" (1 Cor 15:1-3). The same statement is appended by Paul to his instruction about the eucharist (1 Cor 11:23). The contents of what is believed and practiced corresponds to the early preaching in Acts. Paul wrote to the Thessalonians: "Your faith in God has gone forth everywhere . . . how you turned to God from idols, to serve a living and true God, and to wait for his Son from heaven, whom he raised from the dead, Jesus who delivers us from the wrath to come" (1 Thes 1:8-10). Other similar statements occur in 1 Corinthians 15:1-18; Romans 10:8-10. Belief in the resurrection of Jesus assures one of sharing in that resurrection (1 Thes 4:14). Developments occur beyond the theology of Acts, not only Paul's underscoring the second coming of Jesus but also in recognizing Jesus' unique relationship with God the Father, as in the early Christian hymn of Philippians 2:9-11, confessing that Jesus is Lord or *kurios,* the title reserved for God in the Old Testament (cf. Acts 2:36).

Paul recognizes the role of the church and its structure of tradition and authority, not only by admitting that he hands down what he has received (1 Cor 11:23; 15:1-3), but also by recognizing the need of being commissioned to preach the gospel. He wrote to the Romans: "How are

---

29. Cf. Ibid., pp. 255-279.
30. Cf. Marie-Emile Boismard, "La Foi selon Saint Paul," *Lumière et Vie* 22 (1955), pp. 489-514; Joseph A. Fitzmyer, "Pauline Theology," *Jerome Biblical Commentary* 79:125-127.

people to call upon God in whom they have not believed? And how are they to believe in him of whom they have never heard? And how are they to hear without a preacher? And how can people preach unless they are sent? . . . For faith comes from what is heard, and what is heard comes from the preaching of Christ" (Rom 10:14-17; CS). The phrase, "the preaching of Christ," is pregnant with many possible interpretations: The preaching of Jesus during his earthly life (probably not, as Paul does not normally refer to the earthly ministry of Jesus); preaching that Jesus is the Christ or Messiah (very likely); the preaching which reflects the spirit of Jesus in the church (also likely).

In Paul's writings the results of faith show up especially in the justification of the believer. This case is argued at length in Romans 3:6-5:21, developing the statement in 1:16-17, "For I am not ashamed of the gospel; it is the power of God for salvation to every one who has faith. . . . For in it the righteousness of God is revealed through faith for faith; as it is written, 'The one who through faith is righteous shall live.' " Paul here is quoting Habakkuk 2:4 in which the ways of God are beyond human comprehension and explanation; one must wait with trust in a just and compassionate God.[31] Later in Romans 4:3 Paul cites Genesis 15:6 where Abraham "believed the LORD [that many descendants would spring from his marriage with Sarah, despite their advanced age]; and God reckoned it to him as righteousness."[32] Paul argues that we are justified by faith and not by works (Gal 3:16; Rom 3:20). True, he qualifies these works as those "of the law," yet this statement excludes all works. Since the covenant was held in particular esteem by Paul (Rom 7:12; 9:1-5),[33] if its works were considered ineffective for justification, then all other works *ipso facto* were eliminated.

Yet, as we shall see, Paul is not excluding good works from the process of salvation, only works which one may falsely consider the cause of faith. In Old Testament times, Israel could never function as Israel without faith in God who brought them out of the land of Egypt and gave them the gift of the land. This statement stands by itself as the first of the ten commandments for Israel (Ex 20:2). Such faith comes before and sustains all good actions for a faithful Israelite. Faith in Jesus who died and rose for our justification is the absolute condition for any good work as a Christian, inspiring a disciple to work and speak, to die and rise as Jesus did (Rom 4:22-25).

Faith leads to good works, as Paul acknowledges many times. In

---

31. Cf. note 17 and accompanying text.
32. Cf. note 13 and accompanying text.
33. Cf. Phinn Lapide and Peter Stuhlmacher, *Paul: Rabbi and Apostle* (Minneapolis; Augsburg, 1984).

Galatians 5:6, Paul speaks of "faith working through love," and then he enumerates the many fruits of the Spirit, all achieved through and in the human person (Gal 5:13-26). And in 1 Corinthians 15:10, while professing to preach "what I have received," Paul adds that "I worked harder than any of" the other apostles, granted of course that "by the grace of God I am what I am" (Rom 15:9). Through faith Paul is fully alive in his human body: "It is no longer I that live, but Christ who lives in me; and *the life I now live in the flesh I live by faith* in the Son of God, who loved me and gave himself for me" (Gal 2:20).

Faith, as we have seen, incorporates a believer into the body of Christ (Rom 12:3-4), a body which consists of many members, each with their own function (Eph 4:11) but all united in "the unity of the Spirit in the bond of peace. . . .one body and one Spirit, . . . one hope, . . . one Lord, one faith, one baptism, one God and Father of us all" (Eph 4:2-6).

Faith, finally, leads into the knowledge of the mysteries of God (Col 2:1-6), hidden from all ages (Eph 3:3-5, 8-11). Faith, we are told, leads *into;* the Greek phrase here signifies a process, a journey, an ever deepening awareness,[34] which never ceases until faith gives way to vision in the immediate, glorious presence of the risen Lord.

For Paul, Judaism led to a fulfillment in Jesus; faith in Jesus enabled everyone, Jew and Gentile, to live an entirely new life, which acquired its holiness intrinsically from this faith. Faith, moreover, while a totally free gift, presumed good works accomplished by the whole human person, including one's body and mind and all other components. This life in Christ, in fact, led to heroic acts of loyalty and love, anticipating the glory of the resurrection and manifesting a faith reaching beyond human power and human wisdom (1 Cor 1:18-2:5). The one body of the Lord resided within the church in which rested the authority to preach the message of faith (Rom 10:15; Eph 4:7-16). The church celebrated its unity and its growth in faith principally through its assemblies, including the eucharist (1 Cor 11:23-34; 16:1-2).

As in the writings of Paul, likewise in the Fourth Gospel and in the first epistle of John, faith occupies a central position.[35] True, the noun, *pistis,* occurs only once (1 Jn 5:4), but the verb, *pisteuō,* is found ninety-eight times in the gospel and nine times in the first epistle, frequently in the absolute sense without an object, simply "to believe" (Jn 4:54; 5:50;

---

34. See note 37 and accompanying text.
35. Cf. Donatien Mollat, "La Foi dans le quatrième Evangile," *Lumière et Vie* 22 (1955), pp. 515-531; Bruce Vawter, "The Johannine Epistles," "The Gospel According to John," "Johannine Theology: Role of Faith," *Jerome Biblical Commentary* 62; 63; 80:35-38. For the use of *pisteuō* in John's gospel and epistles, see Raymond E. Brown, *The Gospel According to John* (Garden City, N.J.: Doubleday, 1966), pp. 512-515.

6:36), indicating both an attitude and a body of cognitive doctrine. Except in frequency of occurrence, faith is treated somewhat differently in John's writings as contrasted to Paul's. While Paul expended much energy to separate the concepts of faith and works, John coalesces them. To the question, "What must we do, to be doing the works of God?" Jesus responded in John's gospel: "This is *the work of God,* that you believe in him whom God has sent" (6:28-29). While for Paul faith brings justification, John sets up a different parallel: "For God so loved the world that he gave his only Son, that whoever *believes* in him should not perish but *have eternal life*" (3:16). We find a more direct statement in 3:36, "For the one who believes in the Son has eternal life; he who does not obey the Son shall not see life"—with the extension of faith into obedient works. "Whoever hears my word and believes him who sent me, has eternal life; such a one . . . has passed from death to life" (5:24). Eternal life, the blossoming of faith, is evidently not delayed till after one's earthly death. In this latter sense John moves closer to Paul who also sees the believer as a fully alive member of the glorified body of Christ (Rom 6:1-11).

The liturgical setting of Jewish feasts and Christian sacraments is another characteristic feature of the Fourth Gospel[36] which directs our study of faith along a route different from that in Paul's writings. We think of the discussion of baptism with Nicodemus and the statement: "Whoever believes in the Son should not perish but have eternal life [so that] such a one's deeds have been wrought in God" (Jn 3:16, 21). The relation with feast days occurs in many discussions: the Sabbath in chapter 5, the bread of life in chapter 6, the meaning of the feast of booths in chapter 7, possibly the symbolism of baptism in chapter 8, the bonding of Jesus' death with the passover sacrifice (19:14,42), and baptism and eucharist in the mystical meaning of the water and blood which flowed from the side of Jesus, dead upon the cross (Jn 19:31-37).

Two other developments about faith are important in the Fourth Gospel: faith as leading to the person of Jesus and faith as related to knowledge. To believe in the person of Jesus includes not only a strong affectivity of loving devotion but also a growing awareness of Jesus as Messiah and Savior.

---

36. Cf. Xavier Léon-Dufour, *Sharing the Eucharistic Bread* (New York: Paulist, 1987); Bruce Vawter, "The Johannine Sacramentary," *Theological Studies* 17 (1956), pp. 151-166; Raymond E. Brown, *The Gospel According to John,* CXI-CXIV, where Brown writes: "The explanation why the evangelist presented the sacraments through symbolism seems to lie in this principle: the recognition that OT prophecy had a fulfillment in the NT created a Christian sensitivity to typology; therefore it was intelligible to present Jesus' words and actions as prophetic types of the church's sacraments.

While Jesus was preaching in the temple courtyard during the feast of tabernacles (Jn 7:1; 8:2), he declared:

"When you have lifted up the Son of man, then you will know that I am, and that I do nothing on my own authority but speak thus as the Father taught me. And he who sent me is with me; he has not left me alone, for I do always what is pleasing to him." As he spoke thus, *many believed in him* (Jn 8:28-30 CS).

The final phrase, "many believed in him," is expressed in a specific way in the Greek, they believed *eis auton.* The preposition *eis* connotes movement *to* or *toward;* it complements the preposition *en,* which means being stationed *in* a place.

Bruce Vawter commented upon the grammatical phrase, *eis auton:*

[It means to] "believe *into* Christ (or God)." This formula, impossible to reproduce in good English, has been preserved in our creeds, where Credo in Deum [literally, "I believe *into* God"] is a strictly Christian form, replacing the *Credo Deum* or *Deo* [literally, "I believe God"] of classical Latin. Scholars are agreed that this unusual terminology reflects the new theological thinking of the primitive Christian church.[37]

This observation not only brings us back to the early days of Christianity but it also indicates how early Christianity was formulating its faith in a way adapted for worship.

The passage from John 8:28-30 also compresses other aspects of John's theology. The lifting up of the Son of man resounds with rich biblical resonance. For John it includes both Jesus' crucifixion as well as his resurrection and ascension. Each contributes to the glorification of Jesus. From another similar passage in 3:14, "As Moses lifted up the serpent in the wilderness, so must the Son of man be lifted up," the reference to being physically lifted up upon the cross becomes evident. In response to Jesus' request, "Father, glorify thy name," John 12:23-41 introduces these words, as heard from heaven: "I have glorified it, and I will glorify it again." John proceeds to quote from Isaiah 53:1: "Lord, who has believed our report, and to whom has the arm of the Lord been revealed?" This sentence comes from the fourth song of the suffering servant. Growing in one's faith then means to be drawn *into* the mystery of Jesus' suffering, death, and resurrection, to reexperience in oneself what Jesus went through for the salvation of the world. This is "the

---

37. Bruce Vawter, *The Path of Wisdom* (Wilmington, Del.: Glazier, 1986), p. 64.

work of God" when one believes "in him–*eis auton*" and so grows "into" Jesus' likeness (Jn 6:29).

By means of this personal attachment to Jesus and one's growth in faith, one realizes ever more fully the messianic mission of Jesus as savior of the world. We find this sequence of conversation between Jesus, the Samaritan woman, and the inhabitants of Sychar:

> The woman said to him, "I know that Messiah is coming (he who is called Christ); when he comes, he will show us all things." Jesus said to her, "I who speak to you am he." . . . Many Samaritans from that city believed in him [*eis auton*] because of the woman's testimony. . . . [Later] they said to the woman, "It is no longer because of your words that we believe, for we have heard for ourselves, and we know that this is indeed the Savior of the world" (Jn 4:25-26, 39, 42).

Growing into faith in Jesus means an ever stronger awareness of Jesus as the promised Messiah, whose role it will be to save not just the chosen people Israel but the entire world.

This development of faith into the full scope of Jesus' person and work also leads into the mystery of Jesus' divinity. This intensification of faith occurs in a series of "I am" passages:[38]

6:35, 48, "I am the bread of life";
8:12; 9:5, "I am the light of the world";
10:7, 9, "I am the door of the sheep";
10:14, "I am the good shepherd";
11:25, "I am the resurrection and the life";
14:5, "I am the way, and the truth, and the life";
15:1, "I am the true vine."

These passages reach their culmination in several that declare simply without any object, "I am!"

8:24, "You will die in your sins unless you believe that I am" (CS);
8:25, "When you have lifted up the Son of man, then you will know that I am" (CS);
13:19, "I tell you this now, before it takes place, that when it does take place, you may believe that I am"(CS).

These passages of John's gospel relate to the divine name as revealed to Moses in the incident of the burning bush, "I am who I am" (Ex 3:14).

---

38. Cf. Brown, *The Gospel According to John,* pp. 532-538; Senior and Stuhlmueller, *Biblical Foundations for Missions,* p. 295, note 16.

This name is woven into the preaching of the great prophet of the Babylonian exile: Isaiah 43:11-13; 48:12. Here Yahweh states apodictically that "I, yes *I am* the Lord, and there is no savior except me. . . . *I am* God. Indeed from this day onward *I am the one*" (CS). The prophet is not just arguing for monotheism but is equally insisting upon the single savior and re-creator of the universe, none other than Yahweh, the God of Israel. The gospel of John is linking this rich Old Testament theology with the person of Jesus, who alone is the savior of the world, God in our midst. Jesus' listeners, according to John, understood these implications and reached for rocks to stone Jesus as guilty of blasphemy. Jesus did not argue against their suspicions but declared: "I and the Father are one. . . . If I am not doing the works of my Father, then do not believe me; but if I do them, even though you do not believe me, believe the works, that you may know and understand that the Father is in me and I am in the Father." Again they tried to arrest Jesus. As mentioned earlier in this chapter, John links works with faith, the former revealing the intensity of the latter.

In John's gospel, however, Jesus did not stop with the necessity of good works. He was leading the people into the mystery of the Godhead where he and the Father are one, a mystery which resided in himself, the primary object of faith. Faith, moreover, was not to be dependent on touching nor even on seeing Jesus; such physical contacts became impossible for Christians after the death and glorification of Jesus (Jn 29:24-29).[39]

Faith in the person of Jesus shows up in still another way in the writings of John, this time, too, based upon the grammatical nuances of the Greek language. John not only used the preposition *eis* with the accusative, so that belief becomes a journey *into* a new relationship with Jesus. The evangelist also frequently employs the dative after the word, to believe, setting up a personal relationship of affection: 3:15, 16, 36; 5:24; 6:29, 35; 1 John 5:10. This attachment shows up in the passage which blends both modes of faith:

> Whoever believes in him (*autō,* [dative]) may have eternal life. For God so loved the world that he gave his only Son, that whoever believes in him *(eis auton)* should not perish but have eternal life (Jn 3:15-16).

New Testament faith, accordingly, highlights more intensely the *person* of God, present as savior and incarnate in Jesus. The doctrine of the Trinity, however, will have to wait several centuries for clarification.

---

39. Cf. Brown, *The Gospel According to John,* pp. 1046-1051.

The other feature of John's view of faith to be discussed here links faith with knowledge.[40] Knowledge, however, seldom if ever remains at the level of a theoretical discussion of monotheism but reaches out to include the *mirabilia Dei,* the wondrous acts of God, bringing slaves out of Egypt, caring for them in the wilderness, and returning them from exile in the Hebrew scriptures; and in the gospel of John bringing the dead to life (11:1-44) and multiplying bread (6:1-15).

On various occasions John identifies the act of faith with the act of knowing: i.e., in John 8:24 and 28 (CS), "You will die in your sins unless you *believe* that I am" and "When you have lifted up the Son of man, then you will *know* that I am"; in 17:21 and 23, "that they may be one; even as thou, Father, art in me, and I in thee, that they also may be in us, so that the world may *believe that thou hast sent me*" and "I in them and thou in me, that they may become perfectly one, so that the world may *know that thou hast sent me* and hast loved them even as thou hast loved me." At times in John's writings, faith precedes knowledge (6:69; 8:31-32; 10:38), and at other times knowledge precedes faith (4:42; 17:8; 1 Jn 4:16). Both, therefore, go hand in hand.

The knowledge which leads to faith comes through the witness and signs of Jesus who alone has seen the Father (Jn 1:18). We read:

And the Father who sent me has himself borne witness to me. His voice you have never heard, his form you have never seen; and you do not have his words abiding in you, for you do not believe him whom he has sent. You search the scriptures, because you think that in them you have eternal life; and it is they that bear witness to me (Jn 5:37-39).

The Old Testament scriptures find their true meaning through Jesus to whom they bear witness. Jesus gives this witness because the Father has borne witness to him. "God the Father," we read, "set his seal" upon Jesus and attests to the truth of Jesus' words (6:37).

Jesus speaks and acts only according to what he has heard and was told to do (Jn 5:19). This statement is true not just of the humanity of Jesus, always obedient to the godhead, but also of Jesus as God. For as God, Jesus remains in the relationship of son, receiving life in all its totality, and so completely equal to the Father. The bonding between Father and Son is love. "For the Father loves the Son, and shows him all that he himself is doing" (5:20). The bonding of faith and knowledge, therefore, as discussed already, flows from the manner in which John

---

40. Cf. Brown, ibid., pp. 513-514; Alfaro, "Fides in terminologia biblica," p. 500.

sees faith attaching one affectionately to Jesus and leading ever more deeply into the mystery of Jesus.

Jesus always speaks the truth (8:40) and declares that "I am the way, and the truth, and the life" (8:45; 14:6). Truth, we see, is intimately linked with an active "way" of living one's faith and so grants eternal life. Our obedience to the truth draws us into the obedience of Jesus to the Father: "The Son can do nothing of his own accord, but only what he has seen the Father doing" (5:19) and "My food is to do the will of him who sent me, and to accomplish his work" (4:34).

Jesus' works, accordingly, become the object of one's faith. Jesus, we saw already, demanded that people believe in him because of his works:

> If I am not doing the works of my Father, then do not believe me; but if I do them, even though you do not believe me, believe the works that you may know and understand that the Father is in me and I am in the Father (Jn 10:37-38; cf. 5:36; 10:35).

Jesus' works are called "signs," a word which reaches back into the Hebrew scriptures.[41] A sign is not necessarily a "miracle" in our understanding of miracles. For instance, the rainbow in the sky (Gn 9:12-17) or a band of prophets (1 Sm 10:1-13) are designated as signs. At other times signs are truly beyond the normal routine of nature and humanity (Ex 7:9; 8:19). What is always present in a sign, however, is an element of instruction about the mystery of salvation, as in the final verse of the second, major section of the book of Isaiah:

> It [the wonder of the new exodus in the return from exile] shall be to the Lord for a memorial, for an everlasting sign which shall not be cut off (Is 55:13).

Signs, therefore, in John's gospel refer to some unique way, at times truly miraculous but always striking, by which God communicates with people, drawing their attention to a message of salvation which may be otherwise overlooked. Jesus' signs lead to a manifestation of the glory of the Lord (2:11; 11:40). As we are absorbed by obedient faith and prayer into the mystery of God's salvation for us in and through Jesus, we join Jesus (8:21-24) where he resides in the bosom of the Father (1:18).

The major sign to be manifested at the designated "hour" (2:4) when the mystery of Jesus would become clearest and the disciples would believe in Jesus (2:18-22) turned out to be the crucifixion and death of Jesus (12:20-43). To follow Jesus through this mystery required heroic

---

41. Cf. Paul Ternant, "Sign," *Dictionary of Biblical Theology,* 2nd ed.; ed. Léon-Dufour, pp. 545-548.

stamina in one's faith, a willingness to risk being ostracized from one's religious community (9:22, 34) and other kinds of persecution (15:18-16:4).

John's gospel, accordingly, recognizes faith as a gift from the Father (6:44), enabling a disciple to be drawn by loving attraction toward the person of Jesus, even to follow a path that leads into the overwhelming mystery of Jesus. By faith one is expected to follow the heroic way toward the cross and its new life in the resurrection. Jesus does not abandon his followers but instructs them through signs along the path of faith. In the Fourth Gospel and in the epistles of John faith is centered primarily in the person of Jesus, yet through a series of signs includes a wide reach of instruction. The preeminent moment to contemplate the signs and to relive the mysteries symbolically occurs in the sacraments and liturgical assemblies of the believers where the Passion, Death, and Resurrection are memorialized and relived.

PART TWO: THE CATHOLIC PERSPECTIVE

Methodologies for Studying the Bible

As stated at the beginning of this chapter, Catholics share with Protestants the basic methodologies for studying the Bible. In the nineteenth and early twentieth centuries these methodologies were explored and refined principally by scholars of Protestant background. It was only after 1943 and the landmark encyclical of Pius XII, *Divino Afflante Spiritu,* that Catholic scholars ventured more openly into the historical-critical method and form-criticism.[42] Rather than studying biblical doctrine according to a scholastic synthesis of theology, as in the past, Catholic scholars joined the investigation of ancient manuscripts to ascertain the best reading and inquired into the historical setting of the text. Form-criticism divided the biblical text, not according to doctrine, but after the pattern of various literary styles: hymns, supplications, narratives, epic stories, etc. Soon these literary forms were associated with Israel's religious setting, not just of instruction or spontaneous preaching, but especially in sanctuary worship. Liturgy and its development became crucial to biblical study. Still other advances were shared by Catholics and Protestants, like the sociological method which addressed the cultural and political background of a biblical passage or

---

42. Three other documents, important for biblical scholarship, are: "Letter of the Biblical Commission to Cardinal Suhard concerning the time of documents of the Pentateuch and concerning the literary form of the eleven chapters of Genesis"; "Instruction of the Pontifical Biblical Commission Concerning the Historical Truth of the Gospels"; and "Vatican II: Dei Verbum, Dogmatic Constitution on Divine Revelation," *Bible Interpretation,* ed. James J. McGivern (Wilmington, N.C.: Consortium, 1978), pp. 349-352, 391-398, 403-417.

like the canonical method which requires a biblical text to be seen within the larger context of the entire book where it occurs and within the arrangement of books within the Bible.[43]

The liturgical and canonical approaches for understanding faith are the most congenial to Catholic tradition. While these methodological approaches presume an initial inspiration from God or a marvelous intervention by God, they also stress the way in which a community, also inspired by God, memorialized and relived the initial event, with sacred songs and traditional narratives, with sacred ceremonies and symbolic actions, within sacred places of worship, under the guidance of trained personnel called priests, levites, apostles, deacons, and so on. Faith, therefore, becomes a community response to God's presence, reenacting the great deeds of the past. The biblical word and its message of faith required competent, human cooperation to be symbolically and effectively experienced in the liturgy. Faith emphasized equally a body of doctrine or tradition, handed down in the liturgy, as well as an interior response from each individual within the community at worship. Prophets for their part castigated the people if their daily life did not witness to the just, compassionate God proclaimed and worshiped in the liturgy.

In the first section of this chapter we investigated as objectively as possible the biblical view of faith. Yet the attention to a liturgical setting for appreciating one's own faith attests to the Catholic background of the present writer. We will explore some of the consequences of these emphases.

Canonical Methodology

Following the canonical approach, we study individual passages about faith in the context of the larger biblical setting. The exodus tradition became the centerpiece of devotion in Israel's liturgical calendar (cf. Lv 23; Dt 16) and inspired a way of understanding the exile and particularly the return from exile in Isaiah 40-55. Isaiah 7:9, 14 which insists upon a firm faith as the setting for the sign of Immanuel can be investigated within the context of the entire book of Isaiah. Its sixty-six chapters deal continually with signs and with the question of God's justice toward the promises made to the Davidic dynasty and especially the city of Jerusalem. The canonical method in this, as in other instances, highlights the role of sanctuaries and the Jerusalem temple with their ceremonies and priesthood as a major factor in shaping and preserving most of Israel's sacred literature.

---

43. For a summary and explanation of the various methods of biblical study, see *The Bible Today* 26 (January 1988).

Liturgical Methodology

The same procedure—from a wondrous act of God, to its liturgical celebration, and to a tradition and creed—holds for the New Testament. As we investigated the New Testament, from the synoptic gospels, to Acts, then Paul and finally John, we noticed an ever increased role of the community of believers, its leaders, and, with John, its sacraments and liturgy. From this background of canonical criticism—and other details could be mentioned, like the insistence upon the community rather than upon individuals—we recognize how faith relies upon a communal expression within liturgy, presided over by recognized leaders. The Catholic viewpoint of faith has always stressed the necessity of reading the Bible within the context of the church and of church leadership under pope and bishops.

Other consequences of stressing the liturgical setting show up in our understanding of faith. Biblical texts are subsumed within the liturgical seasons of the year like Advent and Christmas, Lent and Easter up to Pentecost, or within major feasts honoring Jesus, Mary, and the apostles. Several important results follow for appreciating one's faith. The sacramental setting—for instance with water for baptism, bread and wine for the eucharist, oil for the anointing of the sick—views these physical elements symbolically. They not only stand for something other than their own reality but they take on a new life: bread and wine as the body and blood of Jesus, water and oil as instruments of a new, specific grace for the believer within the community of the church.

Liturgy invests the passages about manna with an ever richer meaning. In the passage in Exodus 16 and Numbers 11, manna becomes a vehicle for instruction and warning; in Deuteronomy 32:13; Psalms 81:11, 17; 105:39-43; and Wisdom 16:19-21, 25-26, a sign of God's abundant gifts with all kinds of delicious taste; in John 6, a symbol of faith and possibly of the eucharist; in Revelation 2:17, an expression for eternal reward in heaven. Biblical events and texts become *types* with a hidden message which are elucidated by future events and by their explanation in later passages of the Bible, ranging from the Old Testament into the New. Although sacraments and their liturgical celebration are not essential for interpreting the Bible typically, they certainly encourage and find this style of explanation very congenial. The faith which one invests in a biblical passage as the word of God enables it to blossom with new flowers, far beyond the appearance of the original statement. The mysteries within a passage come to light principally in the liturgy where the community gathers under the leadership of its priests and ministers.

Liturgy, moreover, stitches two or more biblical passages together, sometimes longer readings, other times shorter antiphons. Within the setting of the feast or liturgical season each passage releases a new meaning and insight. Each again throws new light upon the other. The text of the Bible and its message of faith are handled in still another important way within the liturgy. Actually the liturgical ministers do not, as in many Protestant churches, read directly from the Bible, but from a *lectionary.* The lectionary consists only of biblical texts, but specific passages of the Bible are chosen, rearranged, at times abbreviated, so that some verses are deleted. In the lectionary, the Bible is placed at the service of the community at prayer. The setting for proclaiming and accepting one's faith is not exclusively the Bible but the Bible within the liturgical tradition of the church.

As a result of directives from Vatican II, an entirely new lectionary of biblical readings was devised, on a three-year cycle for Sundays and a two-year cycle for weekdays. This arrangement has been adopted by some Protestant churches, especially those of a more sacramental or liturgical orientation: the Anglican or Episcopal, the Lutheran, the United Methodist, and the Presbyterian churches. They have tended to extend the readings and to reinsert those verses at times omitted in the Catholic lectionary; they have also maintained, as the Lutheran church for Lent, their own more traditional set of readings as an alternate.[44] Here we see again a significant nuancing of one's attitude toward the Bible as the source of one's faith. The Catholic church has always shown more flexibility in adapting the biblical reading for liturgy. The Catholic church has not backed away from its position that the Bible is the treasured property of the church.

The liturgical setting of biblical passages leads to an extremely serious point of division between Catholic and many Protestant churches toward doctrine and the object of one's faith. Here we witness, not only the control of the Catholic and Oxthodox churches over the scriptures in carefully selecting and editing passages for feastdays, but also the influence which these passages have upon the development of doctrine. An example may elucidate this important variation between the Catholic/Orthodox and the Protestant perspectives toward faith.

A Liturgical Example: Mary

Both the Eastern and the Western churches from early times have honored Mary within their liturgical worship, especially the sleep or dormition of Mary. To this ceremony, honoring the final moment of Mary on earth, we add the ancient feast of Mary's presentation in the temple, known through the apocryphal gospel of James. This feast is

---

44. *Common Lectionary.* The lectionary proposed by the Consultation on Common Texts (New York: Church Hymnal Corporation).

celebrated as well by the Anglican communion and in some mainline Protestant churches. The Byzantine emperor Justinian (483-565) constructed in Jerusalem one of the most expansive churches of Christendom to complement (or rival?) the Church of the Holy Sepulchre which had been built under Constantine's aegis. Because the symbolism of the ancient Jerusalem temple had already been transferred to the Church of the Holy Sepulchre, this symbolism gradually became absorbed as well within the liturgy honoring Mary. It has its basis in Luke 1-2 where many phrases usually associated with the ark and the temple are addressed to Mary.

As a result, the liturgy in Mary's feasts included the singing or proclamation of two sets of biblical passages which developed around the Jerusalem temple, one honoring God as creator, the other celebrating Jerusalem's eternal beauty. Marian feasts therefore, included from very ancient times: 1) Psalms 8, 15, 19A, 24, and Sirach 24 which proclaim the beauty, the sinlessness, and the wonder of the universe as created by God and as seen within the confines and ceremonies of the temple; and 2) Psalms 46-48 which extol the Jerusalem temple as protected against the terrifying forces of evil and as the home of God, the savior of Israel. These psalms hardly ever allude to sin and failure, certainly not to death and corruption, unless as a distant echo of a complete victory over them, an approach shared as well with Isaiah 65:17-66:24 and Revelations 21-22. From this liturgical setting there developed within the Catholic and Orthodox churches (each in its own way since their major split in the year 1054) important doctrines of faith about the place of Mary in the salvation accomplished by God in and through Jesus. Within this liturgical tradition Mary as the new temple of God has come to be honored as immaculately conceived without sin and as bodily assumed into glory after her death. Within the Catholic church these doctrines were not formally defined until the nineteenth and twentieth centuries by Pius IX for the Immaculate Conception and by Pius XII for the Assumption. The Catholic church sees these doctrines of faith as: 1) rooted in scripture; 2) consistently developing in a liturgical setting; 3) gradually clarified and integrated within the larger synthesis of doctrine about Christ and the church; and 4) finally defined as infallible and a necessary part of Catholic doctrine.[45]

From this liturgical background for appreciating the Catholic view toward faith in the Bible, there follows the principle of interpreting the Bible within the church. To base our remarks here upon the preceding paragraph about liturgical celebrations in honor of Mary, we find the

---

45. See Carroll Stuhlmueller, "Old Testament Settings for Mary in the Liturgy," *The Bible Today* 24 (1986), pp. 159-166.

origin of doctrinal development in biblical passages (Lk 1-2) and in the early church at prayer with other sets of biblical texts. From this setting which included biblical inspiration and supernatural instincts of prayer and worship, we move onward to the point where church authority recognizes the feast days and establishes a ritual drawn from the early devotion of the faithful. As these feasts spread across the boundaries of one nation to another, first the feast and then the doctrine implied by the feast become more universal. Hence the ancient dictum: *lex orandi lex credendi*, "the law of prayer [directs] the law of believing." It is from this universal, traditional worship that the Catholic church will define its faith and interpret the Bible.

CONCLUSION

The Catholic viewpoint of faith within a biblical perspective shares the same Bible with Protestantism but moves in a different direction, sometimes with serious results for ecumenical dialogue, by its emphases: 1) upon the Bible as a text to be proclaimed and celebrated within the liturgy, with an important place for the lectionary; 2) upon the way that the Bible is handed down and redacted within a community conscious of its own inspiration and authorized leadership; 3) upon doctrine and knowledge, received as divine revelation from the Bible and communicated within the community. It is important to realize that we are dealing here with emphases rather than with exclusive differences. Yet these variations in emphases, occurring as they did over the stretch of time and often accompanied by violent conflicts and sharp divisions, lead to serious differences in what is considered the biblical heritage of faith. Hopefully by returning to the biblical sources and recognizing more carefully that the differences are basically a variation of emphases, theological disagreements can gradually be reduced to a diversity of spiritualities and of styles of religious leadership.

CHAPTER 6

The Biblical View of Faith: A Protestant Perspective

James L. Price Jr.

INTRODUCTION

"Without faith it is impossible to please God. For whoever would draw near to God must believe that he exists and that he rewards those who seek him" (Heb 11:6). In these words the now anonymous author of the Letter to the Hebrews voices a biblical truism. According to Israel's witness only the fool denies God's existence (Ps 14:1; 53:1) for in "many and various ways God spoke of old by the prophets," and it was "by faith" that they "received divine approval" (Heb 1:1-2; 11:2) (cf. Acts 14:15-18). And now, "in these last days," the Christian author declared (claiming also the heritage from the fathers), God "has spoken to us by a Son," Jesus, "the pioneer and perfecter of our faith" (Heb 12:2).

What meanings are assigned to the concept of faith in the Old Testament and the New Testament? What attitudes and objects of faith have they in common?—and wherein lies the differences? Perhaps in a general sense one may say that the scriptures reveal a view of faith as "an appropriate response" to God's self-initiating activity. The English word *faith* does not of itself provide the contents of this "appropriate response." Indeed, biblical Hebrew has no equivalent for the English noun faith. One New Testament writer, John, never uses the noun for various reasons preferring "to believe," and other verbs of action.

Turning now to the concept of faith in the Old Testament we learn that several verb roots are employed resulting in nuanced expressions of "faith," depending upon their specific contexts. For example, to be firm or reliable, to have confidence in, to obey, to take refuge in, to hope, to wait. The most important among the verb roots, the one expressing nuances of the common English word "faith," is the root *'mn*, appearing often in the *hiph 'il* form (*he 'emin*, to believe). Its special nuance is an attitude associated with the English word "trust." This concept of faith/ trust is used only with respect to personal relationships, preeminently as the acknowledgment of the promises and the obligations based on a sacred covenant originated by Yahweh with the people Israel. It is important to note that the root *'mn* came to influence and to assimilate other, more numerous Hebrew verb roots and stems. Of additional interest is the fact that the translators of the Old Testament into Greek (the Septuagint) attached their concept of faith to *'mn* and its derivatives *pistis* (faith) and *pisteuein* (to believe).[1]

FAITH AND THE EXODUS TRADITION

Some of the most important texts which reveal the Old Testament concept of faith are those relating to Exodus. In this context the scriptures treat God's relationship with the nation as a whole. The meaning of faith for individuals is not a primary element in the tradition of Exodus. The destiny of individuals is organically related to the present and the future fortunes of the nation.

When Moses was called to lead God's people from Egyptian bondage we are told that he protested that the enslaved people would not believe him. To confirm Moses' call, he was given power to accomplish marvelous signs. Moses was also assured that these signs would be believed. When Moses performed marvelous signs in the sight of the people, they "believed." When they heard that the Lord had visited the people of Israel, and that he had seen their affliction, they bowed their heads and "worshiped" (Ex 4:31). But before long, Israel's faith in Yahweh and in Moses weakened (Dt 1:32-33; Ps 78:9-32). Even Moses, according to one source, joined Aaron in a loss of faith in God's power to insure the people's safety in their trek through the barren wilderness (Nm 20:12). In the narrative of the giving of the law, God summons Moses, "Lo, I am coming to you in a thick cloud, that the people may hear when I speak with you and may also believe you forever" (Ex 19:9). Note that in these narratives belief in a prophet as God's reliable messenger is a

---

1. Rudolf Bultmann and Artur Weiser, "Faith," in *Bible Key Words*, Vol. III (New York: Harper, 1960), pp. 1-33.

component of belief/trust in God (Ex 4:1; 19:9. cf. Is 7:1-9; 28:14, 16-22; Jn 3:1-5:2; 2 Kgs 17:9-14).

According to Psalms 78 and 106 the oscillation between faith/trust, on the one hand, and unbelief/distrust, on the other hand, continued throughout the history of Israel. In both of these psalms, faith in God is inspired by the memory of Yahweh's previous acts of deliverance, obedience to his commandments and to his appointed human agents, and a recollection of Israel's repeated acts of idolatry. With regard to the last statement it may be observed that, in the language of the Old Testament, not to believe is not merely an indication of doubt, but an act of apostasy (2 Kgs 17:6-18; Dt 32:15-21a).[2]

In summary one may say that the ideology of the Mosaic covenant prompted a variety of responses, each determined by a particular aspect of the reciprocal relationship between Israel and Yahweh. When God gave a command, order, or commandment, then faith meant obedience (Dt 9:23; Ps 119:66); when attention was focused upon a promise of God, then faith was an acknowledgment of his power to perform it (Nm 20:2-20; Ps 106:24-25).

ABRAHAM'S FAITH/TRUST IN GOD

Abraham was the major patriarchal person to exemplify distinctive qualities of faith/trust according to the Old Testament. The promise of God to Abraham and Sarah concerning the birth of a son led to Abraham's response: "He believed the Lord, and he [God] reckoned it to him as righteousness" (Gn 15:6). The following words of the Christian apostle, Paul, describe succinctly the significance of this part of the narrative of Abraham: "In hope he believed against hope, that he should become the father of many nations; as he had been told, 'so shall your descendants be' " (Gn 14:5-6; 17:2-8, 15-21). "He did not weaken in faith when he considered his own body, which was as good as dead because he was about a hundred years old, or when he considered the barrenness of Sarah's womb. No distrust made him waver concerning the promise of God, but he grew strong in his faith and he gave glory to God, fully convinced that God was able to do what he had promised. That is why his faith was reckoned to him as righteousness" (Rom 4:18-22).

While the terms for believing or trusting are not used in Genesis 22, the story of the binding of Isaac portrays, in a chilling narrative, the quintessence of faith in the Old Testament. Abraham believed that it

---

2. J. M. Ward, "Faith: Faithfulness in the OT," *Interpreter's Dictionary of the Bible*, supplementary volume (Nashville: Abingdon, 1976), p. 330.

was God's will that he sacrifice his beloved son Isaac, the child of promise (Gn 22:2, 12, 16). Abraham's actions established the fact that he was ready, without a word of protest, to make this supreme sacrifice, if his God would have it so. Because of his obedience and his absolute reliance upon God to fulfill his purposes, the child was allowed to live and to become the father of Jacob (Israel), and Abraham was honored as a true exemplar of invincible faith.

FAITH IN THE ISAIAH ORACLES

The prophets made enduring contributions to the development of the concept of faith in the scriptures, especially Isaiah of Jerusalem (ca. 740-701 B.C.E.), and his successor, the so-called Second Isaiah of the Babylonian Exile (after 547 B.C.E.).

When the kingdom of Judah was invaded by a confederation of nations, Isaiah remonstrated with King Ahaz, "If you will not *believe*, surely you shall not *be established*" (Is 7:9).[3] The italicized terms translate two Hebrew verb stems from the same root, a wordplay typical of this prophet's oracles (see also, Is 5:7). Isaiah's contention was that Judah's security was not founded on military might, but rather upon a radical trust in God's power both to deliver believers and to abort the strength of the enemy. This trust entailed believing that God has spoken to the prophet, as in the experience of Moses (Ex 4:1; 14:31).

Consistent with this oracle is another recorded in Isaiah 28:16: "Thus says the Lord, 'Behold I am laying in Zion for a foundation a stone, a tested stone, a precious cornerstone, of a sure foundation: he who believes will not be in haste.' " Isaiah's confidence was that God would ensure that the believing/trusting religious community will not be destroyed. The issue of the nation's real security is also addressed in Isaiah 30:15: "For thus says the Lord God, the Holy One of Israel, '*in returning* and rest you shall be saved; in quietness and *in trust* shall be your strength.' " It is probable that in this text Isaiah coined the Hebrew terms translated "returning" and "trust" (RSV). The second verb stem was based on the root meaning "to feel secure" or "to be confident."[4] This is an illustration of the prophet's enrichment of the scriptures' language of faith.

The meaning of faith in the passages attributed to "Second Isaiah" must be evaluated in relation to the whole of creation, not merely in

---

3. "If you do not stand firm, maintain your confidence, you shall not be made firm, i.e., given power to resist the enemy." C. H. Dodd, *Interpretation of the Fourth Gospel* (London: Cambridge University Press, 1953), p. 181.

4. Artur Weiser, in *Bible Key Words*, p. 23.

relation to Yahweh's covenanted mercies revealed in Israel's history (Is 40:5-8). For this prophet "knowing" was a corollary of "believing": " 'You are my witnesses' says the Lord, 'and my servant whom I have chosen, that you may know and believe me and understand that I am He. Before me no God was formed, nor shall there by any after me, I, I am the Lord, and beside me there is no savior!" (Is 43:10-11; see also Is 44:6-8).

Another way in which Second Isaiah broadened the concept of faith/ trust was to associate it with hope for the future. An early passage in Isaiah suggests that prior to the Exile, while in Jerusalem, the prophet made this connection: "Bind up the testimony, seal the teaching among my disciples. I will wait for the Lord, who is hiding his face from the house of Jacob, and I will hope in him" (Is 8:16-17). Second Isaiah voiced the refrain: "They who wait for the Lord shall renew their strength, they shall mount up with wings like eagles, they shall run and not be weary, they shall walk and not faint" (Is 40:31). In both passages "to wait (patiently) for God" is synonymous with "to hope in him." This waiting and hoping exhibits a faith that does not see the expectation realized but yet believes. Through faith/trust, weakness and despair are overcome by the assurance of God's bestowal of strength (Is 40.29).

THE PSALM WRITERS WITNESS TO FAITH

Because of the prophets' language of faith, especially that of the two Isaiahs, the psalm writers of the Old Testament were provided a vivid and warmly personal vocabulary for the expression of their inmost thoughts and prayers, their fears and hopes. "Our soul waits for the Lord," declared one psalmist, "he is our help and shield. Yea, our heart is glad in him, because we trust in his holy name. Let thy steadfast love, O Lord, be upon us, even as we hope in thee" (Ps 33:20-22; also 22:1-5; 25:1-5; 62:5-10).

The psalmists' devotions give expression to the need for loyalty and obedience as much as for believing and trusting. Indeed, believing God's word, his commandments, was viewed as a hallmark of loyal faith (Ps 119:81, 105-114).

THE FAITHFULNESS OF GOD

Again it is in the Old Testament Psalter that one finds the most frequent declarations that the nation's, and/or the individual's, faith/ trust is established solely upon the faithfulness of God: "The word of the Lord is upright; and all his work is done in faithfulness" (Ps 33:4; also Pss 25:10; 36:5-7; 71:22; 89:1-4; 98:1-3; 100:5; 117:1-2). It was this reality that stirred this people to joyful praise and thanksgiving. God's faithfulness alone, not any human being's, could be trusted, for his faithfulness was revealed to Israel in creation, in the Exodus, and in his everlasting covenant with his people. One psalm writer acknowledged that although at times Israel "had no faith in God and did not trust his saving power. . . yet he, being compassionate, forgave their iniquity and did not destroy them" (Ps 72:22, 33). God's faithfulness was revealed especially in his readiness to deliver, or relieve, the sore oppressed: "The Lord is a stronghold for the oppressed, a stronghold in time of trouble. And those who know thy name put their trust in thee (Ps 9:9-10).

FAITH IN THE NEW TESTAMENT

Early Christian writings disclose the extent to which a common use of the terms faith, to believe, believing, and their antonyms, were inspired by the Old Testament and Jewish traditions.[5] Brief notice will now be taken of this lasting affinity and influence, in the light of which a distinctive Christian development can be seen.

CONCEPTS OF FAITH COMMON TO JEWS AND CHRISTIANS

In the New Testament "to believe" has a variety of complementary meanings. First, to believe is to have faith in God and in his chosen human agents, in Moses and the prophets, and in the scriptures (Lk 24:25; Jn 5:46-47; Acts 24:14; Rom 1:1-2; Gal 3:6-9). Similarly, John the Baptist is to be believed (Mt 11:11-15; Lk 7:24-35; Mt 21:32).

Second, in both Testaments, according to their contexts, obedience is a near synonym of faith and is itself a necessary validation of faith. The apostle Paul wrote that he had "received grace and apostleship to bring about the obedience of faith" (Rom 1:5; 6:17; 15:18; 16:19; Acts 26:19).

Third, in the Old Testament and in Judaism trust is a large element in the concept of faith. This is also true of the New Testament, especially in the synoptic gospels where Jesus challenges his hearers to trust in God and not be anxious, but most of all to have confidence in God's power and readiness to save. In Romans 9:33 Paul, citing Isaiah 28:16, wrote that "he who believes [that is, trusts] in him will not be put to shame."

Additionally, there is in both Testaments a close correlation between trust in God and hope in him. Thus for the writer of the Letter to the Hebrews, Old Testament persons can serve Christians as examples and be seen as fellow pilgrims whose faith was also directed to the future promised by God (Heb 11). In 1 Peter one reads: "Through him [Christ]

---

5. Rudolf Bultmann, in *Bible Key Words*, pp. 62-68.

you have confidence in God, who raised him from the dead and gave him glory so that your faith and hope are in God" (1 Pt 1:21; 1 Thes 1:3; 1 Cor 13:13).

A NEW CONCEPT OF FAITH

Ths distinctively Christian concept of faith is a historic consequence of the apostolic *kerygma* (proclamation, preaching). First and foremost, faith was a believing acceptance of the kerygma, or gospel. In the language of Paul, early Christian proclamation could be described as "the word of faith that we preach" (Rom 10:8; cf. "preaching the faith," Gal 1:23; 1 Cor 1:21-24; 1 Cor 15:14; Acts 8:4, 14). Also one reads that "faith comes from what is heard, and what is heard comes by *the preaching* [literally, "the word"] of Christ" (Rom 10:17).

The content of the apostolic kerygma is cited by Paul in several passages commonly held to be pre-Pauline. The kerygmatic parts of the missionary speeches in Acts also describe the content of this "word of faith" preached by the apostles (Acts 2:22-24; 3:13-15; 10:37-41; 13:26-37).

Two pre-Pauline traditions are: a) "If you confess with your lips that Jesus is Lord and believe in your heart that God raised him from the dead, you will be saved" (Rom 10:8-9), b) "Now I would remind you, brethren, in what terms I preached to you the gospel, which you received, in which you stand, by which you are saved, if you hold it fast— unless you believed in vain. For I delivered to you as of first importance what I also received, that Christ died for our sins in accordance with the scriptures, that he was buried, that he was raised on the third day in accordance with the scriptures, and that he appeared [to chosen witnesses]. . . . He appeared also to me. . . . Whether then it was I or they, so we preach and so you believed" (1 Cor 15:1-11, see also 2 Cor 5:14-15). From these significant passages a person learns that Christian faith consists in the acknowledgment of Christ as Lord and in the acceptance (believing to be true, and true for that person) the witness to Christ's resurrection (1 Thes 1:9-10; Rom 8:11; Gal 1:1; 1 Pt 1:18-21).

The response to the kerygma is epitomized in several formulae supplied by Greek linguistic usage. To believe meant to rely on, to trust (Acts 27:25, Jn 4:50), or to give credence to (Mk 13:21; Jn 4:21). This meaning may be inferred from the use of the dative case for the (personal) object (Acts 16:34; Jn 2:22; 5:46; 8:45-46) or thing (Jn 5:47; Acts 24:14). Sometimes the New Testament writers used the verb "to believe" or "have faith" with or without an additional someone or something, expressed or implied (Lk 22:67; Jn 3:18; also 1:7; 6:36; 20:29). Another common formula may be designated, "to believe that

. . . Jesus died and rose again" (1 Thes 4:14; Rom 10:9); or, "that you are the Christ" (Jn 11:27; Lk 1:45; Jn 8:24; Acts 9:26; Jn 20:31). Ordinarily, this formula is christological and may be translated "to be convinced that."

Peculiar to the New Testament writers is the expression "to believe in (to)." It is found neither in secular Greek nor in the Greek translation of the Old Testament (Septuagint). To have a strong confidence in a person, based on acceptance of the claims made for his person, seems to be the meaning of this expression. Such belief has an element of trust in it, conceived as a personal commitment at the deepest level of one's life (Acts 20:21; Gal 2:16; Phil 1:29; Jn 3:16; 6:40). The expression held special significance for the writer of the Gospel of John. Twice the phrase is used with God the Father as object; thirty-one times with reference to Jesus; elsewhere in the New Testament, eleven times. A synonym used by John, "to come to Jesus," gives proof of the dynamic quality of this belief-formula with its nuance of movement toward Jesus (Jn 6:35; 7:37-38; Acts 24:23).[6]

A variant of belief in (to) . . . is the phrase "to believe *in (to) the name of.* . . ." Used with the verb "to baptize" this preposition "into" may be an abridgement. To be baptized into the name of Christ was to take a step by which a believer passed into ownership of Christ as Lord (Acts 19:4-5; Rom 6:3; Jn 1:12; 2:23; 3:18; 20:31). This expression in both its longer and shorter forms, represents a major New Testament conception of saving faith.

In part, the response of the earliest Christians to the apostolic kerygma was determined by their cultural experiences. Both God and Jesus were proclaimed the objects of faith: Christians "believed in him who raised from the dead Jesus our Lord" (Rom 4:24). For Jewish hearers, accepting the kerygma entailed a revision of the concept of faith in the light of the cross and resurrection of Jesus (1 Cor 1:18-24; 2 Cor 5:19: "God was in Christ reconciling the world to himself."). For Gentile hearers, heeding the kerygma entailed the abandonment of idolatry for the worship of "a living and true God" and a solemn introduction "into Christ" through faith and baptism (1 Thes 1:8-10; Eph 2:11-22).

JESUS AND FAITH: THE SYNOPTIC TRADITION

It is widely recognized that the synoptic gospels, Matthew, Mark, and Luke, manifest three levels of meaning relating to Jesus. The most accessible level is the meaning that a particular saying or incident from

---

6. Raymond E. Brown, *The Gospel According to John* (Garden City, N.Y.: Doubleday, 1966), pp. 512-513.

Jesus' ministry had for a gospel writer. A second level reflects pre-canonical traditions preserved by persons in an oral, somewhat fluid state. And finally, the deepest level of meaning, retaining the actual course of events and the teaching of Jesus, consisted in his actions and words.

Largely due to the disillusionment, if not failure, of modern biographers in their effort to "recover the historical Jesus" (over the heads, so to speak, of the synoptic evangelists), contemporary readers are aware of the inherent subjectivity of all historical reconstructions. It can be presumptuous to speak with precision concerning the inner life of Jesus, his convictions, his intentions and motives—in a word, the faith of Jesus—given the nature of the original source material.[7] But there are numerous readers of the gospels who agree that it is possible to affirm that Jesus' life and teaching revolved around two poles, or two foci of an ellipse, the first of these poles or foci is Jesus' belief in the nearness of the kingdom, or rule, of God (Mk 1:14-15; 9:1; Mt 12:28; Lk 11:20; 14:17-19). The second is Jesus' faith/trust in God's justice and love because the power of his heavenly Father is accessible to persons in distress when they turn to the Father in faith and prayer (Mk 11:22-24; cf. Mt 21:22; Mk 9:14-29).

Jesus offered no new definition of faith. Nonetheless, his own faith (insofar as it can be recovered), and the faith he praised in others, represent a new historical development. He reaffirmed God's promise, enshrined in the scriptures, to redeem his creation from bondage to evil powers, from subjection to disease and other physical disabilities (recall Is 35:3-6; and 61:1-2, cited by Lk 4:16-21). But more than this, Jesus acted upon the belief that, in his own ministry, God's eschatological kingdom was "at hand," had "come near" (Lk 11:20; Mt 12:28; Mt 11:20-24; Lk 10:13-15; Mk 5:34,36).

The meaning of faith as expressed in the stories of Jesus' mighty works is unique in another way. His oft-spoken words, "Your faith has saved you" (made you well), is not found in the alleged "parallels" to the gospel stories either in Jewish rabbinical sources or in popular Hellenistic literature (Mk 2:5; Mt 9:22, 27; Mt 15:28; Lk 8:50). The faith that Jesus commended was not exclusively or specifically Israel's faith, nor was it put forward as evidence of Jesus' messiahship. (That Christ is not himself the object of faith is in keeping with the pre-Easter perspective of these synoptic traditions.)[8] Rather the faith that Jesus expressed was a

---

7. John Reumann, "Faith, Faithfulness in the NT," in *Interpreter's Dictionary of the Bible*, supplementary volume, p. 332.

8. Norman Perrin, *Rediscovering the Teaching of Jesus* (New York: Harper & Row, 1967), pp. 130-142.

trust that God was acting to bestow health and wholeness to needy human beings, a trust not constrained by a person's ideology, religious status, or ethnic origin. Jesus praised and responded to the trustful human requests made by a Samaritan leper, a Roman centurion, and a Syro-Phoenician woman; and he ministered to them in the same way he attended to the need of "a daughter of Abraham" (Lk 17:11-19; Mt 8:10; Mk 7:24-30; Lk 13:10-17).

Along with passages in the gospels in which Jesus commends the faith of suppliants are others in which he expresses consternation and amazement that humans are so lacking in trust toward God. In Jesus' teaching, fearful anxiety is the opposite of trust. "And he [Jesus] said to his disciples . . . do not be anxious about your life, what you shall eat nor about what you shall put on. For life is more than food and the body more than clothing. Consider the ravens. . . . God feeds them. . . . Consider the lilies. . . . God clothes them. . . .How much more will he clothe you, O men of little faith" (Lk 12:22-23; Mt 6:25-33). Winged creatures and plants of the earth rely upon divine providence. If only humans (especially his disciples) could do likewise (Mk 6:6; Lk 17:5-6).

After a storm at sea, Jesus rebuked his disciples for their lack of faith (Mk 4:40; cf. Mt 8:24-26). This incident points up a distinction between the faith/trust of Jesus and the absence or weakness of it on the part of Jesus' closest followers. No storm or other crisis was so threatening as to cause Jesus to doubt God's presence or to question his power and will to save (Mt 14:31; Mk 14:36). "Fear not, little flock," Jesus assured his disciples, "for it is your Father's good pleasure to give you the kingdom" (Lk 12:32).

The earliest gospel, according to Mark, has been described as a kerygma in narrative form. Jesus' ministry is inaugurated with the call to faith: "The time is fulfilled, and the kingdom of God is at hand; repent, and believe in the gospel" (Mk 1:15; 8:35; cf. Mt 16:25; Lk 9:24; also Mk 10:29 and Mt 19:29; and Lk 18:29. For the kerygmatic phrase, "the gospel of God . . . concerning his son," cf. Mk 1:1; Rom 1:1-3).

In the miracle stories reported by Mark, faith is an essential ingredient in anyone's appropriation of God's saving power. Upon hearing that the daughter of Jairus had died before his arrival, Jesus said to this ruler of the synagogue, "Do not fear, only believe" (Mk 9:9, 22b-24).

In Luke's gospel the stories concerning the birth of John the Baptist and of Jesus portray belief in much the same concepts as were depicted in Old Testament stories (which may well have influenced Luke's narratives). Like the prophets of old, the angels of the annunciation are the bearers of God's word; in such a situation, both the message and the messengers are to be believed: "And Mary said" [to Gabriel] "behold I am the handmaid of the Lord; let it be to me according to your word"

(Lk 1:38). The promise of a son to the aged Zechariah and his barren wife, Elizabeth, is reminiscent of the Abraham saga: Zechariah's faith also must prove itself in acts of obedience (Lk 1:5-25).

Luke's editing of the gospel traditions sometimes clearly reflects the mentality of the post-Easter church (Lk 18:8). At other times this mentality is implicit. In the semi-allegorical interpretation of the parable of the sower in the Third Gospel, Satan's purpose is to take away "the word of God" from some persons' hearts "that they may not believe and be saved" (Lk 8:9-12). The apostles' plea to the Lord, "Increase our faith!" was probably Luke's introduction to a saying of Jesus concerning faith's unlimited boundaries, addressed to his contemporaries (Lk 17:5; cf. Mt 17:14-20).

A close examination of Matthew's editing of Mark discloses that while Matthew usually preserved the meaning of faith in this source, he often intensified it by trimming details that detract from its principal elements. Matthew also extended some elements to apply them to the post-Easter church, composed of some persons of little or weak faith.[9]

Examples of Matthew's intensification by abbreviation, in his editing of Mark, may be seen by comparing Mark 5:21-43 with Matthew 9:18-26; also, Mark 10:46-52 with Matthew 20:29-34.

At three places Matthew seems to have substituted a variant for Jesus' word as reported in Mark and Luke. Instead of "your faith has made you well" (or, "has saved you") (with Mk 10:46-52 and Lk 18:35-43, cf. Mt 9:27-31), Matthew wrote, "According to your faith be it done to you" (Mt 8:13; 15:28). Matthew seems to have made a general application of a saying related in his source to single incidents.

Matthew's treatment of two stories in Mark dealing with the appearance of Jesus to his disciples on the sea of Galilee (Mk 4:35-41; cf. Mt 8:23-27; and Mk 6:45-52 and Mt 14:22-33) disclose the evangelist's interest in exploiting their symbolic significance. According to Mark 4:39-41, Jesus simply calmed the disciples' fears; in Matthew's parallel, Jesus responds to Peter's cry, "Lord save me!" by reaching out his hand, and chiding his disciple, "O man of little faith, why did you doubt?" (Mt 14:28-31; cf. Mk 4:40). Note also the christological development reflected in Matthew's version (cf. Mk 6:51 and Mt 14:30, 33; cf. Mk 4:38 with Mt 8:25).

According to Matthew, doubt is the shadow side of faith/trust. Persons of "little faith" are those who are most susceptible to doubt. Over against Mark's "Have faith in God," we read in Matthew, "Truly, I say to you, if you have faith and never doubt. . ." (Mk 11:22; Mt 21:21; Mt 14:31; 28:17).

---

9. Reumann, "Faith: Faithfulness in the NT," p. 333.

FAITH IN THE MAIN LETTERS OF PAUL

The great importance of Paul was clearly recognized in the statements of the early Christian kerygma, and various responses of faith. It was, of course, of great significance that Paul was in major agreement with those "who were apostles before him" (Gal 1:17; 2:2, 9; 1 Cor 15:9-11; 2 Cor 10:5). But Paul's mission to Gentiles opened up an area of discourse which led to his distinctive exposition of the gospel as contained in his letters to the churches.

The Righteousness of Faith

The passages which follow are taken from three letters of Paul namely Romans, Philippians, and Galatians. These passages direct the readers' attention to an interpretation of the gospel which, though not wholly original, was developed in unique ways by Paul. According to many exegetes, especially within the Lutheran and Reformed traditions, justification by faith is the central thesis of Paul's theology. All other themes must be related to this central doctrine if they are to be properly understood.[10] But there are some Roman Catholic scholars, together with several of their Protestant counterparts, who contest the claim that justification by faith is the indispensible key to an understanding of Paul's teaching. They contend that the believer's participation "in Christ," and an anticipation of the new life with him, represents Paul's main salvific theme, which is consistent with, and reenforced by, Paul's eschatology.[11] The prominence given Paul's exposition in his letters of the justification theme is attributed to the frequency of the apostles' heated controversies with Jews and Jewish-Christians over the relation of the gospel and the Law of Moses.

"For his sake [my Lord's] I have suffered the loss of all things and count them as refuse in order that I may gain Christ and be found in him, not having a righteousness of my own, based on law, but that which is through faith in Christ, the righteousness from God that depends on faith" (Phil 3:8-9).

"We know that a man is not justified by works of the law but through faith in Jesus Christ, even as we have believed in Christ Jesus in order to be justified by faith in Christ. . . . By works of the law shall no one be justified" (Gal 2:13-16).

---

10. Günther Bornkamm, *Paul* (New York: Harper & Row, 1971), pp. 115-117, 136-151; Ernst Käsemann, *Perspectives on Paul* (Philadelphia: Fortress, 1971), pp. 60-78.

11. Joseph A. Fitzmyer, *Pauline Theology* (Englewood Cliffs, N.J.: Prentice-Hall, 1967), pp. 51-53.

"But now the righteousness of God has been manifested apart from law, although the law and the prophets bear witness to it, the righteousness of God through faith in Jesus Christ for all who believe . . . (Rom 3:22; cf. Rom 1:16-17).

In these passages Paul draws upon juridical language to express the lasting effects of Christ's death and resurrection, as these events are related to God's purpose of salvation for Jews and Gentiles. Only a few exegetical points can be treated here, phrased as four questions. a) What did Paul mean in declaring that the gospel manifested "the righteousness of God"? b) What meaning did Paul intend in his use of the verb "to justify"? c) Why did Paul emphatically insist that justification was "not by works of the law"? d) How does Paul delineate the meaning of justification-faith?

In response to the first of these four exegetical questions, it should be noted that most Protestant theologians follow Luther and Calvin in interpreting the term "the righteousness of God" as an objective genitive or, more recently, a genitive of source, expressed most clearly in Philippians 3:8-9, the righteousness that is from God, given to the believer and thereby establishing a new relationship (Eph 2:5, 8). Although sinners, believers in Christ stand before God clothed in Christ's righteousness (Calvin's metaphor). This righteousness of faith is *God's* righteousness because it not only proceeds from him but is acceptable to him in lieu of anyone's righteousness based on law (Rom 10:1-4).[12]

Catholic theologians are often in agreement that "the justice of God" (a preferred translation) was written as an objective genitive, but differ from Protestants in holding that a real righteousness is conferred upon believers in Christ, not merely a right standing. By divine grace and sacramental union with Christ sinners are made ethically upright.[13] Some scholars, Protestant and Catholic, however, read Paul's phrase as a subjective genitive, meaning God's own righteousness, not with respect to [God's] divine attribute, but to his activity of saving and judging humankind in and through the eschatological Christ event (Gal 3:23-26; Rom 3:3-6).

In response to the second of the four exegetical questions, it should be noted that the variations of interpretation are more clearly illumined when answers are sought to the question what is the meaning for Paul of the verb usually translated, "to justify." Modern connotations of this verb render Paul's meaning unclear. Accordingly, other English equivalents have been proposed: to acquit; to right-wise; to rectify; to righ-

---

12. J. A. Ziesler, *The Meaning of Righteousness in Paul* (London: Cambridge University Press, 1972), pp. 1-14.
13. Fitzmyer, *Pauline Theology*, pp. 52-53.

teous. Some Protestants insist on the declarative sense: To justify is to acquit, to declare righteous in a relational sense only. God justifies "the ungodly" by freely giving them a new status (Rom 4:5; 5:1-2, 6-8; 8:33). In dialogue with Protestants some Catholic theologians have conceded that this understanding is supported by careful exegesis. Notwithstanding, it is important to remember that anyone's upright status was, for Paul, a consequence of his or her incorporation in (to) Christ through faith and baptism.[14] A vital question remains: Is sanctification an element in justification, as Catholics seem to hold, or its sequel, as Protestant theologians tend to believe? (Rom 15:15-17; 8:29-30; 1 Thes 4:3; 2 Thes 2:13-15; 1 Cor 6:11).

Turning to the third exegetical question, we ask what reason can be given for Paul's adamant position that salvation was "not by works of the law." Several answers have been proposed, more than one of which may reflect Paul's objection. Some scholars contend that Paul had learned from experience that the law could not be followed; therefore hope of salvation by obedience to the law was foredoomed to disappointment. Other scholars have said that Paul came to realize that life under the law led inevitably to legalism and self-righteous boasting. Rather more probable is a third view that Paul's contention was that the gospel manifested God's intention to accomplish his salvation by requiring only faith in Christ, consequently "not by works of the law." Also only on the basis of faith in Christ could Gentiles be saved on the same terms as Jews. In support of this understanding, Paul turned to the scriptures which foretold that Gentiles would share in the legacy of Abraham on the basis of faith/trust (Rom 4: Gal 3; also Rom 9:24-26; 10:20; 15:8-12). Of special importance for Paul was his faith in the kerygma that, in the death and resurrection of Jesus Christ, God offers salvation to all on the basis of faith (Rom 3:26, 28-30; 1 Cor 21-25).[15]

And now to the fourth and final exegetical question, the one concerning the nature of saving faith. Attention has been given to the various ways early Christians expressed their faith, with God or Jesus as its object. Two forms are prominent in Paul's letters: belief that . . ., and belief in (to). . . . For Paul these two forms amount to much the same things: accepting a belief, the kerygma, and being a believer are both directed toward Christ as Lord, establishing a personal relationship which remained the foundation of faith. In short, faith in the kerygma, and in Christ mediated by it, are inseparable.

---

14. Hans Küng, *Justification* (Louisville, Ky.: Westminster/John Knox, 1981).

15. E. P. Sanders, *Paul, the Law, and the Jewish People* (Philadelphia: Fortress, 1983), pp. 17-48.

According to the Greek text of his letters, Paul employs various modes of expression for faith, with Christ as their object. These phrases are usually rendered alike, "faith in Christ." Even when Paul uses "faith" with the genitive "of Christ," which at first sight implies Christ's own faith, most interpreters regard this genitive as defining the person trusted, and translate "faith in Christ." Sufficient attention has not been given by scholars to the question whether or not, by introducing this last expression, Paul has given the language of saving faith a new dimension or depth. The question is not a trivial one because it relates to an understanding of the essential basis of anyone's salvation, a subject treated by Paul in Romans 3:22, 26; Galatians 2:16, 20; 3:22; Philippians 3:9. Does Paul write, "faith in Christ," or "the faith(fulness) of Christ"? In Romans 3:3 Paul alludes to "the faithfulness of God," and possibly his elliptical phrase in Romans 1:17 could mean "from God's faithfulness to man's faith embraced in it."[16] It has been suggested by some biblical theologians that Paul occasionally portrays saving faith in a double-sided sense, especially in treating the subject of Abraham's faith and his true progeny. Drawing upon his knowledge, and that of his readers, of Roman law for the transmission of inheritances, Paul depicts Christ as accepting and fulfilling the role of the testamentary *fidei commissum* ("the faith *of* Christ"). In turn, by trusting Christ, potential beneficiaries become heirs, some receiving the adoption of sons.[17] The analogies are suggestive but convincing only to a minority (Gal 3:23-25; Rom 5:1-2; 2 Thes 3:5; Rev 14:12).

For Paul, faith was expressed as obedience. Already in the Old Testament and in Judaism obedience to God and his commandments was a hallmark of Israel's faith. For Paul it was the complement of "confession" and was the accompaniment of a life of faith, a continuing reliance upon God and not upon one's own resources and achievements. It may be too much to say that for Paul faith was obedience; nevertheless the relation of these two concepts was close. In writing to the Thessalonians he commends them saying, "Your faith in God has gone forth everywhere" (1 Thes 1:8). Later to the same church he warns "those who do not obey the gospel of our Lord Jesus" (2 Thes 1:8). Similarly, in his letter to the Romans he commends his readers "because your faith is proclaimed in all the world" (Rom 1:8), and in the conclusion of the letter he acknowledged, "your obedience is known to all" (Rom 16:19). Paul defined his special mission as designed "to bring about obedience to the faith for the sake of his [Christ's] name (alternate reading: the

---

16. Reumann, "Faith: Faithfulness in the NT," p. 333.
17. G. Howard, "On the Faith of Chirst," in *Harvard Theological Review* 60 (1967), pp. 459 ff.

obedience that is faith). And what is obedience to the gospel? A lifetime of faith/trust.[18]

In ministering to persons in his young churches Paul recognized that there were degrees and differing possibilities of faith. Some who had gladly received the gospel "with full conviction" (1 Thes 1:5) were urged to "hold on" or "stand firm" in their faith (1 Cor 16:13; 2 Cor 1:24; 13:5). "You stand fast only through faith," Paul warned Gentile Christians in Rome, "Do not become proud" (11:20). Amid the vicissitudes of life, the believer must realize the danger of falling (Gal 5:4; 1 Cor 10:12). Since some early Christians exhibit deficiencies of faith, Paul prays earnestly for them (1 Thes 3:10). He "hopes" that as the Corinthians' "faith increases" he may be free to labor in a new field (2 Cor 10:15). Paul's reference to "the work of faith" (1 Thes 1:8) is at first glance a curious paradox since "work" appears to be the antithesis of "faith." Paul's meaning may be expressd in a paraphrase: "In Christ Jesus, neither a work of the law, nor a lack of compliance count for anything, but faith working through love" (Gal 5:6, 24. See also 1 Cor 13:2, 13; 1 Thes 3:6; Rom 13:8-10).

In Christ Jesus . . . Children of God, through Faith

The following are principal passages in Paul's letters on the nature of the new life "in Christ" (or, "in the Spirit").

"It has been granted to you that for the sake of Christ you should not only believe in him but also suffer for his sake" (Phil 1:29)

"Since we are justified by faith, we have peace with God through our Lord Jesus Christ. Through him we have obtained access to this grace in which we stand, and we rejoice in our hope of sharing the glory of God" (Rom 5:1-2).

"Do you not know that all of us who have been baptized into Christ Jesus were baptized into his death? We were buried therefore with him by baptism into death, so that as Christ was raised from the dead by the glory of the Father, we too might walk in newness of life. . . . If we have died with Christ, we believe that we shall also live with him" (Rom 6:3-4, 8).

"If anyone is in Christ, he is a new creation; the old has passed away, behold, the new has come" (2 Cor 5:17).

From the above passages it is clear that Paul's teaching on the role of faith in establishing the new life is linked with his understanding concerning baptism. Sons (and daughters) of God, through faith, have, in

---

18. Rudolf Bultmann, *Theology of the New Testament*, Vol. I (New York: Scribner's, 1951), pp. 314-324; Leander Keck, *Paul and His Letters* (Philadelphia: Fortress, 1979), pp. 50-55.

their act of receiving baptism, "put on Christ" (a reference to a baptismal robe of some sort?). The parallel phrase may be an abbreviation of the believer's "baptism into the name of Christ" (Gal 3:26-27).

More illuminating for an understanding of Paul's own development of this traditional initiatory rite of the early church, and the concepts surrounding it, are the statements in Romans 6. Two important points should be highlighted. First, the whole passage assumes the revision of Jewish apocalyptic eschatology by Paul and others. Instead of the hope of an imminent coming of the End, when God's ultimate salvation and judgment will be manifested, Paul's perspective surveys the "already" and the "not yet." *Already* believers in (to) Christ participate, through their baptism in Christ's death, burial, and resurrection; *already* the believer has "died to sin," that is, freed from bondage to sin; *already* believers have been justified by faith, and so are freed from dependence for salvation upon "works of the law." But *not yet* has the believer been raised with Christ from the dead, an event awaiting Christ's (final) coming. Nevertheless, the believer in union with Christ, and aided by the Holy Spirit, is empowered to lead a new life (Rom 6:7, 4; cf. Eph 2:5-7, but also 1:12-14).[19] Second, Paul's teaching in these passages is not limited to the solitary life of, and hope for, individuals. Through faith and baptism a special union with all other believers is established: "For indeed we were all brought into one body by baptism," wrote Paul, "in one Spirit, whether we are Jews or Greeks, whether slaves or free men" (1 Cor 12-13).

Summary of Paul's Concept of Faith

In summary we may say that Paul proclaimed and taught that to believe/trust, and to be baptized into Christ, means the here-and-now participation in the sphere of Christ's Lordship, in fellowship with all members of his body, and in anticipation of a future resurrection. *Already* the believer in Christ "rejoices in the hope of sharing the glory of God" (Rom 5:2; 25:23).

FAITH ACCORDING TO JOHN'S GOSPEL

The reader of the present chapter is asked to recall what was said earlier about the formation of the traditions in the synoptic gospels. The three levels of meanings that can be distinguished in the make-up of the three earlier gospels are discernible in the Fourth Gospel, the Gospel of John. The difference is not of kind but rather the degree to which the tradition has undergone development and change. Efforts to identify

---

19. James L. Price, "Romans 6, 1-14," in *Interpretation* 34 (1980), pp. 65-69.

various stages in the formation of the Johannine traditions—a separation of the Fourth Evangelist's contributions from that of earlier
sources, oral or written or both, as well as the determination of what
may be attributed to a later editor—are speculative. No consensus
among scholars regarding the history of this gospel's origin has been
reached. For the purposes of this chapter, no resolution of these historical and literary questions is required. It must be acknowledged, however, that the assignment of passages or ideas to the Evangelist, others to
his sources, and still others to one or more editors, complicates our task.
At least it may be said that the Fourth Evangelist has gathered traditions
congenial to his own convictions and that in the course of the narrative
these emerge with some degree of clarity and consistency.

Before the addition of chapter 21, John's gospel concluded with a
statement of purpose: "Now Jesus did many other signs in the presence
of the disciples, which are not written in this book; but these are written
that you may believe that Jesus is the Christ, the Son of God, and that
believing you may have life in his name" (Jn 20:30-31).

John's understanding of Christian faith was, like Paul's, based on
believing the message, *both* the word preached by Jesus *and* the proclamation concerning his messianic role, as the Son sent by the Father to
be the Savior of the world. But unlike Paul, John does not develop a
conception of the way leading to salvation (the righteousness of faith).
His concern is for the right conception of salvation itself (the procure-
ment and enjoyment of "eternal life"). It is probable that this gospel was
written, not as a mission text, but to consolidate the faith of the community in which he served: that its members "may have life, and have it
abundantly" (10:10). To believe and to have life are inseparable. Believers in Christ pass "from death to life" (5:24—a life that is secured in the
name of Christ. 1:12; 16:21; 3:15-16; 6:40, 47; 10:10, 28; 11:25; 12:40-
50; 17:3; 1 Jn 5:13).

John's statement of purpose raises the question of the function of
Jesus' "signs" in the Fourth Gospel. John's account of the inception of
Jesus' ministry notes that Jesus performed a "first" and a "second" sign
(2:11; 4:54). This numeration ends, but, taken along with 20:30, provides some evidence that the Evangelist drew from a "sign source" a
select number of incidents from Jesus' ministry to which he appended
discourses which develop their symbolic significance. An alternative to
the designation "signs" are Jesus' "works" (6:30), although the latter
refer to Jesus' ministry as a whole (17:4; 4:34), while the former are
limited to (what we would call) his miracles.

The Evangelist reports various responses to the signs of Jesus, which
may be grouped in four categories.[20] First, there are the willfully blind

20. Brown, *Gospel According to John*, pp. 530-531.

who refuse to come to the light, who fail to see the significance of the signs (3:19-20; 9:41; 11:47; 15:22). Second, there are the sign-seekers who are disinterested in probing the issue of the identity of Jesus. The belief of these persons is wrongly motivated and therefore not to be trusted (7:5; 2:23-25; 3:2-3; 4:45-48). Third, there are disciples who see the true significance of Jesus' signs. They know who Jesus is, in his relation to the Father, as the Son who manifests the divine glory (2:11; 4:53; 6:69; 9:38; 22:40). Consistent with the conviction that full, saving faith can, like the Spirit, come only after Jesus' resurrection (7:39), John acknowledges that the disciples, in being with Jesus, grew in their faith which became belief unto eternal life (6:60-71; 14:5-12; 20:28). Finally, John wrote of all those who would believe in Jesus without seeing his signs (20:29). Such latter-day disciples would believe the word of those who had been with Jesus and who had received the Holy Spirit (17:20; 20:19-23).

CHAPTER 7

The Systematic Theology of Faith: A Catholic Perspective

Avery Dulles

HISTORICAL PRENOTES

The distinctively Catholic doctrine of faith may be found unofficially in the writings of Catholic theologians and officially in the authoritative teaching of popes, bishops, and councils (the magisterium). Both the theologians and the magisterium have sought to remain faithful to biblical teaching. They have aimed at a balanced synthesis that does justice to the Old Testament and the synoptic gospels but especially to the more developed doctrine of postresurrection faith that is found in the Pauline and Johannine writings. Catholics also refer frequently to the Letter of James as an antidote to a one-sided reading of Paul, and to the Pastoral Letters for their teaching on faith as an objective deposit.

The single theologian who has most profoundly influenced the Catholic theology of faith is undoubtedly Augustine, who pondered the scriptures in the light of his own Greco-Roman culture and his powerful speculative inclinations. Augustine's early anti-Manichaean works are important for the relations between faith and reason. His late anti-Pelagian tracts have become normative for the relations between grace and freedom in the act of faith. Much of the anti-Pelagianism of Augustine was incorporated into official Catholic teaching by the Second Council of Orange (A.D. 529), a local synod that has received numerous approvals from subsequent popes and ecumenical councils.

In the Middle Ages a further shift in the theology of faith came about with the recovery of the lost works of Aristotle. Schoolmen such as Thomas Aquinas (1225-1274), influenced by Aristotle, speculated on the relationship between nature, understood in the Aristotelian sense, and grace, understood as an infused quality or virtue empowering nature to rise above itself. The theological virtues of faith, hope, and love (charity) were studied in relation to the spiritual faculties of intellect and will.

Probably no other treatise in theology has been the object of so many authoritative pronouncements by popes and councils as has the treatise on faith. The official teaching may be found especially in the three modern councils of the whole Catholic church—namely, Trent (1546-1563), Vatican I (1869-1870), and Vatican II (1962-1965). The Council of Trent dealt with faith primarily in its Decree on Justification, a Catholic response to certain questions raised by the Protestant Reformers. Trent agreed with the Reformers that faith was necessary for salvation and that it was a gift of grace. But against the Reformers Trent insisted on the role of human freedom, cooperation, and merit in the life of faith.

Vatican I took up the question of faith and reason in reaction to certain post-Kantian developments in the philosophy of human knowing. It rejected both fideism (the doctrine that faith is an irrational commitment) and rationalism (the doctrine that the human mind can establish the contents of faith by reason without reliance on authority).

Vatican II addressed the question of faith within the wider horizons of ecumenism, interreligious dialogue, and secularization. It affirmed that God gives every human being, including the unevangelized, the assistance needed to achieve faith in the measure required for eternal salvation.

In addition to these councils, we shall refer to certain important documents issued by the Roman magisterium. The reader should be aware of the "laxist" propositions condemned by the Congregation of the Holy Office under Innocent XI in 1679[1] and of the condemnations of certain fideistic[2] and rationalistic[3] positions in the early nineteenth

---

1. Propositions 16 through 23 dealt with errors about faith. See Henricus Denzinger and Adolfus Schönmetzer, eds., *Enchiridion symbolorum, definitionum et declarationum de rebus fidei et morum*, 32nd ed. (Freiburg: Herder, 1963), nos. 2116-2123. This anthology will henceforth be cited DS.

2. Against traditionalism and fideism see, for example, the encyclical of Gregory XVI, *Mirari vos*, 1832 (DS 2730-32), envisioning Félicité de Lamennais; the various theses that Louis Bautain was required to sign (DS 2751-56, 2165-69); and the theses directed against Augustin Bonnetty (DS 2811-14).

3. Against rationalism see Gregory XVI's brief, *Dum acerbissimas*, 1835 (DS

century. Likewise important are the anti-Modernist documents issued from Rome in 1907 and 1910, and the 1950 encyclical of Pius XII, *Humani generis,* which warned against certain tenets of the "new theology" that had surfaced during and after World War II. These and other interventions of the Holy See were intended to safeguard traditional Catholic teaching against unacceptable innovations.

PRESUPPOSITIONS

The doctrine of faith, in Catholic systematic theology, must be seen as organically connected with other points of Catholic doctrine, which are at this stage simply presupposed. Among the presuppositions one might list, for example, the doctrines that God exists and has revealed himself; that Christianity is a revealed religion; that Holy Scripture is a reliable source of doctrine; that the authoritative teaching of the Catholic magisterium is to be accepted (with due respect for the varying weight of different pronouncements), and that the dogmas of the church accurately express divine revelation, albeit in a culturally conditioned manner.

On the basis of presuppositions such as these we may now proceed to examine the nature, contents, properties, rational grounds, and necessity of faith and, finally, the ecclesial dimension of faith.

THE NATURE OF FAITH

Definition

The nearest thing to an official Catholic definition of faith is the statement of Vatican I in its Dogmatic Constitution, *Dei Filius,* that faith is "the supernatural virtue whereby, inspired and assisted by the grace of God, we believe that what God has revealed is true, not because of the intrinsic truth of the contents as recognized by the natural light of reason, but because of the authority of God himself, the revealer, who can neither be deceived nor deceive."[4] A similar lapidary statement was issued by Vatican II: "The 'obedience of faith' (Rom 16:26; cf. 1:5; 2 Cor 10:5-6) must be given to God who reveals, an obedience by which one entrusts (*committit*) one's whole self freely to God, offering 'the full submission of intellect and will to God who reveals' (Vatican I, DS 3008), and freely assenting to the revelation given by him."[5]

2738-40), directed against Georg Hermes; Pius IX's encyclical, *Qui pluribus,* 1846 (DS 2775-86), and the brief directed against Anton Günther, 1857 (DS 2828-31), as well as the summary of previous condemnations in the Syllabus of Errors of 1864 (DS 2901-2980).

4. Vatican I, Dogmatic Constitution *Dei Filius,* chap. 3 (DS 3008).
5. Vatican II, Dogmatic Constitution *Dei Verbum,* no. 5.

Intellectualism

Traditionally, Catholic theologians have tended to stress the intellectual component and to see faith as, in the first instance, a matter of believing what God has revealed. This accent was already present in Trent's reply to the Lutherans, who tended to look on faith rather as trust in God's mercy to oneself.[6] The character of faith as intellectual assent was reaffirmed by Vatican I and by the anti-Modernist documents, which deny that faith is a pious feeling arising from the depths of the subconscious.[7] Vatican II, in an ecumenical advance, accented the elements of trust and commitment but simultaneously reaffirmed the element of intellectual assent.

The official Catholic teaching on this point has been influenced by medieval scholastic theologians who distinguished sharply between faith, as a formally intellectual act, and hope and love, which were attributed rather to the will. In support of this intellectualism, appeal is commonly made to New Testament texts which speak of faith as "believing that" certain things are true (e.g., Jn 11:27; 20:31, Rom 10:8; Heb 11:1-3, 6; cf. Jude 3; 1 Tm 6:20; 2 Tm 1:14), as well as to texts which distinguish faith from hope and love (e.g., 1 Cor 13:13). On the other hand it must be recognized that the Greek term *pistis* (and the Latin equivalent, *fides*) are used in the Bible and in early Christian tradition in a wide variety of senses, so that features such as confidence, trust, fidelity, and obedience may be more prominent than intellectual assent to truth. Vatican II was therefore warranted in including these noncognitive aspects together with intellectual assent in the statement on faith already quoted.

The Virtue and the Act of Faith

Operating in the spiritual climate of Scholasticism, Vatican I defined faith primarily as a virtue, i.e., as the stable disposition to perform acts of faith. Vatican II, convened in a period when actualistic philosophies such as existential phenomenology were dominant, preferred to discuss faith particularly as the act of a believer and only secondarily as a virtue. On this point there is no contradiction between the two councils; they may be seen as mutually complementary, for neither denies that faith is both a virtue and an act.

---

6. Council of Trent, Decree on Justification, chap. 5 (DS 1526) and canons 12 through 14 (DS 1562-64).

7. See Oath against Modernism, A.D. 1919 (DS 3542). This oath was a profession of faith directed against certain Modernist errors and required of all priests, seminary professors, and some church officials until 1967.

The Formal Object of Faith

From the texts already quoted it is evident that the intellectual mo-tive, or formal object, of faith is the supreme authority or trustworthi-ness of God. Considered as an assent, faith subscribes to certain beliefs because they are divinely revealed. In the passage cited, Vatican I speaks of the motive as the authority of God revealing ("*propter auctoritatem Dei revelantis*").[8] The oath against Modernism (1910) states that we believe because of the authority of God who is supremely truthful.[9] Catholic teaching has traditionally emphasized the role of authority in matters of faith. Thomas Aquinas, typifying this approach, wrote that in matters of faith the person whose word is accepted is more central and important than the particular beliefs accepted on that person's word.[10]

CONTENTS OF FAITH

The contents of faith have traditionally been discussed in Catholic theology under the heading of the "material object," as contrasted with the formal object just considered. What can and must be believed on the motive of faith? Vatican Council I, as we have seen, defines faith as the virtue by which we believe that what God has revealed is true.[11] Vatican II asserts that by faith we freely assent to the truth revealed by God.[12] The Council of Trent had described the object of faith as the things that have been divinely revealed and promised. Thus in Catholic teaching faith and revelation are correlative.

Christianity, through the centuries, has developed a rather complete theology of revelation which it would not be possible or necessary to summarize adequately in the present chapter. It may be noted, however, that the revelation attested by the Christian sources is not a haphazard miscellany of divinely authenticated statements but a coherent plan of salvation that has as its center and culmination the figure of Jesus Christ. To know revelation, in the last analysis, is nothing other than to know "Jesus Christ and him crucified" (1 Cor 2:2).

Jesus Christ, of course, is not an isolated figure. He has to be inter-preted against the whole religious history that prepares for his coming—a history set forth for us in the inspired scriptures of the Old Testament, which the New Testament and the church have authenticated as the prehistory of Christianity itself. The meaning of Christ's coming and

---

8. *Dei Filius*, chap. 3 (DS 3008) and canon 2 on Faith (DS 3032).
9. DS 3542
10. Thomas Aquinas, *Summa theologiae*, 2-2.11.2c.
11. Note 4 above.
12. Note 5 above.

earthly career to the early church is recorded for us in the inspired scriptures of the New Testament. But the individual believer is not left to discover the scriptures and to interpret them without assistance. According to Catholic belief, God established the church as the guardian and teacher of the revealed message. Christ promises to remain present to his church to the end of time, directing it by his Spirit, so that the faithful may hear through the church the word of God himself.

Faith may be called "divine" insofar as it assents to the word of God, "Christian" insofar as it takes Christ as "the Mediator and fullness of all revelation,"[13] and "Catholic" insofar as it accepts the authoritative teaching of the church about what is revealed. In the Catholic Christian's act of faith, these three dimensions are simultaneously present. When such a believer confesses, for example, that Jesus Christ is risen Lord, the act of faith is concurrently divine, Christian, and Catholic.

From the Catholic perspective, the contents of faith are summarily indicated in the following sentence from Vatican I: "All those things are to be believed with divine and Catholic faith which are contained in the word of God, written or handed down, and which the church, either in solemn judgments or through her ordinary and universal teaching office, proposes as having been divinely revealed."[14] The distinction between the solemn judgments of the church and the teachings of the ordinary and universal magisterium is further studied in ecclesiology.

The primary object of faith is God—God not simply as he is in himself but especially as he reveals himself in relation to us, for the sake of our salvation. He reveals himself as creator, redeemer, and sanctifier, as the one who calls us into union with himself and who discloses in Christ the way, the truth, and the life. The heart of Christian faith was very early articulated in brief confessional statements such as "Jesus is the Christ," "Jesus is Son of God," "Jesus is risen Lord." Eventually the chief contents of Christian faith were summarized in creeds, and the creeds were further explained by dogmatic declarations to guard against misinterpretations.

Few believers have explicit knowledge of all that the church has taught as divinely revealed. There is no need for the average believer to be thoroughly versed in church history and theology. For the normal Catholic it suffices to adhere explicitly to the central truths of Christianity, which are well known from the New Testament, from Christian preaching and religious education, and from the creeds, which summarize the central articles of faith, and to acknowledge certain well-publicized tenets. The rest of the church's dogmatic teaching is believed by

---

13. Cf. Vatican II, *Dei Verbum*, art. 2.
14. *Dei Filius*, chap. 3 (DS 3011).

"implicit faith." In saying, "I believe the teaching of the church" the Catholic expresses a global assent even to doctrines of which she or he might not be aware.

In modern times there has been much discussion about whether faith is propositional. If the question is whether propositions themselves are the object or content of faith, one must answer with Thomas Aquinas that they are not, "for the act of the believer does not terminate in the proposition but in the reality [signified by the proposition]; for we do not form propositions except to have knowledge of things by means of them, whether in science or in faith."[15]

In a certain sense, however, faith may rightly be called propositional. To some extent, at least, the contents of faith can be set forth in propositions, such as the confessional statements just quoted. To doubt or deny these propositions, if they are understood as the church understands them, is contrary to the faith. Of course the propositions are capable of being misunderstood, and they may have to be translated for the benefit of different audiences, but that is true of propositions in any field of knowledge. Just as it is objectively true to say that Manhattan is an island, so it is objectively true to say that Jesus Christ is the incarnate Son of God. The proposition states the reality.

While respecting the value of propositions, we must avoid the error of confusing the propositions of creed and dogma with faith itself. The propositions depend upon conceptual and linguistic structures and conventions that are tied to certain cultural and historical conditions. They are useful and sometimes necessary instruments for enabling the mind to assent to the realities of faith, but they are not the realities to which they refer. For the sake of effective communication, the church may at times have to change the concepts and language in which it heralds God's revelation. Even when the formulations are clear and accurate, some members of the church may have difficulty understanding what is meant. Those who, for whatever reason, reject the formulations cannot without further ado be judged to have lost the faith. They may be prepared to adhere to the realities of faith but be put off by language that they find opaque and confusing.

Theologians have often debated the question whether a person could have faith in something that was not really, but was only thought to be, revealed by God. It does seem that a poorly instructed believer might give expression to his or her faith by accepting a false statement that was presented as a revealed truth. But, strictly speaking, the virtue of faith would not be the source of the false affirmation. The opinion that such

---

15. *Summa theologiae* 2-2.1.2. ad 2.

a matter was revealed would not come from revelation but rather from human conjecture. Faith affirms only what is contained in the word of God. On this ground Thomas Aquinas maintains that faith never extends to anything false.[16]

Two other subtle questions, still debated in Catholic theology, may here be mentioned. The first has to do with statements of ecclesiastical authority that go beyond the contents of revelation itself and are intended to safeguard or interpret revelation. Granted that the magisterium may legitimately proclaim such truths, it may be asked whether they can be believed on a motive of faith. Theologians rather commonly reply that the individual Catholic, trusting the guidance of the magisterium, should accept such teaching with a kind of faith that is not precisely divine (for it does not go out to God's revelation) but rather ecclesiastical.[17] To dissent from nonrevealed teaching of this kind might be rash and imprudent but it would not be a sin against the theological virtue of faith; it would not be heresay in the technical sense.[18]

The other debated question has to do with private revelation.[19] In the history of the church certain persons have claimed to be the recipients of heavenly messages over and above the contents of the public and apostolic faith. In some cases the church has approved of these private revelations, at least to the extent of declaring that they contain nothing contrary to the faith, and may piously be believed to be from God. The church does not require any of her faithful to accept these revelations as part of their faith. It seems not impossible, however, that God might so certify a private revelation to a given individual that that individual might be bound to credit the revelation as coming from God. In such a case—which is possible in theory, even if not verified in fact—one could have an act of faith that was divine without being, in the technical sense, Catholic.

In the remainder of this chapter we shall be discussing the kind of faith that is due to the public revelation committed to the church as a

---

16. Ibid., 2-2.1.3.
17. On the question of ecclesiastical faith see Yves Congar, "Fait dogmatique et foi ecclésiastique," *Catholicisme hier, aujourd'hui, demain*, vol. 4 (Paris: Letouzey et Ané, 1956), col. 1059-1067.
18. The 1983 Code of Canon Law (canon 751) defines heresy as a baptized Christian's obstinate denial of, or obstinate doubt concerning, some truth that must be believed with divine and Catholic faith.
19. On private revelation see Prudent de Letter, "Revelations, Private," in *New Catholic Encyclopedia*, vol. 12 (New York: McGraw Hill, 1967), pp. 446-448; more fully, Laurent Volken, *Visions, Revelations, and the Church* (New York: Kenedy, 1963).

whole, i.e., faith that is at once divine, Christian, and Catholic. The
marginal cases of "ecclesiastical faith" and of faith in private revelation
will be left aside.

PROPERTIES OF FAITH

Various theologians, in accordance with their systematic presuppositions, list the properties of faith in slightly different ways.[20] But there is a
broad consensus in Catholic theology that faith has the following five
qualities, among others: It is supernatural; it is free; it is certain; it is
obscure; and it is reasonable.

Supernaturality

In calling faith a "supernatural virtue" Vatican I means that acts of
faith, although performed by the human subject, are never performed
without the help of divine grace. In that sense faith is a gift of God.[21]
The Second Council of Orange, in a teaching later reaffirmed by Trent,
had already insisted that faith cannot be achieved by unaided human
effort but that it depends on the free and merciful assistance of God.[22]
Vatican II, with an explicit reference to Orange II, likewise taught that
the act of faith presupposes God's prevenient and concomitant grace or,
in other words, the interior assistance of the Holy Spirit, who moves the
human heart and turns it to God.[23] The help of the Holy Spirit has
traditionally, since Orange II, been characterized in terms of enlightenment and inspiration.[24]

On the supernatural or gratuitous quality of faith there is no real
disagreement between Catholics and Protestants. Like their Catholic
counterparts, the sixteenth-century Reformers were strongly influenced
by the later writings of Augustine, which were quoted or paraphrased by
Orange II. Although the Bible does not itself make the natural/supernat-
ural distinction, Christian theologians, confessions, and councils frequently find the supernatural origin of faith implied in biblical texts
such as John 6:44 ("No one can come to me unless the Father who sent
me draw him"), John 15:57 ("Without me you can do nothing"), and 2

---

20. For standard Catholic approaches see Iosephus de Aldama, *De virtutibus
infusis* in *Sacrae theologiae summa*, vol. 3, 3rd ed. (Madrid: Biblioteca de
Autores Cristianos, 1956), pp. 737-817; Juan Alfaro, *Fides, Spes, Caritas*
(Rome: Pontificia Universitas Gregoriana, 1964), pp. 1-509.
21. *Dei Filius*, chap. 3 (DS 3010).
22. Orange II, can. 5 (DS 375); cf. Council of Trent, Decree on Justification,
chap. 6 (DS 1526) and chap. 8 (DS 1532).
23. *Dei Verbum*, no. 5.
24. Orange II, can. 7 (DS 377).

Corinthians 3:5 ("Not that of ourselves we are qualified to take credit for anything as coming from us; our qualification comes from God").

How the supernatural action of grace influences the mind and the will of the believer is a topic to which we shall return below, at the end of our discussion of credibility.

Freedom

The question of the freedom of faith became an issue at the time of the Reformation, when certain Protestants taught that human freedom, insofar as it could enable one to turn toward God, was extinguished by the Fall. In answer to this position Trent affirmed that, although faith is impossible without the help of grace, grace does not bring about the saving act of faith without the free, though graced, consent of those who receive it. Thus human freedom, although weakened by the Fall, is not extinguished.[25] It remains in sufficient measure for the believer to accept God's grace willingly.[26] The Council did not attempt to solve the theoretical question how the efficacy of God's grace is to be reconciled with the human capacity to refuse it. Nor shall we in this chapter deal with the complex question of grace and free will.

Vatican I reaffirmed the freedom of faith. With Trent it insisted that God's grace is not irresistible.[27] It also asserted, against Georg Hermes, that the human person, even after appreciating the rational force of the arguments in favor of Christianity, remains free to withhold assent.[28] Thus faith is never coerced; it is a truly personal response to a call that comes from on high.

Vatican II in its Constitution on Divine Revelation likewise described faith as a free commitment.[29] In its Declaration on Religious Freedom Vatican II used the essential freedom of the act of faith as the basis for its argument against the use of coercive methods in seeking to impose religious truth.[30]

The freedom of the act of faith is not directly treated in scripture. Such freedom may, however, be regarded as a corollary of the biblical teaching that the refusal to believe is culpable and punishable (1 Jn 3:23; Mk 16:16). God, being just, would not punish people for faults they could not avoid. Inasmuch as a voluntary failure to believe is culpable, it is evident that the freedom of faith does not make faith purely optional. As we shall later see, faith is obligatory under pain of eternal perdition.

25. Decree on Justification, chap. 1 (DS 1521).
26. Ibid., chaps. 5 and 6 (DS 1525-26); canons 4 and 5 (DS 1554-55).
27. *Dei Filius*, chap. 3 (DS 3010).
28. *Dei Filius*, can. 5 on Faith (DS 3035).
29. *Dei Verbum*, no. 5.
30. *Dignitatis humanae*, no. 10.

Certitude

That the content of faith is objectively certain follows necessarily from the fact that faith's object is truth revealed by God, who, as Vatican I puts it, "can neither be deceived nor deceive."[31] The subjective certitude of faith is a more difficult question. Some measure of certitude would seem to be implied in the very concept of faith as conviction, trust, and commitment. A person still in doubt about whether God were provident or whether Christ had risen from the dead could scarcely be said to have faith in these doctrines. Generally speaking, the stronger our faith, the greater will our certitude be. A lack of certitude betokens, to some degree, a lack of faith.

The certitude of faith has a basis in Holy Scripture. In the synoptic gospels faith is regularly set in opposition to fear and doubt; it is associated with courage and confidence. Elsewhere in the New Testament Abraham is praised for his unwavering trust in God's promises (Rom 4:20-22). Paul claims to be utterly confident that nothing can separate him from the love of Christ (Rom 8:38-40). Peter, as quoted in Acts, calls on his hearers to know for certain that Jesus is Lord and Christ (Acts 2:36). And in the nearest thing to a definition of faith in the Bible we read: "Faith is the assurance *(hypostasis)* of things hoped for, the conviction *(elenchos)* of things not seen" (Heb 11:1, RSV).

The Catholic magisterium has reinforced this biblical teaching. In 1679 the Holy Office condemned the proposition that supernatural or salutary faith is compatible with a merely probable knowledge of the fact of revelation or with a real fear that God may not have spoken.[32] In a document directed against the Modernists (1907) the Holy Office condemned the proposition, "The assent of faith ultimately rests on an accumulation of probabilities."[33] Regarding faith as certain, the magisterium normally phrases its professions of faith in terms which express firm assent.[34]

These general principles, based on the nature of faith in the abstract, should not be taken as ruling out legitimate doubts and disputes about whether a given doctrine does or does not belong to the deposit of Christian faith. It is also possible for believers to experience painful involuntary doubts. In the gospels we read of a man who cries out to Jesus, "I do believe; help my unbelief!" (Mk 9:24). Many Christians are weak in faith, and even the saints have sometimes confessed undergoing excruciating doubts while at the same time continuing to adhere dog-

---

31. *Dei Filius*, chap. 3 (DS 3008).
32. Holy Office, Condemned Propositions of A.D. 1679, prop. 21 (DS 2121).
33. Holy Office, Decree *Lamentabili sane*, prop. 25 (DS 3025).
34. E.g. Pseudo-Anthanasian Creed *Quicumque* (DS 76); Lateran IV, Decree *Firmiter credimus* (DS 800); Tridentine Profession of Faith (DS 1862); Anti-Modernist Oath (DS 3537).

gedly to the word of God. Because faith is faith, it is always vulnerable to doubt. Since the object of faith, as we shall see, is neither given in experience nor strictly demonstrated, the believer is conscious of being able at any time to retract the assent of faith without violence to the laws of rationality. Serious temptations against faith may sometimes be the way in which God weans us from an excessive reliance on rational arguments and makes us existentially aware that faith is a free submission to God's testimony apprehended with the help of grace.

Thomas Aquinas gives a brief but helpful analysis of the firmness and precariousness of faith. Faith is firm, he says, inasmuch as it rests on the totally reliable word of God. Yet it has a kind of inbuilt insecurity or mental unrest (which Thomas calls *cogitatio*) inasmuch as the mind remains in quest of a full understanding based on direct vision or cogent reasons. As a mode of knowledge, faith surpasses mere opinion, but falls short of demonstration or self-evidence.[35]

Obscurity

The obscurity of faith is closely connected with its freedom and affects the mode of its certitude. This obscurity can be expounded from several points of view. In the first place, the primary contents of revelation are mysteries, such as the Trinity, the incarnation, and the life of grace and glory. Of these mysteries we can speak only haltingly, since we lack comprehensive knowledge of the subject matter and have to rely on inadequate natural analogies. It is not surprising, therefore, that we cannot adequately understand how it is possible for one God to exist as three divine persons, or how Jesus can be fully God and at the same time fully man. These and other contents of revelation offer endless food for reflection but can never be mastered by the human mind. According to Vatican I "divine mysteries by their very nature so exceed the created intellect that, even after they have been communicated and received in faith, they remain covered by the veil of faith itself and shrouded as it were in darkness as long as in this mortal life 'we are away from the Lord; for we walk by faith, not by sight'" (2 Cor 5:6-7).[36] Paul frequently speaks of the dark and enigmatic character of faith in contrast to the brightness and clarity of the vision for which we hope in the life to come (e.g., 1 Cor 13:12). He claims to impart "a hidden and secret wisdom of God" that cannot be discerned except with the help of the divine Spirit (1 Cor 2:7, 14).

A further reason for the obscurity of faith lies in the fact that its contents are not intrinsically evident but are accepted on external authority. If we could strictly prove that the contents of faith were true we would adhere to them not by faith but by reason. Reason may be able to

---

35. *Summa theologiae* 2-2.2.1.
36. Vatican I, *Dei Filius*, chap. 4 (DS 3016).

show that we have the right and the obligation to believe. However, the arguments of credibility, as we shall presently see, are not stringent; they leave room for the individual to reject the conclusion to which they point. Otherwise faith would not be free.

Reasonableness

A fifth attribute of faith, according to Catholic teaching, is its conformity to reason. This is understood to mean not only that there are objectively valid grounds for professing the true faith but also that sufficient grounds must be perceived. For if one assented without assurance of truth, such assent would be rash and therefore sinful. Faith according to Vatican I is not a "blind movement of the mind."[37]

The reasonableness of the act of faith has to be reconciled with its supernaturality, its freedom, its obscurity, and its certitude. Vatican I was conscious of this problem and proposed the elements of a solution. On the one hand, it stated that the contents of faith are not demonstrable by intrinsic arguments, i.e., arguments that would directly prove the truth of the doctrines themselves.[38] On the other hand the Council maintained that the Christian revelation, and the Catholic church as the bearer of that revelation, have "evident credibility" by reason of the wonderful dispositions of divine providence in favor of the Catholic church.[39] In its discussion of credibility the Council distinguished between "interior helps of the Holy Spirit" and "external arguments" *(argumenta externa)*.[40] These may be separately considered.

By the "interior helps of the Holy Spirit," the Council apparently meant the attractions of grace that incline one to investigate and acknowledge the truth of the Christian testimony. The necessity of such interior helps is implied in the supernaturality of faith, discussed above. The psychological effect of such grace is described in a quotation taken from the Second Council of Orange to the effect that no one can assent to the gospel as necessary for salvation "without the illumination and inspiration of the Holy Spirit, who gives everyone joy (or ease: *suavitatem*) in consenting to the truth and believing it."[41]

The "external arguments of revelation" are also called "divine works" *(facta divina)*.[42] By these Vatican I means the signs given in history,

---

37. Ibid., chap. 3 (DS 3010).
38. Ibid. (DS 3008).
39. Ibid. (DS 3013).
40. Ibid. (DS 3009).
41. Ibid. (DS 3010, quoting Orange II, can. 7 (DS 377). The Latin word *suavitatem* is sometimes translated "ease and joy," as in Josef Neuner and Jacques Dupuis, eds., *The Christian Faith* (Staten Island: Alba House, 1981), no. 1919.
42. Ibid. (DS 3009).

particularly miracles and fulfilled prophecies. More specifically, the Council mentions the signs worked through Moses, the prophets, and the apostles, but especially through Jesus Christ. Several paragraphs later Vatican I refers to the Catholic church herself as being "a great and perpetual motive of credibility and irrefutable testimony to her own divine mission."[43] In this connection the Council speaks of the marvelous expansion of the church, her unity, her durability, her holiness, and her fruitfulness in all that is good. In effect the Council is here claiming that the Catholic church is a moral or sociological miracle—an exception to the general laws governing human societies. Here again, the Council merely indicates the line of argument, leaving it up to theologians to develop it. Before Vatican I issued this statement several theologians had propounded this argument. The Belgian cardinal Victor Dechamps, who was present at the Council, had developed this argument from the church as a living reality in several of his apologetical works.

In summary, Vatican I commended several distinct apologetical approaches to the issue of the reasonableness of faith. It did not press the historical argument from biblical miracles and prophecies to the exclusion of arguments from church history, nor the latter to the exclusion of the former. The Council put its blessing on both types of argument and made no effort to rank them in order of merit. The text of Vatican I could be read as implying that a convergent argument based on both sets of data might be the most persuasive.

A further question is whether the external signs are sufficient to bring conviction without the inner helps of the Holy Spirit. Vatican I did not settle this question. It stated simply that the external signs, in combination with the interior helps given by the Spirit, suffice to render our faith a "reasonable service."[44] The Council thus situated itself in the actual order and did not raise the theoretical question whether reason alone, unaided by grace, could achieve certitude. Conversely, the Council did not raise or decide the question whether the interior inspirations of the Spirit could be so luminous that it would be reasonable for a person to believe without external signs accrediting the revelation. To judge from the language of Vatican I, it would appear that in the normal case the inner and outer helps are simultaneously operative.

DEBATES ABOUT GRACE AND CREDIBILITY

The previous discussion of the properties of faith gives rise to a serious question that has perplexed Catholic theologians and occasioned deeper reflection. The objection may be formulated in terms of the

---

43. Ibid. (DS 3013).
44. Ibid. (DS 3009), with a reference to Rom 12:1 in Vulgate translation.

freedom and certitude of faith. If the evidence is rationally compelling, it would appear that anyone who perceived the evidence would necessarily believe, as Hermes contended. But if the evidence is not compelling, it would seem unreasonable to proffer the supremely firm assent that faith is supposed to be.

An ingenious reply to this difficulty was proposed by the French Jesuit, Pierre Rousselot (1878-1915), in a celebrated article published in 1910.[45] He held that the signs of credibility do not produce a deductive certitude that would compel assent but that they have to be interpreted by a process of discernment which can be, in its own way, fully convincing. He added that the proper discernment of the signs requires that the person be subjectively attuned to their meaning. Just as the lover alone may be equipped to read the meaning of the gestures of the beloved, so a person who is enlightened by divine grace has the needed equipment to interpret the signs of God's presence in history. To a person deprived of grace, the signs would not yield their divine meaning. Such a person would be like a tone-deaf person at a concert. Rousselot's theory accounted neatly for the freedom of the act of faith (since grace invited a free response), for the necessity of grace, for the reasonableness of faith, and for its supreme certitude.

Impressive though it was, Rousselot's position was strongly opposed by the majority of the scholastic theologians teaching in the dominant schools and universities.[46] They insisted that grace is not needed to form a firm judgment of credibility, though faith itself does require interior grace. In 1950 Pius XII, in his encyclical *Humani generis*, seemed to lend his support to this latter view. He declared that the human mind may experience difficulties in forming the judgment of credibility "even though God has provided such numerous and wonderful signs of credibility that the divine origin of the Christian religion could be certainly proved even by the merely natural light of reason."[47] But it is doubtful whether the pope intended to settle such a long and complicated theological dispute by this passing statement. Followers of Rousselot pointed out that in the passage the pope was explaining how it was possible to

---

45. Pierre Rousselot, "Les yeux de la foi," *Recherches de science religieuse* 1 (1910), pp. 241-59, 444-75. Rousselot profoundly influenced many contemporary and later writers on the theology of faith, including Guy de Broglie, Karl Adam, Eugène Masure, Jean Mouroux, Henri Vignon, Felix Malmberg, and Henri Bouillard.

46. In his own day, Rousselot was opposed by Dominicans such as Marie-Dominique Chenu and, even more sharply, by Jesuits such as Christian Pesch, Louis Billot, and Stéphane Harent. On the critical reception of Rousselot see Roger Aubert, *Le Problème de l'Acte de Foi*, 2nd ed., rev. (Louvain: E. Warney, 1950), pp. 470-511.

47. *Humani generis*, AAS 42 (1950) 561 (DS 3876).

resist *both* the external evidences and the interior impulses of grace. The statement about the natural light of reason appeared only in a concessive clause, introduced by "even though." Thus the meaning may have been that resistance to the evidence is possible even if the opponents of Rousselot were correct about the probative value of the signs.[48]

Rousselot had a lasting impact on the Catholic theology of faith, not least because he called attention to certain texts from Thomas Aquinas concerning the illuminative power of grace itself. Rousselot showed clearly that the assent of faith cannot be a mere consequence of the evidential power of the signs, perceived by the cold light of speculative reason. Modern Scholasticism, he charged, excessively preoccupied with the powers of unaided reason, falsified the whole question of the approach to faith, which, as Augustine and Orange II had shown, takes place under the influence of grace. The signs of credibility, perceived by the natural light of reason, could not possibly justify the supremely firm assent of faith. But there was no need for such a natural justification since grace was always at work. While the scholastic authors of the day were trying to justify faith in terms of complicated apologetical arguments, Rousselot was able to show that the normal believer relies not on formal intellectual proofs but rather on a spontaneous perception of the evidence too subtle and complex to be spelled out in syllogistic arguments. For this spontaneous discernment, the "connaturality" produced by grace can surely be important.

Other theologians, while profiting from the insights of Rousselot, have departed on some points from his conclusions, adhering more closely than he did to the full teaching of Thomas Aquinas.[49] They object that Rousselot, unlike Thomas, treated faith itself as though it were an intellectual induction from the signs of credibility. For Thomas, on the contrary, the signs of credibility are inducements rather than proofs. These signs point the way to faith but do not cause it; nor does faith, once achieved, depend on external signs. Rousselot, therefore, demands too much from the signs of credibility.

For Aquinas, the true cause of the assent of faith is divine grace,

---

48. For the interpretation of *Humani generis* on the judgment of credibility see Roger Aubert, "Questioni attuali intorno all'atto di Fede," *Problemi e Orientamenti di Teologia Dommatica* 2 (Milan: Marzorati, 1947), pp. 655-708, esp. note 7, pp. 704-5; also Juan Alfaro, *Fides, Spes, Caritas* (ed. nova; Rome: Pontificia Universitas Gregoriana, 1963), p. 386; and Guy de Broglie, *Pour une théorie rationnelle de l'acte de foi*, Part II (Paris: Institut Catholique, n.d.), p. 76[4].

49. Among the more recent authors who follow Thomas Aquinas in partial opposition to Rousselot are Jan Walgrave, Edouard Dhanis, Louis Monden, Juan Alfaro, and René Latourelle.

impelling the believer to submit to the word of God. We believe not because of the evidence of credibility but because of the uncreated testimony of God himself, recognized by an interior instinct of grace. Without perceiving grace as an object, we allow ourselves to be led by it. The signs of credibility are important because they make it evident that the act of faith is not arbitrary and unfounded. They make it possible for the church to gain a hearing for her message on the part of persons who might be inclined to write off the gospel as an illusion.

THE NECESSITY OF FAITH

The Catholic church has consistently taught, as have the mainline Protestant churches and the Orthodox, that divine faith is necessary for justification in this life and for salvation in the life to come. Many biblical texts assert this.

The theme of justification by faith runs like a refrain through the letters of Paul, especially Romans and Galatians. He frequently asserts that we are made righteous not by performing "works of the law" but by faith in Christ (e.g., Rom 3:28, Gal 2:16). The necessity of faith for eternal life is a constant theme of John's gospel (3:36; 5:24; 8:24). Other texts state that unbelief disqualifies people from salvation (Mk 16:16) and that without faith it is impossible to please God (Heb 11:6).

Following scriptural texts such as these, the Council of Trent declared that faith is "the beginning of human salvation, the foundation and root of all justification."[50] Vatican I stated that it is impossible to be justified without faith and that one must persevere in faith to the end in order to attain eternal life.[51]

These statements, as they stand, can be readily accepted if they have reference only to people who have the gospel credibly presented to them, so that they cannot reject it without sinning against the light. But a difficulty arises when one tries to apply them to the unevangelized. For centuries Christian theologians have tried to grapple with the problem whether and how salvation is possible to those who, without fault on their own part, are ignorant of the biblical and Christian revelation. Are they saved without faith? Does revelation come to them in some other way? Or can they have saving faith without first receiving revelation? Or finally, if salvation is not open to them, can they attain to some natural beatitude short of the beatific vision?

It would be tedious in this chapter to review all the theories that have

---

50. Decree on Justification, chap. 8 (DS 1532).
51. *Dei Filius*, chap. 3 (DS 3012).

been concocted over the centuries to answer questions such as these.[52] We may begin by consulting the official teaching of the church in modern times. Confronted by the threat of liberalism and indifferentism, Pius IX in his encyclical, *Quanto conficiamur moerore* (1863) recalled the necessity of embracing and adhering to the Catholic faith. He added, however, that God would not permit anyone who was free from voluntary fault, and who was outside the true faith through "invincible ignorance," to suffer eternal punishment.[53] He did not directly answer the questions whether such persons are saved and, if so, whether they are saved without faith.

Vatican II registers a further development. In the Decree on Ecumenism it is clearly stated that non-Catholic Christians can have supernatural faith.[54] In the Decree on the Church's Missionary Activity the Council declared that "God, in ways known to himself, can lead those inculpably ignorant of the gospel to that faith without which it is impossible to please him."[55] Again in the Dogmatic Constitution on the Church[56] and in the Pastoral Constitution on the Church in the Modern World[57] the secret working of grace in the hearts of all human beings is affirmed. The Constitution on the Church goes so far as to say that the helps necessary for salvation (presumably including the grace that leads to faith) are not denied to those who, without personal fault, "have not arrived at an explicit knowledge of God, but who strive to live a good life, thanks to his grace."[58]

From the text just quoted it is not clear whether the Council intends to affirm that atheists can achieve eternal salvation without having come to believe in God before they die. On this point a number of theological opinions are tolerated. Many refer to the text from Hebrews which says: "Whoever would draw near to God must believe that he exists and that he rewards those who seek him" (Heb 11:6). Following certain statements of Thomas Aquinas, many of the older theologians surmised that those to whom the gospel has not yet been proclaimed could be saved provided that they had explicit faith in the existence of God and in God's saving providence. After the promulgation of the

---

52. For a rather complete survey, extending the earlier works of Louis Capéran and Riccardo Lombardi, see Maurice Eminyan, *The Theology of Salvation* (Boston: St. Paul, 1960).
53. *Quanto conficiamur moerore* (DS 2866).
54. *Unitatis redintegratio*, nos. 3, 12, 14, and 23.
55. *Ad gentes*, no. 7.
56. *Lumen gentium*, no. 16.
57. *Gaudium et spes*, no. 22.
58. *Lumen gentium*, no. 16.

gospel in a form that effectively reached them, such persons would be obliged to believe explicitly in the Trinity and the incarnation.[59]

These speculations reflected a more objectivisitic perspective on faith and revelation than is common in contemporary theology. Many today would say that the secret workings of grace in the soul provide sufficient light for the individual to make a kind of inarticulate act of faith that is at least minimally sufficient for salvation. Faith is seen primarily as a lived acceptance of, or openness to, the grace of God, which is always present to persons of good will. Even though such implicit faith is deficient in failing to grasp the substantive content of revelation, it does reach out toward that content insofar as it has a dynamism toward the reality of God's redemptive action from which all grace derives. Thus a distinction is made between implicit faith, which cannot affirm its own content, and explicit faith, which adheres consciously to God's redemptive word in history.

Karl Rahner is well known for his thesis that all faith, even that of persons who do not explicitly believe in God, is implicitly or, as he puts it, "anonymously" theistic and Christian.[60] By this he means that such faith lives off God's grace in Christ and brings the believer into a dynamic relationship with God and Christ. Such implicit faith, Rahner would maintain, is sufficient for justification and salvation.

Rahner's theory is by no means free from objections. Many theologians consider that it minimizes the salutary impact of evangelization and the importance of explicit faith. In favor of Rahner's theory, one may say that it gives a plausible explanation of how unevangelized persons might be saved by the grace of Christ and have real supernatural faith without having been told of God's saving deeds in history.

Granted that supernatural faith is necessary, it must further be asked whether it is sufficient for justification and salvation. Martin Luther, followed by many of the early Protestants, held that faith was sufficient. However, by faith he meant more than an intellectual assent to the contents of revelation.[61] Over and above such assent (which he called "historical faith") Luther required a lively personal trust in God's re-

59. See Eminyan, *Theology of Salvation*, p. 24; de Aldama, *De virtutibus*, p. 812.

60. Karl Rahner, "Anonymous and Explicit Faith," *Theological Investigations* 16 (New York: Seabury, 1979), pp. 52-59. Cf. Anita Röper, *The Anonymous Christian* (New York: Sheed & Ward, 1966), with an important Afterword by Klaus Riesenhuber.

61. For the views of Luther and early Lutherans on faith as related to justification see the articles of Eric W. Gritsch, Robert W. Bertram, and John F. Johnson in H. George Anderson et al. eds., *Justification by Faith. Lutherans and Catholics in Dialogue* 7 (Minneapolis: Augsburg, 1985).

demptive work on behalf of oneself (which Lutherans called "fiducial faith" or "faith in the promises"). The Catholics of the sixteenth century, adhering to the scholastic tradition, understood faith to mean a grace-inspired cognitive acceptance of the word of God set forth in scripture and tradition.[62] Such intellectual assent, they maintained, was necessary but not sufficient either for justification or for salvation. These Catholics were able to quote from Paul that faith without love profits nothing (1 Cor 13:2) and from James that faith by itself, without works, is dead (Jas 2:17). The Council of Trent defined against the Lutherans and others that it is possible to lose the grace of God without losing faith itself, and that the faith that remains, even without charity, is the Christian gift of faith.[63] On these points Protestants and Catholics contradicted each other.

Must Protestants and Catholics continue today to deny each other's positions? Both sides are inclined to admit that part of the difficulty, at least, was caused by terminology. The two sides were operating on the basis of different concepts of faith, each having a certain foundation in scripture. In some New Testament texts, faith means an obedient acceptance of the gospel, a full personal response that works itself out through love (cf. Gal 5:6). If faith is understood in this broader sense, both parties can agree that it is sufficient for justification and salvation. Vatican II made a notable ecumenical advance by bringing into the concept of faith, as set forth in the Constitution on Divine Revelation, the factors of trust, obedience, and personal commitment.[64] This advance does not totally overcome the theological disputes inherited from the sixteenth century, but it does allow them to be treated primarily as theological debates and perhaps not as church-dividing doctrines.

THE ECCLESIAL DIMENSION

Influenced by the prevalent individualism, we commonly think of faith as an act or attitude of an individual. There is some truth in this, since it is the individual, in the last analysis, who is a believer and who is to be judged for his or her response to God's grace. But to be realistic we must also recognize that most believers get their beliefs from their parents or from the environment in which they are raised. Faith is a social fact insofar as it is transmitted through the family or community.

The autonomy of the individual varies greatly from one culture to

---

62. On Catholic reactions to Lutheranism see the articles of Jill Raitt, Carl J. Peter, and Avery Dulles, in ibid.

63. Decree on Justification, can. 28 (DS 1578).

64. *Dei Verbum*, no. 5.

another. In tribal societies, which existed long ago in Europe and still thrive in many Third World countries, the individual's religion can hardly be other than that of the social group. To a great extent that is still the case in some Arab countries and even in a highly industrialized society such as Japan. By comparison, Western Europe and North America are highly individualistic. It is relatively easy to lose or change one's religious affiliation without impairing one's status in the society. The society has become secularized with the result that religion is viewed as a private matter.

The latter situation has theological implications. It forces the churches to become, in many respects, voluntary groups, like clubs. Thus it becomes difficult to regard any religious adherence as truly necessary. Churches are seen as gatherings of like-minded believers.

Under these circumstances Catholics have to remind themselves that it is almost impossible to attain Catholic faith except through trusting affiliation with the church as a social body. Faith therefore has an ecclesial dimension.[65] The revelation of God, which forms the object of faith, was originally delivered to a nation, that of Israel. In the early centuries Christians, without loss of their membership in different tribes and nations, saw themselves as members of the People of God of the New Covenant. According to Catholic theology, the church is and remains the believer par excellence. For the individual, to believe means to share in the faith of the church. When popes, bishops, or councils teach what is to be believed, they must transmit the faith of the church. In creeds and confessions believers say together, "we believe" or "we confess." Individuals, even though they are bishops or popes, can lose the faith, but the faith of the church is indefectible.

Not only is the church the great believer; it is also the great witness to the faith. By its very existence, constituted with its unique history and attributes, it is a sign of credibility confirming its own message. Vatican I, as already mentioned, spoke of the Catholic church as the "sign raised up among the nations" inviting all to believe.[66] Vatican II, in numerous texts, called for a renewal of the church in order that the sign of Christ might shine more brightly in our time.[67]

Finally, the church enters into the object of faith. As stated in the creed, "We believe in the church" (credimus . . . ecclesiam). As a sociological reality, the church is open to inspection by anyone who

---

65. See Avery Dulles, "The Church and the Faith of Catholics," *Revelation and the Quest for Unity* (Washington, D.C.: Corpus, 1968), pp. 102-114.

66. *Dei Filius*, chap. 3 (DS 3014).

67. *Lumen gentium*, no. 15; cf. *Gaudium et spes*, nos. 19, 21 and 43; also *Unitatis redintegratio*, no. 4.

looks at the facts, but as the body and spouse of Christ, as the People of God and the temple of the Holy Spirit, the church is discernible only to the eye of faith. Faith is for the Catholic an adherence both to Christ and to the church, for the two are, in the plan of salvation, inseparable.

The sociological Catholicism that currently appears to be on the wane made it in some ways easier to identify fully with the faith of the church. But at the same time, it tended to make the individual too passive. In the religiously fluid situation of our time—at least in the North Atlantic countries—faith is inevitably becoming a more deeply personal commitment. This situation increases the risks of sectarianism, individualism, and loss of faith, but at the same time it encourages the individual to accept full responsibility for his or her religious stance. Free and voluntary participation in the religious vision of the community can make for a more dynamic type of Christianity in which the character of faith as a lived commitment to the unseen God is more vibrantly experienced.

CHAPTER 8

The Systematic Theology of Faith: A Protestant Perspective

Alexander J. McKelway

INTRODUCTION

Martin Luther's (1483-1546) discovery of the evangelical principle of "justification by faith alone," gave the concept of faith its characteristic Protestant definition.

At last, by the mercy of God, meditating day and night, I gave heed to the context of the words, namely, "In the righteousness of God is revealed, as it is written, 'He who through faith is righteous shall live' " [Romans 1:17]. There I began to understand that the righteousness of God is that by which the righteous lives by a gift of God, namely by faith. And this is the meaning: The righteousness of God is revealed by the gospel, namely, the passive righteousness with which merciful God justifies us by faith. . . . Here I felt that I was altogether born again and had entered paradise itself through open gates.[1]

Luther claimed that we are justified—by faith—alone. *Justification* means to be made just by an act of God's righteousness, which from our standpoint can only be understood as an "alien righteousness," not our own. This saving grace becomes ours by *faith*, which, because it is a "gift

---

1. John Dillenberger, *Martin Luther: Selections from His Writings* (Garden City, N.Y.: Doubleday, 1961), p. 11.

of God," is not a product of our decision or action, but which, on the other hand, is always accompanied by our trusting in the action of Christ on our behalf. Because faith is both an act of God and our reception of that act, it encompasses the whole event of salvation. Thus Luther in his famous paratranslation of Romans 3:28 could add the word *"allein,"* so that we are "justified by faith *alone* apart from works of law."

John Calvin (1509-1564) always acknowledged his dependence upon an essential agreement with Luther, and the doctrine of faith was no exception.

> We shall have a complete definition of faith if we say that it is a steady and certain knowledge of the divine benevolence toward us, which, being founded on the truth of the gratuitous promises in Christ, is both revealed to our minds and confirmed to our hearts by the Holy Spirit.[2]

Following Luther, Calvin recognized in the event of faith a dialectical relation between a divine act (a gratuity "confirmed to our hearts by the Holy Spirit") and a human act (of "steady and certain knowledge"). The difference was that Calvin located the original saving action of God in the divine election before creation, and therefore found it unnecessary to invest the faith act itself with the determinative importance characteristic of Luther and his followers (of which more below).

The meaning of faith in Protestantism turns around three assertions: 1) that the *origin* of faith is located in the initiating action of God and not in human will; 2) that the *content* of faith is primarily divine activity and only secondarily our appropriation of, or attitude toward, that activity; and 3) that the *effect* of faith is therefore the actualization of saving grace. It is complete in itself and needs no subsequent belief or action for its authentication. Quite obviously, these three assertions bear the burden of the paradoxical claim that "faith," which by any definition refers to some kind of human thought, is in respect to justification *not* a human activity, but an activity initiated and completed by God. In what follows we will briefly describe the biblical and theological background of this view of faith and then set out the distinctive features of Luther's doctrine and describe the way Calvin appropriated and altered it. It will then be our task to trace the gradual dissolution of the Reformers' dialectical view of faith as theological attention focused more and more on its human aspects. In the debate over "faith and/or works," it

---

2. John Calvin, *Institutes of the Christian Religion*, ed. John T. McNeill (Philadelphia: Westminster, 1960), Book III/Chapter 2/Paragraph 7.

came about that Protestant theology developed a conception of faith *as a work*—a work of doctrinal assent (orthodoxy), of emotional experience (Pietism), of reason (Deism), of subjective feeling (romanticism), and finally of virtue (liberalism). In conclusion we will consider Karl Barth's attempt to recover the meaning of the Reformation doctrine of faith by decentralizing its distinctive form ("justification by faith alone") in favor of its substance ("salvation by grace alone").

BACKGROUND OF THE REFORMATION DOCTRINE OF FAITH

The Biblical Witness

A Protestant account of the biblical view of faith is presented elsewhere in this volume. Here we need only note certain elements of the biblical witness which support the Reformers' interpretation of faith.

The extent to which the Reformers' doctrine of faith was informed by distinctively Old Testament sources is difficult to assess because they always read the Old Testament in light of the New.[3] At the same time, the Reformers were aware of the Old Testament's presentation of faith as not only belief in, assent to, and affirmation of God's promises but as well a matter of "trust" (cf. Pss 37, 40, 62, 115, etc.). More importantly, Old Testament concepts such as *tsedaqah* (righteousness) and *hesed* (faithfulness) suggest that it is only through God's righteousness and faithfulness that human beings are made capable of similar attitudes and actions.[4] Thus, faith in the Old Testament is presented as a result of God's faithfulness and not simply as a firm trust in God's promises. This was confirmed for Luther when, in his early lectures on the psalms, he encountered the cry of Christ in Psalm 22: "My God, my God, why hast thou forsaken me?" For Luther, this meant that faith includes doubt and despair.

Whatever may be learned about the nature of faith from the Old Testament, it is clear that it was from the New Testament, and more especially from the writing of the Apostle Paul, that Luther drew his doctrine of justification by faith alone. Again, we need only note the main lines of Paul's thinking in respect to the origin, content, and effect of faith.

It cannot be denied that Paul understood faith also in terms of human activity. In 1 Thessalonians he speaks of faith as belief in the saving

---

3. Paul Althaus, *The Theology of Martin Luther* (Philadelphia: Fortress, 1966), pp. 93ff. According to Althaus, Luther's interpretation of Abraham's faith in Genesis is simply an extension of his understanding of Romans 4.

4. Gerhard von Rad, *Old Testament Theology* (Edinburgh: Olive and Boyd, 1962), pp. 372-374.

work and promises of Christ, which conviction he obviously takes as a virtue and can even call a "work" (1 Thes 1:3).[5] Furthermore, in 1 Corinthians and elsewhere, Paul makes it clear that faith (in the sense of conviction) must result in love—to which it is inferior (1 Cor 13:13). The understanding of faith as a conviction productive of divine benefit may also be suggested in such statements as: "Abraham believed God and it was reckoned to him as righteousness" (Rom 4:3).

But if Paul can speak of faith/belief as if it were the cause of salvation, "We have believed in Christ Jesus, in order to be justified by faith in Christ," he prefaces that remark (and his whole doctrine) with the reminder that we "know that a man is not justified by works" (Gal 2:15). Paul's insistence that faith is opposed to works makes impossible any definition of faith as dependent upon human capacity or initiative. While Paul does not speak of faith as a gift, it would appear that, for him, not only was the reckoning of faith "as righteousness" a gift (Rom 4:4) but the disposition of faith as well. This seems all the more likely when we consider Paul's strong predestinarianism which places the result of faith (justification) at the end of a series of God's acts of foreknowing, predestining, and calling (cf. Rom 8:30 and Eph 1:11).

For Paul, the *content* of faith appears to have two sides. On the one hand, it involves a knowledge of and trust in the promises of God (as in the case of Abraham) and the life, death, and resurrection of Christ (as in the case of Christians). And yet, this knowledge of God in Christ is, in its salvific power, certainly no work or vigorous "belief," and even less mere "assent." Such a knowledge, such a belief and trust in God, is itself a function of God's grace working through the apostolic witness. Faith too is God's work: "You have come to know God, or rather to be known by God" (Gal 4:9). For Paul, faith contains the act of God—and only in a secondary sense our acknowledgment of and obedience to that act. Thus, because faith is an act initiated and sustained by God, its *effect* is salvation. Because of its divine origin it is complete in itself: "Since we are justified by faith, we have peace with God through our Lord Jesus Christ" (Rom 5:1).

Our conclusion must be that Paul held a polar, or dialectical, view of faith. He could speak of it as God's work and as a human activity of believing and discipleship. But within this dialectic one thing remains clear. When Paul speaks of *saving* faith, he means faith as God's gift—

---

5. In agreement with this aspect of Paul the idea of faith in the gospels leans toward a human "believing" in God's saving activity (Mk 1:14) and trusting in his mercy (Mt 21:22). In the Gospel of John it is mostly a matter of perceiving the saving light of Christ (Jn 1:12). On the other hand, even in those places where "faith" is said to bring about healing (Jn 4:46ff, Mk 2:5) it is perfectly clear that it was *Jesus* who did the deed.

and never our work. When he speaks of our response to that gift, then faith may be understood in terms of human possibilities.

The Tradition

Protestantism's assertion of "justification by faith alone" is essentially a claim about the priority and sufficiency of divine grace over any human capacity or activity. The theological genius behind that assertion was Saint Augustine of Hippo (354-430), the "Doctor of Grace." For Augustine, salvation was the result of a divine predestination by which a person is called and enabled by the power of God's grace to believe and to produce the fruits of righteousness. Grace "goes before him unwilling, that he may will; it follows him when willing, that he may not will in vain."[6] Everything depends upon God—nothing upon the creature. "Grant us what you command and command us what you will."[7]

Augustine puts such stress on the totality of God's initiative, that he must speak of faith also as wrought by God.[8] Even as an act of our will, faith is nonetheless a result of God's prior act. "If God has mercy we also will; our willing belongs to the same mercy."[9] In his *Confessions* Augustine always acknowledges that his coming to faith was not his own work. "Late it was that I loved you. . . . And look, you were within me and I was outside."[10] "Thou didst convert me to Thyself."[11]

We cannot, however, attribute Luther's doctrine of faith to Augustine. For Augustine, the point of the statements cited in the previous paragraph was not to hold up the saving efficacy of "faith alone," but rather to drive home the principle of salvation by "grace alone."[12] Augustine does not conflate grace and faith as Luther does. More often than not, Augustine speaks of faith, not in terms of the decisive point of connection between God and human being, but as "belief." Faith is correct thoughts about God. Thus, in his *Enchiridion on Faith, Hope, and Love*, he speaks of "faith" as merely the disposition to believe, so that "faith may have for its object evil as well as good."[13] Augustine's under-

---

6. Reinhold Seeberg, *Text-Book of the History of Doctrines*, trans. Charles E. Hay (Grand Rapids, Mich.: Baker, 1964), p. 346.

7. Augustine, *The Confessions of St. Augustine*, trans. Rex Warner (New York: New American Library, 1963), p. 236 (X. 29).

8. Seeberg, *History of Doctrines*, p. 347.

9. Ibid., p. 339.

10. Augustine, *Confessions* 235 (X. 27).

11. Seeberg, *History of Doctrines*, p. 340.

12. Ibid., p. 352.

13. Augustine, *The Enchridion on Faith, Hope, and Love*, ed. Henry Paolucci (South Bend, Ind.: Regnery/Gateway, 1961), p. 7 (VIII).

standing of faith is not inconsistent with that of the Epistle of James, where "faith without works is dead." Augustine denies that "those who persevere in . . . wicked courses shall nevertheless be saved on account of their faith . . ."[14] Such a view of faith places it in the service of other virtues, such as love—which for Augustine was always the higher principle: "When there is a question as to whether a man is good, one does not ask what he believes or what he hopes, but what he loves."[15] It was not Augustine's doctrine of faith as such, but the implications of his doctrine of grace that compelled his Protestant successors to interpret the former in light of the latter.

Augustine's emphasis upon grace exercised a similar influence upon Catholic theology long before the Reformation—at least to the extent that faith was presented in terms of a dialectical relation between the initiative of God and the response of the believer. Peter Lombard (c. 1100-1160), for instance, endorsed Augustine's superimposition of God's work over our own. "When God crowns our merit, he crowns his own gifts."[16] The doctrine of merit was never conceived in late medieval theology so as to deny the necessity of grace. The same thing holds true for the doctrine of faith. Even the concept of salvation by faith *alone* was not unknown to the Scholastics.[17] Peter Lombard went so far as to assert that, in faith, righteousness could be imputed to the believer. "Through his very believing [Abraham] received what was promised and was *made* righteous."[18] Augustine's requirement that faith find expression in love was followed closely by the Schoolmen. Faith is a gift, but it is one which provides an infused habit to do good. For Peter Lombard and other Scholastics influenced by Augustine, faith involved works, but neither faith (as human thought) nor works (as human action) were conceived as possible without the prior, initiating, and continuing grace of God. It was only later, under the impact of Nominalism, that there arose a concept of merit as sufficient in itself for the reward of eternal blessedness. Even then, it should be noted, a "congru-

---

14. Augustine, *Enchridion*, p. 80 (LXVII).

15. Ibid., p. 135 (CXVII).

16. H. G. Anderson, T. A. Murphy, and J. A. Burges, eds., *Justification by Faith* (Minneapolis: Augsburg, 1985), p. 150.

17. Ibid., p. 150. Karlfried Froehlich, the author of the chapter: "Justification Language in the Middle Ages," notes that this phrase appears in commentaries on Paul by Marius Victorinus, Ambrosiaster, and, astonishingly, Pelagius.

18. Ibid., p. 151, emphasis mine. Froehlich shows, however, that the meaning given to *sola fide* by Catholic dogmatics moved in quite a different direction from that taken by Luther. The Lombard adopted the interpretation of Ambrosiaster, who held that faith alone is sufficient when there is no time for works, as, for example, in the case of the thief crucified with Jesus.

ous" merit was considered sufficient for salvation either because it was empowered by God's prior grace, or (and more usually) it was graciously "accepted" by God.[19]

We may outline the medieval understanding of faith by employing the specialized vocabulary developed by the Lombard and the later Scholastics in the following way:

I. *FIDES QUAE CREDITUR*	II. *FIDES QUA CREDITUR*
"faith which is believed" (faith as knowledge, as mere content)	"faith by which it is believed" (faith as act)
A. *fides informis* or *historica* a crude acknowledgment of the reality of God and Christ, which under the influence of grace may become	A. *fides divina* faith as initiated by God
B. *fides implicita* a predisposition to believe or, a trust in the superior knowledge of the church	B. *fides actualis* actualization of grace in the heart of the believer, or *fides reflexiva* faith subjectively aware of its object, or *fides specialis* or *propria* a saving faith, trust
C. *fides explicita* a conscious grasp of the essentials of the gospel	C. *fides caritate formata* "faith formed by love" the necessary fulfillment of faith in works of love

Salvation by faith was not a conception alien to late medieval theology—indeed, the notion was inescapable, given the breadth of meaning attached to "faith." From the foregoing it should also be clear that the Protestant doctrine of faith took shape within this framework and differed from the Catholic in the emphasis it placed upon the *fides qua creditur* as initiated by God and actualized in the heart of the believer (II A & B).

FAITH IN REFORMATION THOUGHT

Martin Luther's Doctrine of Faith

In 1521 and 1522, while sequestered in the Wartburg, Luther translated and wrote introductions to the books of the New Testament. His preface to Paul's letter to the Romans includes some important definitions, among them his understanding of the word "faith."

---

19. Ibid., p. 150.

Faith is not something dreamed, a human illusion, although this is what many people understand by the term. Whenever they see that it is not followed either by an improvement in morals or by good works, while much is still being said about faith, they fall into the error of declaring that faith is not enough, that we must do "works" if we are to become upright and attain salvation. . . . They miss the point; in their hearts and out of their own resources, they conjure up an idea which they call "belief," which they treat as genuine faith. All the same, it is but a human fabrication, an idea, without a corresponding experience in the depth of the heart.

Faith, however, is something that God effects in us. It changes us and we are reborn from God (Jn 1:13). Faith puts the old Adam to death and makes us quite different men in heart, in mind, and in all our powers; and it is accompanied by the Holy Spirit. O, when it comes to faith, what a living, creative, active, powerful thing it is. . . .

Faith is a living and unshakable confidence, a belief in the grace of God so assured that a man would die a thousand deaths for its sake. . . . That is what the Holy Spirit effects through faith. . . .It is impossible, indeed, to separate works from faith, just as it is impossible to separate heat and light from fire. . . . Offer up your prayers to God, and ask him to create faith in you.[20]

Luther's doctrine of faith may be summarized from the above quotation as follows: Faith is a gift of God, which, being sustained by the Holy Spirit, creates in us a confidence in God's grace as well as the desire and ability to respond in works of love.

To understand the first principle of Luther's doctrine of faith, namely that it originates in God's action, it is necessary to review briefly his doctrine of justification, from which his notion of faith was never separated. Luther was consumed by the notion of God's righteousness and justice. We are faced, on the one side, with the undeniable fact of continuing and recalcitrant human sin, and, on the other side, with the gracious forgiveness of God through the sacrificial death of his son. Reconciliation with God cannot be achieved by human effort ("works of the law"). Thus the satisfaction of God must (and does) come from God in Christ. The righteousness which God requires of his creatures comes about by God's own act of "justification," which is, literally, a "making just." From this fact there followed for Luther two inescapable conclusions. First, there could be no question of cooperative grace— even if that meant no more than God's gracious "acceptation" of our best, if still inadequate, effort. "Having been justified by grace . . . we

---

20. Dillenberger, *Martin Luther: Selections from His Writings*, pp. 23, 24.

then do good works, yes, [but] Christ himself does all in us."[21] Trust in our own work, on *any* basis "destroys faith and the entire Christ. For it is Christ alone who counts and I must confess this . . . by saying: 'since Christ does it, I must not do it.' For Christ and my own works cannot tolerate each other in my heart; I can, therefore, not put my trust in both of them, but one of them must be expelled—either Christ or my own activity."[22]

By "works" Luther meant any activity believed, on any grounds, to be meritorious before God. He did not, we must note, count as a "work" an act of love undertaken freely in response to divine grace. God alone justifies, and neither the ministry of the church, nor good works, nor the deepest belief can accomplish anything without the prior and sufficient action of God.

The second conclusion is required by the first. Justification makes us righteous in such a way that, while we cannot claim righteousness as our own, we are given an "alien" righteousness that comes from one "other" than ourselves. We do not *possess* it. It is a gift continually to be given. The person who is justified receives various benefits and graces but may or may not manifest them. For this reason Luther often described the life of faith in negative terms. "We perceive that a man who is justified is not yet a righteous man."[23] More often than not Luther describes this righteousness as the result of a negative action of God, who, on the basis of the positive action of Christ, "overlooks," "forgets," "ignores," our sin. "A man is so absolved as if he had no sin, for Christ's sake . . . our righteousness is divine ignorance and free forgiveness of our sins."[24] While righteousness is in that sense a negative thing, brought about by the cancelation of sin and guilt, it is also a positive "recognition," "credit," and "imputation" of the merits of Christ as applied to ourselves, which produces a positive self-assessment.

> This is wonderful news to believe that salvation lies outside ourselves. I am justified and acceptable to God, although there is in me sin, unrighteousness, and horror of death. Yet I must look elsewhere and see no sin. This is wonderful, not to see what I see, not to feel what I feel. Before my eyes I see a gulden, or a sword, or a fire, and I must say, "There is no gulden, no sword, no fire." The forgiveness of sins is like that.[25]

---

21. *Luther's Works*, Vol. 34, ed. Lewis W. Spitz (Philadelphia: Muhlenberg Press, 1960), p. 111.
22. Althaus, p. 225 - WA 37, 46.
23. *Luther's Works*, Vol. 34, p. 152.
24. Althaus, p. 227.
25. Roland Bainton, *Here I Stand: A Life of Martin Luther* (Nashville: Abingdon, 1978), p. 178.

The grace, mercy, and forgiveness accomplished for us on the cross all find expression in Luther's doctrine of justification. Sometimes he employs the concept to indicate the specific action of God in the saving death of Christ—at other times he means by justification the whole complex of activity which includes God's predestinating grace, its actualization for us on the cross, our encounter with Christ in the scripture, and our reception of this saving knowledge. Following Paul, Luther employed the word "faith" to stand for the ways justification takes place and becomes actual in life. In that sense are we saved by faith "alone." The dimension of faith represented by human volition does not compare to the action of God in Christ as the source of our redemption.

For Luther, the *origin* of faith is God. "Let no one assume that he has faith by his own powers, as so many do when they hear about faith and then undertake to gain it by their own ability. They thus undertake a task which belongs to God alone, for having true faith is really a divine work."[26] As we have seen from Luther's preface to Romans, "Faith is . . . something God effects in us," and we ought to pray "to God and ask him to create faith in [us]." Luther's insistence upon the *fides divina*, faith as divine act, was not, as in Augustine, the result of a general theory of divine providence and predestination. Rather, for Luther, it was a response to his absolute conviction that our willing, believing, and doing, whether assisted by God or not, have no effect upon our salvation. Against Pelagius, Augustine taught that, apart from divine grace, our works have no merit before God. Against Augustine, Luther maintained that even in the power of divine acceptation and grace our works have no such potential. This consciousness of our incapacity was so crucial for Luther that he rejected any activity undertaken as if this were not the case. "Since Christ does it, I must not do it."

Because Luther believed faith originated with God, he could make astonishing claims about faith. "Outside of faith God loses his righteousness, glory, riches, etc." "If you believe that he is your father, your judge, your God, then that is what he is."[27] Read in the simplest way these statements could be taken as an extravagant form of self-idolatry, or assertions that only a Ludwig Feuerbach (1804-1872) could make. But if we recall Luther's abhorrence of idolatry, his insistence upon the objective reality of God, and his view of faith as an action of God, they make perfect, even tautological, sense. Since faith is God in action, where faith is God is, where faith is not, God, together with his attributes, is absent. Because faith is God in action, Luther could even assert that "faith is omnipotent as God himself is."[28]

---

26. Althaus, p. 48.
27. *Luther's Works*, Vol 13, ed., Jaroslav Pelikan (Philadelphia: Muhlenberg Press, 1958), p. 7.
28. Althaus, p. 48.

Concerning the *content* of faith, we may again refer to Luther's preface to Romans where we find two distinct, but related, claims. On the one hand, faith not only begins as an activity of God, but continues to be defined by that activity. In faith God addresses himself to a person in such a way that a hearing and believing takes place. Thus the content of faith is God's word, the gospel. It is not thoughts about the gospel; it is not confessional agreement or theological insight or conviction. "Faith is not something dreamed, a human illusion . . . an idea which they call 'belief' . . . a human fabrication." Faith has as its content God's word—a word he "effects in us." It is therefore an encounter with God and the living word, Jesus Christ.

On the other hand, faith contains our response, but it is a response that always looks back upon the prior and sustaining action of God—a *fides reflexiva*. Insofar as this action is realized in life, it becomes a *fides actualis*, it is "a living and unshakable confidence, a belief in the grace of God." Luther put great emphasis upon faith as trust, confidence, and courage—and these, as virtues, as attitudes difficult to attain, might imply an ambivalence at the heart of his doctrine if it were not for the fact that, for Luther, they are not to be understood except as results of God's action. "Offer up your prayers and ask him to create faith in you."

In spite of Luther's acceptance of *Anfechtung* (dread/anxiety) as a necessary preparation for faith, he did not believe that religious experience or feeling (*empfinden*) can produce the trust (*fiducia*) of faith. This is so because the primary experience of God begins with judgment. Our encounter with God, like the Syro-Phoenician woman's encounter with Christ, must begin with a "no," which in itself is no basis for faith. And if it is only that God's " 'yes' is deeply hidden and appears to be a mere 'no,' . . . [yet] our heart feels that there is nothing else than 'no' there."[29] The ambiguity that accompanies religious experience is occasioned by the incapacity of human feeling correctly to receive and assess either God's yes or his no. In either case we seem compelled to faithless self-congratulation or an equally faithless self-condemnation. It is for this reason that Luther recommends that we abandon religious experience as any reliable basis for faith. "So now turn from your conscience and its feeling to Christ who is not able to deceive; my heart and Satan, however, who will drive me to sin are liars. . . . You should not believe your conscience and your feelings more than the word which the Lord . . . preaches to you."[30] So great was Luther's distrust of experience as the proper basis for faith that, for him, "a battle begins in which experi-

---

29. Ibid., p. 58.
30. Ibid., p. 59.

ence struggles against the Spirit and faith."[31] The "trust" and "confidence" which Luther associates with faith obviously do not depend upon the feelings usually associated with those attitudes. "For it happens, indeed it is typical of faith, that he who claims to believe does not believe at all; and on the other hand, he who doesn't believe, but is in despair, has the greatest faith."[32] The trust which Luther assigns to faith is therefore not a matter of deep feeling based on religious experience. It is, rather, an acknowledgment of the power of God which displaces the fear and despair (*Anfechtung*) that must inevitably result from any dependency upon our own religious or spiritual resources.

To what extent does faith have a theological content? As we have seen, the word "faith" has always included the sense of *fides qua creditur*, the faith *that* is believed. The late medieval church supported an increasingly complex system of doctrine which required a *fides implicita* (a willingness to believe what one does not understand) or *fides explicita* (agreement with understanding). Although Luther insisted upon right doctrine and confession of faith, he could, when thinking of the object of faith itself, declare that, even if "I hated this word *homoousion*, and . . . refused to use it, still I would not be a heretic."[33] Luther would not allow doctrinal distinctions to intrude upon the existential encounter of faith. Even less would he identify faith with any implicit assent to doctrine based upon the authority of the church. He disapproved of Augustine's statement: "I would not have believed the gospel unless the authority of the universal church moved me to do so." "That," he said, "would be false and unchristian. Everyone must believe only because it is the word of God."[34] For Luther the doctrinal content of faith is simply that God makes us just through Christ, his cross and resurrection, and these are not so much doctrines as immediate and self-evident truths which accompany the operation of God's grace.

The *effects* of faith for Luther are two: justification and service. When he speaks of justification (or salvation) by faith alone, he means that God's working faith in us brings about our reconciliation. When he speaks of good works as the fruit of faith, what he calls "our proper righteousness," he means an activity which flows so naturally and ef-

31. Ibid., p. 63.
32. *Luther's Works*, Vol. 40, ed. Conrad Bergendorf (Philadelphia: Muhlenberg Press, 1958), p. 241.
33. *Luther's Works*, Vol. 32, ed. George W. Forell (Philadelphia: Muhlenberg Press, 1958), p. 244.
34. Althaus, p. 49. An exception to this rule may be found in Luther's doctrine of baptism, where he accounts for the faith necessary in infant baptism by reference to the "vicarious faith" of the parents and God-parents. (Dillenberger, p. 307.)

fortlessly from a thankful heart that it hardly deserves to be described as a "work," and in no case can be understood as the cause or prior condition of divine favor. Faith and works are in fact so closely related in Luther's thought that "it is impossible, indeed, to separate [them], just as it is impossible to separate heat and light from fire." In that sense our works can hardly be counted as "ours."

> For faith is the work, not of man, but of God alone, as Paul teaches. God does the other works through us and by us; in the case of faith, he works in us and without our cooperation.[35]

John Calvin's Doctrine of Faith

Luther's doctrine of faith was open to the charge that it neglected the moral obedience that belongs to the life of faith. It was left to John Calvin to provide that linkage.

As we indicated in the introduction, Calvin's theology was in basic agreement with that of Luther, and the doctrine of faith was no exception. "Men, being subject to the curse of the law, have no means left of attaining salvation but through faith alone."[36] While we will show how and why Calvin laid more stress on the human side of faith, it is nonetheless clear that he, as much as Luther, saw faith as the result of God's action. Calvin spoke of faith as "the fruit of a supernatural gift that those who otherwise would have remained petrified in unbelief should accept Christ. . . ."[37]

Like Luther, Calvin based his definition of faith upon the doctrine of justification—the need and character of which he defined in much the same way as Luther. "He is said to be justified in the sight of God who in the divine judgment is reputed righteous."[38] Justification by works is clearly impossible, for it would require a life of "such purity and holiness as to deserve the character of righteousness before the throne of God."[39] If this is true, then to be "made just" does not belong to human capability. "Thus we simply explain justification to be an acceptance by which God receives us into his favor and esteems us as righteous persons; and we say that it consists in the remission of sins and the imputation of the righteousness of Christ."[40] Faith, for Calvin, is the means provided by God for our apprehension, acceptance, and conformity to this gift.

---

35. Dillenberger, p. 296.
36. Calvin, *Institutes*, III/11/1 (Cf. also III/3/1).
37. Ibid., III/1/4.
38. Ibid., III/11/3.
39. Ibid.
40. Ibid.

So far, there is no difference between Luther and Calvin. But while Calvin gladly used the formula of salvation (justification) by "faith alone," faith was not as central for him as for Luther. For Luther, faith was the dialectical event of God's grace and our reception. It is God's work and ours, but only ours as a result of God's decision and action. Calvin took the same position but with this difference: What Luther saw as an immediate and momentary *event*, Calvin saw as a *process*—a process in which the action of God and the reaction of the believer are more clearly distinguishable. This is why Calvin could say, on the one hand, that, as an extension of God's action, "faith alone" is the means of our salvation, but on the other, that, "with respect to justification, faith is a thing merely passive," and even more bluntly, "faith . . . of itself is of no value."[41] Here he clearly had in mind not only a mere *fides quae*, with its various forms of knowledge and belief but as well the more substantial *fides qua*, the certain confidence and trust in God that undergirds everything else in Christian life and thought. However indispensible it may be, *our* faith (or faith as our activity) can claim no participation in the work of salvation.

Although Calvin spoke disparagingly of faith as our activity, he established our activity as a form of faith. Where Luther saw faith as a single phenomenon, as a sort of ellipse with two unequal foci, God's work and our response, Calvin posited two kinds of faith. First, faith may be understood as a part of the divine act of justification (and in that sense saves "alone"). In this case the term "faith" often gave way in Calvin's writing to more fundamental terms such as "justification," "grace," or "election." Second, faith could be (and more often was) understood by Calvin to indicate the human response to grace. As such it cannot be said to save, nor can any efficacy be assigned to it. However indispensible, it is merely an "earthen vessel."[42] Because Calvin distinguished in this way the *fides divina* from the *fides actualis*, he could, without intruding upon the priority of God's action, assign to faith definite doctrinal and moral responsibilities necessary for its fulfillment.

In making this distinction between faith (as divine act) and faith (as human response) Calvin was not abandoning faith's connection with justification. On the contrary, he so distinguished faith from faith, because he had already made a similar division within the doctrine of justification, which came about in this way: In the decades leading up to and including the Council of Trent (1545-1563) the Reformation movement was increasingly under attack by Catholic theologians for dissolving Christian obedience and duty into a theory of justification which

---

41. Ibid., III/14/9 and III/11/7.
42. Ibid., III/11/7.

asserted that, as Luther indeed said, "Since Christ does it, I must not do it." Calvin was aware of the anti-works position of Luther's successors, the anti-social behavior of some Anabaptists extremists, as well as the excesses of the libertines in Geneva. On this account Calvin recognized an element of truth in Catholic criticism. He sought to correct the situation, generally, by emphasizing the presence of works in faith, not as a cause, nor as an effect, but as a necessary and inescapable *accompaniment*. Specifically, Calvin signaled the importance of Christian obedience in his system by placing a second and larger exposition of the doctrine of justification after that of regeneration and sanctification.

We may attempt an illustration of Calvin's treatment by an abbreviated comparison of his arrangement of the *ordo salutis* (the steps or "order" of salvation) with that of Luther and Rome. For Catholicism the progression was (roughly) contrition → regeneration → sanctification → justification → glorification. In this system sorrow for sin is followed by the divine gift of new birth, which, accompanied by the virtue of faith, leads to a life of obedience and love. Assisted by sacramental grace, the life so sanctified satisfies the justice of God and obtains salvation (or glorification).

For Luther, the order might be set out thus: [election] → *justification* → (contrition → regeneration → sanctification → glorification). While Luther accepted divine election as absolutely determinative for salvation or damnation, he did not make much use of the idea, considering it an impenetrable mystery unprofitable for the task of evangelical theology. For Luther, the first word that must be spoken about the human condition comes from the justifying work of Christ on the cross. The whole of Christian life, its sorrow for sin, its rebirth, and its growth in grace, is caught up in the "moment" of faith when the reality of God's justification is applied to the individual's life.

For Calvin the order of salvation was somewhat differently conceived. His scheme might be set out thusly: election → justification → contrition → regeneration → sanctification → justification → glorification. The difference lies in the double entry of justification. The one who is elected receives the benefits of Christ's justifying grace by way of faith. The life of faith involves sorrow for sin, conversion, and rebirth into an existence which struggles to obtain holiness. Naturally, the life of faith cannot do this on its own. The righteousness that belongs to human life is always an imputed righteousness—but nonetheless a *real* righteousness. "Whom therefore the Lord receives into fellowship, him he is said to justify; because he cannot receive anyone into favor or into fellowship with himself, without making him from a sinner to be a righteous person."[43] On the other hand (and this is the point of difference between

---

43. Ibid., III/11/21.

Luther and Calvin) the person made righteous in God's eyes by (a first) justification, is thereafter *actually* made into a person whose life can be worthy of (a second) justification. The elect are given both the desire and strength to do the good.

> Christ therefore justifies no one whom he does not also sanctify. For these benefits are perpetually and indissolubly connected. . . . Thus we see how true it is that we are justified, not without works, yet not by works; since union with Christ, by which we are justified, contains sanctification as well as righteousness.[44]

Sanctification is not only a state, it is a process in which life is rendered, by divine assistance, more and more consistent with the righteousness imputed to it in Christ. Such a life can be judged by God as righteous—it is justified. Therefore, for Calvin,

> There is no objection against . . . calling eternal life a reward. . . . So, likewise, it will occasion no inconvenience, if we consider holiness of life as the way, not which procures our admission into the glory of the heavenly kingdom, but through which the elect are conducted by their God to the manifestation of it; since it is his good pleasure to glorify them whom he has sanctified. Only let us not imagine a reciprocal relation of merit and reward.[45]

Just as there is for Calvin a justification that takes no account of works and another that judges the life worthy that God has himself elected and sanctified, so there is also for him a double meaning of faith that accompanies these two views of justification. On the one hand, Calvin insists that faith is a work of God—which "alone" justifies us. On the other hand, he dedicated a large portion of his discussion of faith in Book III of his *Institutes* to faith as human knowledge and action.[46] Concerning faith as knowledge, Calvin, like Luther, denies the *fides implicita*, insofar as that doctrine encouraged a blind acceptance of Catholic teaching. Yet Calvin recognizes a legitimate implicit faith as a prelude to saving knowledge of God in Christ—as (to use his own example) the official who believed in Jesus' power to heal his son (Jn 4:50).[47] Faith for Calvin is also "explicit," not as an understanding of dogma, nor as mere *fides historica* regarding the factual assertions of the gospel, but rather as "a knowledge of God's will toward us, perceived

---

44. Ibid., III/16/1.
45. Ibid., III/18/4.
46. Ibid., III/6-10.
47. Ibid., III/2/2.
48. Ibid., III/2/6.

in his word."[48] Such knowledge will be the result of a "recognition" of God's promises, grasped in "certainty" and providing "peace" to the believer.[49]

Respecting faith as action or works, Calvin rejects the Catholic distinction between an "unformed faith" (*fides informis*, i.e., belief which has not yet the *habitus* of love) and a "formed faith" (*fides formata*, i.e., formed by the practice of love).[50] Yet, for Calvin, "while man is justified by faith alone . . . nevertheless actual holiness of life, so to speak, is not separated from free imputation of righteousness."[51] Sanctification must be actualized in the life of faith by the predestinating and justifying power of God. But both the intellectual certainty and moral steadfastness of faith are possible only insofar as the believer looks to Christ. It is finally the unity of Christ with us that allows Calvin to place such importance upon the actualization of faith in good works. "Not only does [Christ] cling to us by an invisible bond of fellowship, but with a wonderful communion, day by day, he grows more and more into one body with us, until he becomes completely one with us."[52]

To summarize, we may say that Calvin's view of faith differs from Luther's to the extent that he places a greater emphasis upon its human side. Where Luther sees faith as a single event comprised of the action of God and the reaction of man, Calvin posits justification and faith at two places—before and after conversion and regeneration. This double positioning accounts for the special emphasis given to moral duty in the Reformed tradition. In this way the Calvinist doctrine of faith may be judged broader in scope and more open to the Catholic insistence upon the necessity of works as a complement to faith. That Calvin's doctrine of faith failed to achieve the desired rapprochement with Catholicism, was due to his doctrine of election. In contrast to Luther, Calvin could introduce a strong element of works into his conception of justification by faith because his doctrine of God's eternal election had already and without remainder secured the primacy of grace and the incapacity of human being. In seeking a way to connect faith and the moral life Calvin did not contradict the essential concerns of Luther.

Faith in Protestant Confessions

The Augsburg Confession, composed in 1530 by Philipp Melanchthon (1497-1560) in collaboration with Luther, was the first great Reformation statement of faith. Although it was intended to demonstrate the

49. Ibid., III/2/15-16.
50. Ibid., III/2./9-10.
51. Ibid., III/3/1.
52. Ibid., III/2/24.

ecumenical orthodoxy of the new evangelical church, the Confession states Luther's doctrine of faith precisely. Article IV on Justification states: "We receive forgiveness of sin and become righteous by grace, for Christ's sake, by faith, when we believe." And Article XX on Faith and Good Works states, "Our works cannot reconcile us with God . . . for that happens only through faith, when we believe. . . . Faith here spoken of is not [mere belief in] the history of Christ . . . but is a confidence in God and the fulfillment of his promises."[53]

In his "Apology" for the Confession, Melanchthon put more emphasis than Luther "upon the actual righteousness wrought by faith." "Good works are to be done on account of God's command; likewise for the exercise of faith."[54] Luther was accustomed to say that good works were a hindrance to justification. Melanchthon, however, agreed with Calvin that the works of faith, being inspired and empowered by God, were worthy of such evaluation and were in fact necessary for the completion of faith. In spite of the fact that this difference caused no rupture in the theological agreement of Luther and Melanchthon, it became a chief source of conflict among their followers—of which one example must suffice.

The "Majoristic Controversy" takes its name from a contemporary of Luther, George Major (1502-1574), who extended Melanchthon's position to claim that good works are necessary to faith, not because of their inherent merit, but because "no one is saved by wicked works and no one is saved without works. . . . They are necessary to "retain" salvation."[55] Although his position was a reasonable expression of Lutheran orthodoxy, Major stimulated what can only be called a "hyper-Lutheran" reaction from Nikolaus Amsdorf (1483-1565) and Matthias Flacius (Illyricus) (1520-1575). Amsdorf declared that Major's insistence upon the necessity of works for salvation branded him a "Pelagian, a Mameluke, and a denyer of Christ."[56] In attempting to mediate the controversy Melanchthon suggested that "new obedience" was necessary for faith, but that such necessity ought not to be attached to salvation as such. In response Amsdorf and Flacius allowed themselves the same rhetorical vehemence against a liberal Lutheran position that Luther had used against the excesses of popular Catholic theory of merit. Amsdorf declared that "good works are injurious to salvation," and that "God does not care for works."[57]

---

53. Philip Schaff, *Creeds of Christendom* (New York: Harper and Brothers, 1877), pp. 225ff.
54. Seeberg, *History of Doctrines*, p. 338.
55. Ibid., p. 364.
56. Ibid.
57. Ibid., p. 365.

While debate among Luther's successors was by no means restricted to the question of faith (one thinks of Andreas Osiander [1498-1552] and his important attempt to redefine justification), the Majoristic Controversy gave rise to the so-called "antinomian" and "synegistic" controversies. These disputes were also concerned with the relation between divine and human activity in the phenomenon of faith. What is interesting about these disputes is that, while the original Lutheran dialectic of divine and human activity in faith prevailed over distortions pressed from both the right and the left, the very fact that discussion centered upon the role and value of human behavior in faith meant a shift away from Luther's interest in the nature and scope of the divine activity that makes faith salvific. Once the special weighting of Luther's dialectic was lost it was easy enough for later Lutheran dogmaticians to neglect the question of the origin of faith and emphasize more and more its theological content or moral effects.

A similar development can be traced in the history of Reformed dogmatics. In spite of a basic loyalty to Luther's view of faith, the Calvinists tended to elevate the effectiveness of good works performed in and through the power of a divinely inspired faith. The First Helvetic Confession (1536) speaks of faith "as a pure gift and bestowal of God," but also, revealing the Erasmian influence of Ulrich Zwingli (1484-1531), as a human work. It is "the real true service, by means of which we please God."[58]

In the later Reformed Confessions of the 1550s and early 1560s Calvin's thought predominates. The vigorous and straightforward Scots Confession (1560) of John Knox (1513-1572) is, in its treatment of faith, an almost perfect reproduction of the views of his Genevan mentor. Both faith and the works that necessarily flow from it are the work of God.

Our faith and its assurance do not proceed from flesh and blood, that is to say, from the natural powers within us, but are the inspiration of the Holy Ghost. . . . As we willingly disclaim any honor and glory for our own creation and redemption, so . . . also for our regeneration and sanctification; for by ourselves we are not capable of one good thought, but he who has begun the work in us alone continues us in it.[59]

The Heidelberg Catechism (1562) reflects the agreement of Luther and Calvin on the divine origin of faith and its biblical content. In

---

58. Ibid., p. 345.
59. *The Book of Confessions* (New York: The Office of the General Assembly of the Presbyterian Church [USA], 1983), 3.12.

answer to question 21, "What is true faith?" the answer is given: "A certain knowledge by which I accept as true all that God has revealed in his word, but also a wholehearted trust which the Holy Spirit creates in me."[60] The Second Helvetic Confession (1566) states that faith "is not an opinion or human conviction, but a most firm trust and a clear and steadfast assent. . . . This faith is a pure gift of God, which God alone of his grace gives to his elect."[61]

In these early Reformed confessions one finds a view of faith in which emphasis is placed upon both the divine act and human moral response—and placed upon the latter only because it is an effect of the former (i.e., God justifies his own work in our works). At the same time there was increasing interest in the shape and character of Christian life, which found fullest expression in the views of Jacob Arminius (1560-1609), who denied the irresistibility of grace and thereby afforded to human will a cooperative function in the maintenance (but not the origin) of a saving faith. The Synod of Dort (1618) condemned Arminianism in favor of a strict, supralapsarian predestinarianism. God's eternal decree determined before creation for every individual the mission and call of Christ, the bestowal of faith, justification, and sanctification. Faith is a divine gift whereby we are enabled to recognize the decisive act of God in our own election. Thus predestination, and not justification or faith, is the real basis of Christian life. Sanctification takes place because God "infuses new qualities into the will and makes it from dead, living, from evil, good."[62] The life that belongs to faith is not accomplished by moral persuasion, but strictly by the predestinating will of God.

In collapsing faith and sanctification back into the absolute (and necessarily obscure) decree of God, the canons of Dort were only extending the logic of Calvin's doctrine of election. In doing so they may have secured the primacy of God's act in faith from every synergistic tendency. But the question may be asked whether, in making election the theological spring from which must flow every other doctrine (of justification, of faith, of sanctification) the orthodox party at Dort did not in fact reverse Calvin's own procedure. For Calvin, after all, the doctrine of election arose, not from an interest in the absolute power of God, but from the mystery of God's justifying grace in Christ. We may also ask whether, in directing attention away from justification by faith

---

60. *Book of Confessions*, 4.021. Otherwise the catechism shows a decidedly Lutheran influence in avoiding any reference to the requirement of works or to their being, as works of God, worthy of justification. Works are here prescribed only in terms of gratitude.

61. Ibid., 5.112.

62. Seeberg, *History of Doctrines*, p. 423.

toward the eternal decree of a hidden God, the victors at Dort did not isolate Christian faith and life from any vital connection with the grace of God in Christ. In any case, the troubling obscurity of that "terrible decree" forced the Calvinists to seek assurance elsewhere. The result was that both the intellectual content of faith (*fides qua*) and the moral demands of faith (*fides formata*) became increasingly the real focus of the Reformed doctrine of faith—and to that extent became indistinguishable from precisely the Catholic view they wanted to avoid.

THE DISSOLUTION OF THE DOCTRINE OF FAITH

Orthodoxy

Luther's understanding of faith arose from a sense of the immediacy of God's justifying grace in the person and work of Jesus Christ. In spite of the emphasis he placed upon predestination and the sovereignty of God, Calvin never lost sight of Luther's original vision of faith. The same cannot be said, however, for either his or Luther's successors. In the case of the later Calvinists, the relocation of the decisive act of salvation from the justifying work of Christ to the hidden and "terrible" double decree of God meant that faith, having lost its focus upon the concrete expression of God's grace in Christ, looked more and more to human thought and action for its interpretation. Thus the Small Catechism of the Puritans written at the end of the sixteenth century could claim that "there are two things which scripture teaches first of all: what man should believe concerning God, and what duty God demands of man."[63]

Reformed dogmaticians of the seventeenth and early-eighteenth centuries were especially interested in the shape and character of the believing that belongs to faith and undertook to sort out its types, divisions, and functions in a way that closely paralleled that of the medieval Scholastics. Johan Wolleb (1586-1629) distinguished five meanings of faith in scripture: 1) *fides quam credimus*, sincere faith held "in pure conscience"; 2) *fides historica*, the acknowledgment of the fact of God: 3) *fides temporaria*, faith which does not last; 4) *fides miraculorum*, or faith that can "move mountains"; and 5) *fides salvifica*, the faith given the apostles to heal the sick and raise the dead. Johan Heinrich Heidegger (1633-1698) identified a universal *fides communis* which is rather like Wolleb's "historical" and "temporary" faith—which even the reprobate possess—and a *fides propria*, which is true, saving faith given only to the elect. Jean Alphonse Turretin (1674-1737) was interested in the

---

63. Ibid., p. 419.

status of temporary faith, which for him was a grace of illumination, but not of regeneration and adoption. He also defined the category of "miraculous faith" as a conviction arising from a "special revelation and promise" given by God when the generally available word of God is not sufficient. *Fides propria* is "a supernatural virtue poured into man by God," according to Heidegger, and it includes three elements that belong to the understanding and the will. "*Notitia* is the apprehension of the things necessary for salvation. *Assensus* is that by which it is firmly believed that . . . the Word of God [is] true. . . . *Fiducia* is that by which each of the faithful applies the promise of the gospel to himself."[64] Wolleb was insistent that, since faith was *notitia*, it could not be *fides implicita*, "which believes by blind assent, as the Roman Church believes."[65] Gulielimus Bucan (d. 1603) described faith as "knowledge of, assent to, and seeking for . . . grace . . . the firm and sure recognition of the divine benevolence . . . revealed through the Holy Spirit . . . the tool, instrument, and means by which *homo peccator* embraces the whole of Christ . . ." etc.[66] The Leiden Synopsis of Reformed Faith (1625) declared that intellectual assent was not enough, unless "the will also apprehends and embraces" what is believed. The *fiducia* without which saving faith (*fides propria*) is incomplete was described by Johnnes Marck (1655-1731) as "an act by which man adopts God and Christ into himself."[67] Similarly, Peter Mastricht (1630-1706) defined the essence of faith as "an act of a reasonable soul, which consists in receiving God [by] 1) knowledge . . . 2) explicit assent, 3) joy, and 4) hatred and detestation of the things which are contrary to [God]."[68]

It is clear from the discussion of the nature of faith carried on by these Protestant dogmaticians in the seventeenth and early-eighteenth centuries that theological interest had turned away from the prior and efficient action of God to focus more and more on faith *as* works, that is, on the believing subject and the various intellectual, emotional, and volitional aspects of belief. This development was perhaps inevitable during the period of the "wars of religion" and the Catholic Counterreformation. Theological definition and loyalty counted for so much that by the midpoint of the seventeenth century religious controversy throughout Protestantism had reduced the idea of faith to a mixture of civil obedience and doctrinal assent.

---

64. Heinrich Heppe, *Reformed Dogmatics*, ed. Ernst Bizer, trans. G. T. Thompson (Grand Rapids, Mich.: Baker, 1978), p. 530.
65. Ibid., pp. 530-531.
66. Ibid., p. 531.
67. Ibid., p. 533.
68. Ibid.

Pietism

In reaction to the spiritual sterility of Protestant orthodoxy, Pietism emphasized the subjective and emotional aspects of faith. This movement arose in Germany and soon spread throughout the Protestant churches in Europe, England, and the New World. It began in 1765 with the publication of Philipp Jakob Spener's (1635-1705) *Pia Desideria*, which described a program of spiritual renewal involving Bible study, lay ministry, and the cultivation of religious experience. The moral life was emphasized over doctrine, and theological controversy was to be avoided altogether.[69] Faith, for Spener, was above all a matter of inner experience. "Sermons," he wrote, "should not merely incite to external acts of virtue . . . but should lay the foundation [for faith] in the heart."[70] For Spener, and after him August Hermann Franke (1663-1727) and Nikolaus Ludwig Count von Zinzendorf (1700-1760), faith involved a distinct ascetic and mystical element. Introspection and self-examination became the chief requirements for faith, with the result that the Reformer's suspicion of emotional experience was completely forgotten.

Pietism first appeared in England in the Society of Friends, where an immediate experience of the Holy Spirit provided the whole content and meaning of faith. Rather than "saving faith," the Confession of the Society of Friends (1676) speaks of a "saving and spiritual light," which "enlightens the hearts of all . . . in order to salvation. . . . There is an evangelical and saving light and grace in all," and to resist such light is "to make shipwreck of faith."[71] Pietism's greatest impact upon English-speaking Protestantism came by way of John Wesley (1709-1791), who was exposed to Zinzendorf's Moravians in London and later at their community at Herrnhut near Dresden. While attending a pietist devotional meeting at Aldersgate, Wesley heard a reading from Luther's Preface to Romans "describing the change which God works in the heart through faith in Christ [and] I felt my heart strangely warmed."[72] Although Wesley could state that, "The Author of faith and salvation is God alone,"[73] for him (and we may also say for evangelicalism from the Great Awakening to the present day) the nature of faith was understood not so much in terms of divine action as in terms of human response. If emotion is lacking, if the heart is cold, the condition of faith is absent.

---

69. A. C. McGiffert, *Protestant Thought Before Kant* (New York: Harper and Brothers, 1961), p. 157.
70. Ibid., p. 157.
71. John H. Leith, ed., *Creeds of the Churches* (Richmond: Knox, 1973), pp. 327-329.
72. McGiffert, *Protestant Thought*, p. 162.
73. Ibid., p. 166.

Wesley in fact spoke of faith as a human possession, a faculty "whereby the spiritual man discerneth God and the things of God. It is with respect to the spiritual world what sense is to the natural."[74]

Rationalism

If the warmth of Pietism provided a needed corrective to the doctrinal frigidity of orthodoxy, its subjective and emotional view of faith was badly suited to its own age—the age of Enlightenment. In the late-seventeenth and eighteenth centuries there developed a rationalist approach to faith which swept away the fundamental assumptions of Protestantism. Religious rationalism, or Deism, naturally considered faith as *fides quae*, a kind of knowledge, and asserted a parity and even mutual dependency between faith and reason. For John Locke (1632-1704), reason and faith may discover the same truth independently but cannot contradict each other. In his *An Essay Concerning Human Understanding* (1690), Locke defined faith as "the assent to any proposition, not thus made out by the deductions of reason, but upon the credit of the proposer, as coming from God in some extraordinary way of communication."[75] Later, Matthew Tindal (1655-1733) in his *Christianity as Old as Creation* (1730) subsumed faith and revelation under reason and nature. If the Holy Ghost is to deal with us in a way to which we can be held accountable, it cannot act upon us other than by way of the faculties of reason and observation. Revelation, then, must "be a *Republication* or Restoration of the religion of Nature."[76] From this point it was but a small step for Voltaire (1694-1778) to dismiss the specific content of Christian faith ("I certainly do not understand any of this; nobody has ever understood any of this, and this is the reason why people have slaughtered one another!"[77])—and then to reduce the knowledge of God to the second, third, and fifth proofs of Thomas Aquinas (c. 1225-1274).

It is one of the more astonishing facts of theological history that protest against Deism's reduction of faith to reason came, not from theology, but from philosophy. "Our most holy religion," wrote David Hume (1711-1776), "is founded on *faith*, not on reason; and it is a sure method of exposing it to put it to such a trial as it is by no means fitted to endure."[78] One need not imagine that Hume was much concerned to

---

74. Ibid., p. 170.
75. James C. Livingston, *Modern Christian Thought* (New York: Macmillan, 1971), p. 16.
76. Ibid., p. 22.
77. Ibid., p. 28.
78. *The Philosophical Works of David Hume*, Vol. IV, "An Inquiry Concerning the Human Understanding" (Edinburgh: Adam Black, 1826), p. 153.

defend or advance "our most holy religion"; nonetheless he rendered it considerable service, for he marked the entrance to the dead-end street of religious rationalism with warning signs sufficient for any who cared to notice. By employing the ancient law of proportionality, the new scientific law of uniform experience, and his own highly developed logic of inference, Hume was able to dismantle, in turn, Locke's rational defense of miracles, Voltaire's argument from design, and Joseph Butler's (1692-1752) arguments from analogy.

Immanuel Kant (1724-1804) followed Hume with very much the same intention, but with less salutary results. In the Preface to *The Critique of Pure Reason* (1781) Kant argued that when "speculative reason" claims knowledge of God, it must transform deity into an object "of possible experience . . . into an appearance," and on that account he "found it necessary to deny knowledge in order to make room for faith."[79] Knowledge cannot furnish the grounds for faith because "knowledge" operates from experience shaped by universal, but finite, categories of thought (causality, value, etc.). Any argument from the world of finite effects to an infinite cause is bound to fail, because the principle of causality "is applicable only in the sensible world; outside that world it has no meaning whatsoever."[80] Kant's criticism of religious rationalism was, however, not as thoroughgoing as Hume's. Kant held that, if faith cannot claim to be "knowledge," it can nonetheless claim the status of a reasonable *postulate*. By arguing from the universal sense of moral obligation, of "oughtness," to the existence of a universal moral law, and thus to a divine law-giver, Kant was simply stating on other grounds the same argument as Deists such as Butler, namely, that such phenomena can, with reasonable probability, form the basis for a rational belief. If Kant had held to his original agreement with Hume and forgone the reconstruction of Christianity as a rational faith in a universal and divinely governed moral order, he would have rendered better service to theology. As it is, his thought contributed enormously to the dissolution of the Reformers' view of faith as a divine, rather than human, activity.

Nineteenth Century Liberalism

In the latter part of the eighteenth century the reduction of faith to doctrine, emotion, or reason was protested by a romantic movement within Protestantism. Important for this movement were Johann Georg Hamann (1730-1788), Friedrich Heinrich Jacobi (1743-1819), and

---

79. Immanuel Kant, *Critique of Pure Reason*, trans. N. K. Smith (London: Macmillan, 1964), p. 29.
80. Ibid., p. 511.

Samuel Taylor Coleridge (1772-1843), but it must suffice here to address the conception of faith produced by its most significant exponent, Friedrich Schleiermacher (1768-1834).

Like other representatives of the romantic school, Schleiermacher wanted to rescue Christian faith from the liabilities of mechanistic rationalism and subjectivistic Pietism. Critical philosophy had exposed the weakness of Deism. Furthermore, Enlightenment culture generally was contemptuous of the supernaturalism of both orthodoxy and Pietism. Schleiermacher sought in his *Speeches on Religion to Its Cultured Despisers* (1799) to formulate a conception of faith that could withstand those assaults. Accordingly, he preferred to speak not of "faith," but of "religion," "religious feeling," and "God consciousness." Against Kant's universal law, Schleiermacher argued that "religion has nothing to do with . . . knowledge"[81] and that "religion by itself does not urge men to activity at all."[82] Faith is a "feeling," a "self-consciousness" which is also a "world-consciousness," and ultimately a "God-consciousness." It is "immediate," it has no recognizable cause, nor is it a part of any thought process. It is intuition. It is our sense of unity with all things and the dependency of all things on the eternal. "The sum total of religion is to feel that, in its highest unity, all that moves us in feeling is one . . . to feel, that is to say, that our being and living is a being and living in and through God."[83]

Not only in his *Speeches*, but also in his mature work, *The Christian Faith* (1821), we can detect in Schleiermacher an inclination to view faith as the result of the action and presence of God. "Being in relation to God," is in fact, "the consciousness of absolute dependence."[84] To feel, or to sense absolute dependence is also to encounter the presence of the absolute upon which one depends. "God-consciousness" is at the same time a "God-presentness." It is this consciousness that Christ mediates to us and which may be understood as salvific, as "saving faith." Faith for Schleiermacher, therefore, is a human activity of mind and heart, but at the same time it is the result of "the ever renewed

---

81. Friedrich Schleiermacher, *On Religion: Speeches to Its Cultured Despisers*, trans. John Oman (New York: Harper and Brothers, 1958), p. 35.

82. Ibid., p. 57.

83. Ibid., pp. 49-50.

84. Schleiermacher, *The Christian Faith*, Vol. 2, ed. H. R. Mackintosh (New York: Harper & Row, 1963), p. 12. Claude Welch urges the translation of Schleiermacher's *schlechthin* as "utter" rather than the more traditional "absolute." (Claude Welch, *Protestant Thought in the Nineteenth Century*, Vol. I [New Haven, Conn.: Yale University Press, 1972], p. 65, note 16). It is not clear what gain is made by this shift of meaning, or whether it is proper, since Cassell's translates precisely Schleiermacher's phrase, *das schlechthinige Abhängigkeit* as "absolute dependence."

historical communication of the life and light that originates in . . . Jesus of Nazareth."[85] Schleiermacher can even say in *The Christian Faith* that, in respect to justification itself, "an activity of God is implied, and man can be conceived only as passive."[86] Further, he denies that faith as a human volitional event is "the *causa instrumentalis* of justification . . . that faith must be our own work."[87] Here, as at other places in his dogmatics, Schleiermacher demonstrates a Calvinist desire to restore the evangelical emphasis upon the dialectic of faith.

That Schleiermacher's theology did not succeed in this intention was due to the fact that the priority of God's will and act in Christ did not constitute the fundamental presupposition of his dogmatics. Because faith as religious consciousness contained in itself the presence and benefits of God, faith became an end in itself. It was understood as an inwardness and reflection that unites every person with God. The character of saving faith as a divine act was obscured in Schleiermacher by the fact that the subjective experience of faith was given regulative power in his theology. The forgiveness and adoption that makes man "the object of divine favor and love does not happen until he lays hold believingly on Christ."[88] It is *our* feeling of oneness, of dependence, of grace that defines the attributes of God, the nature of redemption and sin. Rather than the gospel determining the content of faith, faith in this scheme appears to determine the content of the gospel. Thus the necessary otherness of God, which gave to the Reformation view of faith its dialectical radicality, is in Schleiermacher lost.

While orthodoxy and rationalism interpreted faith to be one or another kind of thinking, and Pietism and romanticism viewed faith in terms of feeling and intuition, Albrecht Ritschl (1822-1889) associated faith with moral action. Ritschl wanted to reestablish a conception of faith which avoided the subjectivism of romanticism and the objectivism of Catholic and Protestant orthodoxy. Faith, for Ritschl, could not be a *fides explicita*, a knowledge that held doctrines about God as its object. He preferred Luther's definition of faith as "trust." But the problem of knowledge could not be avoided, because the question inevitably arises, what is the basis of such trust? For Ritschl, that basis could not be found in religious consciousness or experience—he was the avowed enemy of all romantic, pietistic, or mystical claims of the knowledge of God. Above all, Ritschl wanted to establish an objective basis for a theological understanding of faith's trust. To discover such a

---

85. Livingston, *Modern Christian Thought*, p. 108.
86. Schleiermacher, *Faith*, p. 500.
87. Ibid., pp. 504-505.
88. Ibid., p. 503.

basis he applied to "the general laws of human conduct and knowledge, for apart from these . . . [theology] could never be understood."[89] Specifically, he employed a Kantian analysis developed by Hermann Lotz (1817-1881), the substance of which was that the categories of knowledge are, fundamentally, only two: "value" and "causation." Religious truth belongs to the knowledge produced by judgments of value. God, like other objects of knowledge, cannot be known in himself but only by his effects upon us. Thus, "God is the power which man worships, which upholds his worth."[90] Or again, "we know the nature of God and Christ only in their worth for us."[91] The divinity of Christ consists in the fact that he represents the value of God for human life.

In his major work, *The Christian Doctrine of Justification and Reconciliation* (1870), Ritschl argued that, since faith depends upon a perception of the actualized value of God, faith cannot be complete without the application of the benefits of grace to the life of the believer. "Justification places sinners in a positive relationship of congruence toward God."[92] For Ritschl this meant that God's justifying grace cannot be known apart from the value it gives to human existence, and since that value cannot be known apart from its moral realization in life, reconciliation becomes a necessary condition for justification. "Insofar as justification is viewed as effective, it must be conceived as reconciliation."[93] This effectiveness finds "practical application only on the condition that the believer takes at once an active part in the recognized purpose of the kingdom of God."[94] Faith in the Ritschlian scheme is the "act through which the new relation of men to God, realized in justification, is religiously recognized and actually established."[95] Against the Reformation doctrine, Ritschl taught that faith not only includes works but may be said to be conditioned by them.

Ritschl's influence was pervasive and reached its apogee in his disciple Adolf von Harnack (1851-1930), who dispensed altogether with Luther's teaching of "faith alone," calling it a "dangerous process," and "convenient misunderstanding." Harnack claimed that "religion is not

---

89. David L. Mueller, *An Introduction to the Theology of Albrecht Ritschl* (Philadelphia: Westminster, 1969), p. 154. The comment is from Paul Lehmann, *Forgiveness: Decisive Issue in Protestant Thought* (New York: Harper and Brothers, 1940), p. 93.
90. Karl Barth, *Protestant Thought from Rousseau to Ritschl* (New York: Harper and Brothers, 1959), p. 362.
91. Albrecht Ritschl, *The Christian Doctrine of Justification and Reconciliation*, ed. H. R. Mackintosh (Edinburgh: T & T Clark, 1900), p. 212.
92. Ibid., p. 77.
93. Ibid., p. 85.
94. Livingston, *Modern Christian Thought*, p. 255.
95. Mueller, *Theology of Albrecht Ritschl*, p. 103.

only a state of the heart; it is a deed as well; it is faith active in love and in the sanctification of life. This is a truth with which evangelical Christians must become much better acquainted."[96] Faith, for Harnack, was a matter of religious sensibility to the moral meaning of God in which we "affirm the forces and the standards which on the summits of our inner life shine out as our highest good."[97]

Liberal Protestantism's reduction of faith to religious self-consciousness and moral striving did not go unchallenged. On the basis of what had already occurred in Friedrich Schleiermacher and Georg Wilhelm Friedrich Hegel (1770-1831), Søren Kierkegaard (1813-1855) was able to predict and protest the inculturation of faith that would later find dogmatic expression in Ritschl. Kierkegaard attacked every interpretation of faith as a product of ethics, science, or history. Faith cannot be reduced to a theory of moral value, because its object, God, makes an absolute claim of obedience which overrides any universal moral imperative. One who has faith "determines his relation to the universal by his relation to the absolute, not his relation to the absolute by his relation to the universal."[98] Thus Abraham, in obedience to the divine command, proves he is a "knight of faith" by attempting to kill his son.

Nor does faith possess God as the object of its knowledge, because, "to be known directly is the characteristic mark of an idol."[99] In Kierkegaard's view, faith contradicts knowledge. The "moment" of faith does not belong to the nexus of cause and effect which produces knowledge. Faith is the encounter of time with eternity between which there exists an "infinite qualitative distinction." The truth of faith is therefore paradoxical and "absurd" and is not based upon historical certainty. The contemporaries of Jesus did not come to faith by what they saw or heard. It pleased God "to walk here on earth in a strict incognito . . . impenetrable to the most intimate observation."[100] "Can one learn from history anything about Christ? No. Why not? . . . He is the paradox, the object of faith, existing only for faith."[101]

For Kierkegaard, faith had the character of an inwardness quite different from Schleiermacher's "feeling," because it corresponds to no

---

96. Adolf Harnack, *What is Christianity?* trans. T. B. Saunders (New York: Harper & Row, 1957), p. 287.
97. Ibid., p. 301.
98. Søren Kierkegaard, *Fear and Trembling*, trans. Walter Lowrie (Princeton, N.J.: Princeton University Press, 1941), p. 80.
99. Karl Barth, *The Epistle to the Romans*, trans. Edwin C. Hoskyns (London: Oxford University Press, 1933), p. 38.
100. Søren Kierkegaard, *Training in Christianity*, trans. Walter Lowrie (Princeton, N.J.: Princeton University Press, 1941), p. 27.
101. Ibid., p. 28.

perception of our relation to the world. The truth of faith has no objective reference. It is radical subjectivity in which the believer learns that he or she is in error (i.e., can know nothing of God objectively) and then holds this "objective uncertainty" with the most "passionate inwardness." This happens only because God himself is the teacher who at once brings this kind of knowledge to the believer and provides the conditions necessary for its understanding. The movement of faith can, from the human side, only be a "leap" away from all certainty and predictability. For Kierkegaard, faith involves as well a recognition and affirmation of such truths as the incarnation, justification, and the law of love. But he believed that these and other specific concepts and ideas had to be appropriated in a context of paradox and absurdity. In this way Kierkegaard's theology offered a corrective to centuries of Protestant neglect of its own heritage. His protest, however, failed to stem the tide of liberalism's dissolution of faith. This was due, in part, to the fact that, having neglected an exposition of God's action in faith, Kierkegaard's theology could be misunderstood as defining faith as a heroic, if also inexplicable, act of existential courage.[102]

The Protestant Doctrine of Faith in the Twentieth Century

It remained for Karl Barth, writing in the midst of the First World War, to denounce in no uncertain terms Protestantism's abandonment of the evangelical doctrine of faith. In viewing faith as a moral, emotional, or intellectual capacity, we actually, wrote Barth, "confound time and eternity."

> We suppose that we know what we are saying when we say "God." We assign to him the highest place in our world: and in so doing we place him fundamentally on one line with ourselves and with things. . . . We press ourselves into proximity with him: and so, all unthinking, we make him nigh unto ourselves. . . . Our arrogance demands that, in addition to everything else, some super world should also be known and accessible to us. Our conduct calls for some deeper sanction, some approbation and remuneration from another world. Our well-regulated, pleasurable life longs for some hours of devotion, some prolongation into infinity. . . . In "believing" on him we justify, enjoy, and adore ourselves. . . . We confound time and eternity."[103]

---

102. Otherwise, the neglect of Kierkegaard's thought can be explained by the fact that his works were not translated out of Danish until the end of the nineteenth century—and also, because his historical situation, in contrast to that of Barth in 1915, was not one in which the failure of liberalism was as yet historically apparent.

103. Barth, *Romans*, p. 44.

As far as Barth was concerned, the traditional distinction between the modern Protestant and Catholic view of faith had vanished. In fact, Barth believed that the Roman position on faith had remained closer to that of the Reformers than had Protestantism. If Catholic dogmatics had steadfastly refused to accept the idea of *sola fide*, they had also from the Council of Trent onward insisted equally upon the primacy of grace in the process of salvation. Moreover, as Barth noted in a 1928 lecture, Catholic liturgy kept before the church the evangelical principle—a principle exemplified in the words of the *Gloria*: "Thou alone art holy, thou alone art God, thou alone art highly exalted, Jesus Christ."[104] In light of this residue of Pauline theology in Catholicism, and equally in light of the collapse of Protestant theology into a celebration of human thought and action, Barth argued that the Catholic church in "its dogma, its ritual of worship, its general attitude . . . does hold before men's eyes something of that . . . without which the whole Reformation would have been purposeless. . . . It is closer to the Reformers than is the church of the Reformation so far as that has actually and finally become the new Protestantism."[105]

Barth's epoch-making *The Epistle to the Romans* (1918) may be understood as a reassertion of Luther's conception of faith as the work of God. Where Paul speaks of faith as salvific, Barth followed Rudolf Liechtenhan in rendering *pistis*, usually translated "faith," as "faithfulness."[106] Thus key passages in Romans are to be read: "For therein is revealed the righteousness of God from *faithfulness* unto faith: as it is written, But the righteous shall live from *my faithfulness*" (Rom 1:17). In Romans 3:28, where Luther interjected the word "alone," Barth places "the faithfulness of God," translating the verse, "For we reckon that a man is justified by *the faithfulness of God* apart from works of the law."[107] "Faith is the faithfulness of God, ever secreted in and beyond all human ideas and affirmations about him, and beyond every positive religious achievement."[108]

In Barth's commentary faith as human activity can only be described in negative terms. The New Testament offers no positive acts of believing, willing, and acting which could constitute some attitude or stance we might call faith. "The activity of the [New Testament] community is related to the gospel only insofar as it is no more than a crater formed

---

104. Karl Barth, *Theology and Church*, trans. L. P. Smith (New York: Harper & Row, 1962), p. 315.
105. Ibid., p. 314.
106. Barth, *Romans*, p. 14.
107. Ibid., p. 107.
108. Ibid., p. 98.

by the explosion of a shell and seeks to be no more than a void in which the gospel reveals itself."[109] Faith is directed to that which is "most deeply hidden" and "contradicts the obvious experience of the senses." It demands that the person of faith be

> sufficiently mature to accept a contradiction and rest in it. . . . Faith is awe in the presence of the divine incognito . . . a shattering halt in the presence of God. . . . Depth of feeling, strength of conviction, advance in perception and moral behavior are . . . no more than unimportant signs of the occurrence of faith, and moreover, as signs . . . they are not positive factors, but negations . . . stages in the work of clearance by which room is made in this world for that which is beyond it. Faith, therefore, is never identical with piety, however pure and however delicate.[110]

Luther's conception of faith as a saving activity of God was to prove elusive for other twentieth-century theologians. Although Paul Tillich (1886-1965) and Rudolf Bultmann (1884-1976) agreed with Barth's attack upon Protestant liberalism's identification of faith with bourgeois values, they could not conceive of faith as other than a human activity. Tillich wanted to reassert the essentials of Luther's doctrine. He embraced what he called "the Protestant principle"—by which he meant "the protest against any finite authority that takes upon itself an infinite claim."[111] He also held the theological principle that in every relation between man and God the action of God is prior and that faith was a condition of "being grasped."[112] "Faith," Tillich wrote, "is not belief and it is not knowledge with a low degree of probability."[113] Nor can faith be restricted to "the subjectivity of mere feeling."[114]

But Tillich could not recover Luther's doctrine of *sola fide*, because, for him, faith is at root a human activity. "Faith is the state of being ultimate concerned."[115] Our concern is "ultimate" if it is about the ground and power of being—which is to say, about God. Thus, Tillich's "Ultimate concern," like Schleiermacher's "Absolute dependence," implies the presence and power of the Ultimate about which one is concerned. But this inclusion of the divine in the human attitude of faith

---

109. Ibid., p. 36.
110. Ibid., pp. 39-40.
111. Alexander J. McKelway, *The Systematic Theology of Paul Tillich* (Richmond: Knox, 1964), p. 33.
112. Paul Tillich, *The Dynamics of Faith* (London: George Allen and Unwin, 1957), pp. 99ff.
113. Ibid., p. 35.
114. Ibid., p. 39.
115. Ibid., p. 1.

was not sufficient to protect Tillich's theory from collapsing the concept of faith into a new form of rationalism. For Tillich, the content of faith is "formed" by the questions raised from an analysis of human existence. Hence faith understands God as "being itself," and Christ as "the New Being," because the human situation requires that revelation be given that ontological form. Whether or not Tillich's method of correlation (of philosophical question and theological answer) succeeds in protecting the substance of revelation from distortion, it is clear that, for him, "faith" is a way of thinking about God—it is "an essential possibility for man."[116]

If Tillich's view of faith tends toward rationalism, that of Rudolf Bultmann recalls the subjective personalism of Pietism and evangelicalism. Bultmann, like Barth and Tillich, wished to avoid an informational interpretation of faith, namely, that of faith as mere *fides quae.* "To believe means not to have apprehended but to have been apprehended."[117] And yet, for Bultmann, faith is prefaced by self-understanding (*Vorverständnis*), actualized by existential decision, and represents a self-appropriation of the benefits of God for life. Faith is, therefore, something we do. "This is what I mean by 'faith': to open ourselves freely to the future."[118] Whatever one may think of Bultmann's program of demythologizing, or his use of Martin Heidegger's (1889-1976) existentialism, there can be no doubt that he holds faith to be a personal act of recognition and inward appropriation. For Bultmann truth is true only in so far as it is true *pro me.* Thus, my own dispostion defines the content of faith—even to the extent that "the saving efficacy of the cross is not derived from the fact that it is the cross of Christ: it is the cross of Christ because it has this saving efficacy [because it helps me]."[119] Bultmann believes that our perception of grace and hope not only defines but establishes the content of faith. That is made unambiguously clear when he asserts that "the event of Easter day . . . is nothing else than the rise of faith in the risen Lord."[120]

Bultmann's reduction of Luther's *solo fide* to an existential preunderstanding, decision, and hope helped to persuade Barth that the doctrine needed a thorough overhauling if it were to play any useful role in Christian faith. "Faith" must be understood not so much as a dialectical event, comprised of divine action and human response but as a polarity

---

116. Ibid., p. 126.
117. Rudolf Bultmann, *Kerygma and Myth* (New York: Harper & Row, 1961), p. 21.
118. Ibid., p. 19.
119. Ibid., p. 41.
120. Ibid., p. 42.

which prohibits any correlation of the divine and human. We have seen that in his *The Epistle to the Romans* Barth denied any substantive qualities to human faith. As a human reality that cannot contain the divine reality, faith could only be the vacuity found in a "crater," "dry stream bed," or "foot print." But later, as his theology developed, Barth discovered in Anselm's concept of faith a recognition of divine activity which makes knowledge of God possible. Barth contended that when Anselm spoke of "faith seeking understanding" (*fides quaerens intellectum*) he meant by "faith" a knowledge "which God himself compels."[121] Thought about God in theology, in worship, in the Bible, or in any other aspect of faith is possible only because God himself empowers thought and language. The epistemological basis of this possibility Barth called the "analogy of faith," because, while all knowledge depends upon analogy, thought and language about God depend upon an analogy made possible by God. It is therefore an analogy of "faith," because, as Luther said, "God does it." God controls the language of faith "elevating our words to their proper use, giving himself to be their proper object."[122] In this way Barth has reaffirmed the *fides divina*—faith as the activity of God. But this conception of faith he employed in the doctrine of revelation and not in the service of the doctrine of "justification by faith alone."

When, on the other hand, Barth turns his attention to faith as human response to the activity of God, he does not mean a "justifying" faith that saves "alone." He means a "spontaneous, a free, and active event" which can only respond to grace and can have no role at all in its effectiveness.[123] This act must be described first as *assensus* ("acknowledgment"), then *notitia* ("recognition"), and finally as *fiducia* (trust or "confession").[124] Throughout his discussion of faith as human action Barth takes pains to emphasize the point that in relation to God's act our faith is "puny," and deserves attention "not at the beginning but—and briefly—at the *end* of our road," i.e., the doctrine of justification.[125]

What then of the doctrine of justification by faith alone? To begin, Barth lays down the rule that "justification by faith cannot mean that

---

121. Karl Barth, *Anselm: Fides Quaerens Intellectum* (London: SCM, 1960), p. 167.
122. Karl Barth, *Church Dogmatics*, Vol. II/1 (Edinburgh: T & T Clark, 1957), p. 23.
123. Ibid., IV/1, p. 758.
124. Ibid., IV/1, pp. 758ff.
125. Barth in fact devotes only 39 pages to the human side of faith, to "faith as act," which, notes Gerhard Ebeling, "by the standards of the *Church Dogmatics*, is an unusually modest length." Gerhard Ebeling, *Word and Faith* (London: SCM, 1960), p. 202.

instead of his customary evil works and in place of all kinds of supposed good works man chooses and accomplishes the work of faith."[126] Saving faith has the character of humility. It is not something about which the believer could in any sense be proud or take personal satisfaction. No correct theology, deep conviction, social consciousness, or evangelical self-surrender can constitute saving faith. At the same time, mere abnegation as such cannot stand for faith. "If faith in its negative form is indeed an emptying, then it is certainly an emptying of all the results of such practice of self-emptying."[127] The void and absence brought to light in his early treatment of faith in *The Epistle to the Romans* is now for Barth filled with the image of Jesus Christ. He is not only the object of saving faith, but as well its subject and content—its "author and finisher" (Heb 12:2). He is the man justified before God, and in him "alone" are we justified. Thus Barth concludes that the doctrine of justification "by faith alone" has meaning and truth only as an expression of justification "by grace alone," which is to say "by Christ alone." "What is the *sola fide* but a faint yet necessary echo of the *solus Christus?*"[128]

Barth's turn toward the activity of God in Christ as the content of saving faith is not characteristic of modern Protestantism, but his shift away from justification by faith alone as its indispensible doctrine is. For instance, although the 1833 Confession of the New Hampshire Baptist Convention speaks sparingly of "justification through faith," the 1925 Statement of Baptist Faith and Message eliminates the reference altogether.[129] The Presbyterian Church's "Confession of '67" barely represents the doctrine of justification by faith in the statement that "those joined to him by faith are set right with God."[130] In the Presbyterians' 1989 Brief Statement of Faith there is no mention of the concept at all—as there is none in the Statement of Faith of the United Church of Christ (1959).[131]

Interestingly enough, confessional withdrawal from the doctrine of justification by faith alone has been paralleled by a continuing emphasis upon faith as "saving knowledge" among evangelical Protestants such as Billy Graham, Jerry Falwell, and others. Here faith is understood to be an effective affirmation; one is "saved" by "accepting Christ."[132] On the

126. Barth, *Church Dogmatics*, IV/1, p. 615.
127. Ibid., IV/1, p. 629.
128. Ibid., IV/1, p. 632.
129. Leith, *Creeds*, pp. 334-343.
130. *Book of Confessions*, I.A.1.
131. Leith, *Creeds*, pp. 590-591.
132. "If you will put that little faith in the person of Jesus, your life will be changed." (*The Quotable Billy Graham*, ed. C. R. Flint [Anderson: Droke House, 1966], p. 74.) Graham can also speak of "all who have been born again

other hand, among Protestant liberation theologians (Robert M. Brown, Letty Russell, et al.) there is an inclination to view faith as *fides formata*, in which peace with God is conditional upon the reconciliation of human conflict and injustice.[133] In either case the Reformers' insistence upon faith as the work of God is lost.

In this situation contemporary Protestantism may be forced to abandon the form of Luther's doctrine of faith in order to preserve its substance. If the dialectical definition of faith as both a divine and human act could be dislodged from its supreme position as the litmus of Protestantism, and elsewhere employed with reserve, then justification could be viewed unambiguously as the gracious and unmerited work of God in Christ, with no danger that our moral life or inner disposition could be construed as a contributing cause of salvation. Faith could be seen as human response to this grace, and theology could proceed to explore the meaning of the assent, knowledge, trust, and obedience that belong to faith without at every turn being burdened by dialectical contradiction. In this way the doctrine of faith could become the occasion for unity rather than conflict between Protestantism and Catholicism. It could become the basis for a new agreement upon the primacy of grace and the practical demands of the faith that belongs to the believer. This, at any rate, seems to have been the intention of Karl Barth—whose thought must certainly have influenced the result of recent Catholic-Lutheran dialogues on justification by faith. The remarkable Common Statement (1985) produced by those discussions provides a fitting conclusion to this chapter.

Our entire hope of justification and salvation rests on Christ Jesus and on the gospel whereby the good news of God's merciful action in

---

by accepting this finished work of Christ," forgetting, apparently, that such birth, according to John 3:6, comes from the "Spirit" and not from the "flesh." (*The Faith of Billy Graham*, ed. T. S. Settel, [Anderson: Droke House, 1968], p. 92). The same view of faith is found in various self-improvement theologies. Norman Vincent Peale, for instance, proclaims, "Make your life what you want it to be through belief in God and yourself," which, as far as P. J. Lee is concerned, puts him in the same category as Graham. Phillip J. Lee, *Against the Protestant Gnostics* (New York: Oxford University Press, 1987), p. 150.

133. "But faith's reality . . . will come only by joining parties and organizations that are authentic instruments of the struggle of the working class." (Robert McAfee Brown, *Theology in a New Key* [Philadelphia: Westminster, 1978], p. 59.) Russell identifies herself with the words of Gustavo Gutiérrez. "Theology of liberation attempts to reflect on the experience and meaning of faith based on the commitment to abolish injustice and to build a new society." (Letty Russell, *Human Liberation in a Feminist Perspective—A Theology* [Philadelphia, Westminster, 1974], p. 20.) These statements accurately reflect the necessary implications of Luther's conception of faith, but not the conception itself.

Christ is made known; we do not place our ultimate trust in anything other than God's promises and saving work in Christ. This excludes ultimate reliance on our faith, virtues or merits, even though we acknowledge God working in these by grace alone (*sola gratia*).[134]

---

134. Anderson, Murphy, and Burges, *Justification*, p. 16.

PART III
FACILITATING GROWTH IN FAITH

CHAPTER 9

Facilitating Growth in Faith Through Liturgical Worship

Louis Weil

INTRODUCTION

An examination of the relation of faith to liturgical worship requires a fundamental distinction between two essential ways in which faith and liturgy are interdependent.[1] The distinction can be succinctly indicated by noting the difference between the two ways in which the term "faith" is commonly used in the Christian tradition. First, there are those contexts in which reference is made to what is called *the* faith, namely, the whole body of Christian teaching as articulated in the Creeds, conciliar documents, confessional statements, the writings of major saints and doctors, and, most important of all, the revealed truths of Holy Scripture. The faith, in this sense, is a complex body of doctrines viewed as essential expressions of the teaching of Christ. Although there are substantial areas of agreement among different Christian communions as to the content of the faith, it is evident that there are also significant differences as to which of the sources listed above make up that fundamental deposit of faith. Yet there would be general agreement as to the nature of this first sense of "faith" as the doctrinal content of Christianity.

---

1. Cf. Charles P. Price and Louis Weil, "Faith and Conversion" in *Liturgy for Living* (New York: Seabury, 1979), pp. 28-29. See also Irénée-Henri Dalmais, "The Liturgy and the Deposit of Faith" in *The Church at Prayer* (Collegeville, Minn.: Liturgical Press, 1983), Vol. I, pp. 273-280.

The other way in which the term "faith" is used is complementary to the first but shifts its focus from the objective content of Christian truth to the human response to God's revelation in a trusting acceptance which leads to and enables a belief in God's redemptive activity in human history. This second sense of faith is generally understood as a gift of God's grace which sustains and nourishes a conviction about the reality of God and about the mighty works of God distinct from and even prior to a rational understanding of that revelation.

These two senses of faith relate to liturgical worship in various ways which will be explored in this chapter. In regard to the first, what we might appropriately call the "propositional" aspect of faith, we shall consider *how* a liturgical rite is a proclamation of faith. Yet, at the same time, it is crucial to the nature of the liturgical act that a didactic purpose not be imposed upon the liturgical texts. Liturgical acts proclaim the church's faith, not in the way that a theological document might set out to present a systematic summary of a particular theological issue, but rather in the way that great poetry lifts up through its images the most profound realities of human existence and intimations of a transcendent dimension. When we consider those times in history when the liturgy has been reordered toward a didactic purpose, we find a fundamental betrayal of this revelatory dimension of liturgical acts.

As to the second sense of faith, we shall consider how authentic liturgical worship is celebrated upon the presumption that those who have gathered are "the faithful," that is, that liturgical rites are celebrated by assemblies of people who are already caught up in the dynamic of a response to God in their lives, and who are consequently, in the liturgical action, lifting up a sign of what is unfolding in their lives. This process of unfolding is not merely an articulation of the human response to God because the liturgy is never one-directional. Liturgical worship signifies both God's initiative action toward the assembly in summoning and nurturing a faithful people, and also the response of that people through gesture, word, and song as they give voice to the faith which has called them to gather and then to go forth to serve in God's name.

Our first concern will be a consideration of how liturgy articulates the faith: What is the specifically liturgical mode in which Christian truth is proclaimed? This will require a consideration of the ancient adage *lex orandi, lex credendi*, which we might freely translate, "praying shapes believing." The interplay between faith and rite is both subtle and complex, and it is often misunderstood. Once certain basic aspects of this relation have been set forth, we shall examine the second sense of faith as it relates to liturgical worship. There is a preliturgical aspect of this sense of faith which requires special attention for an analysis of how liturgical worship is linked to growth in faith and how that worship must be claimed as an essential occasion in which that growth may be nurtured in the ongoing life of the Christian community.

LITURGY AS SOURCE OF THE FAITH

For many centuries the work of theologians on the meaning of worship has been pursued at a theoretical level within the framework of systematic theology. This meant that liturgical theory developed in separation from the reality of the liturgical act as celebrated within the various communities of faith. This approach has not only overlooked what the liturgical texts themselves proclaimed about the nature of corporate worship but also the wider context of the total liturgical experience, in both its verbal and nonverbal dimensions. An important development in recent decades among theologians and liturgists has been the recovery of the bridge which should naturally unite their two areas of investigation.[2] It is in the corporate worship of Christians that the faith finds its most public articulation. Yet for many generations, theologians have, for example, written about the theology of baptism or of the eucharist with little or no reference to the rites which Christians have used in the celebration of those sacramental acts as well as their fuller sociological framework. Today it would be generally agreed that the evolution of liturgical rites and norms of performance offers valuable insight into how Christian theology has developed, shifted in emphasis, or reached out for new images to express the Christian experience of the presence and action of God.

To say, however, that the liturgy is a primary source for the church's faith, that is, the doctrines which Christians are committed to believe, does not mean that liturgical texts may be approached like doctrinal summaries of the faith. The liturgy has a special character, and as a theological source it must be used in a way which is congruent with the nature of the liturgy itself.[3] Earlier in this chapter a comparison was made between the ways in which liturgy and poetry communicate. This

---

2. Lawrence A. Hoffman, *Beyond the Text: A Holistic Approach to Liturgy* (Bloomington, Ind.: Indiana University Press, 1987) offers a new method of approach to the study of liturgy by moving beyond the familiar ground of the study of the ritual texts to the wider context of liturgy as a human activity.

3. Cf. Geoffrey Wainwright, *Doxology* (New York: Oxford University Press, 1980), pp. 218-283. Related material by other authors may be found in *Worship* 57:4 (July 1983), pp. 309-332. See also Aidan Kavanagh, *On Liturgical Theology* (New York: Pueblo, 1984), esp. pp. 73-121.

immediately suggests that the relation of liturgy to the faith must be approached with sensitivity to the particular and highly complex character of human ritual actions. Human activity is, in fact, the first consideration: The liturgy is an action, not merely a text printed on a page. The texts of the liturgy cannot be separated from this dynamic context of *doing*, of movement and gesture and celebration, without distorting the nature of those texts as proclaimed prayer. The text, then, is really only one component within the complex of elements which make up the liturgical whole. The texts are a significant part of the action, but their meaning may be claimed only with reference to the action as a whole. In addition to the textual element of the liturgy, the action involves a range of symbolic movements and gestures, a kind of sacred dance which has a mysteriously efficacious power to communicate the presence of the Holy. This dimension of the liturgy conditions the way in which we may study its texts as a source for the faith. Unlike a doctrinal treatise, the liturgy does not have teaching as its primary goal. This often creates a problem for theologians who examine liturgical texts in the way that a theological document would be studied. By comparison, liturgical texts rely, like poetry, upon metaphor and image. Such texts are often, by the rules of systematic theology, doctrinally vague. Any analysis of liturgical texts which does not take into account its similarity to poetry as a means of expression is likely to be misleading. This is to ask the liturgy to be what it is not by nature intended to be.

To emphasize this holistic understanding of the liturgy is in no sense intended to denigrate the importance of religious education and the need for Christians to study the doctrines of the faith as is appropriate to their intellectual interest and capacity. But it is to insist that this need is not appropriately met within the liturgical context because the nature of the liturgy is not to teach the faith but rather to celebrate it in a symbolic act. Liturgical texts are a fruitful source for theological reflection, but for that fruit to be claimed, the texts must be considered within the wider context of the liturgical action as a whole.

The goal of the liturgy is to enable those who participate in it to live more deeply the mystery of salvation which the rites evoke in signs. Its purpose then reaches further than merely the articulation of correct doctrine. The purpose of the liturgy is to incorporate those who share in its action into a faith which is not only professed but lived. All the elements which make up the liturgical rite have as their common purpose the proclamation of the paschal mystery, that is, the redemptive action of God seen in its most intense focus in the death and resurrection of Jesus. The appointed readings from Holy Scripture, which are a basic element in all liturgical rites, offer the assembly direct contact with a foundational source of the faith. Through the liturgical preaching, the people have brought before them a fuller awareness of how the scripture readings are connected with their own lives in order to deepen their insight into the ways in which God continues to be present and active in the world.

Further, liturgical rites presume a social framework for their celebration. Whereas there is inevitably a private dimension to the response of faith, the proclamation of the faith which is accomplished through the liturgy always unfolds within an assembled community. Because of this communal character which is integral to the nature of liturgical rites, the liturgy offers an intense experience of ecclesial communion. Unfortunately, our culture has tended to interpret religious experience in highly individualized terms, as a matter merely of personal choice. Most of us are so shaped by these inherited attitudes that unconsciously we bring them with us into our participation in liturgical acts, and even interpret those acts through a kind of individualized filter. Yet the liturgy itself communicates its meaning from within a social or corporate model. Its nature is as a common, shared action. This corporate nature of liturgical acts implies the corporate nature of the faith which those acts proclaim. Membership in the church involves membership within a fellowship of faith. The faith which the liturgy proclaims is a faith shared, a faith into which all have been baptized and which is confirmed and nourished in corporate worship. In this perspective, the liturgy images a unity which Christians have traditionally associated with the kingdom of God, and thus in each assembly there is lifted up a sign of the future hope of Christians as the liturgy proclaims the unity of faith in which all mankind is called to participate.[4]

It is precisely because of the nondidactic character of the liturgy that the liturgical tradition manifests a truly ecumenical significance. Whereas the divisions in the church often reflect the disagreements of theologians over one issue or another of Christian doctrine or biblical interpretation, liturgical texts often manifest an open and inclusive ethos which seems to transcend denominational barriers and thus to point to the fundamental unity of all the baptized in a common faith. Diversity of style in the various Christian traditions does not negate the essential unity of faith which manifests itself through the great liturgical texts of the common prayer of the church.

Such diversity in the first instance reflects differences of cultural ethos which have shaped the origins of each of the major Christian traditions. Differences of musical styles or of ritual patterns are not doctrinal in their foundations but are rather reflective of the rich and yet distinct

---

4. Cf. Dalmais, *Church at Prayer*, pp. 240-248.

cultural heritages which have contributed to the particular character of each liturgical family. Yet in addition to such diversity, the divisions among Christians have often contributed to the reshaping of the traditional forms under the impact of a didactic purpose. When the liturgical act is expected to fulfill such a didactic goal, its rites come to be judged more for propositional orthodoxy than in terms of their instrumentality as a means by which faith is celebrated. This imposition of a didactic purpose upon liturgical rites results in the reshaping of the liturgical experience itself.

There are many examples in the history of Christianity which might be noted in this regard, but one major example may suffice to show how the liturgy can come to reflect not unity but separation. The example comes from what is undoubtedly a very complex period in church history, the time of the Protestant Reformation. The reactions of the Reformers in the liturgical realm, however, cannot be separated from the situation which they were seeking to address. During the centuries immediately prior to the Reformation, the liturgy had come to be seen more and more as a private area of clerical responsibility and authority. This situation developed slowly and very much under the influence of forces which were shaping the general culture. As a result, the liturgy had ceased to be experienced by most Christians as the occasion of a proclamation of their common faith. There was a great gulf between clergy and laity, and the laity were denied participation in the sacred rites. So firm was the separation that the rites were celebrated in such a low voice by the clergy that they could not even be heard. In this context, the fact that the language of the liturgy was increasingly not the ordinary language of the street simply confirmed the alienation.

As grim as this picture is, it must be evoked as the backdrop to the reshaping of the understanding of the liturgy which took place at the Reformation. One of the great concerns of the Reformers was to reaffirm the centrality of the Word of God in the lives of Christians as a whole. The inferior status of the laity which dominated in medieval society was accompanied by a general lack of education of the laity, including a lack of education in matters of the faith. The common illiteracy of the laity during this period contributed to the church's failure to accomplish this work. Thus, for the Reformers, the recovery of the central role of the Word of God involved a renewed concern with religious education. We noted earlier the importance of such education for the spiritual health of Christians, but the concern of the Reformers for such education combined with their heritage from recent centuries of a clericalized liturgical tradition, led to an imposition upon the liturgy of this new didactic goal.

The assembly of Christians came to be seen preeminently as an opportunity for the teaching of the faith. There can be little doubt that the didactic aspects of Christian formation had been seriously ignored during the centuries prior to the Reformation. The imposing of this concern upon Christian worship made the liturgy more an occasion of teaching *about* the faith than an occasion of the celebration of faith. What had in the early centuries been characteristically a holistic human activity became essentially a mental activity. The effect of this didactic concern imposed upon the liturgical rites was far-reaching. Liturgical texts became the instruments through which right teaching might be effected, and the rites came to bear the marks of the polemical debates which separated Christians. Thus the liturgy became a sign of separation rather than of unity in faith. To a substantial degree, this didactic distortion of the liturgy affected all churches in which some pattern of liturgical forms were used for public worship.

It can be no accident that within this century the ecumenical movement and liturgical renewal have developed side by side. As the ecumenical movement has attempted to uncover the common ground of faith which all Christians share, so also has the liturgical movement reaffirmed the nature of corporate worship as a celebration of that faith. Not surprisingly, the first stage of liturgical renewal involved the study of primitive texts of the liturgical tradition, texts which are the common heritage of Christians and which are not marked by later polemical debates. Such texts have not only offered models in which Christians of different traditions might pray together but they have also served as a quiet leaven in the reshaping of our liturgical mentality. The study and celebration of early texts have served as a corrective to the overladen and often highly didactic models of recent centuries. These early texts are seen as a privileged witness to apostolic tradition since they permit us to hear the voice of prayer of Christian communities who lived in times much closer to the events of salvation history than our own.

It is in this context that the ancient adage *lex orandi, lex credendi* ("praying shapes believing") is seen to have great significance in regard to the relation between faith and liturgy. The assembly of Christians— and especially at their principal assembly on Sundays—is the place at which the faith of Christians is proclaimed in the shared celebration of that faith.[5] In a corporate action, using words and signs, the faith into which all have been baptized is expressed and at the same time nurtured in each member of the assembly. In proclaiming the faith, the primary purpose of the rites is not a narrow didacticism but rather the formation of the common identity which all share and which is the point of

---

5. Cf. Louis Weil, *Gathered to Pray* (Cambridge, Mass.: Cowley 1986), pp. 123-137.

departure for the mission of Christians in the world. The liturgy is thus a highly complex action, and the mode in which it proclaims the faith is subtle. Although the liturgy may incorporate doctrinal formulations, such as, "Glory to the Father, and to the Son, and to the Holy Spirit," its manner of proclaiming the faith is rather found in its offering access to the experience of the One upon whom faith is centered. The liturgy is thus never static, because the liturgical expressions of a doctrinal statement are set in the vocabulary of the culture and time at which they were written. The liturgy is always grounded in the lived reality of a community of faith. Because of the continuity of the life and witness of the church there is also continuity in the tradition of liturgical forms which articulate and sum up the prayers of generations of believers. Yet the rites are always, although usually gently, in flux, since if the liturgy is to be the authentic prayer of each generation it must incorporate new images from the faith experience of each succeeding age.

Having set forth this modest overview of the relation of faith to the liturgy, we shall now consider how that faith may be nurtured through participation in the corporate prayer of Christians. For growth in faith to take place the liturgy must be seen within the wider framework of pastoral responsibility, since formation in faith touches every aspect of the church's life.

FORMATION THROUGH LITURGY

This chapter has suggested that the primary purpose of liturgy is to celebrate the Christian faith rather than to be the occasion on which that faith is taught. Within the patterns of Christian worship, however, there is clearly an overlapping of these two purposes so that it is impossible to make a rigid distinction between these two intentions. It would perhaps be better to say that the primary intention of liturgical rites is to proclaim and to celebrate the marvelous works of God.

Such an approach to the liturgy will inevitably affect the approach to liturgical norms within any Christian community. The ways in which liturgy shapes the faith life of the members of a particular parish will flow out of the fundamental understanding of what liturgy is about. If the approach is didactic, then there will be specific results, for example, with regard to the doctrinal content in the texts of prayers and hymns. But if, as we have suggested, the liturgy is seen as a celebration of a common faith shared by all members of the community, liturgical priorities will give greater emphasis to the whole human context of the liturgical action as a corporate experience in which that faith is nourished.

Yet the teaching of the faith remains a fundamental and essential imperative for each generation of Christians. Teaching of the faith and celebration of the faith bear a close interconnectedness in that each requires the other if both are to fulfill their respective purposes. Our goal now is to clarify what each is concerned to *do* in the Christian life. We shall find that the purpose of each is related in its own but distinct way to liturgical worship.

Faith in its second sense, as we have commented earlier, is concerned with the human response to God which is characterized by a trusting acceptance, a belief in God's loving providence. Whereas the first sense refers to doctrinal substance, the second refers to a type of attitude, a conviction about the reality of God. But how is that conviction developed and what is its relation to liturgical prayer? Although we have spoken of it as a gift from God, the pastoral experience of the church indicates that there are aspects of the church's ministry to its members which can foster the gift and promote its growth. The problem is that for a great many Christians, faithfulness to the church is often determined by a minimalist model or expectation, namely, attendance at a liturgical service on Sunday morning.

Most clergy would agree that the goals of mature Christian formation within a congregation require an investment of time and energy, an overall commitment which extends beyond the time limits of this weekly attendance at public worship. Yet many laity have been conditioned, often by the attitudes of their parents, to equate that weekly hour of liturgical prayer with the sum of their Christian experience. The church has often failed to hold up a model of Christian living which asks much more that that of the individual. The frustration which grows out of such a situation may help to explain why clergy often feel obliged to use the occasion of the Sunday liturgy as their only didactic opportunity. As a result, it is all too easy to try to exploit the liturgy as a kind of teaching device in which Sunday worship seems the only occasion available to accomplish this other aspect of Christian formation. Our tendency since the Reformation to see the liturgy as a didactic tool reinforces the pastoral imperative. The result is an ineffective conflation in which neither the purposes of Christian formation nor those of corporate worship are adequately achieved. If corporate worship is truly to proclaim that faith which Christians share as the Body of Christ, formation in faith must be seen as a kind of preliturgical priority, a foundation upon which the liturgical signs are sustained and from which they are nourished. Yet the two dimensions are distinct. The liturgy is not a device for creating faith in either of the two senses which we have discussed: The liturgy does not create a disposition of trust in God, nor does the liturgy teach correct doctrine. For those who are "the faithful," the liturgy has a marvelous power to nourish trust in God (faith in the second sense) and to celebrate belief in the mighty works of God (faith in the first sense). To fulfill these purposes, liturgical acts themselves *presume* faith, that is, they are celebrated upon the presupposition that those who gather are in some sense already "in faith." Thus Christian formation in the full sense of that term cannot be accomplished only within the context of liturgical worship.

One aspect of the purpose of formation, as we have seen, is the communication of information. In what we call religious education, this aspect has to do with the passing on of the tradition, the substance of what Christians have believed and why, and how that tradition has been shaped within the wider framework of human history and culture. As we noted earlier, this aspect of Christian formation can be engaged at many different levels of intensity and intellectual sophistication, and there are many Christians of very deep faith for whom this aspect of the tradition takes a very insignificant role. Yet in the overall scope of the church's life this dimension is of great importance because it involves the content of the faith. In regard to faith, that content is not a set of abstract realities. The content of the faith is a mirror to the personal pilgrimage of every Christian. Salvation history is reflected in each individual's salvation history. The content may be called "the Tradition," the passing along of the substance of the Christian inheritance which is the birthright of the baptized. The goal of preaching in the liturgical context is to deepen the awareness of this connection: The saving events in history are proclaimed as an assurance of God's present activity in our own lives.[6]

Yet Christian formation is not limited to the communication of the cognitive content of the Christian faith. Formation has a much wider scope. With the best of intentions, clergy often fail to convey this broader dimension, and limit parish courses to data, information about the faith. The larger picture requires formation for a life of faith, a life of prayer, and help in building the foundations of a Christian lifestyle. Without these dimensions, the liturgy tends to be little more than a formalized ritual and not to accomplish its essential purpose as proclamation of faith.

The content of the faith (information about the tradition) is important, but it is clearly secondary to the more critical concern of the incorporation of individuals into that tradition. Without a commitment of faith on the part of the individual believer, teaching *about* Christian-

---

6. Thomas Downs, *The Parish as Learning Community* (New York: Paulist, 1979) offers practical suggestions by which a parish may become a center for religious education.

ity falls upon ears which have not been tuned to the proper frequency. Personal adherence to the basic claim of Christianity that "God was in Christ reconciling the world to himself" prepares the field in which religious understanding may grow. In regard to faith, there is an essential role for the affective-personal dimension of Christian formation. Formation is thus not merely informative, but rather precisely what the word says, *formative*: Its goal is to touch the whole person, not just the intellect.

It is only within this larger framework that we find the adequate preparation of Christians for a lifetime of sharing in the corporate worship of the community of faith. The didactic dimension, the communication of information, has a legitimate role. For some people the cognitive didactic dimension of the process may play a critical role in their coming to faith, being themselves inclined to question and ponder. Notwithstanding, those who are responsible for the formation in faith of a congregation, both clergy and lay leaders, must not lose sight of the wider holistic framework in which persons come to know and to believe. To know God involves the mind, but also the heart, the feeling aspect of the human being, the dimension which defies capturing in cognitive formulas or concepts. Formation in faith in its fullness is built upon an integration of all dimensions of the human.

FAITH AND THE CATECHUMENATE

Within a number of Christian traditions there has emerged an interest in a liturgical subject which has been neglected for centuries and which has only in recent decades reclaimed its significance in connection with formation in faith, namely, the catechumenate.[7] In contrast to modern programs which see formation solely in terms of cognitive content, the ancient classical catechumenate was not concerned only or even primarily with the communication of information. As the contemporary church recovers the place of the catechumenate in Christian formation, people have become enabled to make the fundamental connections which a mature faith requires: between baptism and ministry, and between worship and their daily lives. Without integrative formation, liturgical rites easily become encapsulated experiences of the Holy which are disconnected from the realities of the human situation. This disconnection became obvious within the pastoral scene during the

---

7. An enormous literature concerning the catechumenate has appeared in recent years. See, for example, Michel Dujarier, *A History of the Catechumenate* (New York: Sadlier, 1979); Raymond B. Kemp, *A Journey in Faith* (New York: Glazier, 1979).

1960s and 1970s when various churches were involved in liturgical revision. During those years, there was much negative reaction to what was perceived as the loss of the sacred dimension, and often this perception focused on the loss of a hallowed liturgical language. This is a complex issue not appropriately discussed in full in this chapter. Nonetheless, we can briefly note that when liturgical rites are said to speak of the sacred precisely because of their separation from what is human and ordinary, there is a grave danger that a fundamental connection between God and the world, integral to faith in the incarnation, has not been made. In the liturgy, what is most fully human is revealed as the domain of God's present action. We must avoid a false sense of "mystery" in Christian worship. The mysterious aspect of Christian liturgy is not found in separation from the ordinary but in its manifestation of God's presence in the ordinary and basic realities of human life: in touch, in water, in food and drink. The goal of the catechumenate is that faith be made explicit in the immediacy of human experience.

All of this is to say that the liturgy has the potential to form the Christian community in faith. This potential is not accomplished primarily through words and concepts but through the whole liturgical experience. The doctrines of the faith which are articulated in liturgical rites are not communicated didactically but rather through images. In other words, the liturgical experience is open, ambiguous, not neatly defined and pinned down in cognitive formulas and definitions. This is not how liturgy has generally been experienced and understood in the centuries since the Reformation, for the priorities of the Enlightenment tended to reinforce the use of the liturgy for didactic purposes. Recent developments in the field of liturgy and related areas, such as ritual studies, have had significant impact upon the inherited view and have brought a judgment upon it. Increasingly, the essential nature of liturgical ritual is being recognized as a sign of the cosmic dance of faith, as an entrance into and celebration of a reality which is beyond definitions and concepts, in which only the evocative language of gesture and movement, color, sound, and fragrance can suggest a transcendent beauty which is at once imprecise and yet absolutely real, in which truth is not limited by the categories of facticity, and which alone is worthy of faith.

It is evident that a whole new approach to the relation of faith and worship is being called for, and, as was noted earlier, the most appropriate language and images of that approach are found not in theological treatises but in the arts. There is a story told about the great dancer Martha Graham. She was once asked what was the meaning of a dance which she had just performed, and so she repeated the dance. Then Graham commented, "If I could say what it meant, I would not have danced it." What does a ring on a hand *mean*? What does a meal shared by friends *mean*? If we attempt to explain marriage and eucharist in definitions, like Martha Graham's questioner, we have missed the point. These wonderfully ambivalent signs point us to the experience of the divine penetration of our humanity at a depth which reason alone can never explain. The liturgy forms us in faith not through a didactic program of sound doctrine but as we are formed in undefinable ways through art, poetry, and music.

The way in which liturgy forms Christians in faith is primarily around such elemental factors as touch and taste and smell, and through the repetitious, yet not monotonous, character of ritual acts. The liturgy forms us as it illuminates the many personal—both shared and individual—meanings which the participants bring into the framework of the liturgical action. It is essentially a corporate and unitive formation as Christians participate together in the mysterious signs of faith in the paschal mystery. We see this pattern set forth in a particularly focused way in the celebration of the various familiar rites of Holy Week, and especially in the powerful constellation of signs which are held together in the Easter Vigil, an ancient rite which has in recent decades recovered a place in the official liturgical books of various Christian denominations. In some parishes there is an enormous continuity and repetitiveness from year to year of the ritual pattern of the Vigil, but for believers who have engaged its signs with their lives the Vigil is never the same twice. To the proclamation of the events of salvation history, the people of God bring, as was indicated earlier, their own salvation history, and most particularly the events of their lives during the past year and which are here considered in the mirror of redemption. In this perspective, they do not simply attend a familiar rite but rather enter into the signs of redemption at a new level, through a deepening awareness of the workings of grace in all the specific realities of their ordinary lives. This is what formation in faith through liturgy is all about.

What has been said about the Easter Vigil may also be applied to the Sunday-by-Sunday assemblies of Christians in local churches all over the world. The rites of the Vigil and its occurrence on an annual cycle give a newness to each encounter with it. But the foundation upon which Christians are formed by the liturgy is seen preeminently in the weekly assembly on the Lord's Day, and in most traditions in the celebration of the eucharist.[8] Why all these assemblies, week after week, year after year in order? What is their purpose? Is it all simply a liturgical routine? Is it in order to make sure that the congregation gets the doctrine correct? Although perhaps no one would give so didactic a

---

reason, is the idea that Sunday worship is a duty, a matter of obedience to the law, any better? The church gathers to worship God each Sunday because it is in this *doing* that we see who we are as the people of God. In worship we take hold of our identity as the body of Christ. In it we are invited into a deeper awareness of the path of faith into the paschal mystery as it is realized—made real—in the life of the community.

This vision of the interrelatedness of worship and faith is not a fact to be learned like an answer in the catechism. Rather it is an experience through which we share in the church's self-realization and are thus formed through this shared identity with the other members of the family of faith. It is baptism which brings this identity into being as new Christians are made "other Christs," and it is the church's corporate worship which celebrates and proclaims this identity as the one body shares the one bread. As Augustine preached to his people at Hippo, "You are the bread on the altar."

The liturgy, then, is the church enacting itself in faith under the gospel of Jesus Christ, at a given time and in a given place, and within the context of a complex pattern of particular circumstances. Such liturgical acts are not celebrated within an other-worldly ideal, some concept of a *pure* church, but by a real community placed in history. It is that community's shared faith which is actualized in the liturgy and which links each particular assembly with other faith communities— often radically different in ethos—all over the world. The common ritual ground of the church's signs of faith establishes the scope of its identity. It is for this reason that ritual patterns resist change: The repeated ritual patterns are a concrete expression of that identity and its continuity. Quixotic liturgical change threatens that identity. Yet if the inner core of the liturgy is not to become a fossil, the outward forms will inevitably and of necessity undergo subtle modification as the dimensions of the community's life change. In the end, the trauma of ritual change is less critical than the imperative of the renewal of the Christian life which is the fruit of a maturing faith.

This assertion points us once again to the fundamental role of some form of catechumenal formation for growth in maturity of faith. Such formation is concerned with the essential connections which each believer must make between the faith which they profess and their manner of living. Without this connection, the liturgy can become a dangerous distraction from the confrontation which must take place between the individual's life and the imperatives of the gospel. Without the type of formation which enables faith progressively to mature, the liturgy can become rather like an exquisite hothouse plant which is beautiful to the eye but which can be maintained only under artificially controlled conditions. Such a situation exists all too often and especially in congregations where the liturgical rites are not experienced within the wider context of Christian education. The result is a rather schizoid attitude toward liturgical acts in which what is *said* in the rite is not lifted up in judgment upon what is *done* in daily life. The moral delusion which this permits is staggering. To address this danger, an educational process in which individuals are challenged to hold up their real lives to the light of the gospel is essential. The goal of such a program is conversion, a fundamental change of direction. Without this critical change within, the signs of the liturgy will remain external in the experience of the individual, unconnected to the process of transformation which faith should be bringing to maturity in that person's life. It is one of the major pastoral responsibilities of both the ordained ministry and the nonordained leaders of religious education to nurture the incipient faith of Christian neophytes so that it may grow to maturity in their daily lives. Without such growth, the liturgy runs the risk of pandering to a superficial religious engagement which never matures into an authentic marriage.

We see then that there is a possible danger to liturgical rites in their relation to faith. Liturgical rites may, as we have suggested, foster faith if preliturgical formation enables believers to make the essential connections between the liturgical symbols and the realities to which they refer.[9] Without such fundamental connections, they are likely to remain no more than a surface religious experience. This danger is a potential betrayal of the whole underlying purpose of liturgical worship, and it is especially severe in those churches in which external aspects of the ritual have a particularly dramatic or formal character. The Gospel of Matthew offers a sobering reminder of Christ's definitive rejection of any religious practices which identify the meaning with the external form *only* (Mt 6:1-6). External rites and practices are an overflowing, an articulation of the working of faith in our lives, or else they are perverse. It is for this reason that a serious program of education is fundamental for the healthy interplay of faith and liturgical worship.

FOSTERING GROWTH

In this perspective, what would the liturgical life of the community of faith look like if it is to be a true signification of the interior life and character of the persons who make up a specific community? The emphasis which has been given to preliturgical foundations is supported and confirmed in insight which we gain from liturgical history.

---

9. Cf. Louis Weil, "Pre-Liturgical Priorities," *Nashotah Review* 11:3 (Summer, 1971), pp. 97-103.

It is well known that during the period of the classical catechumenate (from the third to the sixth centuries), those who were seeking initiation into the church passed through a time of preparation which was often structured according to a three-year model. The texts which have come down to us from that period indicate that the catechumenate was not primarily a time of didactic formation in the tenets of Christian doctrine, but more a time of personal reformation in regard to lifestyle. Theological reflection upon the underlying meaning of the sacramental rites came only after the experience of these rites of incorporation in one's own baptism. Nor was there any indication in the ancient catechumenate of a rush to the font with these (usually adult) candidates. A process of reorientation, of turning one's life in another direction, was taking place in this extended process. The rites of initiation were the public, ritual expression of a type of socialization into the manner of living which the early church held up as normative for its members.

The emergence of Christendom in the Middle Ages and the gradual shift to infants as the usual candidates for initiation turned that process upside down. The resultant loss of the catechumenate contributed to the gradual removal of the laity to an inferior status to the clergy. The loss of the formation process left the laity ill-equipped to speak of their faith with understanding. A complementary consequence was an increasing clericalization of all the public dimensions of the church's life. Clergy gradually became the primary actors in the realm of faith. This was particularly noticeable in regard to the liturgy. Gradually lay participation diminished until second-class status was confirmed in a liturgical passivity which characterized every attendance at a liturgical rite.

We seem to be living at a time in which this pattern is being reversed, but if so, there is still a long way to go.[10] No pattern from a past age can be imposed upon the life of the church at a later time, but it is certainly possible to gain valuable insights from a time when the major process of formation for Christians preceded baptism and not ordination. Our situation today is, however, different in many ways from that of the third or fourth centuries. Infant baptism is a fact in the life of most Christian churches with the result that the majority of practicing Christians are persons who were baptized in infancy. In spite of that fact, the church will fail to facilitate growth unless it can effectively reclaim the preliturgical foundations of its life of faith. The fact that a person has been baptized (often as an infant or young child) does not release the

---

10. Cf. Albert Ottenweller, "Parish Ministry: The Old and the New," and Evelyn Eaton Whitehead, "The Structure of Community: Toward Forming the Parish as a Community of Faith," in *The Parish in Community and Ministry*, ed. E. E. Whitehead (New York: Paulist, 1978), pp. 11-20, 35-51.

church from the pastoral imperative of both the type of formation with which the catechumenate has traditionally been concerned as well as appropriate continuing education. Without this, *any* liturgical pattern will run the risk of remaining external to the lives of churchgoers, and will not realize its significant potential for shaping a mature life of faith.

A complementary aspect of this enablement of the laity is that the clerical domination of liturgical worship must give way to models in which the liturgy is clearly a common action of the whole church assembled. This will not remove the need for sensitive clerical leadership in what is clearly an important area of the church's life, but leadership is a very different thing from a type of clerical domination which understands liturgy as the domain of the clergy. The liturgy does not belong to the clergy; it belongs to the church as a whole rather than to any one group within the church such as the clergy. It is the church's proclamation of faith, the image of its identity. If the liturgy is to be experienced in this way, it must be experienced as the primary event of the Christian community in which its faith is both expressed and nourished.

Finally, if the liturgy is to facilitate growth in faith, there must be an exploration in much greater depth of the connections between any liturgical act and the proclamation of the paschal mystery which lies at the heart of Christian faith and practice. Formation in faith must enable Christians to understand how their own personal stories are mirrored in the great story of redemption. This might seem like a very obvious thing, but any serious conversation with most laity (and perhaps most clergy) reveals that there is a general lack of awareness of how the great events in scripture and the mighty works which the liturgical year commemorates are related to an individual believer's striving to live according to the will of God.

Such a goal will not be achieved by a heavy didacticism. Christians need to be enabled to celebrate the mystery of their participation in the dying and rising of Jesus. Celebration is often marked by dancing, and the liturgy requires such a renewed vision of its purpose. The liturgy is a sharing of the poetry of faith in which the seeds of faith are nourished in the lives of the members of the community. If the liturgy is to be realized in this way, and be fruitful in the lives of the faithful, the church must penetrate more deeply into the signs of the paschal mystery and permit them to form the church anew in the power of God's presence and grace.

At the heart of that mystery is Christ. Christ reveals God's purpose, and the liturgy permits the members of the church, in a visible and human way, to participate in that purpose here and now. At baptism the individual is made a member of Christ's Body. This is not a passive or casual membership. It is an active union. Through baptism, generation after generation of Christians are brought into contact with this mystery of God in Christ. A total sharing in that mystery depends upon an authentic faith. Yet this faith is not an individual or private matter. Christian faith is corporate; it is the faith of the community which finds its highest expression in a corporate act of worship. It is that corporate faith which summons Christians to gather together each Sunday to offer thanks and praise to the One in whom that faith finds its goal. Authentic liturgy, as contrasted with mere ritualism or ceremonialism, gives voice to this faith and connects it to every aspect of human life as the domain in which believers see the wonderful works of God.

CHAPTER 10

Facilitating Growth in Faith Through Social Ministry

Randolph A. Nelson

INTRODUCTION

One of the more vexing issues for both Christian thought and Christian practice is the understanding of the relationship between faith and works. There is within much of the Christian tradition a certain fear of "works righteousness" which means that whatever value is given to activity in the world it does not call into question the agency of God in human salvation. At the same time, there is a clear recognition that the God who saves does so by calling human beings into discipleship and that such discipleship involves "faith active in love."[1]

It is in this vein that Jorge Lara-Brend writes:

The debate about the extent of human capability and human responsibility is an old one. In one form, it appeared in the dispute between Augustine and Pelagius about whether men and women could be saved by grace alone or could cooperate with grace. In the Reformation, the Protestant stress on justification by grace through faith challenged the medieval Catholic view of human action contributing to or earning salvation. The tendency in some Protestant thought to stress justification led to a quietism that rejected the possibility of breakthroughs of true justice, although others recognized that sanctifica-

---

1. A phrase used by George Forell as the title of a book on ethics.

tion was responsible action in the presence of God's grace. There was the further tendency in extreme Calvinist groups to stress predestination to the extent that human beings were completely passive and all events were the outcome of God's decrees. In this century, the rejection of nineteenth-century liberalism by neo-orthodoxy, with its revival of the Augustinian stringency as to the nature and extent of original sin, denied or called into question the possibility of human achievement and any real progress in history. Roman Catholicism, in contrast to Protestantism, has been considerably confident about the human capacity for good because of its much greater attention to people's response to God's grace than to their fall. It is a tradition that trusts men and women far more than it distrusts them. That may be why liberation theology was born in a Catholic continent, even among Protestants. This theology is obstinate in the face of the human negation of grace; it hopes against hope and refuses to give up the human possibility of response.[2]

It is within that general problematic—the relationship of faith and works—that the discussion of this chapter will take place. Our particular discussion will take a more specific focus by concentrating on the relationship of faith to social ministry. Social ministry as used in this context implies ministry that has its roots in the Christian community and thus has a corporate dimension even if in certain instances the specific actions are those of individuals rather than groups. Above all it is ministry directed toward issues in the social order rather than primarily questions of personal morality. Such a differentiation is not without its problems. But the intention is to suggest that social ministry tends to involve institutions, structures, and systems rather than primarily or only interpersonal relationships.

THE FUNDAMENTAL RELATION BETWEEN FAITH
AND SOCIAL MINISTRY

Most discussions of this theme assume faith leads to social ministry, but much less attention is usually given to how social ministry influences faith. Clearly, the movement from faith to social ministry is always important. But by entitling this chapter "facilitating growth in faith through social ministry" the attempt is being made to signal from the very beginning a more reciprocal understanding of the relationship than

---

2. Jorge Lara-Brend, "Latin American Liberation Theology: Pastoral Action as the Basis for the Prophetic Task" in *The Pastor as Prophet*, ed. Earl E. Shelp and Ronald M. Sunderland (New York: Pilgrim, 1985), pp. 157-158.

most discussions assume. With that in mind, we begin this chapter by looking at the reality of faith.

Paul Jersild makes an especially germane point in this regard:

Christians generally would say (and those within the Reformation tradition would say it with particular emphasis) that faith is a gift, which means they are aware that faith is not something which they have generated or produced within themselves. Faith is no achievement of their own, nothing about which they can boast. On the contrary, faith arises when I am addressed by the gospel in such a way that the message illumines my life, revealing myself to myself through the words of that story. It involves a double-take in which I become aware of myself in a new way: I am in the presence of God, and it is Jesus who has brought me there.[3]

To say that faith is a gift is to acknowledge the importance and the priority of God's activity in the life of the Christian believer and the Christian community. Anything that is to be said about the relationship of faith to social ministry is based on an awareness of God's action through which men and women are called into relationship with God. Although the priority of God's grace can be expressed in different ways, most Christian traditions, if not all, ground the possibility of faith in the activity of God. Further, faith is not only dependent on the priority of God's action; faith is itself created by that action. To say then that faith is above all a gift is to say both that God's action is prior to any human response and that God's action creates that human response which is faith; in other words, faith occurs because God creates it.

Understanding faith as God's gift has, however, often made it difficult to describe the way in which faith and social ministry are intrinsically related at the level of human action. Most Christian traditions understand one of the implications of faith to be human action in the service of other persons. To use biblical imagery, faith leads to good works as a tree produces good fruit. Thus, although faith is more God's action than human achievement, there remains room for human response in the form of action that demonstrates a stewardship of creation, a love of one's neighbor, and a commitment to the establishment of peace and justice in the world. There is at the level of theology, at least, an implied naturalness about the relationship between faith and works which would assume that involvement in social ministry could be a taken-for-granted dimension of the life of each Christian person and each Christian community.

---

3. Paul Jersild, *Invitation to Faith* (Minneapolis: Augsburg, 1978), p. 19.

In actuality, however, the relationship of faith to social ministry is often anything but natural; indeed confusion as well as controversy abound. It is a relationship more easily affirmed in principle and in the abstract than in actual practice. Yet it is a relationship essential to the Christian life, one that can neither be ignored nor denied. The need then is to clarify the essential nature and dimensions of the relationship. And in order to make such a crucial clarification, not only must faith's implications for social ministry be explored, but also the way in which faith is facilitated and nurtured through social ministry.

The Dimensions of Faith

The faith that both leads to ministry and is nourished by social ministry is created and developed in the encounter with God. Historically, three distinct but related dimensions of faith have been identified: faith as knowledge, faith as assent, and faith as trust.

Faith knows some things; more importantly faith knows someone: God as encountered above all in Jesus the Christ. Faith, thus, is not primarily facts but neither is it indifferent to facts. The data of history and the interpretation of that history are aspects of faith as knowledge.

Faith assents to what it knows; it acknowledges the truthfulness and the importance of what is known, particularly the truthfulness and importance of the story that is told in and through the history of God's action in the world. Faith accepts and assents to the interpretation given to human history that is transmitted through the Christian tradition.

But faith is, above all, trust. "It is the reliance on the God who has been revealed for our every need. It is a personal relationship of trust and dependence on this God for forgiveness, for life now and eternally. . . . Trust is the heart of faith; it is the most significant element."[4]

Faith as a relationship to God involving knowledge, assent, and trust sets the believer free from the need to "save" her/his own life because that has already been done by God. Faith as a way of being with God enables the believer's attention to be directed away from his/her own well-being secure in the conviction that what is necessary for wholeness of life has been accomplished in the life, death, and resurrection of Jesus the Christ. Thus, freedom from concern for self means freedom for responsible and loving action in the world.

The Dimensions of Social Ministry

Social ministry is one of the ways in which that responsible and loving action in the world is made manifest. It is action on behalf of others whether by attending to their needs as individuals or by attending to the

---

4. Rolf Aaseng, *Basic Christian Teachings* (Minneapolis: Augsburg, 1982), p. 34.

environment, especially the organizations, structures, and systems in which people live. Just as several dimensions of faith can be identified, therefore, so also can several dimensions of social ministry. The first dimension can be described as social welfare and refers to those activities designed to address the needs of individuals and groups adversely affected by neglect, injustice, or tragedy. The second dimension of social ministry can be described with the term social action and refers to activity that seeks to go beyond attention to victims in order to redress the causes that lead to victimization and injustice. Simplistically understood, social welfare has as its immediate concern individuals and groups in some obvious need; social action has as its immediate object of concern the structures and systems which give the social environment its unique and particular shape.

The social welfare dimension of social ministry has characterized the outreach efforts of Christian communities throughout the history of the church. Often, in fact, the Christian community has led the way in developing institutional models for attending to recognized needs in society. Hospitals, orphanages, and educational institutions come to mind as examples of institutional structures created by the church in response to perceived societal needs often in advance of corresponding structures created by political or governmental entities.

The social action dimension of social ministry has been much less common with respect to Christian activity in the world. The reasons are many but clearly some of the characteristics of social action have been seen as too controversial by many Christians and thus have contributed to its relative neglect by the Christian community. Using racism as an example of an issue to be addressed, the emphases that characterize social action have been defined as follows. It is

"1) directed toward the policies or practices of organizations;
2) focused on forces in the environment that shape behavior;
3) concerned about power, influence, rewards, and punishments in which change could take place;
4) concerned about issues; and [includes]
5) such change targets as: influencing legislation, changing hiring practices, helping the poor or "recipients" to be on the boards that direct social service agencies, and eliminating racist attitudes."[5]

Such emphases often mean that social action has the potential for involving its participants in conflict. Furthermore, consensus is often

---

5. Speed Leas and Paul Kittlaus, *The Pastoral Counselor in Social Action* (Philadelphia: Fortress, 1981), p. 3.

not achievable in such situations. Nevertheless, it is a necessary complement to social welfare. It represents part of the prophetic activity of the
Christian community and supplements as well as enhances its other
forms of ministry. "The comforting ministry of a community, one characteristic of which is its pastoral task, can be fully exercised only when
and if the underlying causes of discomfort are exposed and challenged."[6]

Mutual Interpenetration

What is being affirmed in what follows is a reciprocal relationship
between faith and social ministry such that each informs and is informed by the other. Faith gives to social ministry motivation, impetus,
direction, and goal. Social ministry gives to faith expression, embodiment, and nourishment. In attending to the particular realities of the
situation in which social ministry is needed, both faith and social ministry are shaped. It is, thus, the articulation of the reciprocal relationship
between faith and social ministry that is the focus of this chapter.

It is a central conviction of the Christian tradition that the encounter
with God is a transforming experience. What is transformed is not only
the believer's relationship with God but the way in which the believer
lives and acts. There are changes in behavior that follow from the fact
that faith has been created. Some of that behavior is suggested in the
teachings attributed to Jesus by the gospel writers as he describes what
it means to take seriously God's call to repentance and discipleship.

For example, believers are urged to repay no one evil for evil but
rather to love even one's enemies. Moreover, to believe in God and thus
to acknowledge the sovereignty of God is to place one's future in God's
hands to the extent that there is no longer even any need to be anxious
about such necessities as food and clothing. But there is also a more
active stance to be taken ranging from becoming prepared for the full
revelation of the kingdom of God to active service on behalf of the
neighbor.

The New Testament epistles, especially the letters of Paul, continue to
stress the differences that faith in God makes in the lives of the believers. On more than one occasion, Paul speaks of the fruits of the spirit
suggesting that the life of a disciple is characterized by certain virtues
which have behavioral consequences (e.g., Gal 5:22-26; Col 3:12-17).
Such descriptions of the new life in Christ are not directly related,
however, to the kind of behavior that has been identified earlier with
either the term social welfare or social action.

Closer to the dimensions of social ministry are the admonitions to be

---

6. Ronald H. Sunderland and Earl E. Shelp, "Prophetic Ministry: An Introduction," in Shelp and Sunderland, *Pastor as Prophet*, p. 19.

found in the New Testament letter of James. Here action in the world is, to some extent, seen as a *test* of faith and the action identified is not primarily some form of personal morality but rather precisely the way in which other human beings, especially those who are most in need are treated. Thus, the apostle James writes:

> My brothers, what good is it for someone to say he has faith if his actions do not prove it? Can that faith save him? Suppose there are brothers or sisters who need clothes and don't have enough to eat. What good is there in you saying to them, "God bless you! Keep warm and eat well!"—If you don't give them the necessities of life? So it is with faith: If it is alone and includes no actions, then it is dead.[7]

The New Testament writers, therefore, are consistent in their emphasis that faith leads to new behavior. In large measure that new behavior, however, is often more directly concerned with personal virtue or personal morality—refrain from sin—than with activity seeking to care for those victimized by injustice or to change the structures, institutions, or systems of society that cause such injustice.

By contrast the Old Testament prophetic tradition had a much livelier sense of the needs of the poor and oppressed. It also was more vigorous in its emphasis on the importance of action in the pursuit of justice.

There may be several reasons for primary attention being given by the New Testament writers to what was thought to be more central as well as more easily attainable (some control over personal behavior) rather than to the tasks less tractable to individual action (i.e., some change in societal structures or arrangements). One of those reasons for emphasizing the personal over the social was likely a conviction held by the New Testament writers that the consummation of the kingdom of God would occur sooner rather than later. Thus, the language of the New Testament has been described by some scholars as that of an interim ethic. It wasn't until the sense of an immediate parousia declined and the church needed to concern itself with its continued existence in history that more concentrated attention was given to the implication of faith for social ministry.

NEGLECT OF SOCIAL ACTION

Social Welfare

Initially and for much of the church's historical existence the primary expression of social ministry was in the form of social welfare, specifi-

---

7. James 2:14-17, *Today's English Version of the New Testament.*

cally works of Christian charity. Although Jesus suggested that "you will always have the poor with you,"[8] the plight of the poor consistently elicited the concern of the Christian community. It is not only the economically poor who have been the objects of Christian concern. The sick, the widowed, the orphan, as well as the poverty-stricken have received the ministrations of Christians both as individuals and as the gathered community. Such practices have their origins in the early church as described in the New Testament. But such efforts received a more systematic articulation as the church's own internal structure and organization took on more stability. These efforts, as has been suggested, often led to the establishment of specific institutions—schools, orphanages, and hospitals, for example—that became for the whole society models of how to attend to the needs of those individuals who were physically unable or did not have the resources to care for themselves.

Such efforts at social welfare illustrate the inseparable relationship that exists between faith and behavior. As Seifert and Clinebell note, "Religion is a way of life or a quality of man's being and action, rather than a separate segment walled off from the rest of existence. Relationship to God *and* action in the human situation are always to be joined."[9]

Contributing Factors

But, as also suggested earlier, a corresponding emphasis on social action has been less evident throughout the history of the church. There have been courageous individual Christians and prophetic actors, to be sure. Notwithstanding, the Christian community has rarely been as systematic or as consistent in corporately addressing the systemic causes of victimization as it has been willing to respond to the needs of victims themselves. There are a number of factors influencing the difference in response. These factors encompass the theological, the psychological, and the sociological.

Theological factors include the intensely personal nature and character of the experience of faith which has resulted in an emphasis on the personal even private (thus nonpublic) response of faith. Furthermore, because faith is not dependent on any particular external circumstances the conclusion has been drawn that the actual societal situations in which individuals exist have no real bearing on the prospects of salvation or the possibility of faith. Within such a perspective, the hard work involved in seeking situational/environmental change is not as attrac-

8. Mark 14:7, ibid.
9. Harvey Seifert and Howard J. Clinebell Jr., *Personal Growth and Social Change* (Philadelphia: Westminster, 1969), p. 27. Emphasis added.

tive as doing those acts of charity which appear to be more within the control of individual men and women and less likely to lead to conflict.

Another theological factor that plays a part in the neglect of social action for those in the Reformation tradition of Martin Luther has been an understanding of the relationship between political structures and religious structures that is usually described in the terms of the doctrine of the two kingdoms. Whether intended or not, the doctrine of the two kingdoms has suggested that the proper agent for God's rule in the world is civil authority whose responsibility it is to order societal structures in such a way that justice is served. When justice is not served, the implication is that it is the civil authority which ought to seek the necessary changes. The result has been sometimes quite striking indifference on the part of the Christian community in the face of significant, even massive oppression and injustice.

Within the Roman Catholic tradition, John Coleman has pointed to the temptation to be more concerned about community than mission. Such an emphasis has been due in part to the distinction that has been made between sacred and profane history with more attention being given to those inside the church than those outside the church. "The characteristic temptation of religion—and Catholicism in particular—[is] to focus primarily on those already within the fold."[10] Some observers, therefore, have suggested that the Christian community has itself "been an instrument for the reign of injustice."[11]

Theological factors tend to be reinforced by psychological factors. However much faith implies the transformation of the believer's concerns, it does not eliminate sin from the life of the believer, especially the sin of being concerned about one's own well-being. And although faith as depending on God mitigates an excessive concern for one's self, rarely are all traces of self-concern removed. Thus, action that has the potential for placing one in opposition to or in conflict with established procedures, powerful organizations, or authoritative persons is likely to be avoided. Unless a stronger sense of the communal character of faith is developed and the support that comes from a more corporate expression of the faith through the Christian community is experienced the hard work of social action will not get done.

Finally there are sociological factors which play a role in the relative neglect of social action through the church's history. At least two of them deserve special mention. First, for much of the history of the Christian

---

10. John A. Coleman, *An American Strategic Theology* (New York: Paulist, 1982), p. 2.

11. Karen Lebacqz, *Justice in an Unjust World* (Minneapolis: Augsburg, 1987), p. 38.

church in the West, ecclesiastical power and political power worked together, when they were not actually coterminous. Given that situation, concern for the organization and structure of society was not an issue for individual Christians; it was rather a matter for the church hierarchy and the structures were often of the church's own doing.

Second, the development of autonomous systems and structures has been a relatively recent phenomenon. Thus, it is said of Martin Luther in the sixteenth century that he thought of ethics in largely personal terms at least in part because there were few well-organized structures in the political, social, or economic arenas with which to contend. Society in those days was still a rather loosely organized collection of small units held together by strong personalities and traditional ties. Attention to what we have called social action was slow to develop on this account because the organization of society by means of the structures and systems in which such issues emerge is a relatively recent occurrence.

It is only within the last several centuries, then, that social action as a particular activity of the Christian community has assumed such urgency. And it is only within the last several centuries that anything like a social action dimension to the church's witness and faith has received much attention. Instructive in that regard and assuming special importance on the American scene was a development in the early part of the twentieth century that became known as the Social Gospel movement. A brief look at one of its chief exponents will enable us to identify some of what is involved when the implications of faith for social ministry are taken seriously.

The Social Gospel Movement

The Social Gospel movement emerged in the context of the far-reaching industrial changes that were occurring at the end of the nineteenth century in the United States. Industrialization led to instant fortunes for some but long hours of work under difficult working conditions for many others, thus reshaping family and social life. Poverty and exploitation characterized the lives of many urban families and spiritual decay appeared to be gaining momentum.

Among Protestant pastors serving in urban centers of the country, a few began to criticize the prevalent attitudes of the churches toward the urban poor. Out of their ministry they recognized the need for new ways of proclaiming the gospel and they begin to challenge Christians with a theology that called for social action in response to the social problems of the day.

The Social Gospel movement has been criticized for having an overly optimistic assessment of the possibilities of human action. Implied in such a criticism is the conviction that the proponents of the Social

Gospel did not have an adequate understanding of either sin or grace with the result that they overvalued what men and women could do and undervalued what God had done and would still do.

No effort to articulate the relationship between faith and ministry is immune from error or misunderstanding. Still, the Social Gospel movement ought not be dismissed as if it were some form of works righteousness or Pelagian heresy. At least as represented by Walter Rauschenbusch, called by Reinhold Niebuhr the Social Gospel movement's real founder and its most brilliant representative,[12] the concern for social action emerged out of an equally strong concern for a deeply personal and vibrant religious faith. Both concerns were characteristic of Rauschenbusch himself and represented his conviction that social action and faith existed in a mutually enforcing reciprocal relationship. "In conscious intent he sought more than merely to reform the social order or to initiate a social revolution. For any outward change to have meaning and to endure, Rauschenbusch insisted that attention must be given to the deep well of personal religious life."[13]

In 1886, Rauschenbusch accepted a call to a small Baptist church in the section of New York City called Hell's Kitchen. Here he was brought face to face with social problems that he could not ignore. Two other pastors became close friends with Rauschenbusch and together they committed themselves to "cultivating their inner devotional life, ministering to their own congregations and neighborhood, and seeking to engage the attention and affect the life of the working classes of New York City [while] they also were exploring possibilities of effecting changes in the wider life of the church and the nation."[14]

The concern for a deeply personal religious faith led Rauschenbusch to see evangelism as the primary task of the church. Transformation of the social order would not occur without a strong program of evangelism. Hence it became clear to Rauschenbusch that new methods needed to be tried.

To reach the people in his neighborhood outside the church, he sought to appeal to their deepest emotions and saw an emphasis on socialism as promising because "it represented a point of contact with the working classes; it symbolized their aspirations and it was a word which had powerful emotional connotations."[15] His interest in socialism led Rauschenbusch to an awareness of God's activity within and

---

12. Reinhold Niebuhr, *An Interpretation of Christian Ethics* (New York: Harper, 1935), preface.

13. *Walter Rauschenbusch, Selected Writings*, ed. Winthrop S. Hudson (New York: Paulist, 1984), p. 4.

14. Ibid., p. 21.

15. Ibid., p. 35.

through the structures of society as well as through regenerated individuals. He was convinced that a concern for human need and social reform was essential for any adequate theology or expression of faith.

Thus, faith and social ministry were necessarily to be held together. "All social movements would gain immensely in enthusiasm, persuasiveness, and wisdom, if the hearts of their advocates were cleansed and warmed by religious faith."[16] But he was also aware of the importance of seeing that relationship from the other direction as well and understood how involvement in social ministry could have a profound impact on an individual's personal religious orientation. In this vein Rauschenbusch writes: "I set out with the proposition that social Christianity, which makes the reign on earth its object, is a distinct type of personal religion and that in its best manifestations it involves the possibility of a purer spirituality, a keener recognition of sin, more durable powers of growth, a more personal evangelism, and a more all-around salvation than the individualistic type of religion which makes the salvation of the soul its object."[17]

In fact, what he called social Christianity seemed to him not only to enhance the religious life of individual Christians but to be the means by which those outside the church could be brought to God.

The understanding of the relationship between faith and social ministry exemplified by Rauschenbusch receded in currency as the hoped for changes in American society did not materialize and the nation became caught in the throes of the first World War.

The Social Gospel movement was largely a Protestant phenomenon. Meanwhile, American Catholicism, primarily a church of immigrants, spent much of its time and energy seeking to maintain the allegiance of its immigrants and assimilate them into American society well into the twentieth century. Thus, rather than a Social Gospel movement, Catholicism experienced an Americanist program in the 1890s in which an "innocent" acceptance of American life and institutions was central. Accordingly, John Coleman can say that "before the end of the nineteenth century Catholic voices were generally silent or neutral on the major issues of social reform. There was no major Catholic involvement or coherent position on the Jacksonian reforms, the abolition of slavery, the Civil War or post-war reconstuction, and the use of industrial America."[18]

Nevertheless, the more aggressive stance exemplified in the Social Gospel movement, albeit in different forms and with different nuances,

---

16. Ibid., p. 167.
17. Ibid., p. 179.
18. Coleman, *An American Strategic Theology*, p. 169.

has continued to surface at different times on the American scene. More recent manifestations of a more integral relationship between faith and social ministry can be seen in the Civil Rights Movement and the Vietnam War protest of the middle decades of the twentieth century.

During the mid-1800s at least some members of the Christian community understood their faith to imply opposition to slavery, and Christians were involved in abolitionist movements in varying degrees. That legacy was called upon to some extent a century later when Christians once again became more actively engaged in bringing their faith to bear on a public issue—namely, racism—than is usually their wont.

At least some of the social ministry of the Civil Rights period represented an attempt to look at the issue of racism more systematically. In other words, the concern was not just to demonstrate concern about the victims of racism but to find ways to change the policies, practices, and institutions through which the reality of racism was embodied and given public expression. Thomas Pettigrew described the underlying orientation in the following words: "The basic thing the individual should do is start to change the institutions in which he is involved. You change people's attitudes by changing their behavior first. You change behavior by changing institutions."[19]

More often than not, Christians have understood the relationship between attitudes and behavior differently. Usually, the effort is to change attitudes on the assumption that institutional change will be precipitated by changed individuals. In other words, attitudinal change is thought to be a necessary prerequisite to behavioral change both on the personal level and with respect to activity in the structures in which individuals live.

What happened in the Civil Rights movement and the Vietnam War protests was a willingness on the part of some Christians, both lay and clergy, to reexamine the relationship between attitudinal and behavioral change. In doing so they were acknowledging more reciprocity in the relationship between faith and social ministry and they were expanding the vision of social ministry to include social action. Faith intends more than concern for individuals endangered or harmed by policies, practices, and structures that are unjust. Rather faith demands efforts to change the policies, practices, and structures themselves.

That more aggressive stance can also be seen in American Catholicism, especially following Vatican II in 1963. Two examples of that stance are the pastoral letters of the National Conference of Catholic Bishops (U.S.), the first on war and peace (1983) and the second on the economy (1986).

---

19. Quoted in Seifert and Clinebell *Personal Growth*, p. 99.

Both pastoral letters refer to the Catholic social tradition as providing the background for understanding the context in which the letters stand. The biblical vision of the world needs to be elaborated, explained, and applied to the concrete issues of the time such as war and peace and the economy. It is not just the work of the civil community to work for peace. Rather, "the church, as a community of faith and social institution, has a proper, necessary, and distinctive part to play in the pursuit of peace."[20]

Similarly, the bishops write about the economy because faith cannot be separated from everyday life. Thus, the pastoral letter on the U.S. economy "is a personal invitation to Catholics to use the resources of our faith, the strength of our economy, and the opportunities of our democracy to shape a society that better protects the dignity and basic rights of our sisters and brothers both in this land and around the world."[21] The result is to stimulate discussion beyond the church even as the church and its members become actors in a process both political and religious. With respect to such a stance, then, Seifert and Clinebell can write:

Especially since the native habitat of the Christian is on the frontiers of social change, he can always expect opposition and conflict. The experience of persecution is less dangerous to him spiritually than is perpetual peace within the world. Under many circumstances it is as much the work of the church to precipitate conflict as it is to resolve it.[22]

FAITH AS SOCIALLY PROACTIVE

By alluding to the Social Gospel movement, the Civil Rights movement and the Pastoral Letters, it has been our intention to illustrate the conviction that faith is proactive with respect to action against injustice in the world. Faith leads to social ministry even if one of the results is disagreement and conflict. The Christian ought not shy away from the tensions that arise when faith becomes active in the world because faith for the Christian is precisely the willingness to place ultimate loyalty in the God who not only grants forgiveness but seeks justice as well.

---

20. *The Challenge of Peace: God's Promise and Our Response Origins*, NC Documentary Service, Vol. 13, No. 1, May 19, 1983; p. 4.
21. *Economic Justice for All* (Washington, D.C.: National Conference of Catholic Bishops, 1986), p. v.
22. Seifert and Clinebell *Personal Growth*, p. 170.

The Christian faith provides the ultimate security that comes from a realization of acceptance by a loving God. This does not eliminate conflict. On the contrary, it introduces the tensions which arise from the demands of justice for the neighbor. It does, however, make our disagreements less dangerous. . . . In God's forgiveness we find a more ultimate acceptance.[23]

Or again

The Christian has always committed his life to a cause greater than himself for which he is willing to lose himself. In faithfulness to God he has given up the assurance of success in terms of the world. There are times for a lonely/courageous stand in spite of immediate consequences to himself or his organization.[24]

This point can be stated another way. To be a person in God's image "is to use freedom and energetic initiative toward the growth of persons and the improvement of environment. Religion consists not in isolated pious practices but rather in introducing a spiritual quality into the secular world."[25]

Thus far in this chapter, then, we have tried to indicate that social ministry is one of the fruits of faith, that social ministry includes the dimensions of social welfare and social action, and that concrete illustrations can be found within the Christian tradition when faith led to vigorous involvement in social ministry. At the same time, the difficulty that the Christian community has had in maintaining the connection between faith and social ministry including its tendency to concentrate on social welfare and to avoid social action because of the conflictual nature of such activity has also been noted. On the North American scene at least, the performance of the Christian community has rarely been as strong as its rhetoric. Some of the factors have already been noted. In addition, there are differences in denominational positions which may, in turn, be related to sociological and ethnic realities.

Toward a Social Articulation of Faith

But for the purposes of this chapter it is the theological factors that warrant primary attention. Faith's role in drawing forth/eliciting a proactive social ministry will be underdeveloped and social ministry's

---

23. Ibid., p. 184.
24. Ibid., pp. 189–190.
25. Ibid., p. 196.

role in nourishing faith will not be understandable until some theological issues have been addressed.

Elizabeth Bettenhausen, in commenting on the historical quietism of Lutherans may, in fact, be making a more general comment about Protestantism.

> The historical quietism of Lutherans politically and the tendency to separate economic issues from faith is due not simply to a misapprehension of the Reformation teachings about good works as the fruit of faith. It is also due to the separation of the historical self, the *coram mundi*, from the justified self, the *coram deo*, and the substitution of divine agency for human agency in the justified self. Justification by grace through faith is supposed to generate freedom before God, and out of this freedom from self-righteousness neighbor love is to flow. But unless some fuller articulation of sanctification of the social-historical person is made in Lutheran ethics, it is not possible to maintain that it is a human person who is loving the neighbor. . . . In this connection Dorothea Soelle points to a fear in orthodox Protestantism, the fear that God as a result of human development will become less important, that human creativity detracts from the power of divine presence.[26]

The need is to take human action seriously and to value the possibility that it has to be an agent for justice in the world. Bettenhausen suggests that a new theological articulation of justification will have to be made, one which takes the whole individual-social person more seriously and which also takes the interdependence of persons more earnestly by a deeper and more sustained emphasis on the reality of community. "It is the social-historical self who is declared righteous, not a self abstracted from this identity."[27]

José Miguez Bonino urges some of the same rethinking among Protestants in general by raising questions about the interpretation of their own tradition. He wonders why it is that Protestants have generally thought of God's action and human action as "competitive and mutually exclusive" with a corresponding separation assumed between divine and human justice. He asks, "Don't we need to recast the non-negotiable priority of God's initiative and the gratuity of his salvation in terms compatible with the 'partnership' which that salvation institutes—rath-

---

26. Elizabeth Bettenhausen, "Dependence, Liberation and Justification," *Word & World* 7:1 (Winter, 1987), p. 68.

27. Ibid., p. 69.

er the partnership in which such salvation 'consists'? "[28]
The priority of faith as the response to God's redemptive action in
Jesus the Christ can result in a deemphasis on the importance of human
action in the pursuit of justice. Biblical language, however, suggests a
close relationship between faith and love because of what is said to
occur in faith.

If what we are speaking about when we speak of faith is really the
constitution through God's initiative of "a new human subject" do we
not need a new language that is able to express the coherence of faith
and justice both in terms of the synthetic character of God's salvation
and of the human subject?[29]

Within the Catholic tradition, the coherence of faith and justice is
also sought in the work of persons such as Joe Holland and Peter
Henriot who write, "The complete task is to link faith energies with
energies of justice and peace in service of the Living God and social
transformation."[30] The need is to develop gathered communities
throughout the church willing to address the forces threatening the
future of the world and the church.
The Christian community has struggled against both Pelagianism and
legalism. But a fear of Pelagianism cannot lead to a denial of the possibilities of human action, and neither can a concern about legalism lead
to a denial of the need to see justice in concrete terms in relation to the
specific social, economic, and political relationships in which Christians
live.

It is in this two-way transit between our dim discernment of God's
justice operating in our world and calling us to trust it, and the
powerful memory of his justice disclosed and victorious once for all in
the cross and resurrection of Jesus Christ that we try to develop our
theological thinking.[31]

Language such as the "need to recast the non-negotiable priority of
God's initiative" and "the partnership in which such salvation 'consists' " suggests a direction for developing our theological thinking. It is
a direction which would give more emphasis to the second way of

---

28. José Miguez Bonino, "The Biblical Roots of Justice," in ibid., p. 19.
29. Ibid., p. 20.
30. Joe Holland and Peter Henriot, *Social Analysis: Linking Faith & Justice*
(Maryknoll, N.Y.: Orbis, 1983), p. xiv.
31. Bonino, "Biblical Roots," p. 20.

looking at the theme of this chapter namely: the way in which involvement in social ministry enhances and nourishes faith. Social ministry
does, in fact, enhance and nourish faith when intrinsic religious significance is ascribed to social reality and human action is valued on the
basis of what it acomplishes in the social world. And the importance
given to both social reality and human action is fundamentally related
to the understanding of the God who is the creator of faith.

The Seamless Garment of Social Reality and Faith Reality

Social reality is important because reality is of one piece, which is to
say that the distinction and the difference between the reality of God
and the reality of the social world does not entail a dualism at the
practical level such that attention to the reality of God could mean an
avoidance, neglect, or minimizing of the reality of the world. Human
action is also of one piece. Therefore, the difference between faith and
love, for example, does not entail a dualism at the practical level such
that the action of faith could occur and not lead to the action of love.

To say that reality is of one piece is to emphasize the importance of
the social world as an understanding of creation, incarnation, and redemption make clear. The action of God in creation, incarnation, and
redemption indicates the importance of social reality for God inasmuch
as God's own fulfillment does not occur without involvement in the
social world.

Thus, the action of God in creation specifies the reality of God as a
reality in relationship to the actual, concrete world. More is involved
than affirming that what is done in and with the things of the world is
the way in which faith in God is demonstrated. What is done in and
with the things of the world has its effect on God also because of the
intimacy with which God is bound to the social world. It is necessary,
therefore, to understand creation in terms of a mutuality in the God-
world relationship in which the social world is seen as significant for
God as well as vice versa.

The action of God in the incarnation is similar in that here also the
importance of social reality for God as well as God's importance for
social reality is demonstrated. It is not merely the fact that social reality
is the context in which meaning is actualized or discovered. More
important is the fact that the human situation becomes the locus for the
demonstration of God's reality. Social reality becomes a source of meaning and value for the reality of both God and humanity to the extent
that the humanity of Jesus Christ is taken seriously. Human reality and
God's reality become joined in such a way that the reality of God affects
the social world but social reality also has its effect on God.

The action of God in the redemptive event of Jesus affirms that at the center of human fulfillment is an event inseparable from the lived world of men and women. Redemption not only occurs in the context of social reality but is itself a piece of social reality that occurs to men and women engaged in the relationships of the social world. Such a world is not devalued in principle or in practice but is understood in its importance for both God and humanity. Thus, there is strong theological warrant for affirming the importance of social reality as the arena in which human fulfillment is demonstrated and for recognizing the importance of social reality as a source of human meaning and value.

The corresponding importance of human action can also be affirmed. Two things need to be said. First, whatever the priority of justification might be in relationship to sanctification, it cannot be a priority that separates justification from sanctification in such a way that one could occur apart from the other. There is no human action that has significance only with respect to God. In the act of faith, the act of love is already included such that action in the social world is part of an indivisible whole with the grace of God that is said to create faith. In other words, all action has a relationship to the social world; if it has significance vis-à-vis God, it cannot help but have significance for social reality. And if it has no significance in social reality, it has no significance vis-à-vis God.

> Justification is never a private or individualistic event; it is always social or communal, involving the believer, Christ, the entire communion of saints, the church on earth, and the community of all humankind. Justification is not the transformation of an individual's essence but the transformation of one's relationships in life: our relationship with God which includes our relationship to all other people and the rest of God's creation.[32]

The second thing that needs to be said, then, is that this relationship of justification and sanctification points to a commitment in which an absence of positive attention to the social world has the effect of raising questions about justification. In other words, justification does not mean absolute freedom from guidance, restraint, obligation, or duty. Instead, justification pushes to a more serious grappling with the structures and institutions by which life is restrained, upheld, and fulfilled. Positive attention to the social world cannot be avoided by the Christian community and such attention is concerned not only with the motivation of human action but with its effectiveness and results as well.

---

32. Richard Hordern, "Lutheran Theology and the Witness of Peace," *Word & World* 6:2 (Spring, 1986), p. 147.

CONCLUSION

Such theological convictions provide a basis for making some concluding statements which specify most directly how the involvement in social ministry nourishes and nurtures the faith of the individual and the Christian community.

At a very basic level, involvement in social ministry nurtures faith by providing opportunity and occasion for the demonstration of its actuality and practicality with respect to creation and the social world. Faith as trust in God rather than trust in self is evident not only in relationship to God but also in relationship to the things of God. Attention to the needs of individuals together with efforts to overcome injustice concretize one's trust in God in practical ways. Thus, involvement in social ministry prevents a too narrow conception of faith as if it were only the intellect or the will that were transformed in the encounter with God. Rather, faith that results from the encounter with God is a transformation of the whole being and an involvement in social ministry enables faith to explore the freedom of the life in Christ to its fullest.

Involvement in social ministry prevents a too narrow conception of faith in another sense as well by calling attention also to its communal dimension. Because the human being is a social being, faith is never a simple relationship only with God. The person of faith is a person in relationship with other persons, with a social world, and with creation as well as with God. Involvement in social ministry reminds faith of its comprehensive scope and provides expression for the expansive reach of faith by bringing all reality into its purview, thus refusing to allow faith to exclude the created and socially constructed world from its proper attention.

Further, involvement in social ministry enhances the comprehensive character of faith in yet another way by engaging very directly that which stands in opposition to God and the coming of God's kingdom. Precisely with both its opposition to structures of injustice and its efforts to achieve justice, social ministry reminds faith that to be in a right relationship with God does not mean that all is well in the world. Involvement in social ministry precludes a premature acceptance of the way things are. Involvement in social ministry is a reminder that faith exists in the midst of that which militates against faith and stands in opposition to God. Thus, confidence in God does not rest on a naive conception about the health of the social structures in which the individual and Christian community live. By such involvement, faith is prevented from a passive acceptance of the status quo in favor of a stance of active opposition to that which would deny God.

Finally, involvement in social ministry nourishes faith as it seeks to grasp the full reality of God's activity in the world. Rather than being a denial of God's grace and power, such involvement becomes a witness to the mystery of that grace and power. Involvement in social ministry refuses any suggestion that God is limited to specific segments or dimensions of life. Rather, God is to be found where men and women struggle with the unjust realities of life. Social ministry urges faith to go where God's work is yet to be done in order to acknowledge and witness to the mystery of God as the will of God seeks embodiment in the world.

Involvement in social ministry thus becomes the means through which faith knows most fully the God who is its author and shows most concretely the discipleship in which faith lives.

So Jesus said to those who believed in him, "If you obey my teaching, you are really my disciples; you will know the truth, and the truth will set you free."[33]

---

33. John 8:31-32, *Today's English Version of the New Testament.*

CHAPTER 11

Facilitating Growth in Faith Through Pastoral Counseling and Spiritual Direction

Melvin Blanchette

INTRODUCTION

The gift of human existence presents a path to be journeyed by all who become a part of this world. The path is as special and unique as each individual who has been invited to share in the mystery of life. It is a journey to the freedom of self-realization and self-actualization which one walks alone or in the company of others but always in the presence of the giver of life—God. According to Irenaeus, "*Gloria enim Dei vivens homo; vita autem hominis visio*"[1]—the human being radiates the light of God's eternal presence, for the glory of God is the human person fully alive.

The journey of a thousand miles begins with the first step and finds its fulfillment in its own destination. So too, the arduous journey of life has a beginning and an end. For Ignatius of Antioch faith is the beginning, love the end. When these two are found together, there is God, and everything else concerning right Christian living follows from them. He goes on to say that no one sins who lives in faith, and no one hates who lives in love. Life then is a tree known by its fruit. So those who profess to belong to Christ will be known by what they do. For the work one is

---

1. Irenaeus, *Adversus Haereses*, Bk. IV. 20. 7 (Sources Chretiennes), Vol. 100, p. 648.

about is not a matter of words here and now but depends on the power of faith and on being found faithful to the end.[2]

In his letter to the Christian community at Ephesus, Ignatius of Antioch points out the powerful and reciprocal relationship between faith and love. To have faith is a very important dimension of full personality development. Faith helps in the appreciation of what human living has to offer.[3] In a metaphorical sense, faith serves as the key which opens the door to realities unseen. Faith enables maturity because it demands honesty and self-acceptance. Maturity is a concept hard to define. Basically, it has to do with becoming the full and total person one is created to be. Maturity is the fruit of one's human development. Honesty assists in one's quest for maturity by extending an invitation to consider two important components of what it means to become a person. On the one hand, honesty entails an acceptance of all the unique gifts, talents, endowments, and assets that one has or is in the process of developing; and on the other hand, honesty demands an acknowledgment of one's limitations and growing edges, together with the realization of what one has not been given. In short, honesty demands that one tell the truth to and about oneself. Telling the truth about self permits one to receive the gift of self-acceptance. Faith, with its essential message that the human being is not God, clarifies life's fundamental indentity—that being human is being creature. As John Paul II is fond of saying, each person is an unrepeatable act of creation of a loving God. Faith, then, provides an index of true worth. It recognizes each person has dignity because he or she comes from God.[4] It also manifests one's destiny insofar as all are invited to dwell in God's presence forever.

True faith, which is mature and well-integrated into one's personality development, is a result of freedom. Freedom is the act of making choices and knowing the object of those choices. In John's gospel (11:27), Martha says, "I have come to believe that you are the Messiah, the son of God; he who is to come into the world."[5] Faith gives a vision

---

2. *The Liturgy of the Hours*, Vol. III (New York: Catholic Book Publishing Co., 1975), pp. 84-85.

3. For a further explication, see Paul Tillich, *Dynamics of Faith* (New York: Harper & Row, 1957). Although this book is admittedly dated, it does contain a fine appreciation of the meaning of faith and its relationship to doubt, as well as to community, symbol, truth, and courage. These qualities are seen as constitutive of full human development.

4. Pope John Paul II, *Pilgrim of Peace* (Washington, D.C., United States Catholic Conference, October, 1979), p. 178. Pope John Paul II, *L'Osservatore Romano* (English edition), March 9, 1981, p. 20.

5. *Lectionary for Mass* (New York: Catholic Book Publishing Co., 1970), pp. 981-982.

of reality which comes through the person of Jesus. The invitation of life is to address the important questions dealing with existence and expectations.[6] Each person responds to that invitation with either weak or strong faith depending upon a host of other variables. What is so clear is that each person wants to be happy in the process of living. There is probably no reality more elusive than that of happiness. Under the guise of many false illusions, people have been duped into believing that personal fulfillment and the having of many and expensive things is the way to become happy. However, personal fulfillment and the acquisition of material posessions have been found wanting because they do not satisfy the basic urging of the human heart. One need only read the daily newspaper to discover the many tragic reminders of this fact.

What truly contributes to human happiness is a sense of security that comes with having faith which strives to overcome fear in its many forms. Faith is more than an individual's response to the presence of God. It is a community's profession and the shared sense of being with others that gives one the feeling of belonging.[7] This fulfillment of being with and for others not only gives meaning to life but draws one to a deeper understanding of the baptismal commitment to love oneself, others, and God. The insight of Ignatius of Antioch mentioned earlier in this section is helpful because it highlights the connection between faith and love and because it focuses on the importance of faith in the process of becoming human. Faith and love are those qualities which permit truly human development and reveal the way to eternal life.

This chapter explores the ways through which pastoral counseling and spiritual direction can enable and facilitate the growth of faith in the lives of women and men. From the introductory comments already made, it is clearly established how important faith is in personality development. Faith is an essential attribute that includes many dimensions of what it means to be a person: physical, personal, interpersonal, social, political, and economic. Pastoral counseling represents a unique integration of theology and psychology. Therefore, a principal objective of the pastoral counseling process is to assist people in their unique journey of faith by helping them in their understanding of the struggles and challenges of the lived experience of the mystery of faith.[8] Pastoral

---

6. The role of existence and expectation is well described in the writings of Abraham Heschel, and in particular in *Who Is Man?* (Stanford, Calif.: Stanford University Press, 1975).

7. For a fine understanding of faith and community, consult Regis Duffy's, *Real Presence* (San Francisco: Harper & Row, 1982). In particular, the first chapter, "The Cutting Edge of Faith: Commitment," is especially relevant.

8. Thomas Franklin O'Meara, *Theology of Ministry* (New York: Paulist, 1983).

counseling is a witness to that reality through acts of clarification, liberation, and reconciliation. Pastoral counselors are the facilitators of the ministry of clarification through their understanding of where people are in their journey of faith. Effective pastoral counseling and spiritual direction for growth in faith relies on what the client's faith community or denomination posit as the content of faith for that client.[9] The content of faith will be described in this chapter through a series of understandings. However, knowing the content of faith alone is not sufficient for the pastoral counselor to facilitate growth in faith. The content of faith must be understood in the light of structure or the process through which a person comes to mature and integrative faith.[10] For this awareness, pastoral counselors receive direction and insight from many theorists such as James Fowler, a pioneer in the empirical research on faith development. After helping people clarify what their faith is, in whom they have placed their faith, and assessing where they might be in their progress toward mature faith, pastoral counselors reach out through the counseling process with respect for individual mystery. They enable people to celebrate the freedom of what it means to believe. In like manner, they respond to human pain so that it might not dehumanize the person but might be seen as a call to change and an invitation to live life at a greater depth of awareness. Pastoral counseling facilitates growth in faith through the ministry of clarification as part of the ongoing liberating ministry of Jesus. The ultimate objective of pastoral counseling is growth in faith through the lived experience of God's healing.

MINISTRY OF CLARIFICATION

As a ministry of clarification, pastoral counseling relates to the total person, understanding that faith pervades the entirety of the human person. When people encounter difficulties in living and counseling assistance is required, pastoral counseling attempts to understand what part theology or the lived experience of faith might contribute to their pain. It requires being attuned to listening with more than the third ear

---

9. John Macquarrie, *Principles of Christian Theology*, 2nd ed. (New York: Scribner's, 1977).

10. James Fowler is without doubt the one person who has done the most extensive empirical research in faith development. The following texts contain many and rich insights: James W. Fowler, *Stages of Faith* (San Francisco: Harper & Row, 1981); James W. Fowler, *Becoming Adult, Becoming Christian* (San Francisco: Harper & Row, 1984); James W. Fowler and Sam Keen, *Life-Maps: Conversations on the Journey of Faith*, ed. Jerome Berryman (Waco, Tex.: Word, 1978).

and being perceptive in seeing through the many lenses and levels of life that are the causes and sources of peoples' conflicts and difficulties. What people believe can be a source of much distress and pain, hence the so-called understandings which follow are an attempt to explain the content of faith.

Content—Understanding

These are a series of understandings about faith that are necessary for any serious effort at faith living. These understandings will survey the scope of faith, and will describe the domain of faith as it pertains to the total development of the human person. The total development of the human person is, of course, a prime goal of pastoral counseling.

First Understanding. Faith is a life communicated to and shared by persons. It is not merely a cognitive doctrine to be believed or a creed to be recited. The first dynamic of Christian faith is the action of Jesus Christ coming into one's life as a living person with a life-giving message of salvation, of reconciliation, and of love.[11] With this gift comes the expectation of a response. One's holistic response to Jesus becomes the second dynamic of faith. It is a personal acceptance indicating a willingness to be changed and transformed by the spirit of Jesus. That personal response is the beginning of a conversion process.

Second Understanding. Faith is life and is therefore subject to the laws of life. At the organic level to change is to live. Change is a sign of health and vitality. Not to change is to die.[12] A lack of change represents sickness and death. True human life is the ability to relate to all of reality, and in particular to other persons through both knowledge and love. Not to relate to other persons through knowing and loving is to die. These laws of life are irrevocable and inexorable at all levels. These laws express the relational appreciation that faith gives life and demands a commitment to live life fully.[13]

Third Understanding. The awareness of faith is contained in the realization that Jesus enters one's life through the shared human experiences of one another.[14] Paul the Apostle speaks of faith as coming through hearing. Faith is ignited from flesh to flesh. Human experiences

---

11. Katherine Fischer, "Faith and Imagination," *New Catholic World* 225:1350, pp. 257ff. These understandings regarding the content of faith are well nuanced in this fine article which stresses the importance of imagination in the formation of faith.
12. John Henry Neuman, *An Essay in the Development of Christian Doctrine* (Garden City, N.Y.: Doubleday Image, 1960), p. 63.
13. John C. Haughey, *Should Anyone Say Forever?* (Garden City, N.Y.: Doubleday, 1975).
14. Macquarrie, *Principles of Christian Theology.*

of knowing and loving become signals of God's presence among individuals and God's presence becomes visible when one gives evidence of thinking like Jesus and appropriating his style of loving. Through daily lived experiences, Jesus revealed himself and his Father, first to his disciples and through them to those who would follow. This was a process of human contact and conversion to a way of life. Through the daily human experiences that are shared with one another, Jesus continues to reveal himself and his Father. Hence, the reality of human experience mediates the presence of God among people who are searching for the meaning of life.

Fourth Understanding. Faith is contained in the total web of human forces that make up human living. Faith does not function apart from them. It is subject to these human forces, modified and altered by them. Faith is the sense of life and the force whereby persons exist. Faith is the choosing of a frame of reference—the formal factor that infuses, colors, and animates the whole of life. Faith is at home with all different kinds of temperament and character. Accordingly, one's faith life is affected by all the neurotic patterns that have pursued the individual in so many dark ways throughout life.[15] Growth in faith results when a group or an individual is serious and deliberate about doing the "human thing" in the best possible way.

Fifth Understanding. The object of one's faith response and the center toward which all faith is directed is Jesus Christ.[16] The task of Christian theology in any culture is to make the case and explain the fact that Jesus is the absolute bearer of revelation. He is the unique figure in the sweep of history. Jesus is the incarnation of God. Indeed, Jesus is alive in the world and made visible through the witness of believing men and women.[17]

These understandings provide an overview that faith is communicated and shared by Christians. They affirm that Jesus is the embodiment of God. And with Karl Barth, they assert that a Christianity which is not altogether eschatological has altogether and utterly nothing to do with Jesus Christ.[18] Faith is life and, as such, undergoes change and development. A lively faith is not presumed to exist equally in each person or equally in all persons at all times. Human experience is the

15. William A. Barry and William J. Connolly, *The Practice of Spiritual Direction* (New York: Seabury, 1982).
16. Richard P. McBrien, *Catholicism* (Minneapolis: Winston, 1980), in particular Part Three: "Jesus Christ."
17. Monika K. Hellwig, *Jesus, The Compassion of God* (Wilmington, Del.: Glazier, 1983).
18. David L. Mueller, *Karl Barth, Maker of Modern Theological Mind*, ed. Bob E. Patterson (Waco, Tex.: Word, 1984), pp. 125-126.

bearer of God's revelation, and can become the opportunity for witness-ing to the presence of God.[19] Faith is the force that gives people the courage to be and the strength to accept the pain that comes with establishing the kingdom of God on earth.

With these understandings providing a conceptual framework, pasto-ral counselors in dialogue with their counselees are able to derive an index of what constitutes their faith. In the next section, attention is focused on the research findings of James Fowler, who advances empiri-cal evidence gained through interviews regarding the process or struc-ture through which a person passes in the course of growing in a mature and integrative faith.

Process and Structure

As already noted in the previous section, there is a difference between Christian faith and faith development. The understandings about faith provide a global context to assist in the examination of the particular content of faith. These understandings emphasize that the content of Christian faith, which is the message of eternal life proclaimed through the words and actions of Jesus Christ, could be appreciated and system-atically studied from various perspectives as in theology. Faith develop-ment theory with its grounding in empirical research, highlights a series of stages through which a person traverses in the appropriation of the faith content.[20] Both the content and the structure (through which an individual understands and interprets this content) are important factors in faith development. The research of James Fowler traces the direction and movement of faith in a person's life. His research is empirically based on over four hundred interviews with believing persons of several distinct faith traditions.[21] From this accumulation of empirical data, Fowler has devised his theory of faith development. He speaks of faith development as a series of stages of growth. These stages are basically an empirical description containing the manner and mode a person uses to derive meaning. There are no absolutes involved in his description. Nor

19. The understandings of faith might be expressed differently by various theologians such as Avery Dulles, Karl Rahner, Paul Tillich, and Ray L. Hart. However, the basic assumption is that God's self-communication is mediated to us through the experience of the world.

20. In addition to the texts already suggested, I recommend the chapter, "Childhood and Adolescence—A Faith Development Perspective," by Richard Osmer and James W. Fowler, in the *Clinical Handbook of Pastoral Counseling*, ed. Robert J. Wicks, Richard D. Parsons, and Donald E. Capps (New York: Paulist, 1985).

21. Craig Dykstra and Sharon Parks, eds., *Faith Development and Fowler* (Birmingham, Ala.: Religious Education Press, 1986). This book is the most comprehensive account of Fowler's work and evaluation of his theory.

is there any indication of faith in one stage being better or worse than in another stage. What Fowler has attempted is to describe the presence of faith in a person's life. Faith unfolds in a person's life and undergoes change and differentiation. These stages will be reviewed so as to see how they are instrumental to pastoral counselors who are attempting to facilitate growth in faith.

Faith Stage I. The first stage of faith develpment, which Fowler terms "intuitive-projective" is limited to small children. Two words which describe the stage of faith are nonreflective and nonconceptual. Basically, the first stage involves small children repeating words used by their parents rather than a faith process as such. The action is foundational giving rise to further extension and possibility.

Faith Stage II. "Mythic-literal" is the second stage of faith development and is typical of older children and some adolescents. However, some adults will remain in this stage throughout their lives. Faith in this stage is firmly grounded in family and religious traditions. Authority is rarely ever questioned, and persons in this stage absolutize the authority; their faith expressions are legalistic and duty bound. In many ways, the second stage is similar to Lawrence Kohlberg's Punishment and Obedience Orientation.[22]

The either/or quality of this stage in faith development makes it very difficult for some people to see the real purpose and function of the law. Law is a necessity of social life, and rather than viewing it as a restraint of freedom pastoral counseling understands the significance of law as fostering freedom by indicating limits beyond which freedom becomes meaningless because it is unrelational.

Faith Stage III. People who locate their values in the community and who derive a sense of identity from the interpersonal comprise the stage known as "synthetic-conventional." These people have found a synthesis which supports their worldview. They are conventional insofar as they place great value on a set of norms and practices. These conventions and rules are important because they govern the conduct of their lives and determine how they react to one another. To deviate from these recognized conventions and traditions causes people in this stage a great amount of distress. Hence, changes are seen as disruptive.

Faith Stage IV. Early adulthood typically begins around the age of eighteen for most persons. Fowler's fourth stage, a more mature faith, rarely is found before adulthood. The adjectives used to describe this stage, "individuative-reflective," define the locus of authority away from the community to the believer. At this point in a person's journey

---

22. Lawrence Kohlberg, "Moral Education in the Schools: A Developmental View," *School Review* 74:1-3 (1966).

toward maturity there is great emphasis placed on identity and on each person's unique way of being. People in this stage value authenticity and personal integrity. Wrongdoing would be characterized as not remaining truthful to one's own set of values and norms because these values validate the person's sense of integrity. Taking responsibility for one's commitments, lifestyle, beliefs, and attitudes becomes a challenge and an invitation to greater growth in faith.

Faith Stage V. The emergence of Stage V is rarely seen before the age of thirty. This stage is a consequence of a person's deepening life experiences which include the pain of suffering, loss, and injustice. When people enter into this stage, called "conjunctive faith," they are able to reconcile the faith dynamics that have influenced their faith development. They know from whence they have come in the struggle to believe. They have a recognition of the various challenges that the previous stages of faith presented them. Hence, there is present in this stage an explicit call to a greater depth of understanding oneself and others. Believers in this stage have a broad worldview. Alfred Tennyson expressed it so well in saying, they have become part of all they have met.[23] This sense of belonging to a global community motivates them to work actively for peace through justice. One's own reflections and interactions with others determine the content of this stage. As a result, believers in this stage have a vision of life that enables them to respond to the challenges and opportunities which demand commitment and an openness to the future.

Faith Stage VI. This last stage of faith development is called "universalizing faith." It is indeed a rarity. Fowler found only one person in his four hundred interviews who could be identified as possessing this unique response to life. This culmination of growth in faith is derived through human fidelity and divine grace. This stage is universal in the sense that the persons who have it would be recognized as outstanding in holiness regardless of what tradition or value system they hold. Persons in this category would of course be Jesus, Francis of Assisi, Mohandas Gandhi, and perhaps Mother Teresa of Calcutta.

Fowler's social-scientific research provides many implications for pastoral counseling in its efforts at faith facilitation. Human development is multidimensional—sometimes involving vertical growth or regression and at other times horizontal growth involving a widening or deepening of understanding. Most people who enter pastoral counseling relationships will probably be wrestling with issues surrounding either Stages III or IV. As with all stage development theories, people are able to be encouraged to move gradually along the continuum of growth

---

23. Tennyson, "Ulysses," (1842).

both within and between various stages. Under stress and anxiety, it is entirely understandable that people can regress from a more advanced stage of development to an earlier response to life and to the presence of God.

The processes of pastoral counseling and spiritual direction are exquisitely sensitive to the internal framework of faith content in order to appreciate what faith means to a certain person. In similar fashion, pastoral counseling and spiritual direction attempt to clarify what stage of faith development a person might be in, in order to encourage and support satisfaction or a gentle challenge to advance to a more mature expression of faith. If there is one distinctive, identifying mark which sets pastoral counseling and spiritual direction apart and noticeable, it is an overall and pervasive concern for human dignity as presented in faith development. Pastoral counseling and spiritual direction endeavor to treat the human person as a holistic composite of body, mind, emotion, and spirit. This proper expression of concern for human dignity goes beyond the word "respect." It becomes a question of awesome or inspirational respect known as "reverence."

MINISTRY OF FREEDOM

In the New Testament, Jesus is the new Moses and his ministry is the starting point of all Christian ministries. In truth, it is one mission of Jesus with many varied ministries. Jesus' being sent by the Father was not only to give up his life but also to preach the good news of salvation which is essentially an invitation to change and to have faith. Jesus came so that all may have life and have it abundantly (Jn 3:16). Jesus incorporated his mission in terms of the process of freedom which he proclaimed in his messianic manifesto: "The Spirit of the Lord is upon me because he has chosen me to bring good news to the poor. He has sent me to proclaim liberty to captives and recovery of sight to the blind, to set free the oppressed and announce that the time has come when the Lord will save his people" (Lk 4:18-19).

Everything that Jesus did after this "inaugural speech" was a fulfillment of the promises contained therein. He did what he promised, and fulfilled in deeds what he voiced through words. He proclaimed liberty to the captives of sin (Lk 7:36-50) and illusion (Lk 12:11-21) and recovered sight to the physically and spiritually blind (Jn 9). Jesus freed the oppressed from physical and spiritual paralysis (Lk 5:17-25), from rigid and narrow religious vision (Lk 5:33-39), from guilt (Jn 8:1-11), from leprosy (Lk 17:11-19), and from suffering (Lk 8:40-56).

The mission of Jesus as detailed above can be divided into different ministries through which his basic mission is achieved. Four different ministries which have their roots in the gospel are: ministry of the word, ministry of community building, ministry of celebrating, and ministry of healing. What is so noteworthy in the mission of Jesus is the disproportionate amount of time for his healing ministry, namely, helping the burdened and the sick. With ears attuned to hearing, pastoral counselors listen to Jesus saying that people who are well do not need a doctor, but only those who are sick (Mt 2:17). Another implication is that healing can begin with the creation of an atmosphere where respectful listening is established. In that atmosphere, Jesus was *with* others. In like manner, pastoral counselors invite others to examine their scars, lance their wounds, and become open to a new healing presence.

Jesus sent out his disciples with a threefold ministry of teaching, preaching, and healing. The apostolic church continued the healing ministry of Jesus as reported in nineteen accounts in the Acts of the Apostles. The Fathers of the Church continued the same tradition.[24] In nearly every one of the early Fathers—Justin the Martyr, Irenaeus, Tertullian, Cyprian—there is clear evidence of the belief in exorcisms and the power of the church to heal. Pastoral counselors participate, through their experience, education, and choice, in continuing the healing and liberating mission of Jesus. Pastoral counseling is a ministry which aims at achieving wholeness for the individual, a wholeness resulting from a threefold reconciliation with oneself, with others, and with God. However, before reconciliation can take place, people must be freed and their pain must be understood as having meaning and purpose.

Pastoral counseling and spiritual direction fulfill two important functions to those entering a helping relationship. These functions are 1) to enable a person to become free in order to believe and to be responsible, and 2) to enable a person to deal with pain and to understand the deeper significance that pain plays in life.[25]

Many times a person is told to do the responsible thing, or to have faith that things will change. Parents are quick to urge children to act responsibly and to express their faith through prayer, worship, and ritual. However, experience teaches that before a person can believe and be responsible in living, he or she must first experience what it means to be free. As an instructor of pastoral counseling for the past several years

---

24. For other purposes and functions for pastoral counseling, see W. Clebsh and C. Jaekle, *Pastoral Care in Historical Perspective* (New York: Aronson, 1983).

25. These functions of pastoral counseling were first discussed in a chapter entitled, "Theological Foundations of Pastoral Counseling," in *Pastoral Counseling*, ed. Barry K. Estadt (Englewood Cliffs, N.J.: Prentice-Hall, 1983).

in an institution of higher learning, this author used the metaphor that when people come to counseling they seem to be imprisoned within a box. They fear there is no exit. It cannot be emphasized enough how important the counseling relationship is, for once it has been established and the process begun, a person comes to freedom and mature faith is made possible. After a time, a boxed-in quality no longer exists; rather the person has found openings in the box. Windows are raised and doors are opened to possibilities and alternatives.

The second function of pastoral counseling and spiritual direction is to enable a person to deal with the psychological pain generated by human existence. Pain is caused by one's reaction to the expectations placed upon him or her, including both those expectations one places on oneself and those which one allows others to place on him or her. Growth is the result of dealing with the stresses involved in living. What causes one to be human is likewise that which causes anguish, namely, one's ability to be self-reflective and conscious of what he or she thinks humanity ought to be. When one encounters a contradiction between who one is as person and what is expected of him or her, the pain of living humanly enters life. It is this painful awareness which often motivates a person to enter into a pastoral counseling relationship. A person comes to counseling not necessarily to solve problems but rather to experience growth through the relationship established with a pastoral counselor, to relate more appropriately to the struggles and pain life invites all to grapple with and respond to. Hence, the most fundamental function of pastoral counseling, in addition to enabling a person to become free, to believe, and to be responsible, is to relieve psychological pain. Pain comes with problems and tensions of living. It is unfortunate that until only recently pain was seen in negative terms. However, when one comes to the appreciation that something is wrong with the way his or her life is going and pain is experienced, then pain becomes a strong motivation for change. There are many ways that a person might experience pain. A person might perceive pain as a conflict keeping or holding the individual in a state of bondage. Sometimes this conflict prohibiting happiness and joy might be severe. At other times, it might be caused by the inability to communicate well. There are many varieties of pain and conflict-causing situations.

Perhaps the two biggest barriers blocking happiness and causing pain are anxiety and depression. Many counseling textbooks give definitions and causative factors of anxiety and depression. What is clear about anxiety is that it is unpleasant. Everyone wants relief from its burden. The everyday experience of depression is well-known. It might begin as a disappointment, sadness, disillusionment, or despair. Each person knows what is means to become depressed over a loss of some kind. He or she has felt the immobilizing hold depression can have and the resulting sense of powerlessness.

The pastoral counseling process is an effort to reach out to the community of those who bear the marks of pain—the dispossessed, lonely, alienated, unwanted, divorced, those suffering because of sexuality issues, and so on—to serve them in the struggle to believe, to become free and responsible, and to enable them to grow from and through their pain. Pain becomes an all-important call to growth in faith. It is the tension element in life, the situation in which a person comes face to face with the power of life and the power of love. In these confrontations pastoral counseling invites the person to act in a way that will promote personal growth and the growth of faith—for it is only at the cost of pain that one becomes the best.

In the pastoral counseling process the drama of life is seen in all its complexity and variety. Shakespeare has Hamlet say that the player's vocation is to be a mirror to show each age its form and feature. It would seem that the pastoral counselor's task would be to make sure that the image reflected is sound, sincere, and real. Images seen by pastoral counselors run the whole range of mental illness. This complexity of images and variety of forms bring out clearly the need for the ministry of clarification through which pastoral counselors can identify the cause of pain, the source of conflict, and what might bring about freedom and meaning.

It is extremely important to grasp things as they really are. In making a clarification one literally comes to know people through the experience of their story.[26] Images seen and clarified by pastoral counselors include those of neurotic and psychotic persons. In all of these images reflected in humanity's mirror, there is a failure of the individual to deal with a given reality; they thus represent a failure to find socially acceptable gratification for needs and answers to life's questions and the demand posed by faith. The suffering of these individuals stems from the person's distorted view of self, faulty communication with others, and views held about the meaning of existence and faith.

At this point it might be useful not only to deal with images but to illustrate what transpires in the actual pastoral counseling process.[27] These examples are taken from this author's own professional practice. These illustrations are a sharing from personal experience of some of

---

26. Utilizing the practice of diagnosis within the context of ministry is advanced in Paul Pruyser's, *The Minister as Diagnostician* (Philadelphia: Westminster, 1976).

27. Gerald O'Collins quoted the theologian Roy Eckhardt, who maintains that a sensible way to discover what an enterprise means is to look at what its practitioners do, *Foundations of Theology* (Chicago: Loyola University Press, 1971), p. 1.

the important principles that are part and parcel of the author's life and practice. It is hoped that the readers of the following case studies will learn from what is shared as well as be drawn to identify with these experiences. (The former clients, Carol and Brian, have been contacted and their permission obtained to use this material.)

Two Illustrative Cases

The Case of Carol: From Bondage to Freedom. Carol first entered pastoral counseling to become free and to be a richer, fuller, and more mature person. In the first interview she was very fearful and later said she almost did not return. What convinced her of the advantage of pastoral counseling was the fact that she found someone who did not judge her but accepted her as she was. Carol was imprisoned by her fear, and she failed to make choices and then accept the consequences of her decisions. She was approaching middle age but still acted and responded to others as a child. She had a characterological sweetness about her, but beneath this veneer was a great deal of unresolved hostility directed against her parents, former teachers, and employers at work. In addition, she lived out her relationship with God in dread of offending him.

As the weeks and months of pastoral counseling continued, she faced these fears and found a creative force to deal with these important people and relationships. It was painful but she came to realize that she had been setting herself up for many of her own conflicts. She replaced inappropriate behavior with actions more in keeping for a woman of her years. This gave her a great deal of satisfaction. In the course of pastoral counseling she discerned why she disliked her parents so much. They constantly did things for her and thus kept her a child. They had never enabled her to feel free. It must be said that they did this out of love, but it was, in the long run, cruel. Trying to protect her, they never explained to her what should be told a child regarding sexuality and healthy human functioning. Encouraged through the counseling sessions, she read books on human sexuality and asked many questions until she began to act and feel like a woman. At this point, the counselor felt ready to ask her about her body. She disliked her body, and she hated herself. She was overweight and dressed in clothes appropriate for an older woman. (Frequently, it has been found that when persons hate their bodies they end up hating themselves. This observation is in keeping with Sigmund Freud's statement that the ego is first and foremost a body ego: It is not merely a surface entity but is itself the projection of a surface.[28]) As changes happened in Carol's body and she

---

28. Sigmund Freud, *The Ego and the Id*, quoted from *Great Books of the Western World*, ed. Robert Maynard Hutchins (Chicago: Encyclopedia Britannica, 1952), p. 703.

began to lose weight, she dressed more and more in keeping with her chronological age. She became an attractive person and began to like and love the person she was becoming. No longer did she treat her body as a barrier keeping herself imprisoned and alone. She readily accepted encouragement to do nice things for herself. Through this experience, she came to realize she was a good person and one loved by God.

Counseling continued for almost two years, as she unraveled all the reasons why teachers in school disliked her, why employers were fearful of her. The biggest breakthrough to freedom occurred, however, during the Holy Week of her last year in pastoral counseling. It was at that time that she accepted the truth that she could not earn God's love. Until then she had tried to keep herself always in God's grace. However, she did this not because she loved God but rather she feared him as one would a despotic and arbitrary ruler. During this season of hope, Carol learned the lesson Anne Sexton writes about Jesus Christ: "His love was the greatest thing about him—not his death." Coming to the profound awareness that God loved her through Jesus, Carol experienced growth and reconciliation. At last, she was free to be herself and no longer had to endure the frustration of trying to be someone else.

Carol came to freedom through awareness. This process always involves grappling with oneself. It is a painful experience to deal with oneself, with one's parents, and with relationships with other important people. However, there is no substitute if one desires to become free.

Concomitant with Carol's journey to freedom, she matured in Christian faith. When pastoral counseling commenced, she had the naive faith of childhood. She subsequently worked through the more critical faith of the adolescent, and finally she attained the full mature faith of the adult. Carol has embraced all the complexity of being human. She no longer looks for simple answers to complex questions, and she has left behind the egocentric concerns of childhood faith. She came to believe much like the woman in the gospel not because of what others said or did but rather through her personal questing for maturity and adult faith.

The Case of Brian: From Pain to Awareness. Sisyphus was a legendary king of Corinth. Myth tells us that he was condemned in Tartarus to roll a big rock up a hill, and each time it reached the top, it rolled down again. In some ways he is a good example about accepting the rock of the human condition and finding happiness in dealing with it. In addition, he is a reminder to this counselor of another client, Brian, a person who never really accepted himself or the exacting expectations of his life which caused him so much pain. Life can be absurd and as frustrating as rolling a rock up a hill only to have it roll down again. What preserves one from this maddening experience is awareness which creates meaning and presence.

Brian was middle-aged when he first came for pastoral counseling. He was late, had been drinking to get up his courage to face the counselor. He was experiencing anxiety to a high degree, and the source of his anxiety was problems with sexuality. When he began to tell the story of his life history, he was very upset because he was facing financial disaster. He was leading two lives—one by day, another at night. Brian was a homosexual who never integrated this dimension of his life into his total personality. It was always for him a problem to be solved, never something to be accepted, to be understood and dealt with appropriately. He had never stopped rolling the rock up the hill, to stop and ask what the meaning of his life was. It took outside forces to get Brian into pastoral counseling to look inside himself for the causes of his difficulties. Brian was a Protestant minister and his work was suffering terribly because he stayed out all night. During the day he was never sure of the relationships he sought in futile fashion at night. Brian knew very well the expectations that come with existence and was aware that he used alcohol to avoid confronting the demands of his life.

Brian's visit to the clinic to receive help is an unforgettable experience. He looked like a man who had exhausted all his energy and wealth. He was asked if he was willing to work on his problems as he saw them and if he was willing to change. He had had other counselors, been in and out of treatment centers, but never accepted the reality of having a problem. He came to realize that having a problem does not equate with being a bad person. As counseling progressed and Brian with his counselor explored the dynamics of his life, the truth of his life emerged as an impression on a photostatic plate. The image reflected was a person who had never loved himself. He sought love as a young person until he realized he was different. For the rest of his life he defended against his homosexuality and pretended, at great cost, to be someone he was not. He was clearly a man who did not know how to confront the demands of his life. No therapist or psychiatrist ever talked to him about facing the truth of his life. (It must be noted that this author cites this case out of great respect for and profound appreciation of Brian, who responded to God's grace through the instrument of the healing ministry.) It was through mutual conversations that Brian came to understand his uniqueness and his limitations.

Coming to terms with his uniqueness meant to Brian that he was a good person in spite of his homosexuality, that God loved him because he was. When Brian began to realize that he was a good person, as well as a homosexual, as true with Carol and many other people with whom this pastoral counselor has worked, he began to dress better and take care of himself. Brian began to test the counseling relationship in which he could share the heavy burden of his life. It is only through self-revelation that he received the awareness of being loved as he is. The process of risking opened up to Brian the possibility of being loved, and this was transforming. Lastly, Brian affirmed the awareness that if he was to be a ministerial person, he would have to do the work of a minister. This meant accepting the limitations of his life, and particularly how he chose to use time.

From these three levels—sexuality and the goodness of himself, truthfulness and the risk of revelation, and unity of his life and work—Brian came to freedom. This awareness motivated him to change. His faith became dynamic as he realized that life demands honesty in accepting one's endowments as well as the acknowledgment of one's limitations. Faith became for Brian a response which directed all the motives and activities of his life. What he did at night was not integral with his ministry during the day. Gradually, he came to understand that faith is comprehensive and contains all elements of one's life. He never established a loving relationship so there is no happy ending to this story. However, he died a few years after the pastoral counseling ended, with a sense of meaning and being found faithful in the end to his calling.

What These Two Cases Mean for the Ministry of Freedom. Through the case histories of Carol and Brian, the pastoral counseling process as a ministry of freedom through faith has been examined. The two main functions of pastoral counseling for freedom were identified as enabling a person to become liberated so as to believe in himself or herself and God, and helping another deal with the pain caused by the tension between expectation and existence. Certainly, other functions might be included, but it is suggested that in some way they would be subsumed under the functions already mentioned.

With images, poetry, and human history, scripture recounts the story of a people's struggle to become free, to wrestle from both captivity and guilt.[29] With the Exodus, this people celebrates an important moment as they make the shift from a captive people to a free people, living in the land promised to them. In various degrees and with new personalities, the Exodus story is told over and over again as people become bound in guilt and then are invited to return to their God to grow in a deeper covenant relationship.

The freeing experience of the ancient Israelites is the experience of a very ordinary group of individuals. To be sure, this experience has a theological dimension, manifesting the process of salvation. The story of these people is not unlike the story of Brian or Carol, for in each case these two individuals wrestled with painful issues in order to participate in a new and more human way of living their faith.

---

29. Juan Segundo, *The Community Called Church, Volume I: A Theology for Artisans of a New Humanity*, trans. John Drury (Maryknoll, N.Y.: Orbis, 1973).

In this section the actual pastoral counseling process was explained and two important case histories summarized. These case histories are important because they are the vehicle through which the process of salvation may again be discerned. The purpose of this section was to implicate the theological foundations that support the work of the pastoral counselor. In fact, these foundations give pastoral counseling and spiritual direction their meaning as a work of ministry, a work done in and for faith.

Narrative has become a significant tool in the work of Christian ministry. Its significance lies in the fact that the stories of ordinary human experience have the capacity to draw others into the process of that experience. The proclamation of the Word of God is just such an event. Through a proclamation that narrates ordinary events, human persons are summoned to share in the extraordinary.

The original discourse of Christian faith makes a connection between the pastor and shepherd (Jn 10:11). The shepherd serves as one who cares deeply for the sheep. One of the more popular psalms draws such great attention because through the remembrance of the shepherd, people meet God, a pastor who brings comfort and who refreshes the sheep by leading them to green pastures and cool waters. The Hebrew people meet their God as a shepherd. He assumes the pastorate of the people by leading them from exile (Ez 34:11-34; Is 40:10-11). As shepherd/pastor, God stands as a sign of strength, one who can battle against evil (the lions) and lead the nation to its grazing land (Ps 2:9; Is 40:10-11). In their experience of captivity, God promises to the people that they will have a shepherd, a new David, who will establish a lasting covenant of peace (Ez 34:23-27).

As an individual grows in faith and in identification with the Spirit of God, Jesus is portrayed as that new David. He assumes the title of the shepherd who loves his flock as they love him. The common experience of finding the lost sheep becomes an indication of what it is like to experience the reign of God. Jesus, the shepherd, serves as pastor to those for whom he cares, promising to bring comfort to them and to ease the burdens and sorrows that they experience.

The texts of scripture shed light on what it means to be a genuine pastor by taking an understandable image and associating it with God's care. Perhaps the image of the pastoral counselor is just such an image.

A primary resource for the pastoral counselor is the faith which enlivens the counseling dialogue. Just as the relationship between the shepherd and the flock, between God and his people, is marked by both compassion and challenge, so also the relationship between pastoral counselor and client is marked by similar characteristics of growth. If, through the person of the pastoral counselor, a client meets a God who is with his people in their joys and in their sufferings, the client is on a path toward experiencing the freedom which counselors see as the goal.

In the pastoral counseling process, faith is a cornerstone of the relationship between counselor and client. Faith enables both the counselor and the client to understand self as an image of God to all who are encountered. Faith also enables the counselor and client to celebrate the likeness of God as they approach each other as friend.

The friendship of the pastoral counseling relationship comes as a gift of faith to the Christian community. Through the appropriate use of the skills and qualities which pastoral counselors have developed, their work with individuals enables these people to live as believing members of the community and of society. In the next section, the ministry of reconciliation flows as a necessary consequence from the ministries of clarification and freedom.

MINISTRY OF RECONCILIATION

Prior to the pastoral counseling process, the client may be bound in a way that hinders personal growth and thus the fullness of expression of Christian faith. Carol was controlled by a lack of self-acceptance, most obviously expressed by her physical appearance, and Brian was blinded by a judgmentalism which deceived him into believing he could not make worthwhile human choices. Like many clients, neither of them was free; like the people prior to the Exodus were separated from God, both were alienated from themselves and from other people. In fact, they too, were alienated from God.

The Christian community and the pastoral counseling process together affirm that the situation of these people is not hopeless. Pastoral counseling is an experience of growth in faith through the exploration of life and participation in the ministry of reconciliation. The ministry of reconciliation by people of faith goes hand in hand with pastoral counseling, which gives concrete form to the process of reconciliation. For those individuals who lack the experience of God's love the faith stance implicit in the pastoral counseling process provides an opening to that experience.

Post-1970 theology from Latin America reminds all that it is in the experience of the poor and the oppressed that the presence of God may be most keenly felt. This theology points one in the direction of those scriptural events where God, through Jesus, extends himself to those who suffer and who are separated.

In his own time, for example, Jesus related to people held in slavery because through him they realized that they were human beings, even when they were being treated like property. He broke into their history and helped them to see that they possessed a quality of human life that could not be destroyed by others' lack of love and concern. In like manner, Jesus relates to people today through the ministry of pastoral counseling and spiritual direction, helping them to maintain the value of human life and freedom in situations of oppression. The Jesus who relates to today's world is a full human person, the paradigm for what it means to live as a human being. People who focus on the Exodus event understand Jesus is the figure who, in a very pointed and personal way, expressed the desire for all who are burdened to be free from their captivity and to share in the fullness of human life. In the persons to whom Jesus reaches out, the pastoral counselor may see Brian or Carol or other clients. In short, the people who enter into the pastoral counseling process need that love of God to touch them. If a person makes the initial approach, that person is probably ready for that experience to begin; the ground is fallow, and the possibility for new life looms brilliantly.

This is the person of the client prior to the pastoral counseling process. Throughout the process, the client may be understood to have begun a journey of faith which leads to freedom and an alleviation of felt pain. Again, the client is very much like those who walked through desert and wilderness for forty years. For the Hebrew people, the journey of faith had its own set of challenges and beliefs; it helped to constitute them a chosen people directed primarily to God. The client in pastoral counseling similarly faces a set of challenges and beliefs. By getting in touch with the love of God, the client is assisted in making loving choices for him or herself; the developing love of self is itself a freeing experience. Just as the Exodus people came to realize the freedom of a new land and life, in the radiant presence of God—who cared for and loved them, making his dwelling among them—so too, clients are invited to pitch tent on holy ground in the pastoral counseling relationship.

In the beginning of the process the client may often appear to be defensive, much as Brian began the process by defending his homosexual tendencies. Yet, in the faith context, the defensive client faces the same consistent acceptance and love which the unfaithful Israelites met in the words of the prophet Hosea (11:9). Through an ability to be with others in a compassionate and caring way, the pastoral counselor stands in gentle opposition to the client who has been surrounded with notions of unacceptance.

When the goal of the counseling process has been met, the client is a transformed person. This is not to say that the client will engage in the life process without any tensions and difficulties. It does mean that a client will have a new set of resources from which to make positive and loving choices. Whereas prior to counseling one may identify these people with those in the scripture who were most in need of God's love, one may now see in the transformed client those individuals who have been clearly changed through the ministry of Jesus. They have come to a new understanding of faith that walks in light and not in darkness. The change in the disciples, from a group fearfully locked in a room to a community vibrantly proclaiming God's message, dramatically underscores the difference. The goal of pastoral counseling is founded upon the counselor's desire to see clients whose enthusiasm for life and whose ability to make sound choices is greatly enhanced. Breaking out of the locked room of one's myopic existence opens a horizon of new life with new possibilities and a faith that is truly life giving.

If the Exodus event serves as an adequate paradigm for framing the liberating process of pastoral counseling, the same Exodus motif finds its fulfillment in Jesus as the new Exodus. He is the one sent from God, to live as one with humanity and then return to God; he is the one who gathers up to himself to make humanity's identification and oneness with God complete. The ministry of Jesus enables people to live in the freedom of God's Spirit, to live anew as a people consecrated to God. Those who accept the challenge of faith find themselves surrounded by the comforting and awakening love of God; it is a love concretely experienced through the ministry of Jesus and through those who choose to be his disciples.

Pastoral counseling is one form which that ministry of Jesus takes in this age as a genuine service of faith to the members of the Christian community. As a ministry of faith, pastoral counseling follows upon the announcement that the reign of God will bring freedom to those held captive, joy to those in sorrow, sight to those who are blinded. It is shaped by counselors who identify their work with the work of Jesus, who has called people to himself that their sorrows may be comforted and their burdens eased.

For each individual, the sources of captivity, pain, blindness, and sorrow take a unique concrete form. To these forms of evil, sin, or ugliness, the pastoral counseling process holds up the values of the gospel. For it is from the gospel and the life of Jesus that flow the ethical and moral standards which are integral for sound faith living. Where the client enters into the process aware of the concrete forms that ugliness has taken in his or her life, the process enhances vision so that gospel-related values may be seen as viable alternatives in the day-to-day process of living. The pastoral counseling process serves to personalize the liberation of Jesus through its one-to-one relationship between the counselor and client. It personalizes the gospel further by opening up possibilities for living through the specific application of these integral values.

As a dialogic process, pastoral counseling follows upon the patterns of ongoing relationship which can be discerned in the dialogue that continues through history between God and his people. Consequently, pastoral counseling is marked by compassion and gentleness, by an invitation to see more in existence than is evident with a superficial glance. Understanding new possibilities takes the place of coercion to behave in particular ways; such freedom to say "yes" or "no" to God's love undergirds every beckoning which God addresses to the people whom he has chosen.

If perhaps it appears that to live in God's Spirit and to be fully human are one and the same, then the pastoral counseling process has been successful. Even prior to the second century, when Irenaeus wrote that the glory of God is the human being fully alive, the followers of Jesus understood that the reign of God had already broken upon them, to be shared and to live among them as human persons. God's will and the good of the human family are co-terminus; this principle establishes the process of pastoral counseling as a Christian ministry done in faith. Liberation means that human persons are freed to be able to see themselves as a people who share in a new life; the radical transformation of the world which the gospel envisions begins now with the transformation of individuals who are willing and ready to make healthy and loving responses to God's gracious gift of life and love.[30]

At the beginning of this chapter, the words of Ignatius of Antioch were reminders of the connection between faith and love. The pragmatic question: "How can pastoral counselors facilitate growth in faith?" has been answered through the ministries they give so lovingly to people in need. These were the ministries of clarification, freedom, and reconciliation.

---

30. For further discussion of pastoral counseling see Barry K. Estadt, ed., *Pastoral Counseling* (Englewood Cliffs, N.J.: Prentice-Hall, 1983).

CHAPTER 12

Facilitating Growth
in Faith Through
Religious Instruction

James Michael Lee

INTRODUCTION

The teaching of religion stands at the very center of the church's existence and mission. In his words of farewell immediately before his ascension (Mt 28:18-20), Jesus told his disciples that their mission, and thus the mission of the church, is to bring persons into a sharing of divine life and when this is done to help these individuals live as religiously as possible. The first of these dimensions of the church's basic mission, Jesus stated explicitly, is to be accomplished through baptism. The second dimension is to be carried out through teaching.

From the very outset, teaching has always been a central activity and primary focus of the church. Jesus himself was basically a religious educator.[1] He was called teacher (rabbi) by disciples, friends, and enemies. Most of his earthly ministry was devoted to teaching in one form or another. While scripture indicates that Jesus was heavily engaged in teaching religion, it does not record that he baptized anyone, at least with water. Paul the apostle did not baptize much, declaring that the Lord sent him to teach rather than to baptize (1 Cor 1:14-17).

---

1. James Michael Lee, "Religious Instruction and the Bible: A Religious Educationist's View," in *Biblical Themes in Religious Education*, ed. Joseph S. Marino (Birmingham, Ala.: Religious Education Press, 1983), pp. 1-47.

It would appear that religion teaching not only occupied a central place in the ancient church but together with the liturgy was generally esteemed as the most important, the most honored, and the most time-consuming activity of the ecclesia. Historical research suggests that there were three consecutive and interrelated phases in the teaching activity of the ancient church.[2] The first phase, called the kerygma, was intended to so inspire and motivate non-Christians that in cooperation with God's grace they would respond favorably to God's invitation to faith. The kerygmatic phase was followed by the catechetical stage in which persons who had come to faith by God's grace and by kerygmatic teaching would learn what it is to be a bearer of the Christian faith. This stage became formalized into the catechumenate in which persons learned not only the intellectual rudiments of the Christian faith but even more importantly learned to live that kind of Christian lifestyle consonant with faith.[3] The final phase of religion teaching in the ancient church was didascalia. After a successful catechumenate which culminated in baptism, persons were taught by word, by affect, and by deed to widen and deepen their faith. Didascalia was viewed as a lifelong process from baptism until death.

Clarification of Terms

It is generally recognized today that there are three principal forms or subsets of religious education, namely, religious instruction, religious guidance, and the administration of religious education activities.

Religious instruction is the process by which desired learning outcomes are facilitated. Instruction, then, is a synonym for teaching.

Religious instruction is in no way restricted to formal settings, such as the classroom. Rather, religious instruction can and does occur in a wide variety of formal and informal settings such as the classroom, the playground, the worship service, the home, and so forth. Religious instruction is not identified with any one specific teaching procedure, such as lecture or discussion or role playing. Instead, religious instruction encompasses all teaching procedures and all different modes of pedagogical process (e.g., verbal and nonverbal, cognitive and lifestyle). Finally, religious instruction is not aimed exclusively or even primarily at learners of any one age group (e.g., children) but is geared to learners of every age group from infancy to old age.

---

2. André Rétif, "La prédication kérygmatique dans les Actes des Apôtres," doctoral dissertation, Università Gregoriana, 1948; André Rétif, *Foi au Christ et mission d'aprés les Actes des Apôtres* (Paris: Cerf, 1953), pp. 7-32.

3. Justin Martyr, 1 *Apologia*, LXI; Michel Dujarier, *A History of the Catechumenate: The First Six Centuries*, trans. Edward L. Haasl (New York: Sadlier, 1979).

This chapter focuses on only one of the three forms of religious instruction, namely, facilitating the reception and growth in faith through religious instruction.

The Content of Religious Instruction for Faith

Instructional content has traditionally been thought of as that which is taught to learners. In this view, content is distinguished from procedure (the way in which content is taught).

In the twentieth century an alternate view of the nature of instructional content has been advanced by some scholars specializing in educational studies. In this new view, pedagogical process is a content in its own right because the way in which something is taught is also that which is taught.[4] For example, one parent teaches the Ten Commandments to her child using pedagogical procedures which stress cognitive recitation, strict control, and a juridic emphasis. A second parent teaches her child the Ten Commandments using pedagogical procedures which stress lifestyle activites, mild control, and a loving emphasis. Both children learn the Ten Commandments. But each child also learns the Ten Commandments as a cognitive or lifestyle affair, as a matter of strict or mild control, as a juridic or a loving approach to life. The way a content is taught, then, forms a large part of what is taught.

Those scholars who regard instructional procedure as content point to a considerable body of empirical evidence which suggests that the way something is taught often has a more powerful and a more long-lasting effect on learners than the material which was taught.[5] In other words, the way in which something is taught is often more of a content than the material which is taught. For reasons of clarity and accuracy it has been found helpful to use the term "substantive content" to refer to that which was traditionally called content and to use the term "structural content" to refer to pedagogical procedure. In addition to enhanced clarity, the use of the term "structural content" instead of pedagogical procedure underscores that the act of teaching is an authentic content in its own right rather than just a way of facilitating content.

---

4. John Dewey, *Democracy and Education* (New York: Macmillan, 1916), pp. 193-211; J. Cecil Parker and Louis J. Rubin, *Process as Content* (Chicago: Rand McNally, 1966), pp. 1-13; James Michael Lee, *The Content of Religious Instruction* (Birmingham, Ala.: Religious Education Press, 1985), pp. 739-740; Thomas H. Groome, "Walking Humbly with our God," in *To Act Justly, Love Tenderly, Walk Humbly*, ed. Walter Bruggemann, Sharon Parks, and Thomas H. Groome (New York: Paulist, 1986), pp. 56-60.

5. Herbert J. Walberg, "Synthesis of Research on Teaching," in *Handbook of Research on Teaching*, ed. Merlin C. Whitrock, 3rd ed. (New York: Macmillan, 1986), pp. 214-229; Jere Brophy and Thomas L. Good, "Teacher Behavior and Student Achievement," in ibid, pp. 328-375.

CAN FAITH BE TAUGHT?

It is generally agreed by most religious educationists and educators that it is possible to teach *about* faith.[6] But there is a vast difference between teaching about faith and teaching faith. This section will deal with teaching faith.

In terms of teaching faith, there are three principal issues: 1) the nature of instruction; 2) the enhancement of that faith which a person or group already has; 3) the bringing about of faith in a person who does not have faith.

The Nature of Instruction

As noted earlier, instruction is the broad process by and through which learning is caused in an individual in one way or another.

Insofar as all instruction is deliberate and intentional, all teaching is to that extent direct. Still, there is a wide variety of levels and breadths in this directness. For example, [direct] teaching includes giving verbal information to a person, putting a hand on another's shoulder, arranging statues and decorations in a church, smiling or frowning, walking quietly with another person, feeding a homeless individual in a rescue mission, and so forth.

Instruction takes place in an enormously broad variety of substantive contents. The content of teaching may be a product or a process. It may focus on conscious or unconscious modes of human activity. It may be chiefly cognitive, affective, or lifestyle. It may be primarily verbal or nonverbal.

When considering the issue of whether faith can be facilitated or even caused, it is essential to keep in mind the variety of levels of the teaching act. Though empirical research on teaching is still in its infancy compared to research in the older disciplines and fields, nonetheless the available data do suggest that different modes of teaching are necessary to yield different kinds of learning outcomes.[7] Thus, for example, if one

---

6. See, for example, C. Ellis Nelson, *Where Faith Begins* (Richmond, Va.: Knox, 1967), pp. 30-34; Brennan R. Hill, *Key Dimensions of Religious Education* (Winona, Minn.: St. Mary's Press, 1988), pp. 34-35; C. Joseph Sprague and Paul Miller, "Case Study I: Pastors as Religious Educators at Work in Middle America," in *The Pastor as Religious Educator*, ed. Robert L. Browning (Birmingham, Ala.: Religious Education Press, 1989), pp. 210-234; Eichstätt Study Week, "Basic Principles of Modern Catechetics," in *Teaching All Nations*, ed. Johannes Hofinger, rev. and partly trans. Clifford Howell (Freiburg, Deutschland: Herder, 1961), pp. 394-400.

7. Marsha L. Weil and Joseph Murphy, "Instructional Processes," in *Encyclopedia of Educational Research*, ed. Harold E. Mitzell, 5th ed., vol. 2 (New York: Free Press, 1982), pp. 890-917.

conceptualizes faith as primarily intellectual assent to a given body of doctrines, then classroom lectures and pulpit sermons can be effective, at least minimally, in facilitating growth in faith or even in producing faith. But if one conceptualizes faith as a way of life which incorporates psychomotor activity, cognition, affective behaviors, and overt conduct, then cognitively thrusted pedagogical procedures such as lecturing or preaching will not be effective. What is needed in this case are pedagogical procedures which are appropriate to the successful facilitation of all these faith-inclusive behaviors.

Teaching, then, is far wider and deeper than simply standing in front of a classroom and talking, or in the pulpit and preaching. Indeed, teaching of this kind seems to be among the least effective of all pedagogical procedures, even for cognitive outcomes.[8] This is especially true if one conceptualizes faith as holistic rather than as just cognitive.

The Enhancement of Faith

There are a few contemporary religious educationists who contend that faith cannot be taught. For example, Berard Marthaler, a Catholic theological conservative,[9] states that faith cannot be enhanced or otherwise taught; only cognitive beliefs (theologies of faith) are capable of being facilitated.[10] This view is shared by Robert Conrad, a Lutheran theological moderate.[11]

By and large, however, the overwhelming majority of religious educationists and educators of all persuasions assert that faith can be enhanced through religious instruction. All these individuals and groups are keenly aware that faith is a free and unmerited gift of God to which human beings, through the power of God's grace, are enabled to make a free affirmative response. Yet none of these individuals or groups perceive any conflict between faith as God's free gift on the one hand and

---

8. This statement holds true even for teaching conducted in colleges and universities. In the latter connection, one review of the pertinent research concludes that the higher the level of cognitive substantive content, the less effective is the lecture technique compared to other pedagogical procedures. Michael J. Durkin and Jennifer Barnes, "Research on Teaching in Higher Education," in *Handbook of Research on Teaching*, pp. 754-777.

9. Berard L. Marthaler, "Socialization as a Model for Catechetics," in *Foundations of Religious Education*, ed. Padraic O'Hare (New York: Paulist, 1978), pp. 75-76.

10. This position is also advanced by Richard McBrien, "Faith, Theology and Belief," *Commonweal* 101 (November 15, 1974), p. 135.

11. Robert L. Conrad, "If You Really Love Us, then Show Us: A Lutheran Perspective," in *Does the Church Really Want Religious Education?*, ed. Marlene Mayr (Birmingham, Ala.: Religious Education Press, 1988), pp. 82-83.

human teaching to enhance what God has already given on the other hand. There seems to be a common, though often unmentioned, assumption that it is the God-given task of the church in general and of individual church members in particular to fructify, through God's grace, that which God initiated and keeps in existence.

Official religious education documents promulgated by various Christian church bodies take it for granted, and indeed forthrightly state, that a prime purpose of religious instruction is to facilitate growth in faith.[12]

The contention that religious education can and should facilitate growth in faith is one which is shared by Catholic and Protestant religious educationists whose theological orientation is conservative,[13] moderate,[14] and liberal.[15] This position is also held by most religious educationists who are principally identified with a particular focus in the field, such as liberation religious education,[16] intergenerational religious education,[17] religious education curriculum development,[18] and religious education media.[19] Religious educationists who adhere to the

---

12. See, for example, Sacra Congregatio pro Clericis, *Directorium catechisticum generale* (Città del Vaticano: Libreria Editrice Vaticana, 1971), #22 (p. 29); National Conference of Catholic Bishops, *Sharing the Light of Faith* (Washington, D.C.: United States Catholic Conference, 1979), #32 (p. 18); Joannis Paulus II, "Catechesi Tradendae (24 Octobris, 1979), in *Acta Apostolicae Sedis*, LXXI (31 Octobris, 1979), #a 7 (p. 1282) et 19 (p. 1293).

13. Michael Warren, *Faith, Culture, and the Worshiping Community* (New York: Paulist, 1989); C. B. Eavey, "Aims and Objectives of Christian Education," in *An Introduction to Evangelical Christian Education*, ed. J. Edward Hakes (Chicago: Moody, 1964), pp. 60-64; Lawrence O. Richards, *A Theology of Christian Education* (Grand Rapids, Mich.: Zondervan, 1975), pp. 65-66, 213-216; Jim Wilhoit, *Christian Education: The Search for Meaning* (Grand Rapids, Mich.: Baker, 1986), pp. 56-60.

14. C. Ellis Nelson, *Where Faith Begins* (Richmond, Va.: Knox, 1967); Brennan R. Hill, *Key Dimensions of Religious Education* (Winona, Minn.: St. Mary's Press, 1988), p. 34.

15. Randolph Crump Miller, *The Clue to Christian Education* (New York: Scribner's, 1950), p. 35; Charles R. Foster, *Teaching in the Community of Faith* (Nashville: Abingdon, 1982), pp. 65-92; Mary Elizabeth Moore, *Education for Continuity and Change* (Nashville: Abingdon, 1983), pp. 164-168.

16. Daniel S. Schipani, *Religious Education Encounters Liberation Theology* (Birmingham, Ala.: Religious Education Press, 1988), pp. 128-133.

17. James W. White, *Intergenerational Religious Education* (Birmingham, Ala.: Religious Education Press, 1988), pp. 192-215.

18. D. Campbell Wyckoff, *Theory and Design of Christian Education Curriculum* (Philadelphia: Westminster, 1961), p. 79.

19. Ronald A. Sarno, *Using Media in Religious Education* (Birmingham, Ala.: Religious Education Press, 1987), pp. 41-83.

social-science approach to religious education by and large are unanimous in their belief that faith can be facilitated by religious instruction.[20]

Giving Rise to Faith Directly

The issue of whether religious instruction can lead directly to faith in a person who does not yet have faith is usually not discussed explicitly or at length in the religious instruction literature. As a general rule, the proposition that religious instruction is unable to lead directly to faith is assumed rather than proven or otherwise subjected to careful analysis.

Several arguments can be adduced to support the contention that religious instruction can directly lead to faith, and has in fact done so frequently.

First, all the empirical data indicate that every human behavior or set of behaviors[21] is either instinctual or learned. Faith is a human activity, a set of human behaviors. Faith is not an entity "out there." Since faith is obviously not instinctual, it must be learned. Anything that is learned can be taught. After all, teaching is the facilitation of learning.

Second, there is no body of empirical evidence suggesting that faith, or more accurately that cluster of related human behaviors called faith, is learned in a manner basically different from other kinds of learning. Indeed, all the available empirical evidence indicates that faith behaviors are learned in the same general way as other related behaviors are learned.[22]

Third, most Christian religions engage in missionary work at home and abroad in order to "win converts to the faith," among other things. Missionaries in the field consistently provide raw empirical data suggesting that there is a positive correlation between their teaching efforts and conversion to faith. Without the pedagogical activities of these missionaries, God's gift of faith did not seem to have been given. Many

---

20. V. Bailey Gillespie, *The Experience of Faith* (Birmingham, Ala.: Religious Education Press, 1988), pp. 66-88, 233-245; David Arthur Bickimer, *Christ the Placenta* (Birmingham, Ala.: Religious Education Press, 1983); James Michael Lee, *The Shape of Religious Instruction* (Birmingham, Ala.: Religious Education Press, 1971), pp. 182-224.

21. In educational terminology, a behavior is anything which a human being does, e.g., an act of thought, an act of emoting, and so forth. Thus behavior is far wider than overt behavior. Behavior is a descriptive term for a particular act of the organism. It is not exclusively or even primarily linked with any particular viewpoint such as behaviorism, just as the term grace (a descriptor) is not exclusively or even primarily linked to any particular theological viewpoint.

22. André Godin, "Some Developmental Tasks in Christian Education," in *Research on Religious Development*, ed. Merton P. Strommen (New York: Hawthorne, 1971), pp. 109-154.

Catholic parishes in the United States successfully operate weekly instruction classes for those who express an interest in Catholicism. Many members of such classes often come to faith.

Some objections can or have been brought against the above-mentioned arguments.

The first objection is that faith is a supernatural or divine affair and thus is beyond the reach of empirical evidence. This objection is flawed because faith is a human activity and to that extent can be empirically grasped.

The second objection is that because faith is an unmerited gift from God, only God, and not any human teacher is the decisive (and possibly the sole) force in the acquisition of faith. This objection is flawed because the issue is not whether faith is a gift from God but how and in what mode this gift is received. A person necessarily receives the gift of faith (or any gift from any source) according to his or her own nature and operations as a human being.[23]

The third objection is that any claim that religious instruction gives rise directly to faith is Pelagian. This objection is flawed because unlike Pelagianism (at least in its traditional interpretation) the position taken in this chapter is that while God's grace is totally responsible in the ultimate analysis for a person's coming to faith, it is God's grace flowing through the human activity of religious instruction which proximately and effectually gives rise to the acquisition of faith.

SUBSTANTIVE CONTENT IN TEACHING FAITH

Faith as a Construct

The substantive content of teaching faith is faith. If religion teachers are to educate in and for faith, then they must know what faith is.

Faith is not a subsistent reality. Instead, faith is a concept, an abstraction formed by making a generalization from a body of particulars. Concepts are extremely important and powerful in all areas of life, including religious instruction. For example, religious educators rely heavily on such concepts as intelligence, obedience, learning—and faith.

But faith is more than a concept. It is also, and in many ways more importantly, a construct. A construct is a concept which has the added meaning of having been deliberately invented or consciously adopted

---

23. The classic philosophical expression of this point is that all learning occurs according to the mode of the learner. See Thomas Aquinas, *Expositio in Librum Beati Dionysii Divinis Nominibus*, II, 4. In Marietti edition (Torino, 1950), #176. This philosophical point is totally endorsed by psychology from the latter's own unique vantage point.

for a particular purpose. This purpose is enhanced usefulness. The reason a construct is "constructed" is functional, namely, to make a concept more useful. Because a construct is functional, it helps us to analyze a set of particulars more carefully, to discover hitherto unknown but fruitful relationships among various kinds of particulars, and to generate new particulars and new constructs.

For religionists, faith is even more useful as a construct than as a concept. First, as a construct, faith becomes organically integrated into the broader theoretical scaffolding of religion and thus acquires the power to enrich and to be enriched by other constructs present and operative within that theoretical scaffolding—constructs such as grace, salvation, holiness, hope, redemption, time, and so forth. Thus, for example, a religious educator can now assert that self-sacrifice for God is in part a function of faith (a construct), of grace (related construct), of time (another related construct), and so forth. Second, as a construct, faith can be defined, circumscribed, elaborated, and specified in such a way that the particulars encompassed by the construct can be seen as an integrated set, can be fruitfully analyzed both as a set and as singulars within a set and can be measured empirically to a certain extent. Such definition, circumscription, elaboration, and specification are essential if a religious educator is to teach faith successfully because without a knowledge of these properties there would be no genuinely accurate or reliable way of ascertaining what should be taught and how to assess the degree to which the desired learning outcomes have taken place. Third, as a construct, faith takes on the character of what many philosophers and theologians call a cause, or what social scientists prefer to term an independent variable. Hence a religious educator is able to attribute one or another of a learner's behaviors to faith or to lack of faith.

Like all other kinds of constructs, faith can be defined in two general ways, namely notionally and operationally. Each of these has important consequences for religious educators in their work of teaching faith.

A notional definition denotes the meaning of a term by using descriptive words about it. Notional definitions tend to describe the definiendum in terms of essences, together with their accidents or properties. Two prevalent forms of notional definition are the lexical definition and the stipulative definition. A lexical definition is one which reports the accepted or standard use of a word or a phrase. A stipulative definition is one which arbitrarily assigns or deliberately posits a meaning to a word or phrase.

An operational definition is one which gives the activities or "operations" attendant upon a word or phrase. An operational definition concretizes a word or phrase and places that word or phrase in a given here-and-now existential context. An operational definition is a sort of manual of instructions which says: "Do such-and-such in a so-and-so manner." In short, an operational definition gives meaning to a word or phrase by spelling out what must be done to measure it or to facilitate it.

Perhaps an example drawn from a construct related to faith will illumine the basic difference between a notional definition and an operational definition. This related construct is religion. A famous notional definition of religion is that given by an important European theologian of yesteryear, Léonce de Grandmaison: "Religion is the relationship of man, individually and collectively, with God."[24] An operational definition of religion is given by the apostle James in his universal letter, namely, "coming to the help of orphans and widows when they need it, and keeping oneself uncontaminated from the world" (Jas 1:27).

From Construct to Learning Outcome

The realization that faith is a construct which can be defined operationally is absolutely essential for successfully teaching faith. Conversely, without such an explicit or at the very least implicit realization, the religious educator will not be able to facilitate faith effectively, except accidentally.

When religious educators say they are teaching faith or faith-life, they typically mean that they are trying to facilitate some faith-inclusive behavioral outcome in the learner.[25] Such an outcome might be a cognitive behavorial outcome (e.g., knowledge of the doctrine of the incarnation), an affective behavioral outcome (e.g., a positive attitude toward the mystery of the incarnation), or a lifestyle behavioral outcome (e.g., habitually acting in an incarnational manner toward the natural environment in one's immediate neighborhood).

It is pedagogically impossible to teach any one or a combination of these faith-associated behaviors by saying that the educational objective is to teach faith. Faith is a construct. If a construct is taught, then that which is learned is a construct and nothing more. For a religious educator to assert that he or she is teaching faith is, in reality, to assert that what is being taught to learners is an understanding of a construct. To teach faith, then, is always to "teach about" because a construct is descriptive, abstract, and about the bundle of realities from which it is constructed. In order to teach faith as a personally lived reality and not as a construct, the religious educator first ascertains which kinds of

---

24. Quoted in E. Magnin, "Religion," in *Dictionnaire de théologie catholique*, ed. A. Vacant, E. Mangenot, and E. Amann, tome 13, pt. 2, col. 2186 (Paris: Letouzey et Ané, 1939), translation mine.

25. It is important to keep in mind the definition and scope of behavior as delineated on line two of footnote 21 of this chapter.

behaviors are properly included in the construct of faith and then teaches specifically for the attainment of one or more of these faith-inclusive behaviors.

The task of every religious education curriculum and of every religious educator seeking to teach faith is to make faith teachable and thus learnable. In order to accomplish this, the curriculum builder and the teacher initially cast the pedagogical goal of teaching faith into empirical form, since the actual facilitation of a desired learning outcome is itself an empirical act. This empirical form, or to use a more focused phrase, this social-scientific form, includes at least three components, namely, the psychological, the sociological, and the pedagogical. Psychological statements describe the ways in which a person learns the behaviors associated with faith. Sociological statements describe the ways in which social factors promote or inhibit the acquisition of those behaviors associated with faith. Pedagogical statements prescribe the ways in which the behaviors associated with faith can be successfully taught.

The process of operationalizing is of great help in placing the construct of faith into that kind of empirical form in which it can be rendered teachable and learnable. Teaching and learning are definite, circumscribed activities and so are highly congenial or conatural with operationalizing. Operationalizing takes faith out of an abstract generalized construct form and places it into a concrete, here-and-now existential form.

A wide variety of concrete procedures geared to operationalizing desired faith outcomes have been available to religious educators since the early 1960s. Most of those revolve around the necessity of converting broader instructional goals (such as teaching faith) into specific instructional objectives (such as teaching a particular outcome included in the construct of faith). Instructional goals are general and have the pedagogical advantage of serving as an integrative focus for instructional objectives. But their very generality and breadth renders them inherently unteachable. It is only when an instructional goal such as teaching faith is operationalized into a specific faith-associated instructional objective that the overall goal can be attained.

Instructional objectives are statements of desired changes in the thoughts, feelings, or conduct of learners which a particular pedagogical event can bring. One principal benefit offered by instructional objectives is that, by describing learning outcomes in terms of specifying the pedagogical procedure(s) through which these outcomes are to be brought about, effective procedures to facilitate learning are thereby suggested to religious educators.[26]

---

26. The classic work on instructional objectives remains Robert F. Mager, *Preparing Instructional Objectives* (Palo Alto, Calif.: Fearon, 1962).

A large number of leading Catholic and Protestant religious educa-tion curricula designed for school-aged children and youth consciously employ behaviorally oriented instructional objectives to some extent. Many of the instruments prepared by the Religious Education Depart-ment of the National Catholic Educational Association to evaluate faith learnings and to assist religious educators improve their teaching of faith-related outcomes are based on a behaviorally oriented instruc-tional objectives approach. A sizable number of mainline Protestant central-office administrators currently operate on a leadership-by-objec-tives and a teaching-by-objectives approach. The carefully architected structure of many successful conservative Protestant revival meetings and other calls-to-faith rallies is suffused with operationalization and behavioral objectives.

The slow but steady movement in religious instruction away from notionalism and toward operationalism has parallels throughout the world. Thus the classically educated theologian Bernard Lonergan states that the world has passed from a classical mode of dealing intel-lectually with reality to a scientific frame, a frame in which the *a priori* and mentalist mode of thought has been replaced by an *a posteriori* and empirical mode.[27] This is not to say that the classical mode of dealing intellectually with reality is useless or outmoded. Rather it is to assert that for a great many human activities, including religion teaching, the scientific mode of thinking and doing things is more fecund, more useful, and more effective than the classical approach. What Lonergan states in the following quotation applies just as potently both to Protes-tantism and to religious instruction: "To confine the Catholic Church to a classical mentality is to keep the Catholic Church out of the modern world and to prolong the too prolonged crisis within the Church."[28]

Enriching the Construct

Every construct is invented or constructed by some person or group of persons. Consequently, the shape, flow, and content of the construct of faith depends to a significant degree upon the vantage point of its inventor.

Of the many vantage points of the inventor which significantly affect the structure and substance of any construct (including that of faith), three are especially worthy of mention: the psychological, the sociologi-cal, and the physical. In inventing the construct of faith, another van-tage point is involved, namely, the theological.

Psychology. The construct of faith is necessarily the psychological

---

27. Bernard Lonergan, *Doctrinal Pluralism* (Milwaukee, Wis.: Marquette University Press, 1971), pp. 4-12.
28. Ibid., p. 9.

product of a person. Prominent among the psychological factors significantly influencing the formation of the construct of faith is perception. Perception is an immediate discriminatory response. A person does not experience the world as a passive receptor of sense data. Instead, a person immediately experiences the world from the vantage point of his or her perceptions. Perception, then, is an active personal response of the total human organism. What an individual perceives is the result of the dynamic interaction between the objective character of what is perceived and the perceiver's total personality configuration.[29] What a person experiences is, in large measure, what that individual perceives.

Two brief examples illustrate the great power of perception in human life, including the way in which the construct of faith is fashioned. First, persons often perceive sounds and short events that never actually occurred but which one's perceptual processes organize as occurring because they are naturally configured by one's perceptual process to be present.[30] Second, different persons often physically experience similar corporeal realities in a significantly different manner because of their varying perceptions. Thus one classic experimental study disclosed that poor children tended to overestimate the physical size of coins to a greater degree than do wealthy children.[31]

Of the many practical implications of perceptual processes for the shape, flow, and content of the construct of faith, two stand out. First, perceptions are not free-floating but are heavily influenced by the personal needs, feelings, emotions, attitudes, drives, and motivations of the individual.[32] Thus a construct of faith reflects, to a certain extent at least, the personality of its inventor. Second, perception plays a significant influential role in 1) the selection of which experiences are received and which are not and the manner in which experiences are brought into play; 2) how experiences are organized by the person; and 3) how experiences are interpreted. Hence any construct of faith represents to a certain extent the psychologically selective, organizational, and interpretive processes of whomever devised this construct.[33]

---

29. J. Hochberg, "Perception," in *Encyclopedia of Psychology*, ed. Raymond J. Corsini, Vol. 2 (New York: Wiley, 1984), pp. 497-500.
30. Many detective stories make use of this fact in their readers' perceptions. Richard M. Warren, "Perceptual Restoration of Missing Speech Sounds," in *Science* 166 (January 23, 1970), pp. 392-393.
31. Jerome Bruner and Cecile Goodman, "Value and Need as Organizing Factors in Perception," in *Journal of Abnormal and Social Psychology* 14 (January, 1947), pp. 33-34.
32. Karl R. Popper and John C. Eccles, *The Self and the Brain* (New York: Springer, 1977), pp. 272-277.
33. Lawrence A. Pervin, "Personality: Current Controversies, Issues, and Directions," in *Annual Review of Psychology*, vol. 36, ed. Mark A. Rosenzweig and Lyman W. Porter (Palo Alto, Calif.: Annual Reviews, 1985), p. 94.

Sociology. The construct of faith is necessarily the sociological product of the impact of sociocultural settings and forces upon a person. No construct of faith was ever composed in a vacuum. Rather, this construct is tied in with the particular socio-intellectual culture from which it arose (e.g., one or another faith tradition, social surroundings such as monastery or seminary or university or parish, and so forth).[34] A person's behavior, including the cognitive behavior involved in devising the construct of faith, is a function both of the here-and-now relation of that person to the social situation and of the history of that relation.[35] Various sociologists and others involved in sociology have underscored this point from complementary perspectives.

Karl Mannheim contends that all knowledge and all ideas, albeit in different degrees, are bound to a location within the social structure and historical process.[36]

George Herbert Mead holds that the human mind itself is a social product with a social origin. He maintains that if determinants of thought other than society do exist, then these forces can structure mind only through the intermediary of the social relations in which it is necessarily enmeshed.[37]

Peter Berger and Thomas Luckmann view human knowledge as an ongoing dynamic dialectic between society as an objective reality independent of human knowledge and society as a subjective reality. By society as a subjective reality is meant that society is also necessarily constructed from a person's own sociocultural place in existence.[38]

Neo-Marxians such as those of the social-scientific Frankfurt School of Critical Theory underscore that social forces determine all knowledge, including constructs. Thus Jürgen Habermas contends that knowledge is necessarily and always hermeneutic, namely, one in which a person interprets reality in a here-and-now social situation which features interaction with persons and culture. Hence knowledge is always socially personal and participatory. It is conditioned by society and social factors.[39]

---

34. Judith Miller, *The Social Determination of Knowledge* (Englewood Cliffs, N.J.: Prentice-Hall, 1971), p. 72.

35. Talcott Parsons, *The Social System* (Glencoe, Ill.: Free Press, 1951), pp. 68-112, 359-383.

36. Karl Mannheim, *Ideology and Utopia*, trans. Louis Wirth and Edward Shils (New York: Harcourt, Brace, and World, 1954), p. 3.

37. George Herbert Mead, *Mind, Self, and Society from the Standpoint of a Behaviorist*, ed. Charles Morris (Chicago: University of Chicago Press, 1934), pp. 125-134, 214-226, 245-252.

38. Peter L. Berger and Thomas Luckmann, *The Social Construction of Reality* (Garden City, N.Y.: Doubleday Anchor, 1966), pp. 47-183.

39. Jürgen Habermas, *Knowledge and Human Interests*, trans. Jeremy Shapiro (Boston: Beacon, 1971), pp. 43-63, 314-315.

Of the many practical implications which the sociology of knowledge has for the shape, flow, and content of the construct of faith, two can be mentioned. First, the faith community, the scholarly community, or any other social ecology out of which a construct of faith was invented is itself a social reality. Hence to a greater or lesser extent every construct of faith reflects and incorporates features of the social ecology from whence it arose. Second, socially organized practice plays a significant role in determining whether a construct of faith is said to be valid and also the way in which that construct is interpreted. By socially organized practice is meant communal rules governing invocation, recognition, and sanctioning by some formal or informal social unit of any course of action, including cognitive matters of validity and interpretation.[40] A denomination's *ecclesiasticum*, a particular school of theologians, and various subgroups within a church all have communal rules in this regard.

Physics. While physics is not generally thought to be involved in the act of devising a construct of faith, nevertheless profound developments in modern physics lend intriguing support, from a not altogether unrelated perspective, to the view that any construct of faith necessarily reflects to some extent the person or group that devises it.

In sharp contrast to classical physics, modern physics maintains that there is an unavoidable subjectivity in all natural science, including physics. This subjectivity is brought about by the act of human observation of the natural phenomena under investigation. That which is being observed is necessarily disrupted or changed by the act of human observation and measurement, a disruption which is unavoidable due to the existence of the quantum of action.[41] In P. W. Bridgman's words, quantum mechanics "has learned that the object of knowledge is not to be separated from the instrument of knowledge. We can no longer think of the object of knowledge constituting a reality which is revealed to us by the instrument of knowledge, but the two together, object and instrument, constitute a whole so intimately knit that it is meaningless to talk of object and instrument separately."[42] Implicit in quantum physics is not only that a person directly or indirectly (via a measuring instrument) is somehow part of the object under investigation but, even more radically, the object in one sense is brought into being by the person

40. David Silverman, *Reading Castaneda* (London: Routledge and Kegan Paul, 1975), p. 11.
41. N. David Mermin, "Is the Moon There When Nobody Looks?: Reality and the Quantum Theory," *Physics Today* 38 (April, 1985), p. 38.
42. P. W. Bridgman, "The Nature of Physical Knowledge," in *The Nature of Physical Knowledge*, ed. L. W. Friedrich (Bloomington, Ind. and Milwaukee, Wis.: Indiana University Press and Marquette University Press, 1960), p. 22.

participating in the scientific observation.[43] Quantum theory indicates that the world must be actually observed to be objective.[44] Thus the physical universe is a dynamic, inseparable, coproducing whole which always includes the observer not in a tangential manner but in an essential way.[45]

There is always some degree of uncertainty, and thus of inexactitude, in all physical measurement. Quantum theory underscores that far from being exact, physics deals with probabilities.[46] The primary, but by no means the only, cause of this inexactness and approximateness is the human element which, to some extent, is part and parcel of every scientific observation.

Of the many practical implications which modern physics has for the shape, flow, and content of the construct of faith, two stand out. First, no construct, even in the hardest of the hard sciences, is totally objective. Hence no single soft and nonphysical construct such as faith is completely valid. Second, the construct of faith is necessarily inexact, approximate, and changeable. A wide variety of perspectives, nontheological as well as theological, are necessary to come to a really adequate construct of faith.

Theology. No area of scientific inquiry has cognitively explored the construct of faith more than has theology. By its very nature, theological science tends to be significantly influenced by the person or group that is theologizing. Thus there is no one single unified theological position on the construct of faith. Indeed, the constructs of faith devised by theologians have been extremely divergent from one another—so divergent, in fact, that these disparate constructs provided one of the principal rationales for the breakup of Catholicism and the formation of various Protestant denominations.

One way of bringing into order and clarity the widely differing theological conceptualizations of the construct of faith is to use the familiar classification of intellect, affect, and lifestyle. This classification is especially useful in that virtually every theologian considers faith to be inextricably enmeshed in the life of the human being, a life which is characterized by these three primary domains.

It is as tempting as it is overfacile to assert that the concept of faith which is constructed by all the various theologians is a homogenized

43. Max Jammer, *The Philosophy of Quantum Mechanics* (New York: Wiley, 1974), p. 161.

44. Heinz R. Pagels, *The Cosmic Code* (New York: Simon and Schuster, 1982), p. 161.

45. Fritjof Capra, *The Tao of Physics* (New York: Bantam, 1975), pp. 70-71.

46. Werner Heisenberg, *Physics and Philosophy* (New York: Harper & Row, 1958), p. 50.

mix of the cognitive, affective, and lifestyle domains. It is true that many of the theologians and theological groups cited in this section directly or indirectly assert that faith includes all three domains. Notwithstanding, each theologian or group also asserts that one or another of these domains is dominant in faith.[47]

The primacy of the intellect in the construct of faith has been advanced by Christian theologians from the Patristic era down to the present day. Indeed, the overwhelming body of Christian theological opinion from the earliest days of the church until the Protestant Reformation regarded faith as primarily cognitive in nature.

In the early church, Clement of Alexandria (c. 150 - c. 220) looked on faith as a special form of knowledge based on the word of God rather than on natural reasoning.[48] Cyril of Jerusalem (c. 315 - 386) regarded faith as a twofold intellectual activity. Knowledge of doctrine comes by reasoning, while knowledge of the mind of God is the result of a special grace.[49] Basil (c. 330 - 379), one of the Cappadocian Fathers, held that faith is an intellectual assent to those teachings publicly proclaimed by the church.[50] Augustine of Hippo (354-430), the most influential theologian in the early church, agreed with his forerunners that faith is primarily cognitive.[51] Faith, namely belief, shows us not only the object of knowledge but also the reasons for adhering to that knowledge. For Augustine, faith is the assent of the mind to unseen realities; hence the proof of faith differs from the proof of natural science.[52] While a person's motivation for faith is affective and conative, faith itself is intellectual adherence.[53]

In the medieval church, Joannes Scotus Erigena (c. 815 - c. 877) maintains that faith is both an intellectual precondition of faith-knowledge[54] and, more essentially, the unfolding of the intellect during which the person gradually comes to know God.[55] Anselm of Canterbury (1033-1109) conceptualizes faith as fundamentally a cognitive assent to God's truths. Thus faith is more than just knowledge of God (the Truth); it is also an intellectual force seeking further knowledge of God (*fides quaerens intellec-*

---

47. For reasons of space, my treatment of the theologians in this section is necessarily very brief. Thus, while accurate, my treatment is not able to provide the nuances of the positions of the various theologians cited.
48. Clement of Alexandria, *Stromata*, II, 4.
49. Cyril of Jerusalem, *Catecheses*, VI.
50. Basil, *De fide.* in *PG* XXXI, 224.
51. Aurelius Augustinus, *De praedestinatione sanctorum*, V.
52. Aurelius Augustinus, *De fide rerum non videntur*, I-III; Aurelius Augustinus, *Epistola CXLVII (ad Paulinam)*, III-X.
53. Aurelius Augustinus, *Confessiones*, VII, 10.
54. Joannes Scotus Erigena, *In prologum sancti evangeli secundum Joannem*, in *PL* CXXII, 284-285.
55. Joannes Scotus Erigena, *De divisione naturae*, I, 71 (in *PL* CXXII, 516).

tum).[56] Peter Lombard (c. 1100 - c. 1160), an enormously influential theologian, views faith as intellectual assent both to the doctrines of the church and to the twin authorities for these doctrines, namely God and the teaching authority of the church (*magisterium*). Without love, faith does not arrive at its fulfillment. Without love, faith is faith-without-form (*fides informis*). It is love which makes faith come alive (*fides caritate formata*).[57] Thomas Aquinas (1225-1274), the greatest of all the medieval theologians, situates faith in the speculative intellect. Faith is a habit of the mind through which a person's eternal life is initiated. Faith induces reasonable assent to unseen realities.[58] More specifically, faith is intellectual assent to God's truth. While knowable to a certain extent, this truth nonetheless surpasses normal human knowledge.[59]

Responding to the concept of faith-as-affect proposed by most of the Protestant Reformers, the Catholic Counterreformation reemphasized the classical Catholic view of faith as chiefly cognitive. Thus the most authoritative voice of the Counterreformation, the Council of Trent (1545-1562) formally declared that faith is intellectual assent.[60]

The nineteenth century witnessed two important and influential reiterations of the conceptualization that faith is essentially cognitive. John Henry Newman regarded faith as intellectual assent to that which reason is unable to grasp by itself. This assent flows not so much from facts as from probabilities. Probabilities are only probabilities and hence cannot be intellectually proven or advanced as facts.[61] The First Vatican Council (1869-1870) formally defined faith as "the supernatural virtue through which, actuated and continued by God's grace, we believe whatever God has revealed, not because of its intrinsic truth as understood by the natural light of reason, but because of the authority of God the revealer who can neither deceive nor be deceived."[62]

---

56. Anselm, *Proslogion*, I.

57. Hendrikus Berkhof, "The Act of Faith in the Reformed Tradition," in *Faith: Its Nature and Meaning*, ed. Paul Surlis (Dublin: Gill and Macmillan, 1972), pp. 99-100.

58. Thomas Aquinas, *De veritate*, q. 14, a. 2. In ad. 2, Aquinas again states explicitly that faith is a cognitive faculty of the soul.

59. Thomas Aquinas, *Summa Theologica*, Ia-IIae, q. 2, a. 9.

60. Concilium Tridentinum *Decretum de justificatione*, Sessio VI, 13 Ian. 1547, in Henricus Denzinger et Adolfus Schönmetzer, eds., *Enchiridion symbolorum*, editio 32 (Freiburg, Deutschland: Herder, 1963), caput 7 (#a 1528-1531, pp. 371-372).

61. John Henry Newman, *An Essay on the Development of Christian Doctrine* (London: Longmans, 1909), pp. 325-327; John Henry Newman, *Essays Critical and Historical*, vol. 1 (London: Longmans, Green, 1910), pp. 34-40.

62. Concilium Vaticanum I, *Constitutio dogmatica "Dei Filius" de fide catholica*, Sessio III, 24 Apr. 1870, in Henricus Denzinger et Adolfus Schönmetzer, eds., caput III (#3008, p. 589). Translation mine.

In the twentieth century the most influential conceptualization of faith came from the Second Vatican Council (1962-1965) which characterized faith as intellectual assent. Though expanding the locus and context of faith from a strict intellectualism, Vatican I nonetheless asserted that faith is the submission of the intellect to God (the "obedience of faith") in which persons entrust their whole selves freely to God.[63]

Most, but not all, world-class Catholic theologians who wrote after the close of Vatican II significantly broadened the intellectual context of the concept of faith, while still holding to the position that faith is primarily cognitive assent.[64] For their part, some major Protestant theologians began to move in the direction of the Catholic conception of faith as intellectual in character, giving the intellect a greater role than hithertofor in the conceptualization of faith.[65]

The momentous shift in the Christian conceptualization of faith occurred when Martin Luther (1483-1546) made affect the basis of the construct of faith. In Luther's view, faith is far more *fiducia* than it is *fides*. Faith is a living trust of the heart.[66] In a justly famous quotation, Luther states: "Faith is a living and unshakable confidence, a belief in the grace of God so assured that a man would die a thousand deaths for its sake."[67] Luther did, of course, recognize that faith also involves intellectual assent. In his opinion, however, this assent ultimately flows not from cognition, but from total confidence in God. Philipp Jakob Spener (1635-1705), a major Pietist theologian, considered faith as pri-

63. Sacrosanctum Concilium Oecumenicum Vaticanum II, "Constitutio dogmatica de divina revelatione" ("Dei Verbum," 28 Novembris, 1965), in *Acta Apostolicae Sedis*, 58 (24 Novembris, 1965), cap. II, art. 5 (p. 819).

64. See, for example, Jean Mouroux, "The Nature and Structure of the Christian Faith," trans. Thomas F. Malony and Robert Scott Walker, in *Toward a Theology of the Christian Faith*, ed. Michael Mooney et al. (New York: Kenedy, 1968), pp. 78-88; M. D. Chenu, *Faith and Theology*, trans. Denis Hickey (Dublin: Gill, 1968), pp. 2-7; Karl Rahner, "Faith," in Karl Rahner and Herbert Vorgrimler, *Dictionary of Theology*, 2d ed., trans. Richard Strachan et al. (New York: Crossroad, 1981), pp. 167, 169-170.

65. See, for example, Wolfhart Pannenberg, "The Working of the Spirit in the Creation and in the People of God," in Wolfhart Pannenberg, Avery Dulles, and Carl E. Braaten, *Spirit, Faith, and Church* (Philadelphia: Westminster, 1970), pp. 25-27; J. I. Packer, "Faith," in *Evangelical Dictionary of Theology*, ed. Walter A. Elwell (Grand Rapids, Mich.: Baker, 1984), pp. 399-402.

66. Martin Luther, *The Freedom of a Christian*, trans. W. A. Lambert, in *Martin Luther: Selections from his Writings*, ed. John Dillenberger (Garden City, N.Y.: Doubleday Anchor, 1961), pp. 56-61

67. Martin Luther, *Preface to the Epistle to the Romans*, trans. Bertram Lee Woolf, in ibid. p. 24.

marily a matter of the heart and not an assent to doctrinal propositions. In this view, faith flows from and leads to a personal affective devotion to Jesus.[68] Blaise Pascal (1623-1662), a Catholic religious thinker, regards faith as affective. He states forthrightly that faith exists when a person feels God in the heart contrasted to knowing God by reason.[69] Friedrich Schleiermacher (1768-1834) views faith as essentially feeling. As such it is primal awareness. Hence faith is immediate, unmediated in any way by intellectual processes.[70]

Despite the great cleft between conservative and liberal Protestantism which originally arose on a large scale in the latter part of the nineteenth century, both kinds of Protestants by and large clung to the classical Protestant construct of faith as essentially fiducial in nature.

Many leading Catholic theologians since the end of Vatican II have moved significantly toward the Protestant conceptualization of faith, though preserving the traditional Catholic view that faith is essentially cognitive. A few Catholic theologians have even moved totally to the view that faith is basically affective.[71]

The seminal work of Sigmund Freud (1856-1939), Carl Gustav Jung (1875-1961), and other ground-breaking psychotherapists prompted a significant number of psychologically oriented religionists[72] and theologically literate depth psychologists[73] to conceptualize faith as belonging to the zone of the unconscious. Depth psychologists of virtually every psychotherapeutic orientation regard unconscious processes as primary affect.

There has been a growing tendency among certain kinds of theologians since the mid-nineteenth century to conceptualize faith as lifestyle. In general, three broad classes of theologians have been in the

---

68. Philipp Jakob Spener, *Pia Desideria*, trans. Thomas G. Tappert (Philadelphia: Fortress, 1964), pp. 64-67.

69. Blaise Pascal, *Pensées*, trans. W. F. Trotter (New York: Dutton Everyman, 1908), #s 275-282 (pp. 78-80). In a celebrated passage, Pascal remarks that the heart has its reasons which reason does not understand. (*"La coeur a ses raisons que la raison ne connaît pas."*)

70. Friedrich Schleiermacher, *On Religion*, trans. Richard Crouter (Cambridge, England: Cambridge University Press, 1988), pp. 101-107, 128-136, 172-173.

71. See, for example, Avery Dulles, *The Survival of Dogma* (Garden City, N.Y.: Doubleday, 1971), pp. 17-59.

72. See, for example, John A. Sanford, *The Kingdom Within* (Philadelphia: Lippincott, 1970), pp. 156-159.

73. See, for example, Viktor Frankl, *The Unconscious God* (New York: Simon and Schuster, 1975), pp. 60-76. See also Clyde Reid, *The Return to Faith: Finding God in the Unconscious* (New York: Harper & Row, 1974), pp. 59-68. Reid is a Jungian.

JAMES MICHAEL LEE

forefront of this tendency: existentialist theologians, empirical theologians, and liberationist theologians.

Søren Kierkegaard (1813-1855) construes faith as a personal and ongoing existential encounter between a person and God.[74] Faith is an existential plunge of the intensely subjective person into the subjectivity of God, and all this entails. This existential plunge, this leap of faith is inherently risky: danger and dread pervade the encounter.[75] Faith is absurd rationally. Faith lives in and by inner encounter rather than through outward action.[76] Nikolai Aleksandrovich Berdyayev (1874-1948) conceptualizes faith as the concrete living out of one's personal existence in immanent union with God. Faith is born in human experience and authentically exists only in the existential process of human experiencing.[77] Rudolf Bultmann (1884-1976) constructs faith as the concrete here-and-now series of acts by which we realize our own existence. Faith is something we do and the way we do it. Faith is intertwined with revelation, especially biblical revelation. The Bible is saving faith because it is revelation encountering and acting on me in my immediate existential situation.[78] Paul Tillich conceptualizes faith as the state of being ultimately concerned. As ultimate concern, faith is an act of the total personality. Faith is not knowing or believing; it is experiencing with the centered totality of one's whole personal existence. Faith is be-ing. Faith is existentially staking all that one is, namely, one's own existence, on the ultimate ground of being.[79]

Empirical theologians frequently exhibit a marked tendency toward construing faith as a lifestyle. Thus Bernard Meland (1899-) constructs faith as preeminently an act of personal decision. This act is not restricted to any one area of human fuctioning but includes them all holistical-

---

74. Søren Kierkegaard, *Journals and Papers*, vol. 2, F-K, ed. and trans. Howard V. Hong and Edna H. Hong (Bloomington, Ind.: Indiana University Press, 1970), p. 5.

75. Søren Kierkegaard, *The Concept of Dread*, trans. Walter Lowrie (Princeton, N.J.: Princeton University Press, 1957), pp. 139-145.

76. Søren Kierkegaard, *Fear and Trembling*, trans. Walter Lowrie (Princeton, N.J.: Princeton University Press, 1954), pp. 27-77.

77. Nikolai Aleksandrovich Berdyayev, *Christian Existentialism: A Berdyayev Anthology*, selected and trans. Donald A. Lowrie (New York: Harper & Row Torchbooks, 1965), pp. 75-79.

78. Rudolf Bultmann, "New Testament and Mythology," in Rudolf Bultmann et al., *Kerygma and Myth*, ed. Hans Werner Bartsch, trans. Reginald H. Fuller (New York: Harper & Row Torchbooks, 1961), pp. 1-64; Rudolf Bultmann, *Jesus and the Word*, trans. Louise Pettibone Smith and Erminie Huntress Lantero (New York: Scribner's, 1958), pp. 3-15, 87-110, 150-172.

79. Paul Tillich, *Dynamics of Faith* (New York: Harper & Row Torchbooks, 1957), pp. 1-40, 89-105; Paul Tillich, *Systematic Theology*, vol. III (Chicago: University of Chicago Press, 1963), pp. 129-138.

ly. Meland views personal decision as a psychical act in which a person empirically enacts selfhood.[80] Liberation theologians are unabashedly direct in construing faith as lifestyle. Faith is doing justice, doing truth in such a way that persons are thereby emancipated from social, economic, and political enslavement. Faith is quintessentially performative as the practice of justice integratively enacted in and through one's lifestyle.[81] Gustavo Gutiérrez, a Peruvian, constructs faith as the social/political/spiritual process of actively bringing about the kingdom of God in the here-and-now world. To be in faith is to encounter Jesus, and Jesus is most deeply present in this world, especially in persons who are socioeconomically oppressed.[82] Leonardo Boff and his brother Clodovis, both Brazilians, hold that faith becomes faith when its transcendent matrix is radically recast into a revolutionary lifestyle praxis which concretely endeavors to attain justice in the concrete sociohistorical situation. In dialectical fashion, lifestyle praxis integrates one's prayer life and overt action.[83] Jon Sobrino, a Spaniard living in Central America, conceptualizes faith as a personal nontransferable act which is inherently and organically related to the faith of others. Thus faith is one's coresponsibility and coaction with other human beings, especially the poorest, for there is where Christ dwells and saves.[84] Canaan Banana, a Zimbabwean, construes faith as inseparable from good works. Christian faith is internally unified with revolutionary action to such an extent that there is no faith without revolutionary action for justice and God's reign.[85] Johann Baptist Metz, a German and a leading exponent of political theology, conceptualizes faith as a political praxis in history and society. Faith is the ongoing political effort to bring about the eschatological message of Christian hope.[86] James Cone, a major proponent of black or African-American

---

80. Bernard Eugene Meland, *Faith and Culture* (New York: Oxford University Press, 1953), pp. 16-66.

81. Schipani, *Religious Education Encounters Liberation Theology*, pp. 128-135.

82. Gustavo Gutiérrez, *A Theology of Liberation*, trans. Caridad Inda and John Eagleson (Maryknoll, N.Y.: Orbis, 1973), pp. 149-187.

83. Leonardo Boff and Clodovis Boff, *Salvation and Liberation*, trans. Robert Barr (San Francisco: Harper & Row, 1986), pp. 16-18.

84. Jon Sobrino and Juan Hernández Pico, *Theology of Christian Solidarity*, trans. Philip Berryman (Maryknoll, N.Y.: Orbis, 1985), pp. 31-38; Jon Sobrino, *The True Church and the Poor*, trans. Matthew O'Connell (Maryknoll, N.Y.: Orbis, 1984), pp. 47-49.

85. Canaan Banana, *The Gospel According to the Ghetto*, rev. ed. (Gwelo, Zimbabwe: Mambo Press, 1981) pp. 110-116.

86. Johann Baptist Metz, *Faith in History and Society*, trans. David Smith (New York: Crossroad, 1980), pp. 73-77.

theology, construes faith as the concrete dialectical admixture of the biblical story, one's personal story, and the story of a people. Faith is the lived truth about oneself, a trans-subjective reality brought into being and expressed in the above-mentioned three intersecting stories. Faith is the struggle for freedom accomplished through these three enmeshed stories.[87] Peter Hodgson, an American, conceptualizes faith as the personally lived performative response to God. Because the Bible is not so much a linguistic transcription as a word-event, only concrete lifestyle enaction constitutes faith, namely, a lived response to God's word.[88] Schubert Ogden, another American and basically a process theologian, constructs faith as the existence of freedom in freedom for freedom. Faith is a lifestyle performed in utter trust in God's love and in utter loyalty to his cause—these can only be in existence in freedom. Faith is fundamentally freedom because God is fundamentally freedom, and thus it is in freedom whereby God and the human being meet in faith.[89]

Of the many practical implications which theology has for the shape, flow, and content of the construct of faith, three stand out. First, because it has access to divine revelation in a way not available (or acceptable) to other areas of serious inquiry, theological science can provide us with indispensable material from which to fashion an adequate construct of faith. Second, in all eras and within any given era, there have been sharply divergent theological constructs of faith. This fact suggests that theology in and of itself does not provide a sure, unconditional, complete, immutable, or unqualifiedly reliable construct of faith. Third, no theologian in the history of religion has ever devised a construct of faith which captured the nature and operations of the cluster of faith behaviors in their pure unadulterated form or is otherwise free from all personal subjectivity and cultural influence. Every theological construct of faith devised over the centuries has necessarily reflected the psychological state and cultural milieu of its inventor(s). In addition to the general culture in which they were immersed, theologians of every era have operated out of a double-barreled professional (or at least specialty) culture, namely, the science of theology with its unique history and definite methodological parameters and the culture of theologians in collegiality, in professional societies, and so forth.[90]

---

87. James H. Cone, *God of the Oppressed* (New York: Crossroad, 1975), pp. 102-107, 146-151; James H. Cone, *Speaking the Truth* (Grand Rapids, Mich.: Eerdmans, 1986), pp. 35-49.

88. Peter C. Hodgson, *New Birth of Freedom* (Philadelphia: Fortress, 1976), pp. 110-112, 220-221, 332-336.

89. Schubert M. Ogden, *Faith and Freedom* (Nashville: Abingdon, 1979), pp. 43-82.

90. Gordon Childe, *Social Worlds of Knowledge* (London: Oxford University Press, 1949), pp. 5, 7-8.

Constructional Pluralism versus Theological Positivism. The principal point made thus far in this section entitled "Enriching the Construct" is that faith, being a confluence of so many subjective elements, cannot be adequately understood from one vantage point alone. Theology, psychology, sociology, music, art—not a single one of these in and of itself can adequately describe faith or devise a full construct of faith. A pluralism of approaches harmoniously flowing from different sources is necessary. Viewing faith from only one vantage point, fashioning a construct of faith from only one perspective, serves as a severe and crippling constraint upon our consciousness and upon our construction of faith. Both in real life and in artificial construct, faith is organismic in the sense that its roots and its flow are sunk deep and enmeshed wide in a whole host of life areas and so cannot be satisfactorily lived or adequately understood apart from these organismic intertwinings.[91]

There are, then, different valid constructs of faith depending on their source, as for example, theology, psychology, sociology, art, and so forth. Each of these represents a complementary and to some extent a competing interpretation of the reality of faith. The validity of each of these contrasting constructs of faith is objective in the sense that it encapsulates one general global abstraction of the various behaviors classified as faith-constitutive. But the validity of these contrasting constituents of faith is also functional in terms of helping a person understand and deal with the multifaceted reality encapsulated in the construct we call faith.[92]

Strongly opposed to any form of constructional pluralism is theological positivism. According to advocates of theological positivism, only theology is capable of providing positive knowledge, namely, sure information, accurate interpretation, and certain validity about reality.[93] In this perspective, only two types of *fundamentally* meaningful statements and truths exist: those derived directly from theology and those which can be squared with theology on theology's own terms. Theology is thus seen as both the starting point and the final judge for all science, art, technology, education, and human living. The foregoing is preeminently true when it comes to expressly religious reality such as the Bible, liturgy, church organization, religious education—and faith. Proponents

---

91. Peter Hamilton, *Knowledge and Social Structure* (London: Routledge & Kegan Paul, 1974), pp. 139-143.

92. John A. Coleman, "The Renewed Covenant," in *Sociology and Human Destiny*, ed. Gregory Baum (New York: Crossroad, 1980), pp. 101-108.

93. For a further discussion of theological positivism, see James Michael Lee, "The Authentic Source of Religious Instruction," in *Religious Education and Theology*, ed. Norma H. Thompson (Birmingham, Ala.: Religious Education Press, 1982), pp. 147-156.

of theological positivism hold, for example, that the Bible can be validly and truly read only from a theological perspective. Consequently any attempt by sociology to extract sociological information expressed in the Bible, or any attempt by religious instruction to look at the Bible in terms of the teaching procedures described there, is incorrect, unwarranted, and invalid.[94]

Though the vast majority of post-World War II theologians eschew theological positivism, nonetheless a vigorous residue of theologians (usually very conservative ones), some ecclesiastical officials, and interestingly enough a significant number of religious educationists explicitly or implicitly espouse theological positivism.[95]

Theological positivism notwithstanding, it would appear that constructional pluralism is essential in devising an adequate construct of faith. But constructional pluralism in this and other pertinent cases does not mean that theology receives the contributions of other sciences and judges them according to its own canons. This mentality[96] represents unwarranted subordinationism and at bottom is theological imperialism. Theology is not the queen of sciences; it never really was, even though in the past some theologians thought this was the case. Other sciences, as appropriate, are genuine partners in harmoniously devising a valid construct of faith. The task of nontheological sciences or fields in devising a construct of faith is not simply to raise questions or to offer data which are then accepted, modified, or rejected in normative and univocal fashion by theology "in dialogue" with these nontheological sciences or fields.[97] Faith is not the exclusive province of theology. Indeed it is possible, at least in certain circumstances, that faith is not

94. The latter position is advocated by Marianne Sawicki, "Jesus the Pedagogue with Words for Today: A Review," *National Catholic Reporter* 20 (October 12, 1984), p. 20.

95. Joseph Ratzinger, with Vittorio Messori, *The Ratzinger Report,* trans. Salvator Attanasio and Graham Harrison (San Francisco: Ignatius, 1985), pp. 24-26, 71-81; Joseph Ratzinger, "The Church's Teaching Authority—Faith—Morals," in Heinz Shurmann, Joseph Ratzinger, and Hans Urs von Baltissar, *Principles of Christian Morality,* trans. Graham Harrison (San Francisco: Ignatius, 1986), pp. 70-73; Eugene Kevane, *Creed and Catechetics* (Westminster, Md.: Christian Classics, 1978), pp. 254-264; Françoise Darcy-Bérubé, "The Challenge Ahead of Us," in *Foundations of Religious Education,* ed. Padraic O'Hare (New York: Paulist, 1978), pp. 115-120; Kenneth O. Gangel and Warren S. Benson, *Christian Education in History and Philosophy* (Chicago: Moody, 1983), pp. 325-326, 331-345.

96. Many religious educationists hold this view. See, for example, Michael Warren, "All Contributions Cheerfully Accepted," *Living Light* 7 (Winter, 1970), pp. 20-23.

97. For an important variant of this position, see Peter L. Berger, *The Sacred Canopy* (Garden City, N.Y.: Doubleday, 1967), p. 179.

more of a theological province than a province of other sciences. As a human act, faith belongs to all sciences which impinge upon human nature and functioning. Each science has a unique and indispensable contribution to make to a holistic construct of faith. And each science has its own methodological operations which correct the other(s).

Validity of a Construct of Faith

Thus far in this section I have shown that the construct of faith necessarily contains not only a great deal of objective information on the nature of faith but also some necessary psychological, sociocultural, and theological subjectivities of the person or group who devised one or another concept of faith. It must be underscored that this inevitable admixture of a certain subjectivity with the objectivity of faith does not destroy the correctness, usefulness, or validity of this construct. Rather this admixture shows that any construct of faith, no matter how good it might be, is neither absolutely correct, unreservedly useful, or totally valid.

The lack of total objectivity in human experiencing does not mean the absence of all objectivity. Reality as experienced is acceptably objective, namely, it contains a sufficient degree of objectivity to make it stand on its own feet rather than existing as a mental projection. Actually experienced reality typically enjoys a high degree of objectivity. From a purely cognitive axis, we might not be able to prove beyond a shadow of a doubt that the city of Munich exists independent of our experience of it. So too with the construct of faith: There is sufficient objectivity in a well-fashioned construct of faith to make it quite valid, useful, and worthwhile.

The fact that the construct of faith lacks complete exactitude ought not discourage religious educators about the accuracy or usefulness of this construct. In our creaturely world, all knowledge is expressed in degrees of probability. This is true of physics (which is known as an especially "exact science") as well as religious instruction, theology, psychology, and the rest. The more probable a construct of faith is, the more likely it is that it encapsulates some important truth, remembering of course that all knowledge and hence all constructs are tentative and mutable. The task of religious instruction is to discover—and as will be shown in the next section, to fashion for itself—that construct of faith which possesses the highest degree of probability and the highest degree of usefulness.

Religious Instruction. A significant contributor to the development of a well-rounded and genuinely adequate construct of faith is religious instruction. This vital contribution is not only operative within the realm of religion teaching but is also essential for a holistic and valid construct of faith in itself, regardless of the circumstance, field, or setting in which this construct is used.

Because religious instruction deals in large measure with the faith of learners, its enactment provides important information about the nature and workings of faith. In the religious instruction act, faith is not dealt with abstractly as it is in theology or in the other sciences, which are all necessarily cognitive in nature. In the religious instruction act, the behaviors which form the ingredients of the construct of faith are lived, dealt with, and communicated in their actual reality.

Because it is a construct, faith is a logical being abstracted from a wide variety of particular human behaviors we claim are associated with faith. The accuracy of this claim depends upon the actual living out of these behaviors in a real setting. Religious instruction deals with faith-on-the-hoof, with how faith actually develops in learners singly and as a group, with how faith is concretely learned and taught, with the many kinds of actual faith which different individuals have, and so forth. Unlike theologians who necessarily look at faith from the outside when doing theology, religious educators are working with the reality of faith behaviors from the nitty-gritty inside, from the inside of how faith is lived and how it is communicated. This inside view, not of a logical construct, but of the raw lived experiences from which the construct is drawn, provides us with the data and the understanding of here-and-now faith. This inside view also enables us to bring to salience those behaviors which scientists exterior to the religious instruction act might have overlooked or accorded insufficient attention. The inside view also enables us to correct faulty or inadequate notions of what faith is and how it operates in actual reality. Faith is developed and faith is forged in the teaching/learning dynamic. Theology and psychology and sociology might *study* faith, but religious instruction *does* faith. Dealing as it does with teaching/learning/living operations in concrete holistic learners in a wide variety of circumstances, religious instruction provides crucial information for devising a valid, full, and realistic construct of faith.

In order to appreciate the fact that the religious instruction act is a set of dynamic conditions in which faith is facilitated and developed, it is necessary to move away from an outmoded view of teaching as a transmissive activity. The old view held that religion teaching consists basically of transmitting a body of material to the learner.[98] This picture of the religious instruction act was usually composed by theologians or by

---

98. Operative words and phrases used by advocates of this position include "transmitting Christian doctrine," "proclaiming the Christian message," and "heralding the Good News." Notable proponents of this position include Josef Goldbrunner, "Catechetical Method as Handmaid of Kerygma," in *Teaching all Nations*, pp. 108-121; Johannes Hofinger, *The Art of Teaching Christian Doc-*

those religious educators who use theological categories to analyze religion teaching. Most contemporary religious educationists, even those who regard religious instruction as a theological undertaking, have abandoned the transmission view of education (though their grounds for doing so are often shaky theoretically).[99]

Social-scientific analysis of every kind of teaching act, including the act of teaching religion, clearly reveals that there are always four basic elements present in every instructional event.[100] These fundamental ingredients are the teacher, the learner, the substantive content, and the environment. As the religious instruction act is initiated and as it proceeds, these four molar elements interact with one another in a wide variety of ways. What happens in and through this continuous dynamic interaction is that each of the four elements changes. Thus, for example, the learner changes by growing in understanding and doing faith. The teacher changes too. The religious educator is not a catalyst in the religious instruction act;[101] on the contrary, the teacher grows and develops in the religious instruction act. This growth includes the teacher's faith. All the substantive contents, including faith, also change in the religious instruction act.[102] Faith is not transmitted to the learner as an inert shipment of goods or as an entity unaffected by its dynamic interaction with the other three molar variables in the religious instruction act. By virtue of this dynamic interaction, faith changes in the act of teaching it.

The dynamic interaction among the four molar variables means that each of these variables becomes conjoined in actuality.[103] In this conjoinment, each of the elements combines with the others so that singly

---

trine, 2d ed. (Notre Dame, Ind.: University of Notre Dame Press, 1962), pp. 51-73; Alfred McBride, *Catechetics; A Theology of Proclamation* (Milwaukee, Wis.: Bruce, 1966), pp. 147-152.

99. Examples include Randolph Crump Miller, *The Theory of Christian Education Practice* (Birmingham, Ala.: Religious Education Press, 1980), pp. 153-164; John H. Westerhoff III, *Bringing Up Children in the Christian Faith* (Minneapolis: Winston, 1980); Lois E. LeBar, *Education that is Christian* (Old Tappan, N.J.: Revell, 1958).

100. Lee, *The Flow of Religious Instruction,* pp. 233-240.

101. A catalyst is a foreign substance which speeds up a chemical reaction without itself undergoing change.

102. In this instance, and in other cases throughout this chapter that should be obvious, I use the term faith to mean the concrete set of integrated behaviors called faith. In Western language we have so reified the construct faith that the same word simultaneously means a set of behaviors and a construct. For stylistic flow, it is not always helpful to indicate when a set of related behaviors is meant rather than a construct, as is the case here.

103. While each of the four variables as they exist in the religious instruction act can be logically separated for the purpose of intellectual analysis, they are in actuality conjoined in the actual religious instruction dynamic itself.

and as a whole they are subsumed into a new reality. This subsumptional process is called mediatorship.[104] Mediatorship means that faith (as a behavioral substantive content) and the three other molar variables are so united in the religious instruction act that faith no longer exists as faith but now exists under the form of religious instruction (and, concomittantly, that the other three molar variables no longer exist in themselves but under the form of religious instruction). This new reality, this mediated entity, 1) incorporates and retains the essential features of faith, and 2) puts the essential features of faith into a new fused relationship with the three other molar variables so that they are no longer separate but become inextricably combined in an ontically new reality, namely faith-as-taught/learned-in-a-setting.

As can be seen from the two preceding paragraphs about what happens to faith during the act of teaching it, we can readily appreciate that the concrete act of teaching profoundly affects and changes the faith that is being taught/learned. This selfsame analysis also has direct and deep consequences for the manufacture of a valid and full construct of faith. Because the reality of faith is significantly changed in the act of teaching/learning it, then it is helpful to take this changed reality into account when devising any construct of faith which hopes to be meaningful and valid. The actuality of faith, the integrated set of human behaviors we call faith, never exists in isolation. Faith always exists in a human being who is always and inextricably in a concrete here-and-now situation. Since religious instruction activity in its myriad forms is so pervasive in the church, and since religious instruction deals overtly with faith, it is especially important that religious instruction play a crucial and cooperative role in devising a construct of faith.

STRUCTURAL CONTENT IN TEACHING FAITH

Structure as Content

Structural content is pedagogical procedure. As was mentioned near the beginning of this chapter, pedagogical procedure is not a way of delivering content. Rather, pedagogical procedure is a specific and also a global content in its own right. In all teaching, the content which is taught is both what is taught and how the teaching occurs. The content which is taught is not only the substance which is taught but also the structure in and through which the substance flows and is changed. In the religious instruction act, structure at once alters content (substance) and is itself a content (structure).

---

104. Lee, *The Flow of Religious Instruction*, pp. 17-19, 21-22, 300-301.

Procedure is the very being of all creation.[105] Procedure is the making and the made, the creating and the creation. Procedure is the bringing forth and the brought forth.

Three characteristics of all effective procedure, including instructional procedure, should permeate teaching for faith.[106]

First, effective procedure pays great attention to details. Grand vision and noble purpose can be achieved only by unremitting attention to details.

Second, effective procedure vertically integrates the various subprocesses of which it is comprised. Vertical integration is needed in order that the more finely specified procedures flow into the more inclusive ones in a harmonious and reinforcing manner.

Third, effective procedure is rooted in empirical research. All procedure, including teaching, is an art-science, namely, a way of executing a performance based on scientifically verified facts, laws, and theories.[107]

The Components of Structural Content

As noted earlier, there are four components which are always present in every teaching act, including the teaching of faith. These four are teacher, learners, subject-matter, and environment. Each of these four molar variables both changes the others and is itself changed in the religious instruction act. This fact leads to four important general conclusions about teaching faith.

First, subject-matter (in our case, faith) comprises only one of the four molar variables which go to make up the religious instruction act. Hence any religious educator who devotes primary or, worse still, exclusive pedagogical attention to the nature and structure of faith in and of itself is doomed to instructional failure from the outset since such a teacher is working with only one of the four interactive components involved in the here-and-now religious instruction dynamic.

Second, each of the four major variables is a major one. None is minor, secondary, unimportant. Each impacts upon and changes the other in a very significant way. The more the religious educator deliberatively brings into play all the four molar variables, the more potent will be that teacher's faith pedagogy. Despite the wealth of empirical research on the significant effect which the physical/social environment

---

105. Ronald Barthes, "The Structuralist Activity," *Partisan Review* 34 (Winter, 1967), p. 84.

106. These three by no means exhaust the range of important characteristics of effective procedure.

107. N. L. Gage, *The Scientific Base of the Art of Teaching* (New York: Teachers College Press, 1978), pp. 13-24.

has on the quality and duration of learning outcomes,[108] nonetheless the environment appears to be the molar variable most neglected in the field of religious instruction.[109]

Third, the quality of the learner's faith resulting from the religious instruction act does not depend totally or even largely upon the quality of the teacher's own personal faith. The teacher is only one molar variable out of four. Furthermore, the faith of the teacher is significant in the pedagogical event only to the extent to which the educator's faith actually becomes part of the religious instruction act in one way or another. History has repeatedly shown that persons whose faith was weak or at least not healthy in many respects (as judged by conventional religious standards) did indeed facilitate strong faith outcomes in learners.[110] Conversely, the religion teacher's piety is no substitute for pedagogical skill.

Fourth, all teaching, including the teaching of faith, requires that the teacher structure the pedagogical situation in such a way that the desired learning outcome is successfully facilitated. At bottom, then, all teaching consists of structuring the learning situation (SLS). The fundamental model of teaching, the model which is the foundation of every specific form of teaching ranging from cognitive to affective to lifestyle pedagogical methods is the SLS.[111]

Teaching Faith versus Teaching Theology

Theology is a cognitive science which investigates the nature and workings of God using divine revelation as an unshakably fundamental and unique source for intellectual investigation.[112]

Faith, then, differs fundamentally from theology in essence, goal,

---

108. Charles J. Holahan, "Environmental Psychology," *Annual Review of Psychology*, vol. 38, ed. Mark R. Rosenzweig and Lyman W. Porter (Palo Alto, Calif.: Annual Reviews, 1986), pp. 381-407; Barry F. Fraser, "Classroom Learning Environments and Effective Schooling," *Professional School Psychology* 2 (Winter, 1987), pp. 25-41.

109. Harold William Burgess, *An Invitation to Religious Education* (Birmingham, Ala.: Religious Education Press, 1975), pp. 50, 83-84, 119-120, 154-158.

110. Somewhat related to the point of this paragraph is the heresy of Donatism in the early church, and the reasons the *ecclesiasticum* gave at the time for condemning Donatism as a heresy.

111. For a delineation of some important models of teaching, all of which represent forms of the more foundational *S*tructured *L*earning *S*ituation model of teaching, see Bruce Joyce and Marsha Weil, *Models of Teaching*, 3rd ed. (Englewood Cliffs, N.J.: Prentice-Hall, 1986).

112. Avery Dulles, *Models of Revelation* (Garden City, N.Y.: Doubleday Image, 1985), p. 5; Paul Tillich, *Systematic Theology*, vol. 1 (Chicago: University of Chicago Press, 1951), p. 28; Helmut Thielicke, *The Evangelical Faith*, vol. 2, trans. and ed. by Geoffrey W. Bromily (Grand Rapids, Mich.: Eerdmans, 1977), p. 3.

criterion, and method. Faith is a special kind of personally lived affair whereas theology is a scientific endeavor. The goal of faith is to live with God on earth and for all eternity, whereas the goal of theology is to gain a fuller and more precise intellectual understanding of God in himself and in all his works. The criterion of faith is the degree of personal adherence to God's revelation, whereas the criterion of theology is the degree to which it incorporates a validated set of investigative canons which yield cognitive truth which is in general accord with divine revelation (and for Catholics in accord with official ecclesiastical interpretations of revelation). The method of faith is to order one's life in one way or another around God's revelation, whereas the method of theology is scientific investigation.

Faith is essentially subjective (personal) while theology is essentially objective (scientific). Though it is incorrect and indeed imperialistic to define theology as *the* science of faith, it is correct to assert that theology is *one* science of faith (and a uniquely privileged science of faith).

To teach theology is to teach cognitively about faith. To teach faith is to teach experientially in one way or another.

The religious educator who wishes to teach faith has to teach faith primarily and not theology primarily. Theology may or may not be of assistance in teaching faith, depending on the learner and the environment (two of the four molar variables in faith instruction).

The Whole Person

Any effective faith instruction necessarily involves the whole person in one way or another. This is true whether the religious educator construes faith as primarily cognitive, primarily affective, or primarily lifestyle. Naturally, the more that faith is regarded as a lifestyle, the more the whole person of the learner will come into play.

The whole person is always self-in-situation. This situation is historical as well as present. This history inevitably flows through and permeates the person-in-situation.[113] A person may not live in the past, but the past always lives in the person. To teach the whole person is, among other things, to engage the personal and social and cultural background of the learner. For example, human history includes the history of fallen humanity. Hence teaching faith to the whole person necessarily includes an invitation to repentance.[114]

---

113. Neo-Marxian religious educationists have contributed greatly to emphasizing the highly influential historical context of all human action. Representatives of this position include Thomas H. Groome, *Christian Religious Education* (San Francisco: Harper & Row, 1980), pp. 12-15; Malcolm L. Warford, *The Necessary Illusion* (Philadelphia: Pilgrim, 1976), pp. 63-65, 79-83.

114. David M. Stanley, *Faith and Religious Life* (New York: Paulist, 1971), pp. 31-32.

To teach faith as a lifestyle is to engage the whole person of the learner as fully, as humanly, and as experientially as possible. In endeavoring to place faith instruction on a totally lifestyle basis, the religious educator would do well to ground his or her teaching in the five dimensions of religion identified by Charles Glock in his synthesis of the relevant empirical research,[115] namely, 1) the ideological dimension, that is, faith belief; 2) the ritualistic dimension, that is, faith practice; 3) the experiential dimension, that is, faith feeling; 4) the intellectual dimension, that is, faith knowledge; 5) the consequential dimension, that is, faith effects.[116] As lifestyle, faith is the person's actualizing of all five dimensions in concert. From the lifestyle perspective, no dimension, taken in itself, is faith. The religious educator wishing to teach faith as lifestyle should therefore structure the learning situation so that all five dimensions come into play, as appropriate.

Experiential Pedagogy

It is a pedgogical maxim so true that virtually everyone involved in education knows it, that experiential pedagogy is much more effective than nonexperiential or marginally experiential pedagogy. Indeed, the only instructional justification for nonexperiential pedagogy is when experiential teaching is too time-consuming, too costly, too demanding of existing or possible structural conditions such as space, or otherwise just too difficult to enact in a given situation.

Major causes of the superiority of experiential teaching as contrasted to nonexperiential or marginally experiential teaching is that experiential instruction tends to be more personalistic (subjective), more holistic, and more empirical.

Because faith is a lived human experience, it is most fruitfully taught as an experience (substantive content) in an experiential manner (structural content).[117]

The experiential teaching of faith tends to be tied in with the religious educator's construct of faith, assuming that the educator is both consistent and in adequate command of the whole repertoire of instructional procedures. Experientially oriented religious educators who construct

---

115. Since faith is an aspect of religion, Glock's dimensions apply to faith. To make Glock's dimensions more linguistically to the point, I am substituting the word faith for the word religion as originally used by Glock.

116. Charles Y. Glock, "On the Study of Religious Commitment," *Religious Education*, research supplement, 57 (July-August, 1962), pp. s-98-s.110.

117. V. Bailey Gillespie, *The Experience of Faith* (Birmingham, Ala.: Religious Education Press, 1988), pp. 233-248. Unlike James Fowler, who contends that faith grows in abstract stages, Gillespie maintains that faith grows in experiential situations.

faith as primarily cognitive will be inclined to teach faith as a cognitive experience principally. Cognitivist teachers will use a vast array of instructional devices which bring into play a wide variety of pedagogical activities revolving around cognitive experiencing. Such activities include memorizing the catechism, understanding ecclesiastical doctrine, reflecting on one's personal journey in faith, reflecting on the relevance of the gospel to one's own life, and so forth. Experientially oriented religious educators who construct faith as primarily affective will be inclined to teach faith as an affective experience principally. Affectivist teachers will use a vast array of instructional devices which bring into play a wide variety of pedagogical activities revolving around affective experiencing. Such activities include songs, art work, trust walking, sharing dream material, role playing, and so forth. Experientially oriented religious educators who construct faith as primarily lifestyle will be inclined to teach faith as a lifestyle experience principally. Lifestylist teachers will use a vast array of instructional devices which bring into play a wide variety of pedagogical activities revolving around holistic life experiencing. Such activities include projects, field trips, simulation gaming, community service activities, and so forth.

At the heart and at the summit of all experiential pedagogy for faith is religious experience. This is especially true for teaching faith as a lifestyle. From a lifestyle perspective, faith is a form of religious experience. Hence it is obvious that the most successful way to teach faith is through religious experience.

Religious educators who are teaching faith as a lifestyle will do all they can to structure as many religious experiences as possible for learners. Liturgical and paraliturgical services, notably those featuring nonverbal activities and noncognitive variables are helpful in leading learners to religious experience. Environmental factors such as color, light, nature, music, candles, and so forth, are conducive to religious experience.

Communal Pedagogy

A person is not only a self. A person is also a social self.[118] Thus the social world is not a reality forever apart from the individual; it is part-and-parcel of the individual's fundamental personality structure.

Because it is a dimension of the human personality, faith is therefore

---

118. George H. Mead, *Mind, Self, and Society*, ed. Charles W. Morris (Chicago: University of Chicago Press, 1934), pp. 144-164; Philip Blumstein and Peter Kollock, "Personal Relationships," in *Annual Review of Sociology*, vol. 14, ed. W. Richard Scott and Judith Blake (Palo Alto, Calif.: Annual Reviews, 1988), pp. 480-481.

social to the core. Consequently, pedagogy for faith must necessarily be social as well as personal.

As appropriate to its goals and objectives in a given pedagogical situation, faith instruction should take place in one way or another within a social context or at least in light of a social context. This context includes other learners, the parish, the larger local/regional/ national/international faith community, and the "secular" sphere. Robust faith, as all of robust human life, cannot exclude any area of social interaction and growth.

One necessary aim of faith pedagogy is that it can be enacted in such a way that learners enrich the faith of other learners, the parish, the larger faith community, and the "secular" sphere. Because instructional aims are actually statements of desired learning outcomes, any evaluation of the degree to which learners have become richer in faith will necessarily include the ways and the extent to which individual faith impacted upon the lives of other learners, the faith community, and the "secular" sphere.

When faith is viewed as primarily cognitive, the task of religious instruction for social and communal faith will be centered around group intellectual activities such as interpretation,[119] praxis knowing,[120] and so forth. When faith is viewed as primarily affective,[121] the task of religious instruction for social and communal faith will be centered around group feeling-full activities such as encounters of one emotional sort or another. When faith is viewed as primarily lifestyle,[122] the task of religious instruction for social and communal faith will be centered around personal or group activities which emphasize overt conduct such as projects. These personal or group activities also incorporate, as is pedagogically appropriate, cognitive and affective behaviors which are thrusted toward or support the overt activities.

Pedagogy for Active Faith

Virtually everyone writing on the nature of faith and on the teaching of faith repeatedly emphasizes that to live faith and to teach it necessitates human activity. Persons who regard faith as primarily cognitive emphasize that faith is lived primarily through intellectual activity. Individuals who view faith as primarily affective stress that faith is lived

119. C. Ellis Nelson, *Where Faith Begins* (Richmond, Va.: Knox, 1967), pp. 185-198.
120. Groome, *Christian Religious Education*, pp. 139-206.
121. Morton Kelsey, *Can Christians Be Educated?* (Birmingham, Ala.: Religious Education Press, 1977), pp. 109-148.
122. Lee, *The Content of Religious Instruction*, pp. 608-735.

chiefly though affective activity. And those who see faith as primarily a lifestyle emphasize that faith is lived through holistic lifestyle activity.

It is important to underscore that faith does not directly generate cognitive, affective, or lifestyle behavior. To maintain that faith generates behavior assumes that faith is a separate ontic entity in and of itself. But as has been shown earlier in this chapter, faith is only a logical being, a construct devised to intellectually encompass a variety of related concrete behaviors to which the name faith can properly be given. Hence the only truly effective way to teach faith is to teach its constituent behaviors in behavioral fashion, namely, by actively involving learners in those kinds of behaviors logically categorized by the word faith. If one believes faith is primarily cognitive, teaching for active faith means structuring the pedagogical situation in such a way that learners engage actively in a wide variety of cognitive behaviors tied together in the construct of faith. If one believes that faith is primarily affective, teaching for active faith means structuring the pedagogical situation in such a way that learners engage actively in a wide variety of affective behaviors tied together in the construct faith. And if one believes that faith is primarily a lifestyle, teaching for active faith means structuring the pedagogical situation in such a way that learners engage in those lifestyle behaviors tied together in the construct faith. In short, all views on the nature of faith agree that teaching for active faith requires that learners learn in a manner such that they are engaging actively in faith-related behaviors.

In human activity qua human, there seems to be a natural hierarchy of cognition, affect, and lifestyle, with cognition occupying the lowest level. Computers and other forms of artificial intelligence are increasingly replicating and in some ways improving on human cognition, suggesting that cognition is by no means a uniquely human activity which cannot be shared or done by nonhuman entities. But, thus far at least, no artificial device or nonhuman entity has ever satisfactorily replicated, much less improved upon, affective behavior or lifestyle activity. Thus it is not surprising that the relevant empirical research has shown that 1) cognitive teaching generates cognitive learning but does not significantly influence the acquisition of noncognitive outcomes;[123] and 2) affective teaching generates affective learning and also significantly influences the acquisition of cognitive outcomes;[124] lifestyle

---

123. Pleasant Roscoe Hightower, *Biblical Information in Relation to Character and Conduct* (Iowa City, Iowa: State University of Iowa, 1930).

124. Fred M. Zimring, "Attending to Feeling and Cognitive Performance," *Journal of Research in Personality* 18 (September, 1983), pp. 288-299.

teaching generates lifestyle outcomes and also significantly influences the acquisition of cognitive and affective outcomes—something which is self-evident since lifestyle integrates cognition and affect[125]

Selecting Appropriate Pedagogical Procedures

The degree to which faith outcomes are successfully facilitated by the religious educator varies directly with the degree to which the pedagogical procedure used in the teaching act is appropriate for bringing about the desired learning outcome. Hence the selection of appropriate pedagogical procedures in a specific instructional situation is indispensable for teaching faith effectively.

Pedagogical procedure should not be denigrated or even slighted in any way, since pedagogical procedure is in itself structural content, namely, something learned because it is taught. Furthermore, the one thing which makes religious instruction truly distinct from other areas of pastoral endeavor is that it alone has the nature and the power to facilitate desired learning outcomes. The less that religious instruction minimizes or even obliterates its distinctiveness, the less potent it will be—and the less it will be valued both by practitioners in other pastoral areas and by scholars in related fields such as theology and the psychology of religion.

Among the many important general principles governing the selection of appropriate instructional procedures for teaching faith, five are worthy of mention in the present context.

First, effective faith instruction uses a wide repertoire of teaching procedures. It is axiomatic in educational science that no one particular pedagogical procedure is adequate to facilitate all kinds of learning outcomes. For example, a cognitive pedagogical procedure such as reflection is not adequate to facilitate lifestyle learning outcomes. Differential outcomes require differential teaching procedures. The religious educator should carefully select from among the wide variety of available teaching procedures the one which is best suited to the kind of faith outcome to be facilitated (subject matter), the nature and contours of the learner, and the particular environment in which teaching is enacted.

Second, effective faith instruction takes its pedagogical procedures from the whole range of instructional endeavor and not just from any portion of it. There has never been any pedagogical procedure developed specifically or exclusively for teaching faith, or for teaching any other area of religion for that matter. Nor can pedagogical practice ever be developed exclusively for teaching faith because faith is learned in

---

125. Shelly Chaiken and Charles Stangor, "Attitudes and Attitudinal Change," *Annual Review of Psychology* 38, pp. 590-592.

basically the same manner as any other related area of human life. Thus the whole range of instructional procedures is accessible to religious educators and should be used by them, as appropriate, in their efforts to teach faith.

Third, effective faith instruction endeavors as far as possible to use teaching procedures which enjoy empirical support. Empirical research provides proven facts upon which instructional decisions are made. Empirical research assists the religious educator in knowing which procedures will probably be effective and which procedures in all likelihood will be ineffective in a given set of pedagogical circumstances. Basing one's teaching activities on empirical research chases away hit-or-miss instruction for faith.

Fourth, effective faith instruction is one in which there is congruence between substantive content and structural content. The greater is this convergence, the more successful will be the teaching, and vice versa. If the substantive content of faith is conceptualized as primarily cognitive, then cognitively oriented structural content (pedagogical procedures) such as lecture, reflection, and problem solving should be utilized, as appropriate. If the substantive content of faith is conceptualized as primarily affective, then affectively oriented structural content such as songs, trust walk, and attitude builders should be utilized, as appropriate. If the substantive content of faith is conceptualized as primarily lifestyle, then lifestyle-oriented pedagogical structural content such as projects, simulation gaming, and community service should be utilized, as appropriate.

Fifth, effective faith instruction vertically integrates all six levels present in every teaching act, namely approach, style, strategy, method, technique, and step.[126] A lack of vertical integration leads to discontinuous, inconsistent, and structurally clashing pedagogical enactment. For example, a learner-centered teaching style should not be combined with the transmission strategy. Or again, an affective teaching technique should not be used in conjunction with the pedagogical step of giving directions. Careful planning of pedagogical procedure will help insure proper vertical integration of all six levels of the taxonomy of the teaching act.

CONCLUSION

As a general rule, faith instruction should be done within the wider context of religion. The set of behaviors encapsulated by the construct

---

126. For an explanation of these six taxonomic elements of the teaching act, see Lee, *The Flow of Religious Instruction*, pp. 28-38.

faith are located within the broader network of living religion in all its dimensionalities. Ripped away from the web of interactive relationships it has with other aspects of religion, faith cannot subsist and faith instruction will therefore fade.

Among the most important and urgent of these other aspects of religion is love. Though faith might well be the beginning of a person as a Christian, love is the goal of faith.[127] But more than this, faith is formed in love, accomplished in love, and consummated in love. Love empowers faith, directs its path, curbs its abuses, motivates it, enlarges it, fulfills it.[128]

Done in love, with love, and for love, faith instruction can achieve its goal—when competence is present.

---

127. This is the position of one of the earliest Christian saints, Ignatius of Antioch (? - c.110) in his *Letter to the Ephesians*, XIV.

128. These statements about faith, though rooted in social-scientific, philosophical, and theological research, are nonetheless stipulative descriptions. Only when we use empirical procedures to enhance significantly our unidimensional (speculative) grasp of what faith really is and how faith actually works can we gain accurate descriptions of the nature and the operations of faith.

Profiles of Contributors

MONIKA K. HELLWIG is Professor of Theology at Georgetown University. She was born in Breslau in Germany and is a Catholic laywoman. She received her doctorate from The Catholic University of America. Three of Professor Hellwig's numerous books are *Sign of Reconciliation and Compassion* (Glazier, 152 pp.), *Jesus the Compassion of God* (Glazier, 159 pp.), and *Gladness Their Escort* (Glazier, 391 pp.). Her articles have appeared in many scholarly journals including *Journal of Ecumenical Studies, Theology/Philosophy*, and *Theology Today*. She has taught at the University of Notre Dame and at Princeton Theological Seminary. Ten universities have awarded her an honorary doctorate. A past president of the Catholic Theological Society of America, Professor Hellwig has also been the recipient of a Research Fellowship at the Ecumenical Institute of Advanced Theological Studies in Jerusalem and at the Woodrow Wilson Center for Scholars.

JOHN CARMODY is Research Professor at the University of Tulsa. He was born in Worcester (Massachusetts) and is a Catholic layman. He received his doctorate from Stanford University. Three of Professor Carmody's numerous books are *Interpreting the Religious Experience* (Prentice-Hall, 215 pp.), *Bonded in Christ's Love* (Paulist, 232 pp.), and *Holistic Spirituality* (Paulist, 145 pp.). His articles have appeared in many important scholarly journals including *Journal of Ecumenical Studies, Horizons*, and *Theology Today*. He has taught at Boston College, Pennsylvania State University, and Witchita State University. Dr. Carmody was awarded the Lewis Fellowship from Stanford University.

303

LOUIS DUPRÉ is T. L. Riggs Professor in the Philosophy of Religion at Yale University. He was born in Veerle in Belgium and is a Catholic layman. He received his doctorate from the University of Leuven (Louvain) in Belgium. Three of Professor Dupré's many books are *The Other Dimension* (Seabury/Harper & Row, 556 pp.), *Transcendental Selfhood* (Seabury/Harper & Row, 118 pp.), and *Marx's Social Critique of Culture* (Yale University Press, 299 pp.). His articles have appeared in numerous scholarly journals including *Review of Metaphysics, Philosophy and Phenomenological Research*, and *Journal of Religion*. He has taught at Georgetown University. Professor Dupré is a Member of the Royal Academy of Sciences, Arts, and Letters of Belgium, and also is a Fellow at the American Council of Learned Societies. Dr. Dupré is listed in *Who's Who in America, Who's Who in the World*, and *International Scholars Directory*.

JACQUELINE MARIÑA is a doctoral student in religious studies at Yale University. She was born in The Bronx and is a laywoman. She received the prize for the highest scholarship in the graduating class at Yale University Divinity School.

H. NEWTON MALONY is Professor and Director of Programs in the Integration of Psychology and Theology at Fuller Theological Seminary. He was born in Birmingham in Alabama and is an ordained minister in the United Methodist Church. He received his doctorate from Peabody/ Vanderbilt University. Three of Professor Malony's many books are *Wholeness and Holiness* (Baker, 344 pp.), *Christian Conversion* (Zondervan, 192 pp.), and *Glossalia: Behavioral Science Understanding of Speaking in Tongues* (Oxford University Press, 292 pp.). His articles have appeared in many important scholarly journals including *Journal for the Scientific Study of Religion, Review of Religious Research*, and *Journal of Psychology and Theology*. Reverend Malony has been the recipient of the William Bier Award from Division 36 of the American Psychology Association, and a Postdoctoral Fellowship in Clinical Psychology from the National Institute of Mental Health. He has taught at Tennessee Wesleyan College. Dr. Malony is listed in *Who's Who in Religion* and *Who's Who in the West*.

CARROLL STUHLMUELLER is Professor of Old Testament Studies at the Catholic Theological Union at Chicago. He was born in Hamilton (Ohio) and is an ordained Catholic priest of the Passionist Congregation. He received his doctorate from the Pontifical Biblical Institute in Rome. Three of Professor Stuhlmueller's numerous books are his two-volume commentary *The Psalms*, his six volume set *Biblical Medi-*

tations, and *Biblical Foundations for Mission*, with Donald Senior (Orbis, 384 pp.). His articles have appeared in many scholarly journals including *Biblical Theology Bulletin*, *Catholic Biblical Quarterly*, and *The Bible Today*. Dr. Stuhlmueller has taught at the École Biblique in Jerusalem, the University of Notre Dame, and the East Asian Pastoral Institute in Manila. Two institutions of higher learning have awarded him an honorary doctorate. Father Stuhlmueller is past president of the Catholic Biblical Association. He is listed in *Who's Who in Religion*, *Directory of American Scholars*, and *American Catholic Who's Who*.

JAMES LIGON PRICE JR. is Professor Emeritus of Religion at Duke University. He was born in Chase City in Virginia and is a retired ordained minister of the Presbyterian Church (U.S.) He received his doctorate from Cambridge University in England. Professor Price's books include *Interpreting the New Testament* (Holt, Rinehart, and Winston, 624 pp.) and *The New Testament: Its History and Theology* (Macmillan, 489 pp.). His articles have appeared in many major journals including *Journal of the American Academy of Religion*, *Interpretation*, and *Religion and Life*. Dr. Price has taught at Washington and Lee University, and at Rhodes College of Southwestern at Memphis. He was the recipient of the Salem Award from Union Theological Seminary. Reverend Price is listed in *Who's Who in America* and in *Who's Who in Religion*.

AVERY DULLES is Lawrence McGinley Professor of Theology at Fordham University. He was born in Auburn (New York) and is an ordained Catholic priest of the Society of Jesus. He received his doctorate from the Gregorian University in Rome. Three of Professor Dulles's many books are *Models of the Church* (Doubleday Image, 256 pp.), *Models of Revelation* (Doubleday Image, 344 pp.), and *A Church to Believe In* (Crossroad, 200 pp.). His articles have appeared in many scholarly journals including *Theological Studies*, *Journal of Religion*, and *Thomist*. Dr. Dulles has taught as O'Brien Professor at the University of Notre Dame, as Gasson Professor at Boston College, and at Woodstock College. He is the recipient of eight honorary doctorates from various universities. Father Dulles also was a Fellow at the Woodrow Wilson International Center for Scholars and was awarded the Croix de Guerre with silver star from the French government. He is listed in *Who's Who in America*, *Dictionary of American Scholars*, and *Writers Directory*.

ALEXANDER McKELWAY is Professor of Religion at Davidson College. He was born in Durham in North Carolina and is an ordained minister of the Presbyterian Church (U.S.). He received his doctorate from the University of Basel in Switzerland. Professor McKelway's books include *The Systematic Theology of Paul Tillich* (Knox, 280 pp.) and *The Context of Contemporary Theology*, with David E. Willis (Knox, 269 pp.) His articles have appeared in scholarly journals including *Scottish Journal of Theology*, *Perspectives in Religious Studies*, and *Princeton Seminary Bulletin*. Dr. McKelway has taught at Dartmouth College and at Princeton Theological Seminary. The National Endowment for the Humanities awarded Reverend McKelway a fellowship.

LOUIS WEIL is Professor of Liturgics at The Church Divinity School of the Pacific. He was born in Houston and is an ordained priest of the Episcopal Church. He received his doctorate from the Institut Catholique in Paris. Professor Weil's books include *Sacraments and Liturgy* (Blackwell, 115 pp.), *Gathered to Pray* (Cowley, 148 pp.), and *Liturgy for Living*, with Charles Price (Seabury, 345 pp.). His scholarly articles have appeared in many important journals including *Studia Liturgica*, *Worship*, and *Anglican Theological Review*. Dr. Weil has taught at the University of Notre Dame, La Salle College, and El Seminario Episcopal del Caribe.

RANDOLPH A. NELSON is Director of Contextual Education at Luther Northwestern Theological Seminary. He was born in Watertown in South Dakota and is an ordained Lutheran minister. He received his doctorate from the University of Chicago Divinity School. Dr. Nelson published an article in *Word and World*. He has been the recipient of a Fulbright grant, and also a Bavarian State Scholarship award. He has taught at the Lutheran School of Theology at Chicago.

MELVIN C. BLANCHETTE is Associate Professor of Pastoral Counseling at Loyola College in Maryland and has an extensive private practice in pastoral counseling in Washington, D.C. He was born in South Rockwood in Michigan and is an ordained Roman Catholic priest of the Society of Saint Sulpice. He received his doctorate from the United States International University. Dr. Blanchette's books include *Pastoral Counseling*, with Barry K. Estadt and John R. Compton (Prentice-Hall, 304 pp.), and *The Art of Clinical Supervision: A Pastoral Counseling Perspective*, with Barry K. Estadt and John R. Compton (Paulist, 309 pp.) He wrote an article in *Bulletin de Saint-Sulpice*. Father Blanchette has taught at The Catholic University of America, Sacred Heart Seminary, and St. John's Provincial Seminary. He is listed in *Who's Who in the East*.

JAMES MICHAEL LEE is Professor of Education at the University of Alabama at Birmingham. He was born in Brooklyn and is a Catholic layman. He received his doctorate from Columbia University. Three of Professor Lee's many books are his trilogy, *The Shape of Religious Instruction* (Religious Education Press, 330 pp.), *The Flow of Religious Instruction* (Religious Education Press, 379 pp.), and *The Content of Religious Instruction* (Religious Education Press, 814 pp.). His articles have appeared in many journals including *Herder Korrespondenz*, *Religious Education*, and *Living Light*. Professor Lee has taught at the University of Notre Dame, Hunter College of the City University of New York, and St. Joseph's College. He was the recipient of a Senior Fulbright Research Fellowship to Germany and also a Lilly Endowment Fellowship. Dr. Lee is listed in *Who's Who in America*, *Who's Who in the World*, and *Who's Who in Religion*.

Index of Names

Aaseng, Rolf, 224
Abbott, Walter, 22
Abelard, Peter, 60
Achtemeier, Barry W., 39
Adam, Karl, 156
Aiken, Henry D., 64
Aldama, Iosephus de, 150, 160
Aleshire, David, 94
Alfaro, Johannes (Juan), 99, 100, 106, 115, 150, 157
Allport, Floyd, 80
Allport, Gordon, 83, 86, 87, 88, 95
Althaus, Paul, 166, 172, 173, 175
Ambrose of Milan, 8
Ambrosiater, 169
Amsdorf, Nikolaus, 181
Anaximander, 50
Andersen, Francis I., 104
Anderson, H. George, 160, 169, 200
Anselm of Canterbury, 10, 58, 59, 60, 197, 280, 281
Antoine, P., 99, 101
Aquinas, Thomas, 8, 10, 11, 12, 13, 16, 19, 60, 61, 100, 143, 146, 148, 149, 153, 157, 159, 187, 271, 281
Argus, Jacob B., 39
Aristotle, 49, 53, 54, 55, 60, 143
Arminius, Jacob, 183

Ashton, E. B., 69
Attanasio, Salvator, 288
Aubert, Roger, 156, 157
Augustine of Hippo, 8, 9, 11, 56, 57, 58, 61, 62, 67, 142, 150, 157, 168, 169, 173, 175, 216, 221, 280
Aune, David Edward, 105

Bainton, Roland, 172
Balthasar, Hans Urs von, 288
Banana, Canaan, 285
Baron, Salo Wittmayer, 39
Barr, Robert, 285
Barraclough, Geoffrey, 24
Barrett, David B., 24
Barry, William A., 247
Barth, Karl, 78, 79, 80, 86, 166, 191, 192, 193, 194, 195, 196, 197, 198, 199, 247
Barthes, Ronald, 293
Bartsch, Hans Werner, 284
Basham, A. L., 31
Basil the Great, 280
Batson, C. Daniel, 75, 82, 83, 94, 95
Bautain, Louis, 143
Benson, Warren S., 288
Berdyayev, Nikolei Aleksandrovich, 284
Bergendorf, Conrad, 175

Berger, Peter L., 277, 288
Berkeley, George, 72
Berkhof, Hendrikus, 281
Berryman, Jerome, 245
Berryman, Philip, 285
Bertram, Robert W., 160
Berzirgan, Basima Qattan, 46
Bettenhausen, Elizabeth, 236
Bickimer, David Arthur, 270
Billet, Louis, 156
Bizer, Ernst, 185
Blake, Judith, 297
Bleeker, Jouco, 24
Blumstein, Philip, 297
Boff, Clodovis, 285
Boff, Leonardo, 285
Boismard, Marie-Emile, 108
Bonino, José Míguez, 236, 237
Bonnetty, Augustin, 143
Bornkamm, Günther, 134
Bosworth, C. E., 46
Botterweck, G. Johannes, 99
Bouillard, Henri, 156
Braaten, Carl E., 282
Bridgman, P. W., 278
Broglie, Guy de, 156, 157
Bromiley, Geoffrey W., 100, 105, 294
Brophy, Jere, 266
Brown, H., 56
Brown, Lawrence B., 81
Brown, Raymond E., 110, 111, 113, 114, 115, 130, 140
Brown, Robert McAfee, 199
Brown, Roger, 77
Browning, Don, 83, 84, 90
Browning, Robert L., 267
Bruggemann, Walter, 266
Bruner, Jerome, 276
Brunner, Emil, 78, 79, 80, 84
Buber, Martin, 101
Bucan, Gulielimus, 185
Bultmann, Rudolf, 100, 105, 124, 128, 138, 195, 196, 284
Burges, J. A., 169, 200
Burgess, Harold William, 294
Burket, Walter, 50, 51
Burnet, John, 50
Butler, Joseph, 188

Cairns, Huntington, 52
Calvin, John, 16, 135, 165, 176, 177, 178, 179, 180, 181, 182, 183, 184
Cannon, William R., 76
Capéran, Louis, 159
Capps, Donald E., 248
Capra, Fritjof, 279
Chadwick, Henry, 65
Chaiken, Shelly, 300
Chan, Wing-Tsit, 38
Chase, Alston Hurd, 48
Chenu, Marie-Dominique, 156
Childe, Gordon, 286
Childs, Brevard S., 39
Clebsh, W., 252
Clement of Alexandria, 6, 7, 280
Clinebell, Howard J. Jr., 228, 233, 234
Cohen, Abraham, 39
Coleman, John A., 229, 232, 287
Coleridge, Samuel Taylor, 189
Collins, Mary, 21, 106
Cone, James H., 285, 286
Confucius, 35, 36
Congar, Yves, 149
Connolly, William J., 247
Conrad, Robert L., 268
Constantine, 121
Conze, Edward, 35
Coventry, John, 8
Cragg, Kenneth, 46
Creel, J. G., 38
Crim, Keith, 24
Crouter, Richard, 283
Cyprian, 252
Cyril of Jerusalem, 7, 8, 280

Dalmais, Irénée-Henri, 203, 207
Darcy-Bérubé, Françoise, 288
Dasgupta, S. N., 31
Dechamps, Victor, 155
Denny, Frederick Mathewson, 39, 46
Denzinger, Henricus, 9, 21, 143, 281
Descartes, Rene, 18, 62, 63, 64
Dewey, John, 266
Dhanis, Edouard, 157
Diels, Hermann, 50
Dillenberger, John, 164, 171, 175, 176, 282
Dimock, Edward C., 31
Dittes, James, 94, 95

Dodd, C. H., 126
Donaldson, W. J. Jr., 74
Donohue, John J., 46
Downs, Thomas, 212
Drury, John, 258
Duffy, Regis, 244
Dujarier, Michel, 213, 265
Dulles, Avery, 161, 162, 248, 282, 283, 294
Dumoulin, Heinrich, 35
Duplacy, Jean, 99, 100
Dupuis, Jacques, 154
Dykstra, Craig, 90, 92, 94, 248

Eagleson, John, 285
Eavey, C. B., 269
Ebeling, Gerhard, 197
Eccles, John C., 276
Eckhardt, Roy, 254
Eliade, Mircea, 24, 25, 29, 31
Elkind, David, 87, 88, 91
Ellis, Albert, 84
Elwell, Walter A., 282
Eminyan, Maurice, 159, 160
Epstein, Isadore, 39
Erigena, Joannes Scotus, 280
Erikson, Erik, 88, 92, 93
Esposito, John L., 46
Estadt, Barry K., 252, 263

Fairweather, Eugene R., 58
Falk, Harvey, 105
Falwell, Jerry, 198
Faruqi, Isma'il al, 24, 45
Faruqi, Lois Lamya' al, 45
Ferm, Vergilius, 72
Fernea, Elizabeth Warnock, 46
Fernhout, J. Harry, 90
Feuerback, Ludwig, 173
Finkelstein, Louis, 39
Fischer, Katherine, 246
Fitzmyer, Joseph A., 105, 108, 134, 135
Flacius, Matthias, 181
Flint, C. R., 198
Forell, George W., 175, 221
Foster, Charles R., 269
Fowler, James W., 82, 83, 86, 87, 88, 89, 90, 91, 92, 93, 94, 95, 245, 248, 249, 250, 296
Francis of Assisi, 14, 250
Franke, August Hermann, 186

Frankl, Victor, 283
Fraser, Barry F., 294
Freedman, David Noel, 104
Freud, Sigmund, 78, 84, 86, 88, 89, 255
Friedrich, Gerhard, 100, 105
Friedrich, L. W., 278
Froelich, Karlfried, 169
Fuller, Reginald, 284

Gabian, Marjorie, 78
Gage, Nathaniel L., 293
Galloway, Allan Douglas, 7
Gandhi, Mohandas, 30, 56, 250
Gangel, Kenneth, O., 288
Gaster, Theodor Herzl, 105
Gautama, 31, 32, 33
Geertz, Clifford, 25, 46
Gelin, Albert, 99
Gilby, Thomas, 11, 12, 13, 60
Gillespie, V. Bailey, 270, 296
Ginsbuerg, Herbert, 92
Glasse, Cyril, 45
Glatzer, Nahum N., 39
Glock, Charles Y., 296
Godin, André, 84, 85, 86, 87, 89, 270
Goldbrunner, Josef, 290
Goldziher, Ignaz, 46
Good, Thomas L., 266
Goodman, Cecile, 276
Gorsuch, Richard L., 74, 82
Gottwald, Norman K., 39
Graham, Billy, 198, 199
Graham, Martha, 214, 215
Grandmaison, Léonce de, 273
Granet, Marcel, 38
Grazia, Sebastian de, 38
Green, William Scott, 39
Gregory XVI, 143
Gritsch, Eric W., 160
Groome, Thomas H., 266, 295, 298
Günter, Anton, 144
Gutiérrez, Gustavo, 199, 285

Haasl, Edward L., 265
Habermas, Jürgen, 177
Hakes, J. Edward, 269
Hamann, Johann Georg, 188
Hamilton, Edith, 52
Hamilton, Peter, 287
Harent, Stéphane, 156

Harnack, Adolf von, 191, 192
Harrison, Graham, 288
Hart, Ray L., 248
Haughey, John C., 246
Hay, C. F., 168
Hegel, Georg Wilhelm Friedrich, 67, 68, 192
Heidegger, Johan Heinrich, 184, 185
Heidegger, Martin, 68, 69, 196
Heisenberg, Werner, 279
Hellwig, Monika K., 247
Helms, Hal M., 57
Henriot, Peter, 237
Heppe, Heinrich, 185
Heraclitus, 50, 51
Herbert, Lord of Cherbury, 18
Hermann, Ingo, 103
Hermes, Georg, 144, 151, 156
Herrnstein, Richard J., 77
Herzog, Elizabeth, 39
Heschel, Abraham J., 23, 244
Hesiod, 48, 49
Hickey, Denis, 282
Hightower, Pleasant Roscoe, 299
Hill, Brennan R., 267, 269
Hochberg, J., 276
Hodgson, Marshall G. S., 46
Hodgson, Peter C., 67, 286
Hoffman, Lawrence A., 205
Hofinger, Johannes S., 267, 290
Holahan, Charles J., 294
Holland, Joe, 237
Holt, P. M., 46
Holtz, Barry W., 39
Homans, Peter, 83
Homer, 48, 49, 105
Hong, Edna H., 284
Hong, Howard V., 284
Hood, Ralph W. Jr., 82, 95
Hopkins, Thomas J., 31
Hordern, Richard, 239
Hoskyns, Edwin C., 192
Howard, G., 137
Howell, Clifford, 267
Hudson, Winthrop S., 231
Hultkrantz, Ake, 25
Hume, David, 64, 65, 66, 72, 187, 188
Hunt, John T., 16
Hus, John, 14
Hutchins, Robert Maynard, 255

Ignatius of Antioch, 242, 243, 244, 263, 302
Inda, Caridad, 285
Inhelder, Barbel, 92
Innocent XI, 143
Irenaeus, 242, 252

Jacobi, Friedrich Heinrich, 188
Jaeger, Werner, 49
Jaekle, C., 252
James, William, 74, 75, 76, 77, 78, 79, 80, 81, 82, 83, 85, 86, 89
Jammer, Max, 279
Jaspers, Karl, 47, 68, 69, 70
Jeffrey, Arthur, 46
Jepsen, Alfred, 99, 102
Jersild, Paul, 223
John Paul II, 100, 243, 269
Johnson, John F., 160
Johnson, Willard L., 35
Joyce, Bruce, 294
Jung, Carl Gustav, 72, 74, 76, 283
Justin Martyr, 6, 252, 265
Justinian, 121

Kahn, Charles H., 52
Kant, Immanuel, 65, 66, 67, 72, 73, 74, 75, 76, 77, 78, 79, 80, 87, 90, 92, 186, 188, 189
Käsemann, Ernst, 134
Kavanagh, Aidan, 205
Keck, Leander, 138
Keen, Sam, 245
Kelly, George, 90
Kelsey, Morton Trippe, 298
Kemp, Raymond B., 213
Kevane, Eugene, 288
Kierkegaard, Søren, 192, 193, 284
King, Noel Q., 25
Kinsley, David R., 31
Kittlaus, Paul, 225
Knight, Douglas A., 39
Knox, John, 182
Kohlberg, Lawrence, 88, 90, 249
Kollock, Peter, 297
Komonchak, Joseph A., 21, 106
Küng, Hans, 62, 136

Lambert, W. A., 282
Lamenais, Félicité de, 143
Lane, Dermot A., 21, 106
Lantero, Erminie, Huntress, 284

Lapide, Phinn, 109
Lara-Brend, Jorge, 221, 222
Latourelle, René, 157
Lattimore, Richmond, 50
Leas, Speed, 225
Lebacqz, Karen, 229
LeBar, Lois E., 291
Lee, James Michael, 264, 266, 270,
    287, 291, 292, 298, 301
Lee, Phillip J., 199
Lehmann, Paul, 191
Leibniz, Gottfried Wilhelm von,
    63, 64
Leith, John H., 15, 17, 22, 186, 198
Leiva-Merikakis, Erasmo, 61
Léon-Dufour, Xavier, 99, 111, 116
Lessing, Gotthold Ephraim, 64, 65
Letter, Prudent de, 149
Leuba, James, 72, 73, 81, 82
Lewis, Bernard, 46
Liechtenhan, Rudolf, 194
Ling, Trevor, 35
Lings, Martin, 46
Livingston, James C., 18, 19, 187,
    190, 191
Locke, John, 19, 72, 77, 187, 188
Lohse, Bernhard, 15
Lombard, Peter, 169, 170, 281
Lombardi, Riccardo, 159
Lonergan, Bernard, 275
Lopez, Barry, 25
Lotz, Hermann, 191
Lowrie, Donald A., 284
Lowrie, Walter, 191, 284
Luckmann, Thomas, 277
Luther, Martin, 15, 16, 18, 19, 135,
    160, 164, 165, 166, 168, 169, 170,
    171, 172, 173, 174, 175, 176,
    177, 178, 179, 180, 181, 182,
    184, 186, 190, 191, 194, 195,
    196, 197, 199, 229, 230, 282

Mackintosh, H. R., 189, 191
Macquarrie, John, 245, 246
Mager, Robert F., 274
Magnin, E., 273
Maimonides, Moses, 42
Major, George, 181
Malmberg, Felix, 156
Malony, H. Newton, 81, 88, 89, 93,
    94, 95
Malony, Thomas F., 282

Mannheim, Karl, 277
Marck, Johannes, 185
Marino, Joseph S., 264
Marthaler, Berard L., 268
Mastricht, Peter, 185
Masure, Eugène, 156
Mayr, Marlene, 268
Mazrui, Ali A., 46
Mbiti, John, 25
McBride, Alfred, 291
McBrien, Richard P., 247, 268
McClure, Matthew Thomson, 50
McGiffert, A. C. 186
McGivern, James J., 100, 117
McKay, Donald, 93
McKelway, Alexander J., 195
McKeon, Richard, 49
McNeill, John T., 165
Mead, George Herbert, 277, 297
Means, Stewart, 9
Melanchthon, Philipp, 15, 180, 181
Meland, Bernard Eugene, 284, 285
Mencius, 36
Merkle, John C., 23
Mermin, N. David, 278
Messori, Vittorio, 288
Metz, Johann-Baptist, 23, 285
Miller, Judith, 277
Miller, Paul, 267
Miller, Randolph Crump, 269, 291
Mitzell, Harold E., 267
Mollat, Donatien, 110
Moltmann, Jürgen, 23
Monden, Louis, 157
Monroe, Ruth, 78
Moore, C., 31
Moore, Mary Elizabeth, 269
Morris, Charles W., 277, 297
Morris, Ronald J., 95
Mouroux, Jean, 156, 282
Mueller, David L., 191, 247
Muhammad, 42, 43, 44, 45, 46
Munro, Donald J., 39
Munsey, Brenda, 90
Murphy, Joseph, 267
Murphy, T. A., 169, 200

Naipaul, V. S., 46
Nelson, C. Ellis, 94, 267, 269, 298
Neuner, Josef, 9, 154
Neusner, Jacob, 39

Newman, John Henry, 19, 20, 21, 246, 281
Niebuhr, Reinhold, 231
North, Gerald, 89

O'Collins, Gerald, 254
O'Connell, Matthew, 285
O'Donnell, John, 21, 106
Ogden, Schubert M., 286
O'Hare, J. Padraic, 268, 288
Oman, John, 189
O'Meara, Thomas Franklin, 244
Opper, Sylvia, 92
Organ, Troy Wilson, 32
Origen, 6
Osiander, Andreas, 182
Osmer, Richard, 248
Ottenweiler, Albert, 218

Pagels, Heinz R., 279
Pannenberg, Wolfhart, 282
Paolucci, Henry, 168
Parker, Cecil J., 266
Parker, J. H., 56
Parks, Sharon, 90, 92, 94, 248, 266
Parmenides, 51
Parrinder, Geoffrey, 24, 46
Parsons, Richard D., 248
Parsons, Talcott, 277
Pascal, Blaise, 283
Patterson, Bob E. 247
Paul VI, 100
Peale, Norman Vincent, 199
Pelagius, 169, 173, 221
Pelikan, Jaraslav, 173
Perrin, Norman, 131
Perry, Wiliam G. Jr., 48
Pervin, Lawrence A., 276
Pesch, Christian, 156
Peter, Carl, 161
Pettigrew, Thomas, 233
Pfister, Oskar, 89
Piaget, Jean, 78, 87, 88, 91, 92, 93
Pickar, C. H., 101
Pico, Juan Hernández, 285
Pius IX, 121, 144, 159
Pius, XII, 117, 121, 144, 156
Plato, 51, 52, 53, 55, 56, 105
Plaut, W. Gunter, 39
Plotinus, 54, 55, 105
Plutarch, 105

Popper, Karl R., 276
Porter, Lyman W., 276, 294
Power, David, 106
Prebish, Charles S., 35
Price, James Ligon, 139
Price, Charles, 203, 215
Pruyser, Paul, 254

Quinn, Edward, 62

Rad, Gerhard von, 166
Radhakrishnan, Sarvepalli, 31
Rahman, Fazlur, 46
Rahner, Karl, 21, 160, 248, 282
Raitt, Jill, 161
Randall, John Herman Jr., 72
Ratzinger, Joseph, 288
Rauschenbusch, Walter, 231, 232
Reardon, Bernard M. G., 20
Reid, Clyde, 282
Rétif, André, 265
Reumann, John, 131, 133, 137
Richards, Lawrence O., 269
Riesenhuber, Klaus, 160
Ringgren, Helmer, 99
Ritschl, Albrecht, 190, 191, 192
Robinson, Richard H., 35
Roos, H., 9
Röper, Anita, 160
Rosenbaum, Jonathan, 39
Rosenzweig, Mark A., 276
Ross, W. D., 54
Roth, Cecil, 39
Rousselto, Pierre, 156, 157
Rubin, Louis J., 266
Russell, Letty, 199

Sakenfeld, Katherine Doob, 104
Sanders, E. P., 136
Sanford, John A., 283
Sarno, Ronald A., 269
Saunders, T. B., 192
Sawicki, Marianne, 288
Schacht, Joseph, 46
Schaff, Philip, 181
Schimmel, Annemarie, 46
Schipani, Daniel S., 269, 287
Schleiermacher, Friedrich, 19, 20, 21, 189, 190, 192, 195, 283
Schmidt, Herman, 106
Schneider, Carl, 94

Scholem, Gershon G., 39
Schönmetzer, Adolfus, 9, 21, 143, 281
Schüssler-Fiorenza, Francis, 23
Scott, W. Richard, 297
Scotus, John Duns, 13, 61
Seeberg, Reinhold, 168, 181, 183
Segundo, Juan, 258
Seifert, Harvey, 228, 233, 234
Senior, Donald, 103, 106, 113
Settel, T. S., 199
Sexton, Anne, 256
Shakespeare, William, 254
Shapiro, Jeremy, 277
Shelp, Earl E., 222, 226
Shils, Edward, 277
Shinran, 33
Shorey, Paul, 52
Shurmann, Heinz, 288
Silverman, David, 278
Simplicius, 50
Smith, David, 285
Smith, J. A., 49
Smith, Jane I., 46
Smith, Jonathan Z., 25
Smith, L. P., 194, 284
Smith, Norman Kemp, 65, 72, 188
Smith, Temple, 35
Soelle, Dorothea, 236
Sobrino, Jon, 285
Sopher, D., 24
Speight, Marston, 46
Spener, Philipp Jakob, 186, 282, 283
Spilka, Bernard, 82
Spinoza, Baruch, 63, 64
Spiro, Melford, 34, 35
Spitz, Lewis W., 172
Sprague, C. Joseph, 267
Sproul, Barbara, 25
Stallnecht, Newton P., 72
Stangor, Charles, 300
Stanley, David M., 295
Strachan, Richard, 282
Strommen, Merton P., 270
Stuhlmacher, Peter, 109
Stuhlmueller, Carroll, 103, 106, 113, 121
Suhard, Emmanuel, 117
Sunderland, Ronald M., 222, 226
Surlis, Paul, 281
Swartz, Merlin, 46

Tappart, Theodore, 16
Taylor, Rodney, L., 39
Tcherikover, Victor, 39
Telfer, William, 7
Tennyson, Alfred, 250
Teresa of Calcutta, 250
Ternant, Paul, 116
Tertullian, 252
Thales, 49
Thielicke, Helmut, 294
Thomas, Edward J., 35
Thompson, G. T., 185
Thompson, Laurence G., 38
Thompson, Norma H., 287
Tillich, Paul, 86, 87, 88, 89, 195, 196, 243, 248, 284, 294
Tindal, Matthew, 187
Tredennick, Hugh, 53
Trotter, W. F., 283
Tucker, Gene M., 39
Turner, Victor, 25
Turretin, Jean Alphonse, 184
Tzu, Chuang, 35, 36, 37
Tzu, Lao, 35, 36, 37

Ungar, Frederick, 31

Vawter, Bruce, 106, 110, 111, 112
Ventis, W. Larry, 75, 82, 83
Victorinus, Marius, 169
Vignon, Henri, 156
Virgulin, S., 103
Volken, Laurent, 149
Voltaire, 187, 188
Vorgrimler, Herbert, 21, 282

Wainright, Geoffrey, 205
Walberg, Herbert J., 266
Waldo, Peter, 14
Waley, Arthur, 38
Walgrave, Jan, 157
Walker, Robert Scott, 282
Ward, J. M., 125
Warford, Malcolm L., 295
Warner, Rex, 168
Warren, Henry Clarke, 35
Warren, Michael, 269, 288
Warren, Richard M., 276
Watt, W. Montgomery, 46
Weil, Louis, 203, 209, 215, 217
Weil, Marsha L., 267, 294
Weiser, Arthur, 99, 103, 124, 126

Welch, Claude, 189
Wesley, John, 76, 186, 187
Westerhoff, John H. III, 291
Whaling, Frank, 25
White, James W., 269
Whitehead, Evelyn Eaton, 218
Whitrock, Merlin C., 266
Wicks, Robert J., 248
Widengren, Geo, 23
Wilhoit, Jim, 269
William of Occam, 13, 61
Wirth, Louis, 277
Wolff, Hans Walter, 104
Wolleb, Johan, 184, 185
Woolf, Bertram Lee, 282
Wright, Arthur F., 39

Wyckoff, D. Campbell, 269
Wycliff, John, 14

Xenophon, 105

Yang, C. K., 38

Zaehner, R. C., 24
Zborowski, Mark, 39
Ziesler, J. A. 135
Zimbardo, Philip G., 77
Zimmer, Heinrich, 31
Zimring, Fred M., 299
Zinzendorf, Nikolaus Ludwig von, 186
Zwingli, Ulrich, 182

Index of Subjects

Abraham's faith, 125-126
Act of faith, psychological analysis
  of, 86-95
  decisive or emergent, 87-88
  ego identity and, 88-89
  faith development, 89-95
    cognitive view of faith, as, 89-
      90
    criticisms of, 93-95
    maturation and, 92-93
    stages in, 90-91
Active faith pedagogy, 298-300
Actualism, 145
Ad gentes, 159
Affect, faith as, 4-5, 14-16, 19-21,
  34, 101-102, 104, 105-106, 110-
  111, 125-139, 145, 160-161, 166-
  167, 174-175, 185, 186, 189-190,
  204, 224, 282-283, 298
African-American theology, 285-
  286
African nonliterate religion, 26-27
'Aman, 99, 101-106
American Indian nonliterate
  tradition, 26-27
Anfechtung, 174-175
Anselminanism, 10, 58-60, 197,
  280-281
  Barth's view of, 197
  philosophical, 58-60

theological, 280-281
Answer to problems, faith as, 75-76
Antinomianism, 182
Anxiety, psychological, *see* Pain,
  psychological
Appropriate response, faith as, 123
Aristotleanism, 53-56, 143
  base for scholastic theology of
    grace, 143
  boulesis, 55
  contemplation, 54-55
  intelligibility in, 53
  theory of forms, 53
Arminianism, 76, 183, 184
Artificial intelligence, 299
Assensus-notitia-fiducia, 192
Attitude, faith as, *see* Affect, faith
  as
Attitudes, 233
Augsburg Confession, 180-181
Augustianism, 8-9, 56-57, 168-169,
  280
  philosophical, 56-57
  theological, 8-9, 168-169, 280
Australian nonliterate religion, 27-
  28

Baptism, 138-139, 219-220, 264-
  265
  early church and, 139, 265

317

Baptism cont.
  justification and, 138-139
  liturgical formation and, 219-220
  Paul's vocation and, 264
  religious instruction and, 264-265
Barthianism, 193-195
Bātah, 101
Behavior, definition of, 270
Behaviorist perspective on faith, 81
Biblical view of faith, 99-141
  Catholic perspective, 99-122
    Acts of the Apostles, 107-108
    cognition, faith as, 100-101
    Greek New Testament, 105-107
      Hebrew Bible, impact on,
        105
      pisteuō/pistis, use of, 106
      Synoptics, 106-107
    Hebrew Bible, 101-104
      continuous condition, 102
      liturgy, 104
      personal relationship, 102
      practice, lived, 102-103
      trust, 101-102
    Johannine Gospel, 111-117
    methodologies for biblical
      scholarship, 117-122
      canonical, 118
      form-criticism, 117
      historical-critical, 117
      liturgical, 119-122
      sociological, 117-118
    more than cognitive, 100-101
    Pauline texts, 108-111
  Protestant perspective, 123-141
    Abrahamic faith, 125-126
    Exodus tradition, 124-125
    God's faithfulness, 127
    Isaiah oracles, 126-127
    New Testament, 128
      Jewish-Christian
        commonalities, 128-129
      Johannine Gospel, 139-141
      new concept, 129-130
      Pauline texts, principal, 134-
        139
      Synoptic Gospels, 130-133
    Psalm writers, 127
    word meanings, 123-124
Bhakti, 30-31
Black theology, *see* African-
  American theology

Bodhisattvas, 32
Boulesis, 55
Buddhism, 31-35, 67
  bodhisattvas, 32
  Ch'an/Zen Buddhism, 33
  East Asian cultures, in, 34-35
  Enlightenment, 32
  Four Noble Truths, 32
  Hinduism and, 31-32
  Mahayana form of, 32-33
  Nichiren form of, 33
  nirvana, 32
  samsara, 31-32
  Shintoism and, 33
    kami, 33
  sila, 33
  Three Jewels, 32
  Tibetian form 34
  tripitaka, 32-33
Bultmannism, 195-196, 284

Calvin's doctrine of faith, 16, 135,
  165, 174-184
  definition of faith, 165
  fides divina et fides actualis, 177-
    178
  human side, emphasis on, 180
  justification, 176-180, 184
  Luther, constrasted to, 176-184
  obedience of faith, 177-178
  origin of faith, 182
  orthodoxy of faith, 16
  predestination, 165, 183
  righteousness of God, 135
  sanctification, 179-180
  works and faith, 181
Canonical methodology of biblical
  study, 118
Cartesianism, 62-63
Case histories in pastoral
  counseling, 255-260
  Brian, 256-258
  Carol, 255-256
  meaning of, for freedom, 258-260
Catalyst, educator as, 291
Catechesi tradendae, 269
Catechetics, as phase in ancient
  religious instruction, 265
Catechumenate, 213-218, 265
  liturgy and, 213-218
    church enacting itself in faith,
      216-217

Easter Vigil and, 215-216
goal of, 214
lifestyle content and, 213
nonverbal dimension of, 214-
215
rites and, 217
religious instruction, 265
Ceremonialism, contrasted to true
liturgy, 220
Certitude of faith, 152-153
Ch'an/Zen Buddhism, 33
Chinese traditions, 35-38
amalgam, as, 35
Confucianism, 35-36, 37-38
moral practice and, 35-36
The Way and, 37-38
Taoism, 36-38
harmony with the Tao, 37-38
The Way and, 37-38
Christology, 5
Civil rights movement, 232-233
Clarification, ministry of, in
pastoral counseling, 245-251
content-understanding, 246-248
Christ-centered, faith as, 247
holistic, faith as, 247
living, faith as, 247
personal, faith as, 246
shared human experience, faith
as, 246
goals of, 245-246
process and structure, 248-251
holism and, 251
stages of faith development,
248-251
Clericalization, 218-219
Code of Canon Law, 149
Congregation of the Holy Office,
143, 152
Cognition, faith as, 6-13, 16-22, 51-
68, 73-74, 89-95, 100-101, 110-
111, 115-117, 145, 152-158, 185,
187-188, 203-204, 224, 280-282,
298
Common Statement, 199
Commonalities in concept of faith,
Jewish and Christian, 128-129
Communal pedagogy, 297-298
Comparative religions, faith in, 24-
26
Buddhism, 31-35
Chinese traditions, 35-39

Confucianism, 35-36
Taoism, 36-38
Hinduism, 28-31
Islam, 42-46
Judaism, 39-42
nonliterate religious traditions,
25-28
African, 26-27
American Indian, 26-27
Australian aboriginal, 27-28
Eskimo, 25-26
Siberian, 25-26
perished cultures, 24
Compassion, 104, 106-107, 109,
128
Computers, 299
Confessions, Protestant,
Reformation era, 180-184
Augsburg Confession, 180-181
First Helvetic Confession, 182
Heidelberg Catechism, 182-183
Majoristic controversy and, 181-
182
Reformed confessions, 182
Scots Confession, 182
Second Helvetic Confession, 183
Confession of the New Hampshire
Baptist Convention, 198
Confession of the Society of
Friends, 186
Confidence, faith as, *see* Affect,
faith as
Conflict, social action and, 226-227
Confucianism, 35-36, 37-38
moral practice and, 35-36
The Way and, 37-38
Construct, faith as, 271-292
concept, compared to, 271-272
definition and, 272-273
notional, 272-273
operational, 272-273
enriching the construct, 275-289
physics, 278-279
psychology, 275-277
sociology, 277-278
theology, 279-289
learning outcome, relation to,
273-275
classical mode and, 275
operationalizing, 274-275
theory, place in, 272
usefulness of, 272

Construct cont.
  validity and, 289-292
  religious instruction in
    contributing to, 289-292
  subjectivity and, 289
Constructional pluralism, 287-289
  faith and, 287-289
  nature of, 287
  necessity of, 287-289
  nontheological sciences and, 288-289
  theological positivism versus,
    287-289
Content, types of, 266
Conaturality, 157
Conversion, 270-271
Cornerstone of counselor-client
  relationship, faith as, 260
Counterreformation, 16-17, 185,
  281

Dance, liturgical, 219
Declaration on Religious Freedom,
  Vatican II, 151
Decree on Justification, Council of
  Trent, *see Decretum de
  justificatione* , Concilium
  Tridentinum
Decretum de justificatione,
  Concilium Tridentnum, 145, 150,
  151, 161, 281,
Definition, types of, 272-273
  notional, 272-273
  operational, 272-273
*Dei Filius, see Dogmatic
  Constitution "Dei Filius" of the
  Catholic Faith*
*Dei Verbum, see Dogmatic
  Constitution "Dei Verbum" on
  Divine Revelation*
Deism, 166
Depression, psychological, *see Pain,
  psychological*
Depth psychology, 283
Dharma, 28-29
Dharmakaya, 38
Dhikr, 44
Dialetical relation, faith as, 165
Didascalia, as phase in ancient
  religious instruction, 265
Directorium catechisticum generale,
  269

Discovery, faith as, 72-73
Dissolution of Protestant doctrine
  of faith, 184-200
  nineteenth-century liberalism,
    188-193
  orthodoxy, 184-185
  Pietism, 186-187
  rationalism, 187-188
  twentieth century, 193-200
Divino Afflante Spiritu, 117
*Dogmatic Constitution "Dei Filius"
  of the Catholic Faith*, 144, 146,
  147, 150-155, 158, 162, 281
*Dogmatic Constitution "Dei
  Verbum" on Divine Revelation*,
  144, 147, 150, 151, 161, 282
Donatism, 294
Dort, Synod of, 183
Doubt, 133, 152-153, 166
Dualism, philosophical, 6
Dum acerbissimas, 143

Ecclesial dimension of faith, 161-163
Ecclesiastical authority, Catholic,
  see Magisterium
Ecstasy, 25
  see also Entsasy
Ecumenism, liturgy as fostering,
  207-209
Ego identity, 88-89
Election, *see* Predestination
'Emeth, 104
Empirical theology, 284-285
Enchiridion symbolorum, 144
Energy, faith as, 234-235
Enstasy, 29-30
Eros, 52-54
Eskimo nonliterate religion, 25-26
Eudaimonia, 52-53
Existentialism, 68-70, 145, 78-79,
  284
  philosophical, 68-70, 145
  theological, 78-79, 284
Exodus tradition, 124-125
Experiential pedagogy, 296-297
Explicit faith, see *Fides explicita*

Falsity, 148-149
Faith development theory, 89-95,
  248-251
  cognitive view of faith, as, 89-90

criticisms of, 93-95
maturation and, 92-93
pastoral counseling and, 250-251
stages in, 90-91, 248-250
Fideism, 143
Fides caritate formata, 281
Fides explicita, 159-160, 170, 175,
179-180
Fides formata, 180
Fides implicita, 147-149, 159-160,
170, 175, 179, 185
Fides informans, 281
Fides qua creditur, 170
fides actualis, 170
fides caritate formata, 170
fides divina, 170
Fides quae creditur, 170
fides explicita, 170
fides implicita, 170
fides informis (seu historica), 170
Fides quaerens intellectum, 197,
280-281
First Helvetic Confession, 182
Form-criticism, biblical, 117
Formal object of faith, 146
Formed faith, *see Fides formata;
Fides caritate formata*
Formiter credimus, 152
Four Noble Truths of Buddhism, 32
Fowlerism, *see* Faith development
theory
Frankfurt School of Critical Theory,
277
Freedom, 143, 151, 243-244, 251-
260, 285-286
liberation theology and, 285-286
mature personality and, 243-244
ministry of, in pastoral
counseling, 251-260
biblical base, 251-252
case histories as illustrative,
255-260
faith as cornerstone of
counselor-client relationship,
260
happiness, 253-254
pain, psychological, 253-254
Trent, Council of, and, 143
Vatican I, Council of, and, 151
Vatican II, Council of, and,
151
Freudianism, 78, 283

Functional religion, 84-86, 89
active synthesis and, 85
interpretation, 85
presence, 85
higher motives and, 89
wish-based, as, 84-85

Gaudium et spes, 159, 162
Gnosticism, 6
God's faithfulness, 127-128
Great Awakening, 186

Hākah, 101
He 'emin, 124
Hegelism, 67-68
Heidelberg Catechism, 182-183
Hell's Kitchen, 231
Helvetic Confessions, 182, 183
Heresy, 149
Hesed, 104, 166
Hesiodian myths, 49
Historical-critical method, biblical,
117
Hinduism, 28-31
bhakti, 30-31
dharma, 28-29
karma, 31
meditation, 30
moksha, 29
puja, 31
samsara, 29
Vedic scriptures and, 28, 30, 31
yogin, 29-30
History of religious concept of faith,
3-23, 142-144, 164-200, 280-286
Graeco-Roman culture, 3, 142
Hebrew scriptures, 3-4
Middle Ages, 9-14, 143, 280-281
modern era, 18-22, 143-144, 185-
200, 281-286
New Testament, 4-6
Patristic era, 6-9, 280-281
Reformation, 14-18, 164-184,
282-283
Catholic Counterreformation,
16-18, 281
Protestant, 14-16, 164-184,
282-283

Homerian myths and tales, 48-49
Homoousion, 175
Hope, 100

Humani generis, 144, 157
Humeanism, 65-66

Image, 4
Implicit faith, see *Fides implicita*
Individualism, 161-162
Initiation, rite of, *see* Baptism
Injustice, social, 225-228, 232-234,
   285-286
Intellectual act, faith as, *see*
   Cognition, faith as
Involvement in social ministry, 240-
   241, 285-286
Isaiah oracles, faith in, 126-127
Islam, 42-45
   Five Pillars, 42
   lifestyle and, 42-45
   Muhammad and, 43-44
   Qur'an, 43

Jewish concept of faith, 3-4, 39-42,
   128-129
Jinn, 43
Johannine Gospel, 111-117, 139-
   141
Judaism, 39-42
   Kabbalism, 41
   lifestyle and, 42
   Maimonides's summary of, 42
   Mishnah, 39, 41
   priestly faith, 40
   prophetic faith, 40
   rabbinic writings, 41
   Sapiential faith, 40
   Torah, 39-40, 42
Jungianism, 72, 74, 76, 283
Juridical language, 135
Justice, socioeconomic, 225-228,
   232-234, 285-286
Justification, 9, 14-16, 109, 143,
   164, 171-200, 236, 239
   see also Righteousness

Kabbalism, 41
Kantianism, 65-66, 67, 72-80, 87,
   90, 92, 186, 188-189
Karma, 29, 31
Kerygma, 129, 132, 265
   gospel usage, 132
   Pauline usage, 129
   phase in ancient religious

instruction, 265
Kierkegaardism, 192-193, 284

Laity, empowerment of, 219-220
Lamentabili sane, 152
Language, theological, 148
Lateran IV, Council of, 152
Laxist propositions, 143
   see also Modernism
Lecture technique, 268
Leibnizism, 63-64
Leiden Synopsis of Reformed Faith,
   185
Lessingism, 64-65
Lex orandi, lex credendi, 204, 209
Liberation theology, 23, 260, 285-
   286
Lifestyle, faith as, 35-38, 39-42, 42-
   45, 68-70, 102-103, 106-107,
   112-115, 163, 192-193, 195-196,
   213, 283-286, 296, 298
Liturgy, 99, 103-104, 106-107, 117-
   122, 203-220, 264-265
   Bible and, 99, 103-104, 106, 107,
      111
   biblical scholarship, as method
      of, 117-122
      lectionary and, 120
      nature of, 119-120
      sacraments and, 120
         Marian example of, 120-122
      tradition, as congenial to, 119
   catechumenate, 213-218
   church as enacting itself in faith
      through, 216
   formation through, 210-211
   fostering faith growth, as, 217-
      220
      laity, empowerment of, 218-219
      sharing in Christ, 219-220
   goal of, 205-207, 210-211
   meaning of faith, and, 203-205
   religious instruction and, 264-265
   source of faith, as, 205-210
      corporate action and, 209-210
      ecumenism and, 207-209
      liturgical celebration and, 207
      liturgical goals and, 206-207
      liturgical texts and, 205-206
      liturgical theory and, 205
   sociological context, 205-207
   theology and, 205-206

Love, 110, 138, 221, 224, 237, 244, 302
Lumen gentium, 159, 162
Luther's doctrine of faith, 15-16, 18-19, 160, 164-166, 168-182, 184, 186, 190-191, 194-197, 199, 229-230, 282
  affective, as, 15, 186, 190-191, 282
  anxiety and, 18
  Augustine and, 168-169, 175
  biblical background, 166, 170
  Calvin, contrasted to, 176-180
  cognitive content in, 16
  content of faith, 174-175
  effects of faith, 175-176
  gift of God, 171
  Heidelberg Catechism and, 182
  justification, 160-161, 164-165, 170-176, 184, 194-197, 199
  meritoriousness, 172
  origin of faith, 173
    fides divina, 173
  Peter Lombard and, 169-170
  sociopolitical structures, relation to, 229-230

Magisterium, 143, 144, 149, 152, 281,,295
Mahayana Buddhism, 32-33
Majoristic controversy, 181-182
Manicheanism, 142
Maturity, psychological, 243
Mediatorship, in religious instruction, 292
Medicine man, *see* Shaman
Mental health, 75
Metaphor, poetry and, 205-206
Methods, teaching, *see* Procedures, teaching
Milesian monism, 49
Mirari vos, 143
Mishnah, 39, 41
Modernism, 21, 145, 146, 152
Moksha, 29
Molar variables in teaching process, 291-295
Mother goddess, 27-28, 30
'mn, 124
Mystery, false sense of, 214
Mystical awareness, faith as, 74-75

National Conference of Catholic Bishops, 233
Native American nonliterate religion, *see* American Indian nonliterate religion
Necessity of faith, 71-72, 158-161
Neo-Marxism, 277, 295
  see also Liberation theology
    Praxis
Nichiren Buddhism, 33
Nirvana, 32
Nominalism, 62
Nonliterate religious traditions, 25-28
  African, 26-27
  American Indian, 26-27
  Austrialian aboriginal, 27-28
  Eskimo, 25-26
  shaman in, 25-28
  Siberian, 25-26
Nonverbal behavior, 205, 214-215
Notional definition, 272-273

Oath against Modernism, 145, 146, 152
Obedience of faith, 108, 137-138, 144, 177
  see also Rule of faith
Obscurity of faith, 153-154
Operational definition, 272-275
Operationalism, 274-275
Orange, Second Council of, 9, 142, 150, 157

Pain, psychological, 253-254
Paschal mystery, 219-220
Pastoral counseling, 242-263
  clarification, ministry of, 245-251
    content—understanding, 246-248
      Christ-centered, faith as, 247
      holistic, faith as, 247
      living, faith as, 246
      personal, faith as, 246
      shared human experience, faith as, 246
    goals of, 245-246
    process and structure, 248-251
      holism and, 251
      stages of faith development, 248-251
  freedom, ministry of, 251-260

Pastoral counseling cont.
  biblical base, 251-252
  case histories as illustrative,
    255-260
  Brian, 256-258
  Carol, 255-256
  meaning of, for freedom,
    258-260
  faith as cornerstone of
    counselor-client relationship,
    260
  happiness, 253-254
  pain, psychological, 253-254
  precondition to reconciliation,
    as, 252
  reconciliation, ministry of, 260-
    263
  relationship to faith, 242-245
  theology, integration with, 244
Pelagianism, 9, 142, 169, 221, 231,
  237, 271
  see also Works, faith and
Perception, 72-73, 79-80, 82, 276
  faith as, 72-73
  selective perception in, 79-80,
    82
  role in devising construct of faith,
    276
Performative theology, 285-286
  see also Operationalism
Phenomenology, 81, 145
  existential, 145
  psychological, 81
Philosophical faith, as term, 47-48
Philosophy and faith, 47-70
  Greek, 48-56
  Aristotle, 53-56
  myths and poems, ancient, 48-
    49
  Plato, 51-53
  Plotinus, 54-55
  pre-Socratic, 51-53
  medieval Christian, 56-62
  Anselm, 58-60
  Augustine, 56-58
  nominalism, 62
  Thomas Aquinas, 61-62
  modern, 62-77
  Descartes, 62-63
  Hegel, 67-68
  Kant, 65-67
  twentieth century, 68-70

philosophical faith, term, 47-48
Physics, 278-279
Pietism, 166, 186-187, 189, 282-283
Pisteuō, 99, 101, 103, 105-107,
  110-111, 124, 145, 194
Pistis, see Pisteuō
Platonism, 51, 52
  changelessness in, 51-52
  eros in, 52-53
  eudaimonia in, 52-53
  knowledge in, 51-53
Pluralism, constructional, *see*
  Constructional pluralism
Poetry, liturgy and, 205-206
Political theology, 285-286
Pontifical Biblical Commission, 117
Positivism, theological, *see*
  Theological positivism
Praxis, 285-286, 298
  see also Liberation theology
    Neo-Marxism
Preaching, Bible and, 99
Predestination, 167, 178, 183-184
  see also Calvin's doctrine of faith
    Freedom
Prehistoric traditions, *see*
  Nonliterate religious traditions
Preliturgy, 204-205, 217
Pre-Socratic philosophy, 49-51
  Anaximander, 50
  Heraclitus, 50-51
  myth to rational discourse,
    movement of, 50
  Parmenides, 51
  Thales, 49
Private revelation, 149
Proaction, social, 234-239
Probability, faith as, 20, 152, 281
Procedure, teaching, *see* Structural
  content in teaching faith
Proclamation view of religious
  instruction, *see* Transmission
  view of religious instruction
Prophecy, 103
Propositional, faith as, 148
Pseudo-Athanasian Creed
  Quicumque, 152
Psychology of faith, 71-95
  act of faith, 86-95
  decisive or emergent, 87-88
  ego identity, essential for, 88-89
  faith development, 89-90

answer to problems, faith as, 75-76
discovery, faith as, 72
gift, faith as, 75
mystical awareness, faith as, 74-75
nature and parameters, 71
necessity of faith, 71-72
perception, faith as, 72
perspectives on faith, broad, 81
practical reasoning, faith as, 73-74
selective perception, faith as, 79-80
uniqueness of faith, 81-86
Psychotherapy, 283
Puja, 31
Pythagoreanism, 55

Qāwā, 101
Quanto conficiamur moerore, 159
Quantum physics, 278-279
Qui pluribus, 144
Quicumque, 152
Quietism, 236

Rasul, 43
Rationalism, religious, 143-144, 187-188
    Catholic condemnation of, 143-144
    Deism, 187-188
    Kantianism, 188
Reaction to stimulus, faith as, 76-78
Readiness, faith as, 126
Reasonableness of faith, 154-155
Reconciliation, 252, 260-263
    freedom, as precondition for, 252
    ministry of, in pastoral counseling, 262-263
Reformed Confessions, 182
Reification of faith, 75, 271-272-, 291
    see also Construct, faith as
Religious education, *see* Religious instruction
Religious experience, 81, 186
Religious instruction, 147, 148, 205-207, 210-213, 264-302
    center of church's mission, as, 264-265

content, distinction between major types, 266
    contrasted to other forms of religious education, 265-266
    definition of, 265
    liturgy as primarily noneducational, 210-213
    love and, 302
    nature of, 267-268
    structural content in teaching faith, 292-301
        active faith pedagogy, 198
        communal pedagogy, 297-298
        components of, 293-294
        experiential pedagogy, 296-297
        procedures, selection of pedagogical, 300-301
        structure as content, 292-293
        teaching for faith versus teaching theology, 294-295
        whole person, 295-296
    substantive content in teaching faith, 271-292
        enriching the construct, 275
        physics, 278-279
        psychology, 275-277
        sociology, 277-278
        theology, 279-289
        faith as construct, 271-273
        from construct to learning outcome, 273-275
        validity of a construct of faith, 289-292
            religious instruction's role in, 289-292
            subjectivity and, 289
    teachability of faith, 267-271
        enhancement of faith, 268-270
        giving rise to faith directly, 270-271
        nature of instruction, 267-268
    theological content in, 147, 294-295
    theological language in, 148
Revolutionary action, 285-286
    see also Liberation theology
        Praxis
Righteousness, 134-139, 166, 167, 169, 171-201, 221-222
    see also Justification
Rite of Initiation, *see* Baptism
Ritschlism, 191-192

Romanticism, 166
Rule of faith, 6

SLS model of teaching, *see*
Structuring and the Learning
Situation
Sacraments, 139
justification and, 139
see also Baptism
Samsara, 29, 31-32
Sanctification, 221-222, 239
see also Justification
Schleiermacherism, 19-20, 189-190,
192, 195, 283
Scots Confession, 182
Second Helvetic Confession, 183
Self-acceptance, 243
Shaman, 25-28, 35
African, 26-27
American Indian, 26-27
Australian aboriginal, 27-28
Chinese, 35
Eskimo, 25-26
Siberian, 25-26
Sharia, 28, 45
Shintoism, 33
kami, 33
Siberian nonliterate religion, 25-26
Sila, 33
Skepticism, philosophical, 72-73
Small Catechism of the Puritans,
184
Social action, 225-234
conflict and, 226-227
definition, 225-227
neglect of by churches, 227-234
contributing factors, 228-234
psychological, 229
sociological, 229-230
theological, 228-229
social welfare, 227-228
see also Social ministry
Social Gospel movement, 230-234
Catholic dimension, 232-234
Protestant dimension, 230-232
Social ministry, 211-239
expanding one's faith, as, 240-241
faith as socially proactive, 234-
240
enmeshment of social reality
and faith reality, 238-239
faith as energy, 234-235

social articulation of faith, 235-
238
neglect of, by churches, 227-234
contributing factors, 228-234
psychological, 229
sociological, 229-230
theological, 228-229
social welfare, 227-228
relation to faith, fundamental,
222-227
dimensions of faith, 224
dimensions of faith ministry,
224-226
mutual interpenetration of
social ministry and faith,
226-227
nature of faith, 222-227
works, righteousness and, 221-
222
Social proaction, faith as, 234-239
Social self, 297
Sociological construct of faith, 277-
278
Sociological factors in social
ministry, 229-230
Sociological method of biblical
scholarship, 277-278
Soteriology, 5
Spinozism, 63-64
Spiritual direction, *see* Pastoral
counseling
Statement of the Baptist Faith and
Message, 198
Steadfastness, faith as, 138
Structural content in teaching faith,
292-301
active faith pedagogy, 298-300
communal pedagogy, 297-298
components of, 293-294
importance of all, 293-294
subject matter, 293
experimental pedagogy, 296-297
love and, 302
procedures, selecting pedagogical,
300-301
principles of, 300-301
structure as content, 292-293
characteristics of effective
procedure, 293
teacher's personal faith, 294
teaching faith versus teaching
theology, 294-295

whole person, 295-296
Structuring the Learning Situation, model of teaching, 294
Substantive content in teaching faith, 271-292
enriching the construct, 275-289
physics, 278-279
psychology, 275-277
sociology, 277-278
theology, 279-289
faith as a construct, 271-273
from construct to learning outcome, 273-275
validity of a construct of faith, 289-292
religious instruction's role, 289-292
subjectivity and, 289
Supernaturality of faith, 150-151
Syllabus of Errors, *see Enchiridion symbolorum*
Synod of Dort, 183
Synoptic Gospels, faith in, 106-107, 130-133

Tantra, 34
Taoism, 36-38
harmony with the Tao, 37-38
The Way and, 37-38
Taxonomy of the teaching act, 301
Teachability of faith, 267-271
enhancement of faith, 268-270
giving rise to faith directly, 270-271
nature of instruction, 267-268
The Way, 36-38
Theological positivism, 287-289
constructional pluralism versus, 287-289
faith and, 287-288
nature of, 287-288
nontheological sciences and, 288-289
Theology of faith, systematic, 143-200
Catholic, 142-163
contents of faith, 146-150
credibility, debates on, 155-158
ecclesial dimension of, 161-163
grace, debates on, 155-158
historical prenotes, 142-144
nature of faith, 144-146

act of faith, 145
definition, 144
formal object of faith, 146
intellectualism, 144
virtue of faith, 145
necessity of faith, 158-161
presuppositions, 144
properties of faith, 150-155
certitude, 152
freedom, 151
obscurity, 153-154
reasonableness, 154-155
supernaturality, 150-151
Protestant, 164-200
dissolution of doctrine of faith, 184-200
nineteenth-century liberalism, 188-193
orthodoxy, 184-185
Pietism, 186-187
rationalism, 187-188
twentieth century, 193-200
justification and dialectical relation, 164-166
Reformation doctrine of faith, 166-184
biblical witness, 166-168
Calvin's, 176-180
Luther's, 17-176
Protestant Confessions, 180-184
tradition, 168-170
Theory, role of construct in, 272
Thomism, 8-13, 16, 19, 60-61, 100, 143, 146-149, 153, 157, 159, 187, 271, 281
Three Jewels of Buddhism, 32
Tibetian Buddhism, 34
Tillichism, 86-89, 195-196, 243, 248, 284, 294
Torah, 39-40, 42
Transmission view of religious instruction, 290-291
Tripitaka, 32-33
Trent, Council of, 16-17, 143, 145, 150-151, 177, 281
Trust, faith as, *see* Affect, faith as
Tsedaqah, 166

Uncertainty, principle of, 279
Unformed faith, 180

Uniqueness of faith, psychological, 81-86
  belief and, 83-84
  faith-states, 82-83
  functional religion and, 84-86
  perception and, 82
  transempirical experience, 82
Unitatis redintegratio, 159, 162

Vatican I, Council, 21-22, 143-146, 150-151, 281
Vatican II, Council, 22, 143-144, 146, 150-153, 282-283
Vedic scriptures, 28, 30, 31
Vertical integration in teaching procedure, 293, 301

Vicarious faith, 175
Virtue of faith, 145
Voluntarism, 13-14, 61

Way, The, *see* The Way
Whole person, teaching the, 295-296
Works, faith and, 75, 110, 136, 165-166, 169, 175-177, 179, 181, 185, 221-223, 227, 231, 285-286
  see also Justification
Worship, *see* Liturgy

Yáhal, 101
Yogin, 29-30